Non-Western Colonization, Orientalism, and the Comfort Women

Non-Western Colonization, Orientalism, and the Comfort Women

The Collective Memory of Sexual Slavery under the Japanese Imperial Military

Ako Inuzuka

LEXINGTON BOOKS
Lanham • Boulder • New York • London

Published by Lexington Books
An imprint of The Rowman & Littlefield Publishing Group, Inc.
4501 Forbes Boulevard, Suite 200, Lanham, Maryland 20706
www.rowman.com

6 Tinworth Street, London SE11 5AL, United Kingdom

Copyright © 2021 by The Rowman & Littlefield Publishing Group, Inc.

All rights reserved. No part of this book may be reproduced in any form or by any electronic or mechanical means, including information storage and retrieval systems, without written permission from the publisher, except by a reviewer who may quote passages in a review.

British Library Cataloguing in Publication Information Available

Library of Congress Cataloging-in-Publication Data

Names: Inuzuka, Ako, author.
Title: Non-western colonization, orientalism, and the comfort women : the collective memory of sexual slavery under the Japanese Imperial Military / Ako Inuzuka.
Other titles: Collective memory of sexual slavery under the Japanese Imperial Military
Description: Lanham : Lexington Books, 2021. | Includes bibliographical references and index.
Identifiers: LCCN 2021003088 (print) | LCCN 2021003089 (ebook) | ISBN 9781498598378 (cloth) | ISBN 9781498598385 (ebook)
Subjects: LCSH: Comfort women—Korea—History. | World War, 1939-1945—Women—Abuse of—Korea. | Service, Compulsory non-military—Japan. | Reparations for historical injustices—Korea. | Sexual abuse victims—Korea. | World War, 1939-1945—Atrocities—Japan. | World War, 1939-1945—Reparations. | World War, 1939-1945—Japan—Claims. | Collective memory—Korea. | Japan. Rikugun.
Classification: LCC D810.C698 I588 2021 (print) | LCC D810.C698 (ebook) | DDC 940.54/05—dc23
LC record available at https://lccn.loc.gov/2021003088
LC ebook record available at https://lccn.loc.gov/2021003089

Contents

Acknowledgments　vii

Preface　ix

1. Introduction: Collective Memories of Sexual Slavery under the Japanese Imperial Military　1

2. The Memories of Sexual Slavery in Japan from 1945 to the 1960s: Romantic Stories of Forbidden Love　35

3. The Memories of Sexual Slavery in Japan from the 1970s to 1990: Japanese War Guilt, Victims, and Romanticized Memories　61

4. The Memories of Sexual Slavery from 1991 to 2015: Nationalist Memories　91

5. The Memories of Sexual Slavery from 1991 to 2015: Progressive Memories　125

6. The Memories of Sexual Slavery in Japan from 2015 to the Present: The 2015 Bilateral Agreement and "Comfort Women" Statues　161

7. Reflections on the Memories of Sexual Slavery in Japan and South Korea　203

Appendix A: Timeline　215

Bibliography　217

Index　229

About the Author　239

Acknowledgments

This book would not have been possible without the support and assistance of many. I am deeply grateful to Omar Swartz for his careful reading of the manuscript and constructive feedback. I also wish to thank J. Michael Sproule for thoughtful advice throughout the writing process.

I am indebted to the University of Pittsburgh at Johnstown for the award of a College Research Council Grant that allowed me to travel to Japan and for granting me a sabbatical leave during the 2018 fall semester. I owe thanks to the Asian Studies Center of the University of Pittsburgh for a Japan Studies Small Grant that enabled me to travel to South Korea to conduct my autoethnography. I also wish to express my appreciation to my colleagues at the Humanities Division and the Communication Department of the University of Pittsburgh at Johnstown for their support and understanding throughout this lengthy project.

My special thanks go to Nicolette Amstutz, Sierra Apaliski, and the staff of Lexington Books for both their continuous assistance and patience.

Finally, I owe my heartfelt appreciation to my family: my late father, Yoshisuke Inuzuka, who inspired me on topics of history and my mother, Naomi Inuzuka, for her warm encouragement and support throughout my life. I am also indebted to my partner, Thomas Fuchs, who has been a tough yet helpful critic and a dedicated husband and father. I am also blessed with two sons, Tobias and Adrian, one of them a prolific author himself (*Dog in a Box*, *Ninja Cook Book*, and others). They have both been extremely patient with their busy mom and excited about her book. They have always made me smile and brightened my day.

Preface

In June 2018, I visited South Korea. Although my project concerns the memories of sexual slavery by the Imperial Armed Forces of Japan (1871–1945) in contemporary Japan, I wanted to visit and experience commemorative sites in South Korea because my focus is on Korean victims and survivors. The victims of sexual slavery under the Imperial Japanese Army, widely known as "comfort women," were young females forced into sexual servitude for Japanese soldiers during the Asia-Pacific War. The majority of them are believed to have been Koreans.[1] I thought that taking this opportunity to reflect on my personal experience in this particular cultural and societal context through autoethnography[2] might allow me to critically analyze "power and cultural politics from within."[3]

I selected three prominent Korean memorial sites of sexual slavery frequently mentioned in the media and literature: the "Wednesday demonstrations" to demand that the Japanese government take legal responsibilities, held weekly in front of the Japanese Embassy in Seoul; the *Statue of Peace* or so-called "comfort women" statue, in front of the Japanese Consulate in Busan; and the House of Sharing and its affiliated museum, where some of the survivors reside. Due to their reputation as contested sites, either as locations that challenge the Japanese government to redress the crimes of its past or as "anti-Japan" places, I thought they would serve as useful locations for me to consider autoethnographically the collective memories of sexual slavery.

I arrived at the site of the Wednesday demonstrations in front of the Japanese Embassy in Seoul, South Korea, at around 11:00 a.m. Though it was supposed to start at 12:00 p.m., I was surprised to see many people waiting, including high school students holding their own handmade signs. Later, I found out that the day was a holiday due to a national election, explaining the greater presence of high school students.

There were barricaded areas in which people were walking. I was not sure if I was allowed to do so, so I stood by one of the barricaded areas, feeling like an "imposter." I was there because I agreed with the cause, yet I am not Korean, but Japanese. Do I look Japanese? Do they notice I am Japanese? Suddenly, a police officer spoke to me in Korean, gesturing me to go into the barricaded area. I said "Sorry, I don't understand" in English because of my limited understanding of Korean. He paused for a couple of seconds and replied in English, "You shouldn't be standing here. You're blocking traffic." I asked, "Should I go in there?," pointing to the barricaded area. "Ah, yes," he said. Feeling that I now have permission, I sat on the ground in the barricaded area next to other people. The demonstration began. Speakers ranging from high school students to older people came up to the stage and spoke. Though many speakers addressed the crowd, the overall atmosphere was fairly relaxed. Many of the speakers had smiles on their faces, and some speakers sang and danced on the stage. People around me, mostly high school students, applauded and chanted "Repeal! Repeal!" once in a while.

Their chants referred to the bilateral agreement of December 28, 2015, through which the Japanese and South Korean governments had intended to lay the decades-old issue to rest once and for all. The Japanese government had hoped it could erase the memories of sexual slavery by enforcing the resolution, which stipulated that neither country would bring up the issue again. However, the demonstrators pointedly refused to "forget." Recalling the images of Koreans in demonstrations fanatically shouting anti-Japan messages in Japanese media reports, I felt nervous about being there, but the relaxed atmosphere eased my mind. Halfway through the demonstration, one female high school student gave an emotional talk, crying and shouting toward the Japanese Embassy building, "Ilbon, Ilbon!" [Japan, Japan]. After her presentation, the next speaker was again smiling and relaxed. For the rest of the time, I could not stop thinking about the outpouring of emotions against Japan.

About one hour later, it was over. I saw many people, especially high school students, taking group photos together with the statue of the "comfort woman," smiling and looking happy, unlike the images of angry Koreans in demonstrations the Japanese media would report. The "Statue of Peace," the official name of the statue, symbolizing "comfort women" was installed by the Korean Council for the Women Drafted for Military Sexual Slavery by Japan (currently, the Korean Council for Justice and Remembrance for the Issues of Military Sexual Slavery by Japan), a major support organization for survivors, in front of the Japanese Embassy in Seoul in 2011. I also saw a long line of people handing over money, receiving a small pin, and then writing something. I figured they must be making donations, so I stood at the end of the line. "I only have a little cash," I realized. I looked in my wallet and saw only W 30,000 (about $26). I took it out and waited. When my turn came, I handed the money to a person from the Korean Council, feeling embarrassed. She smiled and handed me several pins. Feeling relieved, I asked her what the people were signing. She said that it was a petition demanding an apology from the Japanese government. I signed and wrote in "Pennsylvania, USA," as the location of my residence. While I do live in Pennsylvania, I also wanted to hide that I was Japanese because I felt that it would be inappropriate for a Japanese person to be there, though it may have nevertheless been very clear to her from my name.

The next day, I went to Busan to see another statue of the "comfort woman" in front of the Japanese Consulate. This statue was erected by the Korean Council one year after the 2015 resolution in protest against it. As the Japanese government demanded its removal, it developed into a diplomatic controversy between the two nations. After a two-and-a-half-hour ride of the KTX, South Korea's high-speed train, I arrived in Busan. At the station, I went to the information counter and saw a young man with the sign "English" in front of him and I asked him in English, "Could you please tell me how to get to the Japanese Embassy?" Looking irritated, he said, "There is no embassy here. There is only a consulate." "That's what I meant," I replied. He said, "You have to take the subway and get off at Choryang station, the next station. The consulate is right there." "How long would it take if I walked?" I asked. He spat back, "15 to 20 minutes but it's easier to take the subway." "OK, I'll do that then. Where is the subway station?" I asked again. He said, "Take exit 7 and you'll see it." I thanked him and walked to exit 7. The subway station was difficult to see because of ongoing construction. "What an unfriendly guy," I thought, wondering if he was always that unfriendly or if he was simply having a bad day. Or was it because I am Japanese?

Immediately after I arrived at Choryang station and took the stairs up from the exit, I saw two young police officers chatting. I asked them for directions to the Japanese Consulate, and one of them gave them to me. Being relieved at their polite reply because I was nervous that they might act irritated like the guy at the information counter, I thanked them and began to walk. Then, after only 20–30 meters, the statue appeared unexpectedly. It was identical to the one in front of the Japanese Embassy in Seoul. Having seen the one in Seoul surrounded by so many people before, during, and after the demonstration, I must have been expecting the statue to be surrounded by people, but it was surrounded instead by yellow plastic barriers, and there were half-dry flowers on the ground. She quietly sat there, staring at the building of the Japanese Consulate. I began to take pictures and looked closely at the statue. While I was standing there, taking photos and examining the statue, nobody

Figure P.1 The "Statue of Peace" in Busan. *Source*: Photo by Ako Inuzuka.

else stopped. Once in a while, passersby gave curious looks to a tourist taking photos of the statue.

Was this small statue the one that caused so much diplomatic controversy? Obviously, the symbolic power of the statue was enough to cause the Japanese government to take offense. Yet, people's seeming indifference to it was an interesting contrast to the scope of the controversy and to Japanese media reports of South Koreans fanatically protesting against Japan. Obviously, they have their own lives to worry about, and the issue of sexual slavery is not on their minds all the time. Just like there is heterogeneity in the memory of sexual slavery among the Japanese, there must be differences in feelings toward the issue among South Koreans.

While walking around the area, there was a statue of General Li Sunsin, who died in battle defending Korea from Japan's invading troops in the sixteenth century, as the trilingual (Korean, English, and Japanese) plates explained. The statue faces Japan, and its location near the Japanese Consulate is probably not a coincidence, but rather another reminder of Japan's past aggression. The statue can also remind people of the resilience the Koreans demonstrated when facing Japan.

Two days later, I was to attend an English tour at the House of Sharing. As instructed, I went to Gangbyeon station in eastern Seoul, where volunteers took the tour participants, about ten of us, mostly from the United States and Canada, to the House of Sharing in a van. The van left Seoul and drove into the countryside. I saw fields with many greenhouses, and the van drove by a big river. Over an hour's drive from Gangbyeon station, we finally arrived.

The House of Sharing is located in the countryside. Later, one of the tour guides explained that they had to relocate it several times because of neighbor complaints. Although it appears most South Koreans are united in support of the survivors of sexual slavery, or *halmŏni* [grandma] as they are referred to at the House of Sharing, many South Koreans did not want them to live nearby due to a traditional prejudice against women who were engaged in prostitution, regardless of the circumstances.

The master narrative of the English tour at the House of Sharing proceeds from the *halmŏni*'s victimhood to their activism for survival and energy for their cause: the Japanese government's apology and acceptance of legal responsibility. The tour started with a showing of the film *Apology*, briefly explaining sexual slavery under the Japanese imperial military and the Japanese government's position on the issue while featuring three survivors from three different countries: South Korea, China, and the Philippines. Then, the tour was led outside the main building, where statues of survivors were

Figure P.2 The Statues of Survivors at the House of Sharing. *Source*: Photo by Ako Inuzuka.

situated. After a brief explanation of the museum and the artworks on the exterior of the building, the visitors were encouraged to take photos.

The tour then moved inside the building. In a section where visitors could see photos of the Japanese imperial military's official documents and a large map of Asia illustrating Japan's occupied areas together with confirmed and estimated lotions of comfort stations, the visitors learned the background and general information on the "comfort" system. The photos of the documents are used as evidence of the Japanese military's involvement. During this initial part of the tour, the visitors heard a story of the recruitment experienced by one of the survivors, describing how she was kidnapped from her home. One of the tour guides addressed me, saying that I was doing a great thing and that it must not be easy for me to come to the House of Sharing as a Japanese person. I smiled. Later I repeated it to myself: "I'm doing a great thing." I am not like nationalist Japanese who are in denial. I am not like [Japanese prime minister] Abe. I am a good Japanese person.

The tour moved to the next area, "a place of experience." The visitors could go down a set of stairs into a dark basement with a reconstructed comfort station room. The room was small, barely large enough for a small bed, with a small washing area that was earlier explained as the place where both women and soldiers were supposed to wash their genitals and the women had to wash condoms due to supply shortage toward the end of the war. Small wooden pieces with women's names in Japanese hung outside of the room. One of the tour guides explained that that was how they indicated which women were available; the name plates of those who were not available on that day were hung backward. The tour guide explained that it was a practice adopted from Japanese restaurants, where unavailable food items were covered, underscoring the objectification of the women. The visitors then heard another testimony from one of the survivors, Chong Ok-Sun,[4] read aloud by one of the guides, in which she described how those who caught venereal disease were treated with 606 shots, Salvarsan-based syphilis medication, which led to infertility, or simply a hot iron stick, and how those who became pregnant were made to abort. Those who had complications simply "disappeared." Alternatively, they would be killed in front of others, who were told that the body would be used to feed other Korean women. The story was terrible, and one of the tour guides became emotional and had to wipe her tears away.

I felt disoriented while taking the stairs up on the other side, as we entered a bright spacious room with black and white woodblock prints of *halmŏni*. One of the tour guides explained that one can hear a testimony by pressing a button, and she pressed the one of Kim Hak-sun, one of the three survivors who sued the Japanese government in 1991. Soh writes that, in the South Korean mainstream discourse on "comfort women," they are unambiguously depicted as victims without complicity,⁵ so I had expected to see the same here. However, while the main focus of the tour was on the women's victimhood, we also heard a few stories of complicity about how some Koreans were involved in the recruitment, the South Korean government's indifference to the issue after the war, and how Koreans themselves silenced survivors after the war.

In another area, one could hear about the Wednesday demonstrations and the names of numerous individuals and groups that made donations were listed on a wall. All of this served to show their efforts toward redress and support for these efforts. In another building that looked like a temple, visitors could see exhibits of artworks, which the *halmŏni* painted as part of art therapy. The visitors could see photos of some of the survivors who had passed away, with their personal possessions on display.

After examining some of the monuments outside, we finally went into the building in which some of the survivors reside. Two of the survivors were sitting there, surrounded by volunteers, and another one soon came to join them. They were small and looked like any old women you see in Japan. It was a somewhat surreal and simultaneously familiar scene. I almost could not believe that survivors of sexual slavery were actually sitting only a few meters away from me. I had read about them so much. They went through unspeakable situations. They are so courageous to speak up. Yet, the scene before me looked just like old women in a nursing home in Japan. A tour guide introduced them in English; in the meantime, one of them stood up and left. He explained that the *halmŏni* like to watch TV; the women had smiles on their faces, and the overall atmosphere was relaxed.

The two women briefly talked about their experiences in Korean, while one of the volunteer tour guides translated into English. One of them talked about her experience of being beaten by a Japanese soldier with a stick, and she showed a scar on her head to everybody. Then, she asked if there were any Japanese there. I hesitantly raised my hand and a couple of tour guides pointed to me. Then, she addressed me in Korean as the tour guide translated into English. She showed me the scar on her head again while talking, being visibly upset. The interpreter calmly translated: "A Japanese beat me and I still have a scar. The Japanese did terrible things to Koreans during the war. . . . They did a lot of terrible things during colonial times. . . . Because of the terrible things they did to Koreans, she doesn't want Japanese to come here." Initially, I was not too surprised or shocked, as I agreed with her overall sentiments. I agree that the Japanese did terrible things to Koreans. The Japanese government has not been sincere about their past wrongdoing. I was thinking that, yes, I agree with you. However, when the interpreter said that "she doesn't want Japanese to come here because of what they did during colonial times," my heart began to beat very fast. I realized that, in her eyes, I was one of the evil Japanese! I was screaming inside that I was not one of them! I am a good Japanese person who supports her cause! So many ideas flooded my head, among them the tour guide's comment that "I am doing a great thing." I suddenly felt embarrassed by the thought that I felt content at this comment. I felt exposed, as if my self-satisfaction had been revealed. I thought I was doing a great thing by confronting my country's past and tackling the issue. The image of the high school girl at the Wednesday demonstration shouting "Japan, Japan!" came back to me again. I felt like an imposter. In the meantime, the interpreter continued to translate the survivor with the same calm tone, in contrast to the upset *halmŏni*: "But she doesn't hate the Japanese people, just the Japanese government." After that, the tour participants were encouraged to go to shake hands with the survivors, but I could not. I felt embarrassed and wanted to leave. Then, the interpreter came to me and gave me a small pin as a gift and said, "Sorry, I hope you are not offended. As she said, she doesn't hate Japanese people." I had been feeling tense but, suddenly, I broke down in tears. I felt even more embarrassed and did not want the *halmŏni* to see me. Compared to how completely destroyed their lives had been, my crying over something like this seemed almost insulting. I thanked her, said I completely understood, and waited until everybody else finished greeting the survivors.

Even after coming back to the United States, I could not stop thinking about the *halmŏni*'s outcry. She is entitled to hating the Japanese as well as the Japanese government, I felt. After all, it was individual Japanese people, the soldiers, who beat her up and raped her repeatedly, and it was the Japanese government's colonial policy that placed her and many other Korean women in that situation. If the same thing happened to me, I would hate the whole nation and its people as well.

As Ellis and Bochner argue, autoethnography makes researchers vulnerable.[6] I had thought that I would be rendering myself vulnerable by going to places where I would be forced to confront my country's past and wrongdoings. Instead, my autoethnography ended up exposing the arrogance of my thinking of myself as a "good Japanese" or "conscious Japanese." I had thought that I was committed to the cause, believing that South Koreans' anger at Japan's past wrongdoing is justifiable, especially because the Japanese government had not been sincere in dealing with the nation's past. However, when I actually had to face a Korean woman who was not just angry about the abstract idea of Japan's wrongdoing but had suffered directly because of it, I was more affected than I thought I would be.

This book is my personal journey of making sense of present-day Japan's collective memories of sexual slavery in particular and the Asia-Pacific War in general. By exploring how sexual slavery and its survivors have been remembered in Japan, I have struggled to make sense of what I learned and felt while growing up in Japan, my own role as a Japanese researcher of the collective memory of sexual slavery, the role of the nation of Japan, and the potential for survivors' healing.

Having grown up in Japan in the 1970s and 1980s, I am a product of Japan's postwar *heiwa gakushū* (peace education), and I proudly call myself a pacifist. I have always thought that war is terrible, causing ordinary everyday people to suffer, and I feel fortunate to live in a time when my country is at peace. In Japan's peace education, primary and secondary schoolchildren learn about the importance of peace by learning about the brutal nature of war. The focus is Japan's victimhood; typically, Japanese children learn about the atomic bombs dropped on Hiroshima and Nagasaki and air raids on Japanese cities through hearing survivors' personal narratives of their traumatic war experiences. For instance, when I was in sixth grade, I went on a field trip to the Nagasaki Atomic Bomb Museum. I was shocked by the photos of severely injured people and the story narrated by a survivor, and I remember having a hard time sleeping that night. The overall message of peace education is, "War causes much suffering. Therefore, war is bad. We should appreciate today's peaceful society." I learned the same message through popular culture. Beginning in 1961 and continuing today, Japan's public broadcaster, Nippon Hōsō Kyōkai's (Japan Broadcast Association or NHK) has aired the serialized drama *Renzoku Terebi Shōsetsu* (*TV Novel Series*). During the late 1970s to the 1980s, this featured female protagonists overcoming hardships during World War II. While I can today recall the detailed storylines of only a few such series, I distinctly remember female protagonists running to find shelter during air raids and an evil *kempei* (special Japanese military police) who made the lives of the protagonists difficult. My knowledge that both my grandfathers died in the war and the stories my parents told of their suffering while growing up without fathers were consistent with what I learned through peace education and the media's focus on Japan's victimhood: "War is bad. Many people (Japanese) suffered. Therefore, peace is important."

As I matured, I, of course, became aware of Japan's past aggressions, such as the Nanjing Massacre and sexual slavery. Yet, it did not significantly challenge the overall memory of the war I had formed: "War makes ordinary people do terrible things. Other Asians may have suffered, but we, the Japanese, greatly suffered as well. Therefore, war is bad." At the same time, I began to develop certain unsettling feelings regarding how to reconcile Japan's role during the war between victimhood and its aggressive past. My feelings changed after I moved to the United States as a graduate student. I learned that National Pearl Harbor Remembrance Day is still observed in the United States, though it is not in Japan. I learned that many Americans believe that dropping the atomic bombs was a good thing because it hastened the end of the war and, as a consequence, saved American lives. Having seen photos of people, including children, who were severely injured and disfigured by the blasts and by radiation exposure, and having heard the stories of people dying in Nagasaki, I could not believe how anybody could call killing hundreds of thousands of people a "good thing." When I met people from Korea, Taiwan, or China in the United States, I also learned that the people from other Asian countries saw the Japanese as nothing but aggressors.

These were just a few of my experiences with the socially constructed nature of memories, and I became interested in collective memory studies, especially memories of the Asia-Pacific War. I became interested in why some topics evoke such strong emotions and why some people try hard to defend the ways past events are remembered. This project is my personal journey to reconcile "victim" memories with "aggressor" memories—my way of trying to make sense of the *halmŏni*'s outcry and my role as a researcher and Japanese person.

NOTES

1. Sang-hun Choe, "Professor who Wrote of Korean 'Comfort Women' Wins Defamation Case," *The New York Times*, January 25, 2017, National Newspapers.

2. Carolyn Ellis, *The Ethnographic I: A Methodological Novel about Autoethnography* (Walnut Creek, CA: AltaMira Press, 2004), xix.

3. Satoshi Toyosaki, "Toward De/postcolonial Autoethnography: Critical Relationality with the Academic Second Persona," *Cultural Studies/Critical Methodologies*, 18, no. 1 (2018): 33.

4. Throughout the book, Japanese and Korean names are written in the East Asian manner, with the family name first, followed by the given name.

5. C. Sarah Soh, *The Comfort Women: Sexual Violence and Postcolonial Memory in Korea and Japan* (Chicago: University of Chicago Press, 2008).

6. Carolyn S. Elllis and Art P. Bochner, "Analyzing Analytic Autoethnography: An Autopsy," *Journal of Contemporary Ethnography* 35 no. 4 (2006): 433.

Chapter 1

Introduction

Collective Memories of Sexual Slavery under the Japanese Imperial Military

In the period from the late 1930s to 1945, mostly during the Asia-Pacific War,[1] an estimated 50,000–200,000 women were assigned to the Japanese imperial military's "comfort" system.[2] On its surface the "comfort" system was a governmentally sanctioned scheme of organized prostitution, operated by the military with the purpose to improve the moral of the troops, prevent the spreading of sexually transmitted diseases (STDs), and protect the population of occupied areas from sexual violence. However, a wealth of evidence, ranging from military documents to testimony from survivors and soldiers, has shown beyond doubt that the majority of "comfort women," a euphemism for the tens of thousands of victims, did not voluntarily join, nor were they prostitutes to begin with. Most young women were actually recruited in occupied areas, especially Korea, and were either coerced to join or lured into the system under false pretenses. They were then, often for years, held in slave-like conditions serving the sexual needs of soldiers in so-called comfort stations. Many of them died of diseases, killed themselves, or were killed in enemy attacks especially when they were sent to the frontlines. Those who survived had often contracted STDs, suffered from infertility, long-term psychological trauma, and frequently became addicted to drugs or pain medications due to the physical and psychological pain they had endured. Those who prevailed took many years to muster the strength to openly confront their abusers.

Despite the weight of historic evidence and a view of history that is shared in broad strokes by Japan's neighbors and even Japan's Western allies, the memories of the "comfort women" in Japan are not uniform and can be strikingly at odds with internationally accepted histories. So how are the "comfort women" remembered in Japan and what contributed to the formation of these memories?

For decades the collective memories of the Asia-Pacific War have been contested sites where Japan's neighbors and progressive Japanese challenge mostly conservative nationalist politicians and scholars in their attempts to whitewash Japan's wartime atrocities. The memories of sexual slavery orchestrated by the former Japanese military are one of these battlegrounds where histories clash and memories are in flux. By illustrating how memories of sexual slavery in Japan have changed over the past seventy-five years, I aim to provide a better understanding of the present-day international controversy surrounding this issue.

Japan's militaristic expansion in Asia during the late nineteenth century and the first half of the twentieth century is still a sensitive issue in Asia even more than seventy years after Japan's defeat. Japan's neighbors are paying close attention to how the nation is dealing with its past. For example, Japanese politicians' visits to the Yasukuni Shrine, a Shinto shrine honoring those who died for their country, including fourteen Class A War Criminals,[3] are causing international controversy almost every year. The tense relationship to its history can also be seen in Japan's internal struggles to deal with its past. For instance, the final decision about the content of history textbooks lies with the Japanese Education Ministry, which has been repeatedly accused of revisionist censorship by Japanese historians and textbook authors. That criticism culminated in a series of "textbook trials" (the "Ienaga trials"), spanning more than thirty years (1965–1997).

Ienaga Saburō, a Japanese history textbook author, questioned the constitutionality of textbook screening by suing the Japanese Education Ministry three times. He first sued the ministry in 1965 for rejecting his 1962 textbook and ordering to delete 274 parts from his 1963 textbook. Ienaga's textbooks were constantly ordered to modify to whitewash the actions of the Japanese imperial military during the war or were even rejected at times as a result of the ministry's textbook screening. For instance, one of the descriptions that Ienaga was ordered to eliminate from his 1963 textbook was: "The war was idealized as a 'holy war' and the defeats of the Japanese military and their atrocities were all concealed from the general public in Japan. As a result, the majority of the Japanese were placed in a situation where they could do nothing but eagerly cooperate with this reckless war" (my translation). As grounds for the education ministry's demand to eliminate the above description, the ministry stated that certain of Ienaga's expressions—"idealized," "the atrocities of the Japanese military," and "reckless war"—were based on his one-sided criticisms of various situations and the acts of Japan and were not designed to help students understand the situations and the acts of the country. Similarly, he sued the ministry again in 1967 and 1984 for being ordered to delete some parts from his textbooks. While he lost in the first trial, he won the second one and the third trial was a partial victory for him (the

Supreme Court ruled that modifying four of the nine parts was illegal though they maintained that textbook screening per se was constitutional).[4]

Japanese history textbooks have also become a diplomatic issue. In 1982, Japanese newspapers reported that the Japanese Education Ministry made history textbook writers replace the word *shinryaku* (invasion) with less direct *shinshutsu* (advancement) when referring to the Imperial Japanese Army's actions in Asia during the war. When the governments of China and South Korea protested the euphemism, a diplomatic conflict ensued. After this, the Japanese government revised its textbook screening criteria to include the *kinrin shokoku jōkō* ("neighboring nation clause"), which required that passages relating to modern and contemporary events in history be sensitive to the need for harmony with neighboring countries.

Despite the textbook trials and diplomatic controversies, the situation has not improved by much. Books still have to pass a rigorous and—according to many critics—biased screening process, and the results have not gone unnoticed. For example, in April 2005, the release of a junior high school history textbook whitewashing Japan's wartime past led to international media coverage and anti-Japan protests throughout China, where they suffered from Japan's aggression during the war. Thus, it should not be surprising that the issue of the Imperial Armed Forces' government-sanctioned sexual slavery and Japan's unwillingness to take full moral and financial responsibility have continued to sour the diplomatic relationship between Japan and its neighbors, most notably South Korea, from which most of the former "comfort women" came from.

JAPANESE MODERNIZATION AND MILITARISM

Before we continue with the discussion of the "comfort women," let me provide some historical context by explaining Japan's modernization that began in the middle of the nineteenth century and the subsequent militarization and militarism.

The Meiji Restoration of 1868 marked the beginning of Japan's modernization and the Meiji era (1868–1912). Before the Meiji era, Japan was governed by the Tokugawa Shōgun (Edo Period: 1603–1868) under the feudal system. During the Edo period, the nation closed its borders for trading with all other countries except for China and the Netherlands under the policy of *sakoku* (national isolation). In 1853, U.S. Naval Commodore Perry threatened Japan with military action if Japan did not sign treaties that would allow trading with the West. Japan ratified the treaty with the United States (and later with Britain, France, Russia, and the Netherlands) although the treaty was disadvantageous to Japan (e.g., Western countries could dictate the tariff on Japan's imports from and exports to Western countries; Japan could not prosecute Westerners who committed crimes in Japan).⁵ Thus, Japan ended its policy of *sakoku*, and its modernization began.

Japan's modernization was about embracing Westernization and militarization, as represented in such slogans as *datsua nyūō* (leave Asia, enter Europe) and *fukoku kyōhei* (rich country, strong military). Japan's governmental officials considered that the unequal treaty would be revised by Japan becoming a strong, wealthy, Westernized nation. Westernization and industrialization were heavily promoted during the Meiji era. As Ian Buruma has argues, Westernization was "meant to show foreigners that Japan was a serious modern country, worthy of respect."⁶ To Japanese officials at that time, the best way to be equal to the West was to emulate the West.⁷ At the same time, in the process of Westernization, many Japanese also developed a racist contempt for other Asians. Fukuzawa Yukichi (1835–1901), an influential Japanese thinker and advocate of Westernization who is credited with the authorship of *Datsuaron* (*Discussions on Leaving Asia*), urged Japan to separate itself from Asia. Urs Matthias Zachmann argues that Fukuzawa was concerned with Westerners' Orientalist representations of Asia, especially China and Korea, as backward, despotic countries, which led him to suggest Japan dissociating itself from those countries to avoid being lumped with them.⁸ According to Zachmann, Fukuzawa thought that Japan should treat China and Korea in the same way Westerners treated Asian countries, that is, with imperialist expansion through military force.

In addition to Westernization, another area of focus for Japanese officials was creating strong military forces while industrializing the nation to become wealthy (*fukoku kyōhei*). Japan's modernization was closely tied to its continuous invasion of Korea, China, and Southeast Asia.⁹ Japan won in the Sino-Japanese War (1894–1895) and acquired Taiwan as its first colony. Japan also won in the Russo-Japanese War (1904–1905) and acquired the southern half of Sakhalin and railroad rights in Manchuria (northeastern part of China). Inoki states that whereas Japan's victory in the Russo-Japanese War was surprising news to the rest of the world, the victory also promoted Japan to the position of a "major country" or a "first-class country."¹⁰ Zachmann also argues that Japan's desire to become an imperial power was, at least initially, to gain equality with the Western powers and maintain independence.¹¹ To many Japanese, becoming an imperial power and defeating other countries—especially Western ones—enabled Japan to finally achieve equal status with the Western powers.

While Japan did abolish the unequal treaties with Western countries after the Russo-Japanese War, that did not end its imperialistic, militaristic ambitions. Japan annexed Korea as its second colony. Japan declared war against Germany during World War I based on the Anglo-Japanese Alliance

(1902–1923). As a result, after the armistice, Japan received control of the former German territories in Asia such as the Shandong Province in China, the Republic of Palau, and the Marshall Islands. Japan also sent troops during the Siberian Intervention (1918–1922) and acquired the northern half of Sakhalin. Further, in 1931, the Imperial Japanese Army bombed part of the railroad owned by Japan in Manchuria, accused Chinese dissidents of the attack, and used the incident as a pretext for invading Manchuria (the Mukden Incident). During the following year, Japan established the puppet state of Manchukuo, Manchuria. Conflicts between the Chinese and Japanese military units continued from the 1920s to the 1930s; Japan stationed members of the Imperial Japanese Army in China, purportedly to protect Japanese residents. In 1937, Japanese troops under training near the Marco Polo Bridge reported shots fired toward the troops. Within days, the Marco Polo Bridge Incident developed into an all-out armed battle. The Second Sino-Japanese War (1937–1945) officially began.

Japanese military officials used the slogan "*Daitōa Kyōeiken*" (the Greater East Asia Co-Prosperity Sphere) to justify Japan's wartime invasions into other Asian nations and the Pacific Islands. Japanese officials claimed that their war efforts would liberate Asian nations from Western colonial powers; they said that once the war was over, Asian nations would coexist in co-prosperity under the Japanese empire's guidance.[12] The propaganda was widely promoted among the residents of Japan's occupied areas in Asia and the public in Japanese. Consequently, Japan called the war the "*Daitōa Sensō*" (the Greater East Asia War). After the war, when the Allied occupation forces banned the word *Daitōa*, the phrase was replaced with the "*Taiheiyō Sensō*" (the Pacific War). Tsuzuki has argued that this slogan initially attracted some activists, advocates of "Asia for the Asiatics," in other Asian countries suffering under Western imperialism.[13] However, the essential problem with *Daitōa Kyōeiken* was that they were proposing a united Asian empire led by Japan instead of suggesting a united empire of countries with equal standing—replacing Western imperialism with their own.

THE "COMFORT WOMEN"

The origin of organized sexual slavery under the Japanese imperial military can be traced back to the late 1930s. The main reasons why the Japanese imperial military established the "comfort" system are commonly believed to be: (1) the control of STDs, which was a problem when soldiers visited local prostitutes in Japan's occupied areas; and (2) to deter soldiers from assaulting local women in occupied areas. Other possible benefits were the prevention of information leaks to the local population and boosting troop morale.[14] Japanese military officials realized that STDs had the potential to significantly weaken their armed forces and consequently attempted to implement a system to provide "safe" women under the control of military doctors. To illustrate this point, there were 1,109 documented cases of hospitalization due to STDs during the Siberian Intervention (1918–1922) when Japanese military units were stationed.[15] More than one thousand STD patients in a conflict that resulted in 1,399 casualties on the Japanese side must be an alarming number for any commanding officer.

Sexual assaults on local women by Japanese soldiers were a common occurrence in occupied areas in Asia. Military officials had to worry about discontent among local residents, which could make it more difficult to control those areas. Providing soldiers with a "safe" opportunity for sexual release would therefore take care of a host of problems: it would decrease the spread of STDs, appease civilians in occupied areas, prevent information leaks, and improve the morale of the troops.

As time would tell, the "comfort" system was not effective in reducing the number of Japanese soldiers contracting STDs nor did it put an end to rapes committed by Japanese soldiers. The number of soldiers contracting STDs stayed roughly the same and, if anything, increased from 11,983 in 1942 and 12,557 in 1943 to 12,587 in 1944.[16] An anecdotal report by a military physician indicates that soldiers continued assaulting local women despite the program. Unfortunately, it was considered permissible to rape "enemy's women" among soldiers. It was also cheaper than visiting comfort stations and some officers even condoned these actions labeling them "energizing."[17]

As Catherine MacKinnon has pointed out, rape is often regarded as "an inevitability of armed conflict"; she calls it "an act of domination."[18] While her work specifically focuses on the mass rapes of Muslim and Croatian women by Serbians during the conflict in the former Yugoslavia—what she calls "ethnic rape," this might also illustrate Japanese soldiers' mass rapes of Chinese women:

> [This is] not only a policy of the pleasure of male power unleashed; not only a policy of defile, torture, humiliate, degrade, and demoralize the other side; not only a policy of men posturing to gain advantage and ground over other men. It is rape under orders, not out of control, under control.[19]

Because rape was officially banned in the Japanese military and Japanese military officials attempted to stop it by establishing the "comfort" system, "ethnic rape" may not have been their official policy yet it is important to note that perpetrators were not prosecuted in many cases. MacKinnon discusses rape as being motivated by xenophobia and ethnic hostility. Rape during war times is about humiliating the enemy as well as male domination and sexual release, motivated by hatred toward the enemy. In this context, we should not be surprised that Japanese soldiers continued to rape Chinese women even after the "comfort" system was established.

Japan's Imperial Armed Forces were not alone in their preoccupation with preventing STDs among soldiers. Scott Stern's study on the American Plan describes the United States' efforts to prevent STDs among soldiers.[20] Under that plan, tens of thousands of prostitutes, "promiscuous" women, and "reasonably suspicious" women were detained and forcibly quarantined without due process. Initially, this occurred only near military bases in the United States around the time of World War I, but eventually, it spread to cities all over the country and were carried out throughout World War II and, in some states, until the 1970s. Both the American Plan and Japan's "comfort" system were based on a patriarchal ideology that men have uncontrollable sexual desires that must be sated. Within those patriarchal structures, both attempted to protect their male troops by controlling women. In the end, both programs were ineffective in reducing the number of STD cases among soldiers.[21]

The first confirmed "comfort station" mentioned in military documents was built in Shanghai, China in 1932.[22] However, according to the memoir of Okamura, the officer in charge of constructing and running the station, there had already been earlier "comfort stations" operated by the imperial navy. Initially, the military planned to recruit Japanese prostitutes for the Shanghai station but when it began operating, most of the women were local Chinese who were forcibly recruited. Later on, Japanese women would account for a small portion of the "comfort women." Japanese "comfort women" are generally believed to have been prostitutes who volunteered for the assignment. However, it is questionable whether the term voluntary is applicable considering the circumstances under which the women were recruited. Until the end of the Asia-Pacific War, prostitution was not much of a choice of any kind, rather, the vast majority of women ended up in this profession in exchange for their family's debts (i.e., they were sold into prostitution by their families). These women lived under close supervision and received little payment, the majority of which was deducted for various "living expenses." Consequently, their debts would rarely decrease. When they were offered to enlist as "comfort women," they were typically promised better payment, which could be used to eventually buy their freedom (similar to slaves in ancient Rome[23]). Essentially, they had to choose between two forms of sexual slavery and many chose what they believed to be the lesser evil.

As the war between Japan and China escalated and the Japanese-controlled territories increased in size, the number of "comfort stations" also went up drastically and more and more women were needed. Although Chinese women continued to be "recruited" as "comfort women" especially in China, the military, worried about information leaks, did not consider it safe to have soldiers in close contact with Chinese women. Chinese "comfort women" were also not very popular among Japanese soldiers because they did not speak their language. Japanese prostitutes, on the other hand, frequently had STDs, which led Asō Tetsuo, a military doctor to suggest that women with no experience in prostitution would be more appropriate as gifts to soldiers of the emperor's military.[24] However, the Japanese military could not force Japanese women who were not prostitutes already to work as "comfort women." Apart from the likely public outcry, the knowledge that their loved ones might be working in a "comfort" station would have negatively impacted soldiers' morale. The women who, preferably, were non-prostitutes, were less likely to leak information to the enemy, and were able to speak at least some Japanese had therefore to come from somewhere else.

This is the most plausible reason why most victims of the "comfort" system were recruited in Japan's former colonies, Korea and Taiwan, with Korea contributing the majority of women. The Japanese language was an official language and taught in schools in both countries under the *kōminka seisaku*, a policy to assimilate Koreans and Taiwanese into Japanese culture.

There were, however, also a significant number of local women in occupied areas who, contrary to claims of protecting civilians, were forced into the "comfort" system. These include Chinese, Philippina, Indonesian, Vietnamese, Burmese, and even Dutch women who were captured after the Japanese imperial military seized Indonesia, a former Dutch colony.[25] The total number of victims of the "comfort" system is a matter of ongoing debate since most military documents were destroyed at the end of the war. Estimates range from 50,000 to as many as 200,000 women.[26]

There is little doubt that the "comfort" stations were under the control of the Japanese military. Usually confiscated buildings in occupied areas such as hotels and large homes were used. When no suitable building was available, new facilities were constructed. The buildings were divided into small rooms with barely enough space for a bed, separated by screens made of grass or thin wooden boards. Each room contained either a small bed or a futon mattress and the personal belongings of the "comfort women" who lived in them. All "comfort women" had to register with the military officials, providing information such as where they came from or if they had any debt. The lives of the "comfort women" were tightly controlled. They were forced to engage in sexual acts with twenty to thirty soldiers a day with few or no days off. If they resisted, they were severely beaten by soldiers or comfort station managers.

Soldiers who used the "comfort stations" had to pay in most cases. This made them feel as if they were paying for prostitutes, which was legal in Japan until the 1950s. However, many of the women did not receive compensation for their services. Even most of those who did receive payment would eventually lose their money because they were paid in the special military currency issued by the Japanese military, which could be used only in Japan's occupied areas and became worthless after the war. Those from former Japanese colonies who deposited money in Japanese postal accounts lost access to their accounts after the war.

The "comfort" system included a variety of facilities serving slightly different purposes. The living conditions of those confined in the system may have varied considerably and how they were treated depended in part on the type of facility. Differences in purpose were reflected in the appearance of the facilities themselves. Soh categorizes "comfort" stations into three categories with various subtypes.[27] The three main categories are "concessionary," "paramilitary," and "criminal" facilities. "Concessionary" facilities were operated for profit and run by civilian proprietors who were mostly Japanese and Korean yet regulated by the military. These can be further divided into two subcategories: "houses of entertainment" and "houses of prostitution." Houses of entertainment were comprehensive comfort facilities similar to a specific type of restaurant, *ryōtei*, found in pleasure quarters in imperial Japan. Houses of entertainment served food and provided entertainment as well as prostitution. They were usually reserved for officers only, and most frequently found in urban areas. Houses of prostitution were mostly for the rank and file soldiers although some officers also frequented them as they were cheaper than houses of entertainment. At houses of prostitution, only officers were allowed to stay overnight. The majority of Korean survivors seem to have been stationed in houses of prostitution. While many claimed that they never received payment, a few women acknowledged the receipt of payment. Concessionary facilities were located both in cities and remote areas where military units were stationed.

The second type of comfort facilities, paramilitary facilities, were set up and managed directly by particular units of the military.[28] This category can be subdivided into the "maidens' auxiliary" and the "quasi-brothel." The "maidens' auxiliary" belonged to a particular unit of the military and it was usually located in a remote area close to the frontline. The "comfort women" in a maidens' auxiliary were expected to play various feminine gender roles such as washing for the soldiers and taking care of the injured as well as sexual labor. The "quasi-brothel" was also located in remote areas but unlike in "maidens' auxiliaries," women at "quasi-brothels" were expected to perform sexual labor only. They were "exempt" from manual labor and they sometimes served multiple units at the same time. With permission from their commanding officers, soldiers were able to visit quasi-brothels on certain days of the week for specific lengths of time.

"Criminal facilities," the third type, differed significantly from concessionary and paramilitary facilities. They were makeshift facilities constructed after sex crimes were committed by individual soldiers against local women near the frontlines in Japan's occupied areas, like the Philippines. Japanese soldiers abducted local women, often after raping them, and confined them in these facilities to continually satisfy their sexual needs. That this happened mostly during the final years of the war is likely attributable to the increased difficulty of transporting Korean or Japanese women to the far-flung battlefields.[29]

A BRIEF SUMMARY OF A DECADE-OLD CONFLICT

It is not surprising that memories of sexual slavery orchestrated by the Japanese imperial military constitute an "inconvenient past" for many Japanese, most notably members of Japan's conservative leading party, the Liberal Democratic Party (LDP). Until 1991 when three Korean survivors of sexual slavery took legal action against the Japanese government, the "comfort women" were virtually absent from Japan's official war histories (e.g., "comfort women" were not mentioned in middle school history textbooks until 1997).[30]

In December 1991, Kim Hak-sun and two other Korean survivors supported by the Association for the Pacific War Victims, a South Korean organization, filed a lawsuit at the Tokyo Local Court against the Japanese government to seek compensation. In 2001, they lost the case on the grounds that war compensation for Koreans had been settled between the Japanese and South Korean governments in the 1965 bilateral agreement. However, the lawsuit garnered much public attention both in and outside of Japan. (The women appealed to the Tokyo Higher Court, but the case was dismissed again in 2003; their subsequent appeal to the Supreme Court was dismissed in 2004.)

The lawsuit as well as the discovery of additional evidence confirming the involvement of the Japanese imperial military in the operation of "comfort stations"[31] forced the Japanese government to issue a formal apology in 1992 and the so-called Kōno Statement in 1993. In this statement, Japan, for the first time, acknowledged the former Japanese military's involvement in the "comfort" system. Although the statement also acknowledges the forceful and deceptive recruitment of women into sexual slavery, the later administrations remained ambivalent about the actual role of the military in the coercive and deceitful recruitment of the women, directly or indirectly placing the blame for this solely on nonmilitary contractors, and some politicians maintained the position that most women willingly participated in this "high risk, high reward job."

The Kōno Statement marked a significant turning point in Japan's "comfort women" policy, yet the issue has remained controversial in and outside of

Japan. One contributing factor is the refusal of the Japanese government to pay reparations to survivors of sexual slavery. This refusal is based on a war reparations agreement with South Korea from the 1960s (stipulating that all claims have been met).[32] As a result, the Asian Women's Fund, a fund offering compensation to survivors of sexual slavery, was established by donations from the Japanese public but not the Japanese government. The attitudes of high-ranking Japanese politicians toward the issue of sexual slavery have also drawn international criticism, especially from South Korea where the majority of the victims were taken.[33]

In 1996, Radhika Coomaraswamy, a Sri Lankan jurist and the United Nations' special rapporteur on violence against women, submitted a report on the "comfort women" based on research in South Korea, North Korea, and Japan to the UN Human Rights Commission.[34] In her report, Coomaraswamy criticizes the Japanese government for failing to meet its responsibilities and calls for the following steps:[35]

- Acknowledge . . . violations of international law and accept . . . legal responsibilities.
- Pay compensation to former "comfort women."
- Establish a governmental screening organization for providing compensation.
- Punish those who were involved in the conscription.
- Include classes in schools that would enhance public awareness of the "comfort women" issue.

To date none of these conditions have been met except for the last one that the education ministry temporarily satisfied by including a brief description of the "comfort women" in junior high school history textbooks. However, this passage was removed by 2014. The Japanese government argues that there is no legal obligation to follow these demands because Japan had not ratified the Den Haag and Geneva treaties that stipulate conduct during war.[36]

The Coomaraswamy report has been discredited by Japanese nationalists. One main point of criticism is that it cites Yoshida Seiji's confessional books in support of claims of the former Japanese military's coercive recruitment of Korean women. Yoshida, a former Japanese soldier, wrote two books about "hunting" Korean women in *Chōsenjin Ianfu to Nihonjin* [Korean Comfort Women and the Japanese] in 1977 and *Watashi no Sensō Hanzai* [My War Crimes] in 1983. By the early 1990s, the truthfulness of his accounts was called into question by nationalist historians who oppose the "comfort women's" redress movement, as well as progressive historians who support the movement.[37]

In another development, Michael Honda, a Japanese American Democrat from California, proposed a nonbinding resolution in the U.S. Congress in

January 2007 that would call on Japan to unequivocally acknowledge and apologize for its brutal mistreatment of women during World War II.[38] In response to the proposed resolution, on March 1, 2007, former prime minister Abe Shinzō (in office: 2006–2007 and 2012–2020) denied the former Japanese military's role in forcing women into sexual slavery.[39] He stated that "there is no evidence to prove there was coercion." Abe's remarks resulted in official protests from several of the countries where the "comfort women" were abducted and garnered even more support for the pending resolution. It was jointly proposed by 167 representatives and passed the U.S. House Foreign Affairs Committee with the overwhelming support of 39–2 votes on June 26, 2007.[40] Abe, since then, did apologize to the former "comfort women";[41] however, he maintained his position that there is no evidence for "direct" coercion of women into sexual slavery (e.g., members of the military actively being involved), while he acknowledged the possibility of "indirect" coercion (e.g., private contractors collecting women for the military). These statements, again, caused controversy on a national and an international level.

In 2014, the *Asahi Shimbun*, a liberal Japanese newspaper, supportive of the redress movement, retracted several of its articles that cited Yoshida's accounts concluding that Yoshida's books were, in fact, fabrications. Since then, Japanese nationalists have used the *Asahi Shimbun*'s retraction to argue that the whole "comfort women" issue is a fabrication.[42] Japanese prime minister Abe, seeking to have the Coomaraswamy report modified, sent Satō Kuni, Japan's ambassador in charge of human rights issues, to meet with Coomaraswamy. Coomaraswamy, however, rejected Abe's request, arguing that Yoshida's accounts constituted only a small part of the evidence for the Japanese imperial military's coercive recruitment of "comfort women."

In a new development on December 28, 2015, Prime Minister Abe and South Korean president Park Geun-hye reached a "final and irreversible" agreement on the sexual slavery issue.[43] According to the agreement, the Japanese government is going to issue another apology and donate $8.3 million dedicated to the care of surviving victims. In return, the South Korean government will abstain from any future claims. Yet again, the agreement is controversial because the victims had no voice in negotiating it and it does not include an admission of legal responsibility by Japan (the payment is considered a humanitarian gesture not reparations[44]). Also, Japan made the payment contingent on the removal of a statue symbolizing the "comfort women" in front of the Japanese Embassy in Seoul—a move that further irritated many Koreans.[45] The statue was installed by a civic group, the Korean Council for the Women Drafted for Military Sexual Slavery by Japan, in 2011 and the group labeled the agreement "a humiliating diplomacy."[46]

More fuel was added to the fire when a new statue signifying a "comfort woman" was erected in front of the Japanese Consulate in Busan, South

Korea, on December 30, 2016. The Japanese demanded the immediate removal of the monument, a demand that was not met by the new South Korean government (President Park Geun-hye, negotiator of the "final and irreversible" agreement was impeached in December 2016). The Japanese government considered this a violation of the 2015 bilateral agreement and the issue has strained the diplomatic relationship between the two countries since then (i.e., the Japanese government called back Nagamine Yasumasa, Japanese ambassador to South Korea in protest[47]).

THE HUMAN RIGHTS DISCUSSION

After the 1991 lawsuit instigated by Kim Hak-sun and two other Korean survivors of sexual slavery, it became a major point of debate whether sexual slavery under the Japanese imperial military should be considered a human rights violation or not. The 1948 United Nations Universal Declaration of Human Rights that "is generally agreed to be the foundation of international human rights law" lists thirty articles of fundamental human rights. Among those, several apply to the case of sexual slavery under the Japanese imperial military. For instance, Article 4 states that "[n]o one shall be held in slavery or servitude; slavery and the slave trade shall be prohibited in all their forms." Article 5 reads: "No one shall be subjected to torture or to cruel, inhuman or degrading treatment or punishment." Also, as Shashi Tharoor put it simply, human rights violations are about coercion: "where coercion exists, rights are violated."[48] To progressive scholars, writers, and activists such as Yoshimi, as the survivors were forcibly and deceitfully confined into sexual servitude with threatened or actual use of violence , the "comfort" system clearly violated these articles.[49] Interestingly, Article 8 states, "Everyone has the right to an effective remedy by the competent national tribunals for acts violating the fundamental rights granted him by the constitution or by law." According to this article, not redressing the issue after human rights violations were committed constitutes a human rights violation in itself. Nationalist scholars and writers, on the other hand, challenge the "forced" aspects of the "comfort" system arguing that the women were "paid prostitutes" who voluntarily engaged in this occupation and, therefore, no human rights violations occurred. Following this argument no redress is necessary.

According to Swartz, there are three general categories of human rights.[50] The first category or first-generation rights are concerned with civil and political liberties. That would include the rights to freedom of speech, religion, freedom of the press, rights related to criminal law, and political rights. Second-generation human rights are then cultural, social, and economic rights affirming the dignity of the individual. Third-generation human rights are about collective group rights, especially in developing nations including the rights to self-determination and national development. Survivors of sexual slavery were coerced or deceived into a state of sexual servitude and forced into inhumane situations where basic human needs are not met. This constitutes an example of a violation of second-generation human rights although a memory of such violations is not shared by nationalist scholars.

JAPANESE WAR MEMORIES

Through *heiwa gakushū* (peace education) promulgated in contemporary Japan, Japanese children have been taught the importance of peace by learning about the horrendous nature of war. As part of this, Japanese children have typically been taught about the suffering inflicted on the Japanese, such as the atomic bombs and air raids by the Allies, instead of the suffering the Japanese caused during the war. Thus, many Japanese today view themselves as victims of the Asia-Pacific War, as victims of the nuclear attacks on Hiroshima and Nagasaki, or as victims of the numerous air raids on Japanese cities.[51]

Cold War politics after the war may have contributed to Japan's selective amnesia concerning wartime atrocities. Japan became a critical U.S. ally in East Asia when the Korean War broke out, and China became a communist nation. This meant that Japan's past crimes in Asia, especially those committed against communist Chinese, were conveniently "forgotten" by many people in the United States. To be an influential U.S. ally, Japan now had to be viewed in a positive light. In addition, as will be discussed in more detail in chapter 2, the Japanese were discouraged by the Allied occupation forces from remembering the Great Japanese Empire in postwar Japan, and this made it easier for the Japanese to forget the nation's colonial past and exploitation of its colonies.

This Japanese indifference to the nation's past as aggressors is in stark contrast to the ways in which Germans remember the war and their war responsibilities. Julian Dierkes points out that since the 1960s, public discourse in West Germany, including media accounts, literature, and education, has acknowledged and widely discussed National Socialist atrocities and Germans' collective involvement. This did not change after the unification.[52]

Memories casting the Japanese in the role of aggressors contradict the victim role taught through *heiwa gakushū*. This is one reason why memories of sexual slavery are contested among Japanese today; they challenge the dominant memory of the Asia-Pacific War and, thus, part of their heritage, identity, and worldview. Collective memory is frequently viewed as a construct heavily influenced by concerns of the present. An analysis of past materials on sexual slavery such as Japanese films and books will enable me to provide accounts of period-specific memories and identify some of the concerns that make the "comfort women" memory controversial in Japan today.

COLLECTIVE MEMORY

One way to look at collective memory is as "a set of ideas, images, feelings about the past—[that] is best located not in the minds of individuals, but in the resources they share."[53] Following this approach, we make sense of the past, utilizing a variety of resources. This active process of memory formation is motivated by our personal experiences and goals, by what we believe we are and what we aspire to be, but the process is facilitated or impeded by our surroundings and artifacts available to us. Another defining criterion of collective memories is that they are shared among people and they constitute histories that are accepted by a significant portion of a community or society.[54]

There is a wealth of literature on collective memory ranging from sociology to history and communication. The studies of collective memory that are closest to my own views have all in common that they approach collective memory as a relationship between the present and the past.[55] The formation of collective memory is an active, dynamic process: motivated by worldviews, traditions, political interests, and personal desires. In short, for me, collective memory is people's appropriation of the past in contemporary society. Rhetoric of the past is used to influence the beliefs, attitudes, and values of others. Different narratives, advanced by different proponents, are competing for audiences, fall on fertile ground, or meet with resistance. How rhetoric of the past is used to serve the needs of the present or to influence others is of considerable interest to me and other rhetorical critics.[56]

It is important to realize that an absence of certain events in artifacts can also greatly influence the formation of memories. What is left out of a story can be just as telling as what remains. When Irwin-Zarecka discusses collective remembering and forgetting, she argues that an "absence of memory is just as socially constructed as memory itself."[57] How events or a group of people are "forgotten" and omitted from official history is often ideologically or politically motivated and a fight to be "remembered" can challenge the current power structure and cultural assumptions. Wen Shu Lee and Philip Wander describe discursive amnesia as "a group's inability or unwillingness to recall certain people, events, and offenses" and contend that this systematic collective forgetting "perpetuate[s] privilege and interest" among certain groups of people.[58] In the following chapters, I will examine what memories of sexual slavery have been suppressed in Japan and how this collective forgetting has privileged certain people and ideologies.

Intrigued by the socially constructed nature of collective memory, a number of communication scholars have studied memories of various past events. For instance, Hasian,[59] Owen,[60] and Ehrenhaus[61] have examined the memories of the Holocaust in popular sources such as films and a museum. The memories of World War II have been studied by Prosise[62] and Biesecker.[63] Other past events communication scholars have written about include: the Vietnam War (e.g., Hariman and Lucaites[64]), slave revolt (e.g., Hasian and Carlson[65]), race violence (e.g., Owen and Ehrenhaus[66]), and the Asia-Pacific War (e.g., Inuzuka,[67] Inuzuka and Fuchs,[68] Inuzuka[69]). Although, in recent years, the number of publications on memories from non-Western countries has increased (e.g., Aoki and Jonas's work on the Rwandan genocide,[70] Cole's 2018 work on the Liberian civil war,[71] Blackmore's 2018 essay on the memory of the dictatorship of Rafael Trujillo in the Dominican Republic,[72] and my own works on memories of the Asia-Pacific War), there remains a strong Western bias in collective memory studies in communication, which is indicative of a Western bias in rhetorical criticism in particular and communication in general where whiteness is "the norm" and non-Western topics are discussed only in intercultural communication.

ORIENTALISM

An important and maybe somewhat surprising aspect of memories of the "comfort women" is that they lend themselves to be discussed within an "Orientalist" context. Orientalism is characterized as the ways in which Western colonial powers viewed the non-West. When the Japanese adopted colonialism from the West, they also adopted a worldview not unlike that of Western colonizers. By examining colonial memories of sexual slavery, memories of mostly Korean victims who, as colonial subjects, were "remembered" by former Japanese colonizers, I will show that "Orientals" can "Orientalize" each other.

In his groundbreaking *Orientalism*,[73] Edward Said argues that Orientalism was a way for the West to dominate and control the Orient, that is, colonization. He also discusses some of the characteristics of "Orientals" presented by Orientalist scholars. One of these characteristics is the distinction between the West and the Orient, which was associated with the idea of Western supremacy and Oriental weakness. Said argues that while Westerners were considered to be "rational, developed, humane," and superior, Orientals were seen as "aberrant, underdeveloped," and inferior.[74] Similarly, Orientalists believed that Orientals were incapable of rational, logical thought. Oriental women were typically depicted as exotic and sexually suggestive.

From Western colonizers' perspectives, non-Western colonized countries had no culture or history and "no independence or integrity worth representing without the West."[75] Authors are "shaping and shaped" by their country's history and "culture and the aesthetic forms it contains derive from historical experience."[76] In this sense, an analysis of the depictions of sexual slavery in Japan to learn more about the nature of memories of sexual slavery is meaningful because the perceptions of each Japanese author/movie director are shaped by Japan's history and the authors' representations of sexual slavery derive from historical experience.

Some scholars in my field have applied postcolonial theories to their collective memory studies. For instance, Hasian and Shugart critique the representations of French colonization of Vietnam in the movie, *Indochine*,[77] and Hasian examines military Orientalism in the movie, *Zero Dark Thirty*.[78] However, postcolonial analyses in collective memory studies in particular and postcolonial studies in general tend to focus on Western colonization of the non-West. I will apply postcolonial theories to a case of non-Western colonialization and discuss how Korean victims of sexual slavery are remembered by their former Japanese colonizers in similar ways former Western colonizers remember colonized "Orientals." In doing so, I will illustrate how Orientalism is about power and domination—not necessarily about a "superior West" or an "inferior East," and how, in memories of Korean victims, exoticism is used as an excuse/justification for sexual exploitation.

Even among postcolonial studies in general, the number of studies focusing on non-Western colonization is very small. Among those few, for example, Tessa Morris-Suzuki discusses the decolonization process of Korea after Japan's defeat in the Pacific War and its effects in Japan.[79] Morris-Suzuki specifically focuses on two occasions in the 1950s when the Japanese government attempted to return a large number of Koreans who had stayed in Japan after the war, so that the nation could restore the myth of an "ethnically homogeneous Japan." This myth, promoted and popularized in postwar Japan, contrasted starkly with the multiethnic ideology of the Greater East Asia Co-Prosperity Sphere that had been promoted by the Japanese empire to justify Japan's militaristic expansionism in Asia. The underlying discrimination against Koreans in Japanese society must have been an instigator for the Japanese government's action of sending Koreans back "home."

In another study focusing on non-Western colonization, Lionel Babicz compares Japan's colonization of Korea to France's colonization of Algeria, discussing the similarities and differences between the two forms of colonization and postcolonial relations between former colonizers and formerly colonized nations.⁸⁰ Among the similarities were the assimilation policies employed by France and Japan in Algeria and Korea, respectively. Both France and Japan forced their colonial subjects to adopt their cultures—French culture for Algerians and Japanese culture for Koreans. Babicz paints a somewhat more favorable, humane picture of Japan's treatment of Koreans during colonization or its postcolonial relationship with South Korea than others have depicted.

Jung-Bong Choi critiques Western-centered postcolonial studies. Many influential postcolonial critics in Western academia come from former Western colonies such as India, East and North Africa, the Caribbean, and Palestine (e.g., Edward Said, Homi Bhabha). These scholars are familiar with and heavily influenced by British or French imperialism. When they critique colonialism, they critique the West, particularly British and French imperialism.⁸¹ Their attempts to tear down a Western Eurocentric worldview have often resulted in the opposite, a phenomenon described as "oppositional Eurocentrism." Choi defines this as "the contradictory mechanism by which the recalcitrant endeavour of postcolonial criticism to dethrone Eurocentric consciousness ends up enshrining and re-placing the West as the sacred hub of world history."⁸² Discussions that locate every evil in the West but identify the same West as the potential cure for every problem tend to marginalize not only former colonies but non-Western cultures in general because they are assumed to be too helpless to subvert the imperialistic power structure. Studies that focus on non-Western colonialism can help alleviate this problem. The study of Japanese colonialism, an Eastern power that joined the ranks of nineteenth-century colonizers, shows that non-Western cultures were not necessarily inept, disorganized, or (unfortunately) incapable of committing great injustice. What could make the subject problematic is that Japanese imperialism was inspired and heavily influenced by its Western counterpart, which means that comparisons cannot be avoided. Therefore, Japanese imperialism might be held against a Western "gold standard," which could lead to a dilemma similar to "oppositional Eurocentrism."

RESEARCH ON SEXUAL SLAVERY UNDER THE JAPANESE IMPERIAL MILITARY

Sexual slavery under the Japanese imperial military has received little attention from scholars and writers before the 1970s. Senda Kakō, a Japanese journalist, wrote *Jūgun Ianfu: Seihen* [Military Comfort Women: Main Edition] in 1973 and *Jūgun Ianfu: Zokuhen* [Sequel: Military Comfort Women] in 1978 that are considered the first systematic reports on government-sanctioned sexual slavery. Senda himself had no knowledge of the issue until the 1960s when he saw photos of Korean survivors fleeing together with Japanese soldiers from the Allies at the end of the war when the Allies' counterattack became fierce.[83] For his books, Senda interviewed former Japanese soldiers who frequented "comfort stations," a few Japanese survivors of sexual slavery, and Korean witnesses of abductions. He also examined diaries and letters written by former Japanese soldiers. In Senda's books, the "comfort women" are depicted as victims of the "comfort" system who were destroyed in the process of "comforting" soldiers and who suffered from physical and psychological trauma until long after the war. However, in his work, the "comfort" system is not viewed as a war crime for which the perpetrators should be held accountable. A second early account on the "comfort women" stems from Kim Il Myon, a Korean resident of Japan, who wrote *Tennō no Guntai to Chōsenjin Ianfu* [The Emperor's Military and Korean Comfort Women] (published in 1976), focusing on the experiences of Korean "comfort women." Pointing out that Korean women were targeted most frequently as potential "comfort women" and that Korean "comfort women" were stationed under harsher conditions than their Japanese counterparts, he argues that the "comfort" system was a case of ethnic cleansing with the goal to decimate the Korean people.[84]

After the trial in 1991, the "comfort women" received considerably more public and scholarly attention. The term, "sexual slavery," became associated with the "comfort women" and the issue was now considered a potential war crime. While some progressive scholars such as Ueno Chizuko,[85] a sociologist from Tokyo University, and Yoshimi Yoshiaki,[86] a historian from Chuō University, argue that sexual slavery was a war crime the nation is responsible for, nationalist scholars such as Hata Ikuhiko, a historian from Chiba University, maintain that "comfort women" were paid prostitutes and the women who came forward did so solely for monetary reasons.[87]

In the West, Dai Sil Kim-Gibson, a Korean American filmmaker and author, published, *Silence Broken: Korean Comfort Women* in 1999, compiling interviews with mostly Korean survivors of sexual slavery.[88] She vividly describes the survivors' stories starting from their "recruitment" to repeated rape and violence at "comfort" stations. In her book, many of the survivors also relate the hardships they had to endure after the war such as infertility, psychological trauma, and failed romantic relationships because of their past. Kim-Gibson also directed a documentary under the same title in the year 2000. Also, George Hicks, an Australian writer, published, *The Comfort Women: Japan's Brutal Regime of Enforced Prostitution in the Second World War* in 1997, describing the operation of the "comfort" system illustrated by survivor's testimonies.[89]

Yonson Ahn contributed a chapter, "Japan's 'Comfort Women' and Historical Memory: The Neo-nationalist Counter-attack," to the anthology,

The Power of Memory in Modern Japan published in 2008, examining memories of sexual slavery constructed and promoted by neo-nationalists in contemporary Japan. She describes how Japanese neo-nationalists, for the purpose of fostering patriotism among school children, attempt to replace a "masochistic view" of Japanese history—a view emphasizing negative aspects of the nation's past, with more positive narratives. Toward this end, neo-nationalists have embarked on a campaign to counter the redress movement for sexual slavery survivors. Neo-nationalists take an extreme positivist position, only trusting official documents by the Japanese military/government and disregarding the women's testimonies as "unreliable" or "mere oral accounts." As a result, they deny the involvement of the former Japanese military and government in the coerced or deceitful recruitment of women. Japanese neo-nationalists also tend to present the women as prostitutes who voluntarily participated in this "high risk, high reward" work. They also claim that military brothels have existed in the armies of many countries due to men's uncontrollable sexual desires. Following this argument, the "comfort" system was a necessity to prevent soldiers from raping local women. Furthermore, neo-nationalists contend that one cannot pass judgment on sexual slavery during times of war from today's perspective (i.e., a different moral code applies to times of war).[90]

In 2008, C. Sarah Soh, a Korean American anthropologist, published *The Comfort Women: Sexual Violence and Postcolonial Memory in Korea and Japan*, compiling her interviews with mostly Korean survivors of sexual slavery and Korean and Japanese activists of the redress movement. In her work she challenges the dominant, paradigmatic discourse in South Korea that "Korean 'comfort women' were coercively or deceitfully recruited under Japan's national wartime policy of *Chŏngsindae* (Korean) or *Teishintai* (Japanese) [Women's Volunteer Labor Corps] and that they were all held in slave like conditions."[91] While the Japanese military, guided by imperial Japan's paternalistic ideology and racist colonial policy, was the driving factor behind the "comfort" system, colonial Korea's patriarchal system and classism were also contributing factors as they rendered young Korean women vulnerable to deceptive recruitment by, often civilian, Japanese or Korean proprietors. Many of the survivors' testimonies reveal that they ran away from home when young to escape oppressive family conditions. In pursuit of independent lives as working women, they accepted deceptive offers of employment as "factory workers" in Japan. Detailing the experiences of these women before, during, and after the war, she concludes that the victims-survivors' experiences varied greatly depending on their socioeconomic and personal backgrounds and she questions the paradigmatic discourse on the "comfort women's" lives.

Soh's criticism of Korean patriarchy and classism and the Japanese empire's racist and patriarchal colonial policy provides an interesting contrast to a contemporaneous U.S. situation Stern describes. The American Plan also mainly targeted and detained impoverished, nonwhite women with the purported motive of "protecting troops from venereal disease."[92] Certain types of women—poor women, "promiscuous" and "reasonably suspicious" women, and minority women—were predominantly targeted by these programs.

In the field of communication, only a few studies have been conducted on sexual slavery. Most of these studies focus on the public apologies issued after the sexual slavery lawsuit in the 1990s because apologia is an important topic within rhetorical criticism, a subfield in communication. Edwards analyzed Japanese prime minister Murayama Tomiichi's apology.[93] Izumi examined the role of apologies in the "comfort women" reparations discourse in the 1990s and argued that the topic of apology shifted from a discourse on legal responsibility to a discourse on moral responsibility.[94] Studies on collective memories of sexual slavery are even less common in communication. One exception is Sarah Vartabedian's recent analysis of the "comfort women" statue in Seoul.[95] She argues that the statue constitutes an objective "witness" on behalf of the actual survivors because rape survivors are frequently seen as irrational, hysteric narrators of their own trauma. She claims that the statue, as an objective and implacable witness, accuses those who need to be held accountable.

Overall, although a number of books about sexual slavery under the Japanese imperial military appeared in several countries including Japan, South Korea, and the United States especially since the 1990s, most of them are reports on what the "comfort" system was and how it was operated, with a focus on testimonies from survivors, former Japanese soldiers, and witnesses, and military documents (e.g., Senda,[96] Kim-Gibson,[97] Hicks[98]). Most of the few articles on sexual slavery in communication focus on apologies. However, very few publications explore how sexual slavery is remembered in contemporary society. While Soh discusses memories of the "comfort women,"[99] her focus is clearly on South Korea. Considering how controversial the ways in which the Japanese remember the Asia-Pacific War in general and the "comfort women" in particular have been in East Asia, it is essential to have a thorough, in-depth analysis of how sexual slavery has been remembered in Japan.

APPELLATIONS

How to refer to the women who fell victim to sexual slavery under the Japanese imperial military has been another subject of debate. They are most commonly referred to as "the comfort women" (*ianfu* in Japanese, used without quotes in its English translation). A similar variation, *jūgn ianfu* [military comfort women], was first used by Senda Kakō in his 1973 book, *Jūgun*

Ianfu, a first systematic report on the issue, and has therefore been attributed to him.[100] During the war, a variety of other appellations were employed ranging from euphemisms such as *shakufu* [alcohol serving women] or more directly, *shougi* [licensed prostitutes], *joushi gun* [girls military], and *onna* [a woman or women] to the more derogatory *shūgyōfu* [women of indecent occupation] or sometimes even *pi* or *Chōsen pi* [Korean pi]. For instance, in *Shunpūden* [Story of a Prostitute][101] and *Inago* [The Locust],[102] two novels about "comfort women" that will be discussed in more detail later, the "comfort women" are simply referred to as *kanojo* [she/her], *kanojotachi* [they/them/their], or *onna* [woman/women] by the narrator. However, when addressed by soldiers, they are referred to as *pi*. The origin of *pi* is not clear. Some hold that it comes from the English word prostitute, but many believe it comes from a Mandarin Chinese term for female genitals.[103] Writers such as Senda and Soh claim that soldiers also called them *kōshū benjo* [public toilets].

After Kim Hak-sun's trial in the 1990s, the "comfort" system was, for the first time, recognized as sexual slavery.[104] Consequently, more and more people, especially those in support of the redress movement have tried to avoid the term, "comfort women," because it does not do justice to the abuse the women had to endure. But the term is also not popular with those who oppose the redress movement, especially in its variation "*jūgun ianfu*" [military comfort women]. The term, *jūgun* refers to *gunzoku*, civilians who officially worked for the military. As some Japanese nationalists take the position that the Japanese military and government were not directly involved in the recruitment of women and the operation of the "comfort" system, the use of *jūgun* is problematic for them and women who were simply "paid prostitutes" had no such status in the military.[105]

Soh notes that while some survivors adopted the term, "sex slaves," others disliked it because of its degrading connotations.[106] She states that the South Korean general public also reacted negatively to the term, "sex slaves," because the term is so negatively laden that it was hurtful to their self-esteem though the term may more accurately represent many women's experiences than "comfort women." Nonetheless, Soh explains that "sex slaves" has been widely used in the international community including the United Nations since the 1990s. In postwar Korea, the term *chŏngsindae* (Women's Volunteer Corps) was historically used synonymously with "comfort women."[107] This is a misperception because most "comfort women" were recruited before 1943 while the Women's Volunteer Corps was not established until 1944. Instead, South Koreans widely adopted the term, *halmŏni* [grandmother], referring to the Korean survivors with respect.[108] Traditionally, Koreans use kin terms such as "grandmother," "grandfather," "anti," or "uncle," when addressing strangers with respect in accordance to age differences between the addressors and the addresses. While the practice of referring to the survivors as *halmŏni* or grandmothers has been adopted even outside of South Korea (e.g., on the Philippines or in Taiwan) there are also issues with this terminology. For example, speakers' perceived generational distance is not always accurate. Some people who address the survivors as *halmŏni* may be of the survivors' children's generation.[109] Another problem is classism surrounding the appellation. Although meant to be polite and respectful, women of high social status would never be called *halmŏni*.[110] Soh also problematizes the desexualizing effects of the appellation as well as the erasure of individual differences among the survivors, calling for individualized appellations referring to them.[111]

While I agree that there is a need for differentiation among victims and, therefore, will use individual names whenever possible, I still have to employ a collective, general term for the sake of analysis. Individual names are not always available especially in texts, fiction or nonfiction, before the 1990s because the authors tend to discuss the women's experiences collectively, using witnesses' testimonies or former military documents. When discussing the collective memories of these women held by others, the Japanese public during different time periods, differentiation is not feasible because such memories often do not differentiate. Generalization is a common theme and the term "collective" frequently also applies to their content. However, *ianfu* or the comfort women clearly feels inappropriate. Since this term is widely known and used, scholars such as Izumi have used it in parentheses.[112] It is easily recognizable to readers who may not be familiar with the subject and the term is also used in many of the texts I am analyzing in this book. Consequently, I will follow this example and use the term in parentheses. Whenever possible, I will use, "sexual slavery survivors" which in my opinion better reflects the majority of the women's experiences and acknowledges their strength and agency. Although they led misfortunate lives under circumstances that were mostly out of their control, before, during, and after the war, reading their testimonies, we learn that many of them were strong and determined women who did not accept their fate and do not fit the classic victim role. Many of those who came forward after the war have taken an active part in the redress movement and continue to fight back to this day.

CHAPTER ORGANIZATION

I will examine how sexual slavery under the Japanese imperial military has been remembered over the past seventy years, following the Asia-Pacific War. I further divide this period into four stages: (1) from 1945 to the 1960s, (2) from the 1970s to 1990, (3) from 1991 to 2015, and (4) from 2015 to the present. The beginning of the 1970s is used as a first divisive point because the 1970s mark a time period when a number of articles and books on the former Japanese military's atrocities in Asia were published in Japan and it is interesting to see how sexual slavery was remembered before and after Japan became morally "conscious" of these events. This development may have been precipitated by the activism of the 1960s when student protests against the Vietnam War and the military treaty between the United States and Japan created a fertile environment for historical/political discourse. For instance, Honda Katsuichi, a Japanese journalist, published articles titled, *Chūgoku no Tabi* [Travels in China], in *The Asahi Shimbun* [Asahi Newspaper] in the 1970s, based on his interviews with Chinese survivors of the Nanjing Massacre of 1937[113] and other Japanese atrocities committed in China. Ienaga Saburō, a Japanese history textbook author who took the Japanese Education Ministry through a series of trials for downplaying Japanese war crimes, won the second of his three textbook trials in the 1970s. In this context, Senda published a first systematic study on sexual slavery in 1973 and Kim Il Myon wrote his report on sexual slavery in 1976.

I have selected the year 1991 as a second turning point marked by the lawsuit three South Korean survivors, Kim Hak-sun and two other women, filed against the Japanese government. The trial constituted a paradigm change, as it was the first time that the military "comfort" system was viewed as a potential war crime.

The year 2015 marks a third turning point because in this year the governments of South Korea and Japan agreed on their "final, irreversible" resolution of the "comfort women" issue. As mentioned earlier, many people, some of the survivors of sexual slavery included, are opposed to this resolution. As a result, one year later, a statue signifying the "comfort women" was erected in front of the Japanese Consulate General in Busan, which promptly rekindled the conflict, clearly showing that the issue is far from resolved.

I will illustrate how sexual slavery has been remembered during each of these periods. I have selected some of the most widely cited books (including three movies and one museum) of each time period as my texts. While this does not necessarily provide the most "accurate" histories of sexual slavery, I argue that "popular truths" are rarely the most accurate and collective memories are "opinions" accepted and shared by the majority of a community. Therefore, the availability of a source to the public can be more important than its historical accuracy in determining its impact on the formation of collective memories.

Thus, chapter 2 that focuses on the memories of sexual slavery from 1945 to the 1960s examines four texts: *Shunpūden* [Story of a Prostitute] published in 1947 and *Inago* [The Locust] published in 1964, two novels written by Tamura Taijirō, a writer who himself served in the Asia-Pacific

War, the movie of the same title, *Story of a Prostitute* that was released in 1965 (directed by Suzuki Seijun), and another film based on the same novel, *Akatsuki no Dassou* [Escape at Dawn] released in 1950 (by Taniguchi Senkichi, the director, and Kurosawa Akira, the screenwriter). All of these sources are dominated by one subject, the romance between a low-ranking Japanese soldier and a "comfort woman" (or comfort singer in *Escape at Dawn*) that ends in tragedy. Although based on the novel, *Story of a Prostitute*, *Escape at Dawn* greatly differs from the original text and the second movie adaptation from 1965. The considerable differences in the 1950 version can be attributed to censorship by the General Headquarters (GHQ) of the Allied occupation forces. Kurosawa was apparently ordered to rewrite his screenplay seven times.[114] One of the objectives of the GHQ's censorship was to "re-educate the Japanese with an 'anti-war humanism.'"[115] As discussed in more detail in chapter 2, there are certain ideas the GHQ wanted to prevent from spreading among the Japanese public and the changes to the movie seem to have been based on the GHQ's censorship guidelines.

Chapter 3 examines the memories of sexual slavery in Japan from the 1970s to 1991. During this period, the perception of the "comfort women" changed and portrayals of the "comfort women" as victims emerged for the first time. However, most of the stories from that period are related by former Japanese soldiers and not by former "comfort women." The main texts I examine in this period are *Jūgun Ianfu: Seihen* [Military Comfort Women: Main Edition] (published in 1973) and *Jūgun Ianfu: Zokuhen* [Sequel: Military Comfort Women] (published in 1978) written by Senda Kakō, *Tennō no Guntai to Chōsenjin Ianfu* [The Emperor's Military and Korean Comfort Women] by Kim Il Myon (in 1976), *Chōsenjin Ianfu to Nihonjin* [Korean Comfort Women and the Japanese] (in 1977) and *Watashi no Sensou Hanzai* [My War Crimes] (in 1983) by Yoshida Seiji, and *Akarenga no Ie* [House with a Red Brick Roof] (in 1987) by Kawata Fumiko. *Jyūgun Ianfu: Seihen* is considered the first systematic report on sexual slavery in Japan. As mentioned earlier, the authenticity of Yoshida's autobiographic accounts was cast into doubt in the early 1990s. The *Asahi Shimbun* retracted several articles citing Yoshida's accounts in 2014 and they are now regarded as fabrications by most experts. Yet, at the time of their publication, Yoshida's books were widely read and cited and the likely impact of his writings on the formation of memories of sexual slavery during this period cannot be overlooked.

Chapters 4 and 5 cover the third period, from 1991 to 2015. Since the beginning of the 1990s, mostly because of the lawsuit initiated by three Korean survivors, sexual slavery has drawn the attention of scholars, journalists, and the general public. Since then, a number of books and scholarly essays have appeared on the topic. There has been much controversy between progressives who support the redress efforts of the former "comfort women" and nationalists who downplay the role of the Japanese military and government in operating the "comfort" system. Not in small part owing to the lawsuit much of the discussion pivots around the question whether or not the Japanese government should be held responsible for the "comfort" system. Here, I analyze differences in how progressives and nationalists remember sexual slavery. Chapter 4 focuses on nationalists' memories while chapter 5 examines progressives' memories. As sources of nationalist memories, I examine *Ianfu to Senjō no Sei* [Comfort Women and Sex in Battlefields] (published in 1999) by Hata Ikuhiko; *Shin Gomanism Sengen: Dai 3 Kan* [New Gomanism Declaration: Volume 3] (published in 1997) by Kobayashi Yoshinori; *Rekishi Kyōkasho Tono 15nen Sensō* [A 15-Year War with History Textbooks] (1997) edited by Nishio Kanji, Fujioka Nobukatsu, Kobayashi Yoshinori, and Takahashi Shirō; and *"Jūgun Ianfu": Asahi Shimbun vs. Bungei Shunjū* ["Military Comfort Women": Asahi Newspaper vs. Bungei Shunjū] (in 2014), an anthology edited by Bungei Shunjū, a conservative literary magazine. Hata, Nishio, Takahashi, and Fujioka are history professors while Kobayashi is a cartoonist. Kobayashi's cartoons that propagate his positions on various issues have been popular among the Japanese youth.

In chapter 5, to examine a progressive point of view from the same period (1991–2015), I examine *Jūgun Ianfu* [Military Comfort Women] (in 1995) by Yoshimi Yoshiaki; *Nashonarizumu to Jendā* [Nationalism and Gender] (in 1998) by Ueno Chizuko; *Jūgun Ianfu* [Military Comfort Women] by Nishino Rumiko; *Jūgun Ianfu to Rekishi Ninshiki* [Military Comfort Women and History Understanding] (in 1997) edited by Arai Shinichi, Nishino Rumiko, and Maeda Akira; *"Ianfu" Mondai ga Toutekitakoto* [What the "Comfort Women" Issue Has Led us to Question] (in 2010) edited by Oomori Noriko and Kawata Fumiko; and *Jūgun Ianfu to Sengo Hoshō* [Military Comfort Women and Postwar Compensation] by Takagi Kenichi. Yoshimi, Ueno, Arai, and Maeda are professors while Oomori and Takagi are lawyers who represented sexual slavery survivors in their trials against the Japanese government and Nishino and Kawata are writers and activists. Many of these writers, including Yoshimi, Nishino, Arai, and Kawata, have been officers and active members of *Nihon no Sensō Sekinin Shiryō Sentā* [Center for Research and Documentation on Japan's War Responsibility]—an NPO that supports redress for survivors of sexual slavery.

For the period from 2015 to the present, chapter 6 will discuss memories of sexual slavery after the 2015 bilateral agreement. Various events surrounding sexual slavery such as the erection of "comfort women" statues, the *Asahi Shimbun*'s retraction of its articles citing Yoshida's confessions, and the 2015 bilateral agreement reenergized scholars and activists. This chapter covers both nationalist and progressive memories of sexual slavery because of its short duration. For the nationalist side, I analyze *Kokuren ga Sekai ni*

Hirometa "Ianfu = Seidorei" no Uso: Junēbu Kokuren Hakendan Hōkoku [A Lie Spread All Over the World Through the United Nations, "Comfort Women = Sex Slaves": Reports by a Team that was Sent to Geneva for the United Nations' Meetings] (in 2016) edited by Fujioka Nobukatsu, *Ianfu Mondai no Kessan* [Settlement of the Comfort Women Issue] (in 2016) by Hata Ikuhiko, and articles from the newspaper *Sankei Shimbun*. For progressive memories, I analyze *Q & A Chōsenjin "Ianfu" to Shokuminchi Shihai Sekinin: Anatano Gimon ni Kotaemasu* [Q & A Korean "Comfort Women" and the Responsibility for Colonization: We Will Answer Your Questions] (in 2015) edited by Kim Puja, a professor at Tokyo University of Foreign Studies, and Ryūta Itagaki, a sociology professor at Dōshisha University, articles from the *Asahi Shimbun*, exhibits at the Active Museum: Onnatachi no Sensō to Heiwa Shiryōkan [Women's Active Museum on War and Peace] in Tokyo, and *Shusenjō: The Main Battleground of the Comfort Women Issue* (in 2018), a documentary film directed by Japanese American filmmaker Dezaki Miki. The Women's Active Museum on War and Peace (WAM) was opened in Tokyo in 2005 by the nonprofit organization *Sensō to Josei he no Bōryoku: Research Action Center* [Violence against Women in War Research Action Center] (VAWW RAC). Irwin-Zarecka discusses collective remembering and forgetting.[116] The bilateral deal between Japan and South Korea in 2015 and the Japanese government's insistence on the removal of the statue may constitute examples of such an attempt to promote "collective forgetting." On the other hand, South Korea's refusal to remove the statue could be interpreted as a fight to be remembered and may be challenging the present hegemonic official memories of sexual slavery in Japan.

Finally, in the concluding chapter, I will discuss the overall memories of sexual slavery under the Japanese imperial military and their potential problems. Discussing the differences in memories of sexual slavery over the last seventy years in Japan, I will also reflect back on my experience of visiting South Korea. By reflecting upon my autoethnographical accounts and my research on the overall memories of sexual slavery in Japan, the chapter will consider the roles of problematic memories of past events in society.

By analyzing these artifacts to examine what memories of sexual slavery under the Japanese imperial military exist and how they changed over time promoted by political and other concerns of their time, I hope to be able to provide a more in-depth understanding of the international and domestic controversy surrounding collective memories of sexual slavery. As Hasian argues, when we study "'history' that is filled with tangled ethnic relations, intercultural politics, and competitive postcolonial needs," we are reminded of the multiplicity and socially constructed nature of collective memories.[117] Thus, we can make politics and power relations that have influenced certain memories visible by critically examining memories of such "history." Careful analysis of such memories can provide valuable insights into current situations.[118] Additionally, by focusing on the memories of Korean survivors of sexual slavery, I attempt to contribute to postcolonial studies, providing a case of non-Western colonization of the non-West.

NOTES

1. Although it is widely considered that the (Asia)Pacific War spanned between 1941 and 1945 marked by Japan's attacks on the Allies in 1941 and Japan's surrender in 1945, some scholars such as Fujitani, White, and Yoneyama argue that because of the multitude of the war, it should be considered as the Asia-Pacific Wars. For instance, Dirlik states that for the Chinese, World War II was part of the War of Resistance against Japanese Aggression that began with Japan's invasion of northeastern China in 1931 and the subsequent establishment of the Japanese puppet state of Manchukuo and the full-scale war between China and Japan started in 1937. Similarly, in Japan, the war is referred to as the "15 nen sensō" [15-year war] that started against China in 1931 and ended in 1945. Following this convention, in this book, when I use the term, the Asia-Pacific War, I refer to the war(s) during 1931 and 1945.

T. Fujitani, Geoffrey M. White, and Lisa Yoneyama. "Introduction," in *Perilous Memories*, eds. T. Fujitani, Geoffrey M. White, and Lisa Yoneyama (Durham, NC: Duke University Press, 2001), 3; Arif Dirlik, "'Trapped in History' on the Way to Utopia: East Asia's 'Great War' Fifty Years Later," in *Perilous Memories*, eds. T. Fujitani, Geoffrey M. White, and Lisa Yoneyama (Durham, NC: Duke University Press, 2001), 302.

2. Yoshimi Yoshiaki argues that at least 50,000 women fell victims to this form of sexual oppression during the war. Media sources such as *BBC news* ("Japan's lack of apology,") estimate the number was 200,000. About 80% of them are believed to have been Koreans. "Japan's lack of apology on war-time past to affect South Korea ties – Yonhap," *BBC Monitoring Asia Pacific*, April 30, 2015, LexisNexis Academic.

3. Class A War Criminals are mostly Japanese military officials and politicians of high rank found guilty of committing "crimes against peace," labeling the act of hostile invasion a war crime, at the International Military Tribunal for the Far East (Tokyo trial). It was held by the Allies in Tokyo from 1946 to 1948. Twenty-eight Japanese politicians and military officials were prosecuted and all except for three who either died or was sick were found guilty. Seven including Tojō Hideki, a former prime minister and imperial army general, were executed in 1948. The seven who were executed and another seven who died in prison were enshrined as "Showa Junnansha" [Showa (era) martyrs] at the Yasukuni Shrine in 1978.

4. Kazu Kobayashi, "Hajimeni" [Introduction], in *Ienaga Saburo Taidanshū* [Collections of Interviews with Ienaga Saburo], ed. Ienaga Saburo (Tokyo: Minshusha, 1995), 2–6.

5. Kiyoshi Inoue, *Nihon no "Kindaika" to Gunkokushugi (Japan's "Modernization" and Militarism)* (Tokyo: Shinnippon Shinsho, 1966), 16.

6. Ian Buruma, "Suicide for the Empire," *The New York Review of Books*, November 21, 2002, 25.
7. Norimitsu Onishi, "Ugly Images of Asian Rivals Become Best Sellers in Japan," *The New York Times*, November 19, 2005, A1.
8. Urs Matthias Zachmann, "Blowing up a Double-Portrait in Black and White: The Concept of Asia in the Writings of Fukuzawa Yukichi and Okakura Tenshin," *Positions* 15, no. 2 (2007): 250–255.
9. Masamichi Inoki, *Gunkoku Nihon no Kōbō* (*The Rise and Fall of Militarist Japan*), (Tokyo: Daisan Bunmei sha, 1995), 33.
10. Inoki, *Gunkoku*, 66.
11. Zachmann, "Blowing up a Double-Portrait in Black and White," 345.
12. William L. Swan, "Japan's Intentions for its Greater East Asia Co-Prosperity Sphere as Indicated in its Policy Plans for Thailand," *Journal of South East Asian Studies* 27, no. 1 (March 1996): 139.
13. Tsuzuki Chushichi, *The Pursuit of Power in Modern Japan, 1825–1995* (New York: Oxford University Press, 2000), 256.
14. Yoshiaki Yoshimi, *Jūgun Ianfu* [Military comfort women] (Iwanami Shoten: Tokyo, 1995), 52–56.
15. Yoshimi, *Jūgun Ianfu*, 17–19.
16. Yoshimi (1995) cites documents from *Daitōa Sensō Rikugun Eiseishi* [History of the Great East Asia War Army Medicine] edited by the Self-Defense Army Medical School.
17. Yoshimi, *Jūgun Ianfu*, 43–47.
18. Catherine MacKinnon, "Crimes of War, Crimes of Peace," in *On Human Rights: The Oxford Amnesty Lectures 1993*, eds. Stephen Shute and Susan Hurley (New York: Basic Books, 1993), 88–89.
19. MacKinnon, "Crimes of War, Crimes of Peace," 89.
20. Scott Wasserman Stern, "The Long American Plan: The US Government's Campaign against Venereal Disease and Its Carriers," *Harvard Women's Law Journal* 38 (2015): 373.
21. Scott Wasserman Stern, *The Trials of Nina McCall: Sex, Surveillance, and the Decades-Long Government Plan to Imprison "Promiscuous" Women* (Boston: Beacon Press, 2018).
22. Yoshimi, *Jūgun Ianfu*, 16–17.
23. Mark Cartwright, "Slavery in the Roman World," *Ancient History Encyclopedia*, accessed June 4, 2020, https://www.ancient.eu/article/629/slavery-in-the-roman-world/
24. Kakō Senda, *Jūgun Ianfu* [Military Comfort Women] (Tokyo: Sanichi Shobō, 1978), 43–47.
25. Yoshimi, *Jūgun Ianfu*, 175–184.
26. See note 2.
27. Soh, *The Comfort Women*, 117–132.
28. Ibid., 124–130.
29. Ibid., 130–132.

30. Although all seven textbooks included passages on the "comfort women" in 1997, in 2002, the number decreased to only three out of eight textbooks and, by 2014, the "comfort women" completely disappeared from middle school textbooks. In 2015, a middle school history textbook with a passage on the "comfort women" published by Manabisha, a new publisher, has been approved for use in 2016 by the Education Ministry although they had to include the Japanese government's position that "there is no evidence that proves the direct involvement of the Japanese military in the forcible recruitment of 'comfort women'" ("Govt's stance on comfort women").

31. On January 11, 1992, *The Asahi Shimbun*, a Japanese liberal newspaper, reported on Yoshimi Yoshiaki's discovery of documents, in the Self-Defense Library in Tokyo, that indicate the involvement of the military and the government in the "comfort" system. It was reported that one of the documents Yoshimi discovered is a letter written by the Military Department signed by high military officials such as Umezu Yoshijiro on March 4, 1938, ordering a unit of the Japanese military stationed in China to establish comfort stations under their control in collaboration with *kenpei* [Japanese special police] ("Iansho gunkanyo shimesu shiryō").

32. "Ianfu mondai de kōshiki shazai" [Official apologies for the comfort women issue], *Asahi Shimbun*, January 17, 1992, 1.

33. "No Comfort: [Editorial]," *The New York Times*, March 6, 2007, A20.

34. "Japan Urged to Set up War-Crimes Tribunal on Forced Prostitution: UN Criticizes Tokyo for Ignoring the Issue of So-Called Comfort Camps," *The Vancouver Sun*, February 7, 1996, A9. LexisNexis academic.

35. Ryūichi Ōtsuka, "Govt urged to pay 'comfort women.'" *The Daily Yomiuri*, February 7, 1996, *1*. LexisNexis academic.

36. "Japan urged," A9.

37. Soh, *The Comfort Women*, 154–155; Ikuhiko Hata, *Ianfu to Senjō no sei* [Comfort Women and Sex in Battlefields] (Tokyo: Shinchosha, 1999), 240.

38. Norimitsu Onishi, "Tokyo Outraged by a Familiar Face: Japanese-American Fights for Apology Over 'Comfort Women.'" *The International Herald Tribune*, May 12, 2007, 1. LexisNexis academic.

39. Ibid., 1.

40. Aya Igarashi, "'Comfort Women' Vote Passes," *The Daily Yomiuri*, August 1, 2007, 1. LexisNexis academic.

41. Onishi, "Tokyo Outraged," 1.

42. Martin Fackler, Rick Gladstone, and Choe Sang-hun. "Japan, Seeking Revision of Report on Wartime Brothels, Is Rebuffed," *The New York Times*, October 17, 2014, 4. LexisNexis academic.

43. Anna Fifield, "An Early Roadblock for Landmark 'Comfort Women' Deal," *The Washington Post*, January 1, 2016. LexisNexis academic.

44. Jonathan Soble and Choe Sang-hun, "'Comfort Women' Deal Angers Some," *The New York Times*, December 30, 2015, *A07*. LexisNexis academic.

45. Justin McCurry, "Former Sex Slaves Reject Japan and South Korea's 'Comfort Women' Accord; Deal Made Us Look Like Fools, Say Women Forced to Work in Japanese Wartime Brothels," *The Guardian*, January 26, 2016. LexisNexis academic.

46. Soble and Sang-hun, "'Comfort Women,'" A07.
47. "Impasse over Busan Statue Drags On," *The Japan Times*, February 9, 2017. LexisNexis academic.
48. Shashi Tharoor, "Are Human Rights Universal?" *World Policy Journal* 16, no. 4 (1999/2000): 4.
49. Yoshimi, *Jūgun Ianfu*, 170.
50. Omar Swartz, *The Rule of Law, Property, and the Violation of Human Rights: A Plea for Social Justice* (London: Foxwell & Davies Scientific Publishers, 2007).
51. Fujitani et al., "Introduction."
52. Julian Dierkes, *Postwar History Education in Japan and the Germanys: Guilty Lessons* (London: Routledge, 2010), 3–4.
53. Iwona Irwin-Zarecka, *Frames of Remembrance: The Dynamics of Collective Memory* (New Brunswick, NJ: Transaction Publishers, 1997), 4.
54. For example, Marouf Hasian and Robert Frank. "Rhetoric, History, and Collective Memory: Decoding the Goldhagen Debates," *Western Journal of Communication* 63, no. 1 (1999): 95–114.
55. For example, Carole Blair, Greg Dickinson, and Brian L. Ott, "Introduction: Rhetoric/Memory/Place," in *Places of Public Memory: The Rhetoric of Museums and Memorials*, eds. Greg Dickinson, Carole Blair, and Brian L. Ott (Tuscaloosa: University of Alabama Press, 2010), 6–7; Kathleen J. Turner, "Rhetorical History as Social Construction: The Challenge and the Promise," in *Doing Rhetorical History: Concepts and Cases*, ed. Kathleen Turner (Tuscaloosa: University of Alabama Press, 1998), 10; Bruce E. Gronbeck, "The Rhetorics of the Past: History, Argument, and Collective Memory," in *Doing Rhetorical History: Concepts and Cases*, ed. Kathleen Turner (Tuscaloosa: University of Alabama Press, 1998), 56.
56. For example, Gronbeck, "The Rhetorics of the Past."
57. Irwin-Zarecka, *Frames of Remembrance*, 119.
58. Wen Shu Lee and Philip C. Wander, "On Discursive Amnesia: Reinventing the Possibilities for Democracy through Discursive Amnesty," in *The Public Voice in a Democracy at Risk*, eds. Michael Salvador and Patricia M. Sias (Westport: Praeger, 1998), 151–172.
59. Marouf Hasian, "Remembering and Forgetting the 'Final Solution': A Rhetorical Pilgrimage through the U.S. Holocaust Memorial Museum," *Critical Studies in Media Communication* 21, no. 1 (2004): 64–92.
60. A. Susan Owen, "Expertise, Criticism and Holocaust Memory in Cinema," *Social Epistemology* 25, no. 3 (2011): 233–247.
61. Peter Ehrenhaus, "Why We Fought: Holocaust Memory in Spielberg's *Saving Private Ryan*," *Critical Studies in Media Communication* 18, no. 3 (2001): 321–337.
62. Theodore O. Prosise, "The Collective Memory of the Atomic Bombings Misrecognized as Objective History: The Case of the Public Opposition to the National Air and Space Museum's Atomic Bomb Exhibit," *Western Journal of Communication* 62, no. 3 (1998): 316–347.

63. Barbara A. Biesecker, "Remembering World War II: The Rhetoric and Politics of National Commemoration at the Turn of the 21st Century," *Quarterly Journal of Speech* 88, no. 4 (2002): 393–409.

64. Robert Hariman and John Louis Lucaites, "Public Identity and Collective Memory in U.S. Iconic Photography: The Image of 'Accidental Napalm,'" *Critical Studies in Media Communication* 20, no. 1 (2003): 35–66.

65. Marouf Hasian and Cheree Carlson, "Revisionism and Collective Memory: The Struggle for Meaning in the *Amistad Affair*," *Communication Monographs* 67, no. 1 (2000): 42–62.

66. A. Susan Owen and Peter Ehrenhaus, "Communities of Memory, Entanglements, and Claims of the Past on the Present: Reading Race Trauma through *The Green Mile*," *Critical Studies in Media Communication* 27, no. 2 (2010): 131–154.

67. Ako Inuzuka, "Remembering Japanese Militarism through the Fusosha Textbook: The Collective Memory of the Asian-Pacific War," *Communication Quarterly* 61, no. 2 (2013): 131–150.

68. Ako Inuzuka and Thomas Fuchs, "Memories of Japanese Militarism: The Yasukuni Shrine as a Commemorative Site," *The Journal of International Communication* 20, no. 1 (2014): 21–41.

69. Ako Inuzuka, "Memories of the Tokko: An Analysis of the Chiran Peace Museum for Kamikaze Pilots," *Howard Journal of Communications* 27, no. 2 (2016): 145–166.

70. Eric Aoki and Kyle M. Jonas, "Collective Memory and Sacred Space in Post-Genocide Rwanda: Reconciliation and Rehumanization Processes in Mureithi's *ICYIZERE*," *Journal of International and Intercultural Communication* 9, no. 3 (2016): 240–258.

71. Courtney E. Cole, "Commemorating Mass Violence: Truth Commission Hearing as a Genre of Public Memory," *Southern Communication Journal*, 83, no. 3 (2018): 149–166.

72. Lisa Blackmore, "Collective Memory and Research-Led Filmmaking: Spatial Legacies of Dictatorship in the Dominican Republic," *Popular Communication*, 16, no. 2: 90–105.

73. Edward W. Said, *Orientalism* (New York: Vintage Books, 1978), 95.

74. Ibid., 300.

75. Edward W. Said, *Culture and Imperialism* (New York: Vintage Books, 1993), xix.

76. Ibid., xxii.

77. Marouf Hasian and Helene A. Shugart, "Melancholic Nostalgia, Collective Memories, and the Cinematic Representations of Nationalistic Identities in *Indochine*." *Communication Quarterly* 49, no. 4 (2001): 329–349.

78. Marouf Hasian, "Military Orientalism at the Cineplex: A Postcolonial Reading of *Zero Dark Thirty*," *Critical Studies in Media Communication* 31, no. 5 (2014): 464–478.

79. Tessa Morris-Suzuki. "Defining the Boundaries of the Cold War Nation: 1950s Japan and the Other Within," *Japanese Studies* 26, no. 3 (2006): 303–316.

80. Lionel Babicz. "Japan-Korea, France-Algeria: Colonialism and Post-Colonialism," *Japanese Studies* 33, no. 2 (2013): 201–211.

81. Jung-Bong Choi, "Mapping Japanese Imperialism onto Postcolonial Criticism," *Social Identities* 9, no. 3 (2003): 325–327.

82. Choi, "Mapping Japanese Imperialism," 331.

83. Senda, *Jūgun Ianfu*, 219.

84. Il Myon Kim, *Tenno no Guntai to Chōsenjin Ianfu* [The Emperor's military and Korean comfort women] (Tokyo: Sanichi Shobō, 1976), 14–21.

85. Chizuko Ueno, *Nashionarizumu to Jenda* (Tokyo: Seidosha, 1998) 140.

86. Yoshimi, *Jūgun Ianfu*, 163–192.

87. Hata, *Ianfu*, 177–192.

88. Dai Sil Kim-Gibson, *Silence Broken: Korean Comfort Women* (Parkersburg, IA: Mid-Prairie Books, 1999).

89. George Hicks, *Comfort Women: Japan's Brutal Regime of Enforced Prostitution in the Second World War* (New York: W.W. Norton & Company, 1995).

90. Yonson Ahn, "Japan's 'Comfort Women' and Historical Memory: The Neo-Nationalist Counter-Attack," in *The Power of Memory in Modern Japan*, eds., Sven Saaler and Wolfgang Schwentker (Folkestone, UK: Global Oriental, 2008), 32–53.

91. Soh, *The Comfort Women*, 3.

92. Stern, *The Trials of Nina McCall*, 49–50.

93. Jason A. Edwards, "Community-Focused Apologia in International Affairs: Japanese Prime Minister Tomiichi Murayama's Apology," *Howard Journal of Communications* 16, no. 4 (2005): 317–336.

94. Mariko Izumi, "Asian-Japanese: State-Apology, National Ethos, and the 'Comfort Women' Reparations Debate in Japan," *Communication Studies* 62, no. 5 (2011): 473–490.

95. Sarah Vartabedian, "No Cause for Comfort Here: False Witnesses to 'Peace,'" *Southern Communication Journal* 82, no. 4 (2017): 250.

96. Senda, *Jūgun Ianfu*; and Kakō Senda, *Jūgun Ianfu: Zokuhen* [Sequel: Military comfort women] (Tokyo: Sanichi Shobō, 1978).

97. Kim-Gibson, *Silence Broken*.

98. Hicks, *Comfort Women*.

99. Soh, *The Comfort Women*.

100. Soh, *The Comfort Women*, 70.

101. Taijirō Tamura, *Shunpūden* [Story of a Prostitute] (Tokyo: Chikuma Shobō, 1947).

102. Taijirō Tamura, *Inago* [The Locust] (Tokyo: Chikuma Shobō, 1964).

103. Nagasawa Kenichi, *Kanko Iansho* (Kanko Comfort Station) (Tokyo: Tosho Shuppansha, 1983), 234.

104. Ueno, *Nashionarizumu*, 122.

105. Nobukatsu Fujioka, *Ojoku no Kingendaishi: Ima, Kokufuku no Toki* [Shameful modern history: Now, time to overcome] (Tokyo: Tokuma Shoten, 1996), 36.

106. Soh, *The Comfort Women*, 72–73.

107. Ibid., 71.

108. Ibid., 72–76.

109. Ibid., 73–74.
110. Ibid., 75.
111. Ibid., 75–76.
112. Izumi, "Asian-Japanese," 473.
113. According to Honda Katsuichi, within a few months after the Japanese military defeated China's nationalist military at Nanjing in 1937, the Japanese military massacred Chinese POWs and civilians, raped thousands of women, and plundered. The City of Nanjing estimates that the number of casualties was about 300,000.
114. Kyōko Hirano, *Tennō to Seppun* [The emperor and kiss] (Soushi sha: Tokyo, 1998) 144–149.
115. Tetsushi Marukawa, "The Representation of 'Asia,' 'Occupational Forces,' and 'Women' against the Backdrop of Post-War Japanese Culture: from the System of Censorship to the Present," *Inter-Asia Cultural Studies* 6, no. 2 (2005): 277.
116. Irwin-Zarecka, *Frames of Remembrance*, 119.
117. Marouf Hasian, "Critical Intercultural Communication, Remembrances of George Washington Williams, and the Rediscovery of Leopold II's 'Crimes against Humanity,'" in *The Handbook of Critical Intercultural Communication*, eds. Thomas K. Nakayama and Rona Tamiko Halualani (West Sussex, UK: Wiley-Blackwell, 2010), 312.
118. Jolanta A. Drzewiecka, "Public Memories in the Shadow of the Other," in *The Handbook of Critical Intercultural Communication*, eds. Thomas K. Nakayama and Rona Tamiko Halualani (Sussex, UK: Wiley-Blackwell, 2010), 290.

Chapter 2

The Memories of Sexual Slavery in Japan from 1945 to the 1960s
Romantic Stories of Forbidden Love

The years immediately after the end of the Asia-Pacific War were marked by silence. The trauma of a lost war, a lost empire, and nuclear strikes loomed large and ushered the demoralized losers in a victim role that perhaps favored forgetting over remembering. Most military documents had been destroyed by the end of the war and the court-martial of the victors nurtured a collective amnesia. In a beaten and occupied Japan there was no room for national pride. This was not an environment for differentiated historic discussions. History is written by the winners, but it is interesting that the "comfort women" had no place in this history or the tribunals following the war.[1] There are only very few texts during this time period that touch on the "comfort women" and the ones that are available are found in popular literature. As a result, all four texts analyzed in this chapter go back to a single author Tamura Taijiro, a popular writer and former Japanese soldier. Two are novels written by Tamura and the other two are films based on one of his novels. Nevertheless, the texts had a wide audience at the time and, because of a lack of alternative sources, they had substantial impact on the formation of collective memories of "comfort women" in Japan. As discussed in later chapters, there are aspects of these memories that have carried over to artifacts produced in more recent years.

The four artifacts analyzed are the novels *Shunpūden* [Story of a Prostitute] (published in 1947)[2] and *Inago* [The Locust] (in 1964)[3] by Tamura Taijirō and two films based on *Shunpūden*, *Akatsuki no Dassou* [Escape at Dawn] (released in 1950, directed by Taniguchi Senkichi)[4] and *Shunpūden* (released in 1965, directed by Suzuki Seijun).[5]

Tamura Taijirō's success as a writer was due in no small part to his war memories that served as his inspiration and provided the backdrop for several of his novels. He is considered a central figure in what is known as "literature of the flesh," a genre that became popular in postwar Japan in reaction to the oppressive moral code before and during the war. Tamura also published *Nikutai no Mon* [Gate of Flesh] in 1947, a story about Japanese prostitutes in occupied Japan and *Nikutai no Akuma* [Devil of Flesh] in 1946, a story of a forbidden love affair between a beautiful prisoner of war from the Chinese Communist military and a Japanese soldier. Tamura was troubled by a break in perception from pre- to postwar Japan displayed by the younger generation of writers who celebrated sexual freedom around the same time.[6] To Tamura, prewar thought and consciousness were continuous with postwar life and thought despite differences on the surface, that is, although extreme stoicism and spiritualism were forced upon people before and during the war, more "primitive" urges were always present and he witnessed firsthand the preoccupation with basic physiological needs in military camps. To him, the pursuit of sexual freedom and satisfaction of physical desires were the true human nature and the liberation from the prewar moral codes became his goal. *Inago* [The Locust] has not been as widely cited or discussed as the other artifacts analyzed in this chapter, but it is one of the very few works on Korean "comfort women" from this period. Considering Tamura's success as a writer and the popularity of the genre, "literature of the flesh," it is reasonable to assume that the story was also widely read.

In *Story of a Prostitute*, both the novel and the 1965 movie version, a beautiful, passionate "comfort woman," Harumi (she is Korean in the novel but this is not made clear in the film) seduces Mikami, a submissive orderly in an attempt to get back at Narita, an arrogant adjutant. Soon, however, Harumi finds herself in love with Mikami. After being injured and captured by the Chinese, Mikami is returned to a Japanese military base in China and faces the death penalty (being a POW was considered a dishonor in the Japanese military). In the end, Mikami and Harumi commit suicide together.

In *Escape at Dawn*, the 1950 movie version of *Story of a Prostitute*, the romance between Mikami and Harumi follows the original storyline. However, the rest of the plot differs considerably from the original novel and the 1960s movie version. Harumi appears to be Japanese although this is not explicitly made clear and she and other women are "comfort singers" not "comfort women." Harumi is attracted to Mikami before she even meets Narita and falls in love with Mikami. Harumi never becomes Narita's mistress despite Narita's advances and, in the end, Narita kills Mikami and Harumi with a machinegun when they try to escape after a failed suicide attempt. The considerable changes in the 1950 version of the movie are the result of extensive censorship by the GHQ of the U.S. occupation force. Kurosawa Akira, the screenwriter, was ordered to rewrite his screenplay seven times.[7]

The Locust is also a love story, in this case between the Japanese soldier Harada and Hiroko, a Korean "comfort woman." Harada and other soldiers are on a mission, transporting empty urns and Korean "comfort women," including Hiroko, to their unit at the Chinese frontline. Harada has been one of Hiroko's customers and they have developed affection toward each other. Throughout their trip, they are all troubled by locust swarms that keep bothering them. When Hiroko is critically injured by enemy fire, Harada tries to rescue her. However, he finds it impossible to carry both her and the essential military supplies and he ends up leaving her behind to die. After arriving at his unit, he visits a "comfort" station to spend time with another Korean "comfort woman." When they are about to have sex, Harada feels a sharp pain at his loins and finds a big locust on the woman's body that prevents them from having intercourse.

When analyzing artifacts created during the period immediately after the war, we have to consider the influence of censorship by the U.S. occupation forces after the war. The following section outlines censorship conducted by the occupation force before moving to an analysis of the artifacts.

CENSORSHIP

From 1945 to 1951, the GHQ led by Douglas MacArthur enforced censorship over a wide range of communication media channels in Japan. These included mail, telephone, art (such as theatrical plays), and mass media such as newspapers, magazines, books, radio, and films. Etō lists the guidelines for censorship stipulated by the GHQ in November 1946 as follows:

Items that should be deleted or banned:

1) Criticism of the Supreme Commander of the Allied Forces
2) Criticism of the Tokyo Military Trial
3) Criticism of the fact that the GHQ wrote the constitution
4) References to the censorship system
5) Criticism of the United States
6) Criticism of Russia
7) Criticism of England
8) Criticism of Korea
9) Criticism of China
10) Criticism of other Allied Countries
11) Criticism of the Allied Countries in general
12) Criticism of the treatment of Japanese people in Manchuria
13) Criticism of policies held by the Allied Countries before the war
14) References to potential World War III
15) References to "the Cold War" between the Soviet Union and Western countries

16) Promotion of positions defending the war
17) Promotion of the idea of Japan as a divine country
18) Promotion of militarism
19) Promotion of nationalism
20) Promotion of the Greater East Asia Co-Prosperity Sphere
21) Other types of promotion
22) Defense of war criminals
23) Relationships between Allied soldiers and Japanese women
24) Situation of black markets
25) Criticism of the Occupation Force
26) Exaggeration of starvation
27) Instigation of violence and nonpeaceful actions
28) False reports
29) Inappropriate references to the GHQ and its local offices
30) Reports on unreleased news[8]

The GHQ was mostly concerned with criticism of the United States, including the occupation force and its policies in Japan, and other former Allied countries, as well as ideologies that were promoted in Japan before and during the war such as nationalism, militarism, and the Greater East Asia Co-Prosperity Sphere.

MEMORIES OF SEXUAL SLAVERY DURING THE POSTWAR PERIOD

By examining the two novels and two films, several themes emerge: (1) "comfort women" as paid prostitutes who voluntarily chose their profession, (2) tragic love between a Japanese soldier and a "comfort woman" (or singer), (3) exotic "comfort women," (4) passionate "comfort women" with insatiable sexual desires, and (5) criticism of the Japanese imperial military. Each theme will be discussed in more detail below. An absence of memory can be just as relevant as memory itself and how a group of people is "forgotten" and omitted from official history is often ideologically or politically motivated. Therefore, memories that are absent in these sources will also be discussed, and ideologies that may have played a role in this collective "memory loss," as well as who and what ideology are privileged by this discursive amnesia,[9] will be discussed. Themes missing from all or some of the examined artifacts are as follows: (1) suffering and pain, (2) the nationalities of the "comfort" women," (3) criticism of the "comfort" system itself and the military's role in operating it, and (4) memories of the "comfort women" and hence the "comfort" system as a whole have also been suppressed, perhaps in a misguided attempt of Allied censorship.

"Comfort Women" as Paid Prostitutes Who Voluntarily Chose Their Profession

The first theme of "comfort women" as paid prostitutes, which is consistent with the claim made by contemporary Japanese nationalist scholars (see chapters 4 and 6 for more details), is ubiquitous. In the movie, *Story of a Prostitute*, the opening scene specifically introduces Harumi as a "prostitute" when describing the end of her previous relationship with a man who married another woman.[10] The narrative opens with, "Harumi ha Tenshin no baishunfu dearu" [Harumi is a prostitute in Tianjin]. The novel explains that Harumi and other Korean "comfort women" sold themselves (or they were sold by their families) into prostitution to help their poor families:

> They [Harumi and two other "comfort women"] were all from a peninsula that is connected to this [Eurasia] continent. They have been using Japanese names instead of their real names since they were sold in Tianjin to pay for the debts of their families. (My translation)[11]

It was not uncommon in prewar Japan that daughters from extremely poor families would sell themselves (or be sold) into prostitution. Japanese readers who read the above passage would not doubt that the "comfort women" were prostitutes.

In *The Locust* as well, Hiroko's job is described as a "business earning a lot of money" (arakasegi no kagyō), that is, prostitution:

> Among the women who were at the brothel, Hiroko was the nicest one and she was kind to soldiers. To soldiers, women's faces were not important but Hiroko had a somewhat attractive face. And for a woman in the business of earning a lot of money, her skin was smooth, pale, and transparent. (My translation)[12]

Later in the novel, *The Locust*, soldiers from a frontline unit want to "play" with the women because they are distressed about the prospect of potentially dying the following day. Harada temporarily sends off the women to that unit. But when they return, the women are angry because the soldiers did not pay them.[13] Again, this passage implies that "comfort women" were paid prostitutes though they have to comply with the directives from a commanding officer. There is also no indication that "comfort women" are forced to serve the sexual needs of Japanese soldiers. Throughout the novels, *Story of a Prostitute* and *The Locust*, and the movie, *Story of a Prostitute*, the "comfort women" who come to the Japanese military base are portrayed as doing voluntarily and enjoying the sexual intercourse with soldiers. For instance, in the beginning of the movie, *Story of a Prostitute*, when Harumi and two other "comfort women" are on a military truck on their way to a military base in China, they are attacked by Chinese guerrilla fighters and one Japanese soldier dies. The two other women insist on returning to Tianjin but Harumi wants to stay. Importantly, there is an element of choice here: those who want to leave can leave. In the same scene, Harumi states that she wants to have sex with many men (while in the novel, she wants to have sex with many men to forget her previous lover). She elects to start her "business" right after she arrives at the base despite the comfort station manager's suggestion to wait until the following day.[14]

Even in the case of a Korean "comfort woman" in the movie, *Story of a Prostitute* (while they are all Koreans in the novel, many of them seem to be Japanese in the film), we do not get the sense that she was forcibly or deceptively brought to the base. In one scene, she is talking to a Japanese soldier, Uno, about going with a dispatch troop:

> I'm thinking about going with the dispatch. I know it'll be dangerous but I've heard that I could get paid the same amount of money as Japanese women. If I stay here, my debt will never be erased. (English subtitles)[15]

While it is implied that Korean "comfort women" were discriminated against, her statement also suggests that she is a prostitute who receives money for her services and that she became a "comfort woman" because of her family's debt rather than being coerced or deceived. "Comfort women" who were forced or deceived into sexual slavery are forgotten both in the novel and in the film. Instead, we are presented with lustful prostitutes described in ways similar to Oriental women in Western Orientalists' accounts as those with "untiring sensuality" and "unlimited desire."[16]

Even in the case of Japanese "comfort women" who are generally considered prostitute volunteers, feminist scholars such as Ueno question whether they can truly be considered "volunteers." Until the 1950s, prostitution in Japan was legal and government controlled. Under this system, prostitutes were typically sold for their families' debts. They lived in slave-like conditions and were under constant surveillance to prevent them from escaping. When these women were offered to join the "comfort" system in exchange for their debts, most of them may have agreed but it is questionable whether this truly qualifies as free choice.[17]

Of course, there is the possibility that Tamura actually believed that Korean "comfort women" were paid prostitutes. According to sources reviewed by Yoshimi Yoshiaki, a progressive historian, soldiers did pay for sexual acts in most cases yet the women did not always receive payment.[18] In some areas, the ways in which "comfort" stations were operated were fairly similar to brothels in Japan (e.g., there were stations where women were shown to potential customers in order to choose). It is entirely possible that Tamura who served in China for seven years and likely frequented "comfort" stations there may have believed that the women were paid prostitutes who were in that profession for the usual reasons. This would explain why Tamura promoted such memories but ultimately it would not change the fact that he promoted memories of "comfort women" as paid prostitutes to a wide audience. In other words, Tamura had a significant part in forming these memories regardless of his motivations in the same way a body of literature produced by Western novelists and poets contributed to the creation of a certain knowledge of the Orient by Western Orientalists as Said suggests.[19]

Tragic Love between a Japanese Soldier and a "Comfort Woman/Singer"

The theme of tragic love between a Japanese soldier and a "comfort woman" (or singer) is found in all the novels and films. The relationships are depicted in a romanticized way and end in tragedy. *Story of a Prostitute*, both the novel and the 1965 movie, presents the relationship between Mikami and Harumi as tragic, forbidden love between a low-ranking soldier and a prostitute who is the mistress of his superior. In *Escape at Dawn*, the 1950 movie adaptation, Harumi is not Narita's mistress but Mikami feels that he should not be with Harumi because of Narita's advances (unwelcome as they are). In *The Locust*, nothing strictly prohibits Harada and Hiroko from forming a relationship. In this case, it is mainly a sense of duty that gets in the way of love. The conflict between romance and duty is dramatized when Harada faces the dilemma of choosing between Hiroko and the supplies. In the end, he decides to leave her behind and she dies from her injuries. Tragic endings of forbidden love are a common element in romantic literature. In the case of relationships between soldiers and (alleged) "prostitutes," it conveniently avoids the problems of a happy ending. Marriages with former prostitutes as well as mixed marriages between Korean women and Japanese men were rare and frowned upon in pre- and postwar Japanese society. It would have been difficult to sell such an ending to a broad audience.

The Floating World or the pleasure quarters were glamorized in literature and arts in feudal Japan, contrary to the slave-like conditions that the women endured.[20] The idea of romance between a man and a *geisha* or a prostitute became a common motif in literature (e.g., *Sonezaki Shinjū*). Since historically Japan was a patriarchal society, women's chastity was greatly valued and, consequently, prostitutes were ostracized. At the same time, until the end of the Asia-Pacific War, most marriages were arranged by parents or relatives. Therefore, a relationship with a *geisha* or a prostitute was one of the few places where romance could be found. When a man's passion proved stronger than the societal hurdles, he could marry a *geisha* or prostitute after buying her freedom. If this was not possible, the relationship turned into forbidden love, which was a common male fantasy and literary motif at the time.

Exotic "Comfort Women/Singers"

The next theme exoticizes "comfort women" or singers. In both of Tamura's novels, they are explicitly and accurately portrayed as Korean and their "Koreanness" and "foreignness" are emphasized. In both novels, all "comfort women" speak broken Japanese, using soldiers' idioms. Most Korean "comfort women" had only limited knowledge of the Japanese language when they were recruited. Although Japanese was an official language and was taught in schools in colonial Korea, most "comfort women" came from poor families in rural areas and did not attend school.[21] As a result, their Japanese language skills were initially limited. Over time, though, they gradually picked up Japanese, mostly from soldiers who spoke a hypermasculine form of the Japanese language. In that sense, Tamura's depiction of Korean "comfort women" who spoke a broken, masculine Japanese is not inaccurate; however, the discursive amnesia[22] regarding women who spoke fluent Japanese and the emphasis on their speech with broken Japanese reinforce the women's foreignness. Consequently, it privileges native Japanese speakers who are presented as "the norm."

Interestingly, Harumi's nationality is ambiguously depicted in the 1965 movie version of *Story of a Prostitute* while Harumi, like the rest of the women, is Korean in the novel. In the movie, the nationality of Harumi's character is never stated and there is no mention of her background or hometown although we do learn that another "comfort woman" comes from a town in northern Japan. When Harumi remembers her childhood, the scene only depicts the ocean, small portions of houses devoid of people, providing no clues as to which country she is from. Considering that there is a Korean "comfort woman" in the movie who speaks with a foreign accent and, at one point, even wears a traditional Korean dress, Harumi appears Japanese without being officially labeled Japanese. The Japanese actress playing Harumi has no foreign accent, yet, we see her exoticized—she appears in front of an "exotic" painting together with "exotic music" in the beginning and when she and Mikami are captured by the Chinese military, she sings in Chinese. I believe that the ambiguities in Harumi's character can be explained by appeals to the audience on two levels. The filmmakers probably wanted to depict Harumi as Japanese to ease general viewers' anxiety over international relationships especially between Japanese and Korean people. As discrimination against ethnic Koreans is still prevalent in Japan today, it is not difficult to imagine how negatively Japanese–Korean relationships must have been viewed in the 1960s. Similar to Western colonizers' view of colonized Orientals as inferior, "subordinated intellectually to the West" and "acqui[ring] all the marks of an inherent weakness" as Said discusses,[23] Koreans were seen as inferior by Japanese colonizers. This view persisted in postwar Japan, possibly to the point where a romance between a Japanese and a Korean was too problematic to be depicted in a mainstream movie. While Harumi's and other women's Koreanness was retained in Tamura's original novel, it is interesting that his most successful novel, *Nikutai no Mon* [Gate of Flesh] published in 1947, with six movie adaptations including one as recent as 2008, does not involve international relationships. At the same time, the filmmakers may have wanted to maintain the "foreignness" of Harumi in order to appeal to former Japanese soldiers who must have constituted a significant portion of their audience in 1965. The existence of the "comfort women" was no secret to them and they must have known that most of them were Korean. By implying the "foreignness" of Harumi (or "Koreanness" to former Japanese soldiers), the filmmakers may have intended to resonate with more "authentic," nostalgic memories of "comfort women" held by this part of their audience.

Similarly, in *Escape at Dawn*, the 1950 movie adaptation of *Story of a Prostitute*, Harumi appears Japanese (although her nationality is not explicitly stated), yet she maintains a somewhat "foreign" or "exotic" atmosphere. When Mikami and Harumi are captured by the Chinese army, Harumi speaks Mandarin Chinese fluently. In responding to a Chinese doctor's question, "Why do you speak Chinese so well?" she responds, "I attended a school in Beijing." Although it is not completely unrealistic that Japanese women in the 1940s have been educated in Beijing, this scene does not exist in Tamura's original novel and was added by the filmmakers. In the original novel, Harumi does not speak Chinese:

> "Bu Su, Bu Su," Harumi murmured. She felt so frustrated that she couldn't say anything better but she meant, "No, no." She couldn't come up with anything else with her limited Chinese. (My translation)[24]

In *Escape at Dawn*, Harumi also changes her Western-style clothes to a Chinese dress that is offered to her at the Chinese military base because her own clothes became dirty. This scene was also added by the filmmakers. Other than the overall impression, there is no clear indication that she is indeed Japanese. When comfort singers talk about their homes in Tokyo, Harumi does not say anything. Some comfort singers complain that they cannot go back to *naichi* (that literally means "inside land" referring to the original Japanese territories in contrast to *gaichi* or "outside land," referring to Japanese colonies such as Korea and Taiwan and Japan's occupied areas in Asia). A few of them even cry because they are missing *naichi*. However, we never see Harumi missing *naichi*. In the movie, the character of Harumi is played by Yamaguchi Yoshiko, which significantly adds to the "foreignness" of the character of Harumi.

The popular actress, Yamaguchi, was born to Japanese parents in 1920 in Manchuria, the northeastern part of China, which was occupied by Japan from the early 1930s to the end of the war. She grew up speaking both Mandarin and Japanese and started her career as a Chinese actress under the name Li Xianglan (or Ri Kōran in Japanese pronunciation). Later, she starred in many Japanese propaganda films, one of them *Shina no Yoru* [China Nights] released in 1940 where she played the role of a Chinese anti-Japan activist who falls in love with a Japanese sailor. In *China Nights*, she realizes that she is in love with the sailor when he hits her. She exclaims, "Forgive me! It didn't hurt at all to be hit by you. I was happy, happy! I'll be better, just watch." Vitello argues that the underlying ideas of these films are "an oppressed China, resisting the occupation at first, soon embraces Japan as its rescuer."[25] Because of her involvement in these propaganda films, the Chinese government tried her for treason after the war—a crime that carried the death penalty. Fortunately, her Japanese citizenship was proven by her family registry and she was released and deported to Japan. Soon after her return to Japan, she resumed her acting career. Yamaguchi's dramatic and "exotic" past as well as her real nationality were public knowledge at the time and probably contributed to her exotic flair while implying her as Japanese.

As mentioned earlier, the screenplay of *Escape at Dawn* was heavily influenced by GHQ censorship. After Japan lost all of its colonies and occupied territories, the GHQ attempted to avoid all references to those former parts of the empire. After the outbreak of the Korean War, this trend even accelerated, especially regarding references to Korea. One reason may be that the GHQ wished to suppress nostalgic memories of Japanese people about the empire. Another reason could be that, as discussed in chapter 1, as Japan became increasingly important as a U.S. ally in East Asia in Cold War politics, it had to be viewed in a positive light. Japan's past crimes, including its exploitation of Koreans, had to be purged. This GHQ policy is the likely reason why Harumi's nationality has been altered in *Escape at Dawn* and it has been suggested that the avoidance of its colonial past contributed to Japan's later inability to cope with its wartime responsibilities in colonized territories.[26]

Although Harumi's "Koreanness" was suppressed and "comfort women" turned into comfort singers in *Escape at Dawn*, many male viewers in 1950 who were former Japanese soldiers likely understood this as a story about "comfort women" (e.g., *comfort singers* traveling between Japanese military bases near the frontlines were uncommon; it was even less common that comfort singers would stay with the same unit for an extended period of time. The plot takes care of this problem by bombing a nearby bridge in another departure from the original novel.). Probably to avoid that viewers would think of Harumi and the other singers as "comfort women," GHQ censorship may have cunningly directed to add a number of scenes where characters clarify that they are not "comfort women." In one of them, a singer says explicitly, "We are not comfort women!" Also, when the women arrive at a bar on the military base where they are going to stay after the nearby bridge was bombed, one of them, Yuri, asks their manager, Tachibana, what they will have to do there:

Yuri: What are we going to do here?
Tachibana: Well, we cannot leave until the road is fixed.
Yuri: So until then?
Tachibana: Well, I would feel bad if you just hung out. You will have to help out at the bar.
Yuri: They sell alcohol here, right?
Tachibana: Alcohol, finger foods, cigarettes, and sweets.
Yuri: All we have to do is sell those, right?
Tachibana: They may ask you to serve alcohol.
Yuri: And then?
Tachibana: And, you may have to sing once in a while.
Yuri: And then? That's all, right?
Tachibana: Yes, that's all.
Yuri: You're sure that's all?
Tachibana: Yes. (My translation)[27]

In this conversation, Yuri, the leader of the comfort singers, makes sure that she and the rest of the women will not perform the functions of "comfort women," assuring the viewers that they are not "comfort women" at the same time.

The replacement of "comfort women" with *comfort singers* was probably related to the GHQ's direction to suppress the depiction of antisocietal activities such as crime, gambling, suicide, and prostitution.[28] Consequently, censorship officers attempted to make sure the women would not be perceived as "comfort women" because they were widely considered prostitutes. At the same time, the filmmakers may have wanted to maintain some measure of "authenticity" to appeal to the audience of former Japanese soldiers. Former soldiers must have known that most "comfort women," especially those who had interactions with soldiers, were Korean. Making Harumi more "foreign" could have been an attempt to appeal to nostalgic feelings in this group of viewers.

Passionate "Comfort Women" with Insatiable Sexual Desires

In the novels and the films, women are depicted in a similar fashion to "Oriental" women portrayed by Western Orientalists as passionate and lustful. For instance, in the beginning of the novel, *Story of a Prostitute*, Harumi and the other women are introduced as follows:

> They [Harumi and other Korean "comfort women"] refused customers they did not like, yelling at them, but they bought food and drinks for customers they liked even by borrowing money from others. They sang when they were happy and they cried loudly when they were sad. They lived carefree lives. They lived passionately. They did not behave based on logic or knowledge from books but lived instinctively. They loved the things their bodies liked and hated the things their bodies abhorred. Their expressiveness demonstrated the power of their temperament. They who bit into garlic and ate chili peppers had bodies that were a manifestation of their strong wills. And they never regretted living passionately following their feelings. (My translation)[29]

The depiction of foreign women as temperamental and passionate is consistent with Western Orientalists' characterizations of "Orientals" as capricious and passionate.[30] In the above passage, we can also see that Korean "comfort women" are presented as simple-minded beings following their bodily instinct rather than logical thinking, which is also consistent with Western Orientalists' designation of Orientals as "the childish primitive."[31] A similar portrayal is also found in the description of Harumi's past relationship with a Japanese man in Tianjin. Both the novel and the 1965 movie version have a scene where Harumi threatens her lover's wife with a knife and bites his tongue when he apologizes to her for marrying someone else. Also, in the film, when she cannot see Mikami anytime she wants, Harumi throws a tantrum.

The women are also equipped with insatiable sexual desires similar to Oriental women who were believed to be licentious and have "unlimited desire" by Western Orientalists.[32] As mentioned earlier, in *Story of a Prostitute*, both in the original novel as well as the 1965 movie version, Harumi wants to sleep with many men to help her forget her previous lover. In the movie, even on the day when Mikami and Harumi return from the Chinese military base, Harumi gets right back to work when even the "comfort" station manager suggests to rest. According to her, this will distract her from Mikami's fate. In addition, at the beginning of the movie, when Harumi and other women are transported to the military unit, she talks about the soldiers' bodies:

> They look strong. The men in Tianjin can't compete with these soldiers.
> I want to throw my body against lots of different men. (English subtitles)[33]

We can also observe this trait in other women in the film. From a conversation among other "comfort women," we gather that they enjoy sleeping with soldiers. In one scene, one of them talks about sex with the adjutant:

> If you once have sex with the Adjutant, it's over. You lose your mind. (English subtitles)[34]

In *The Locust* as well, Hiroko has insatiable sexual desires. After degrading sex with a number of soldiers, she wants to sleep with Harada to feel better about herself:

> Hiroko's slightly fatty arms, in contrast to her small face, held on to Harada's neck. Harada could tell Hiroko was excited. She wanted to make sure that her body still belonged to her by having sex with Harada. What the other soldiers did to her earlier merely separated her body from her mind. When the soldiers left her body, her body completely left her. To make certain to herself that her body is still hers, Hiroko had to make love to Harada. (My translation)[35]

Although Hiroko states that she is exhausted from having sex with a number of soldiers earlier that night, more sex with somebody she likes is the only way for her to feel that "her body is still hers."

Even in *Escape at Dawn*, the movie version that has been purged of any association with "comfort women" and replaced them with *comfort singers*, there are still traces of this carnal portrayal of Oriental women, as Harumi is the one who is more passionate about Mikami and their relationship. Even after Mikami rejects her by slapping her, Harumi does not give up and continues to seduce him. Shimizu Akira, a movie critic who wrote a review of the film in 1950, thought that Harumi's behavior of seducing Mikami was "unlike Japanese" and too "foreign."[36] Harumi's mix of Japanese and exotic attributes was perceived as too exotic by some viewers at the time yet this criticism rested on the assumption that Harumi was Japanese. Therefore, it could be argued that this reflects a compromise that would satisfy the GHQ while giving a nod to those in the audience who were familiar with "historic reality," or in this case the seed of male fantasies.

It has been suggested that the original *Story of a Prostitute* is based on Tamura's fantasies of Korean "comfort women," which were inspired by his wartime experiences.[37] Tamura viewed Korean "comfort women" as "having a dual nature—one of primitive sexual urges and the other being a tender-hearted partner for Japanese men."[38] Part of Tamura's success as a writer was that these views probably resonated with his readers, many of whom were former soldiers. Tamura's sexual fantasies of Korean "comfort women" are also comparable to Western Orientalists' view of the Orient as Said suggests. The Orient was considered as the place of "freedom of licentious sex" and "escapism of sexual fantasy."[39]

One might argue that Tamura's Orientalist depictions of Korean women as passionate, illogical, and driven by sexual urges can be attributed to the genre, "literature of the flesh." The stories revolve around physical urges rather than rational thinking, defying oppressive wartime moral codes. However, there are clear differences in his depictions of Japanese prostitutes in *Nikutaino Mon* [Gate of Flesh]. Although the Japanese prostitutes in *Gate of Flesh* live like *kemono* [beasts], they rarely experience sexual pleasure. They live in the basement of a destroyed building in postwar Tokyo. Ranging from eighteen to nineteen years old, they barely bathe and have sex outdoors with their customers (Tamura actually refers to the women finding customers as *kari* [hunting]). To them, sex is merely a means of survival.[40] These descriptions, written by the same author within the same genre, are in stunning contrast to his portrayal of Korean "comfort women" who like to have sex, at least with certain customers, even after sleeping with many men every day.

Although exotic, Orientalist depictions of Korean "comfort women" are ubiquitous in the artifacts analyzed, there are also contradictory aspects supported by research on "comfort women" (see chapter 1). According to the latter, both Japanese military officials and individual soldiers preferred "Japanese like" "comfort women." One example would be giving Japanese names to non-Japanese "comfort women."[41] According to Nishino, Korean "comfort women" were more popular among soldiers than other non-Japanese "comfort women" because they spoke at least some Japanese.[42] Similarly, some survivors state that those who spoke Japanese well were treated better.[43] This observation is also in line with the Western colonial agenda of "civilizing the uncivilized." Western colonizers attempted to Westernize colonized natives despite a belief that those colonized natives could never fully become like Westerners.[44] While Japanese military officials attempted to "Japanize" Korean "comfort women" (as did Japan's colonial policy of 1939 that forced Koreans to adopt Japanese names), Korean women are still remembered as exotic and foreign during this period. The success of Tamura's fantasies of exotic "comfort women" supports the view that such memories were shared by, or at least resonated with, former soldiers. At the same time, Tamura's fiction reinforced and shaped those memories and made them accessible to a wider audience. Thus, Korean "comfort women" were assimilated into

Japanese culture, while, at the same time, continuing to be perceived as foreign and exotic, which perhaps were equally attractive attributes for soldiers. Although it seems that the hierarchy among Asian "comfort women" was mostly based on the degree of their Japanization, this was apparently not the case with Western "comfort women." By examining testimonies from Dutch survivors of sexual slavery such as Jan Ruff-O'Herne, we learn that Dutch women were reserved for officers only like Japanese women. This is probably related to Japan's lopsided Western-centered internationalization process that began in the late nineteenth century and, while inspiring the country's own nationalism and colonial ambitions, also planted ideas of Western supremacy in many Japanese people.[45] As mentioned in chapter 1, Japan's modernization was about Westernization. In order to catch up with "superior" Western civilization, the nation made efforts to Westernize itself. To do so, many Western teachers were employed to teach various subjects ranging from literature and Western languages to sciences at Japanese universities and high schools. Tanabe writes that Western teachers' salaries were three times more than their Japanese counterparts.[46] Fujimoto also explains that Japan's internationalization has been a *whitenization*, identifying with and privileging white Westerners.[47] This *whitenization* among Japanese military officers may have placed Dutch women high in the hierarchy.

Criticism of the Japanese Imperial Military

Criticism of the Japanese imperial military can be ubiquitously observed both in the novels and in the movies. Interestingly, none of that criticism, despite its abundance throughout the texts, is related to the "comfort" system or the military's role in operating it. Wayne Booth argues in *The Rhetoric of Fiction* that an author's position is always present in a text, either explicitly or implicitly. Even if we eliminate all explicit judgments made by an author, an author's presence is still revealed by their authorial decisions. Narration, therefore, becomes a place to find an "author's voice" in fiction. Another place is "nihilism." Booth defines nihilistic works as those in which "we find lost characters whose only discovery can be that there is nothing to discover, or whose final action is suicide or some other gesture of despair."[48] Nihilism is a theme that can be identified in all versions of *Story of a Prostitute* and *The Locust*.

In both the novel, *Story of a Prostitute* and the movie of the same name, Mikami and Harumi commit suicide (their suicide attempt fails in *Escape at Dawn* possibly because the GHQ considered suicide an antisocietal idea). The reason they do this is the treatment of Mikami by the Japanese military. Mikami is supposed to be executed because he was captured by the Chinese military and being captured alive was considered dishonorable by the

Japanese imperial military. Both in the novel and in the two films, the criticism is obvious. For instance, in the original novel, when it is decided that Mikami will be court-martialed, the narration provides the following criticism perhaps revealing an "authorial voice":

> It was not taken into consideration that Mikami was unconscious as a result of being injured when he was captured, that his comrades did not bring back the unconscious Mikami, and that Mikami did not say anything during interrogation and unequivocally demanded his return to the Japanese military. He would have attempted to escape if his physical condition had allowed for it. Absolutely nothing was taken into consideration. (My translation)[49]

Similar criticism carries over into the two movies. In *Story of a Prostitute*, one of the "comfort women" says, "I wonder why they couldn't bring back Mikami though they were able to bring back his machinegun." In *Escape at Dawn*, one of the soldiers also points out the fact that Mikami was abandoned when he was injured while his machinegun was saved. In another scene, a gloating Narita tells Mikami that he will be executed by a firing squad that will put holes into him like a honey comb. Another soldier overhears the conversation and, after Narita leaves, states, "I don't want to believe this is how the Japanese military works."

In the two movies, we can also observe criticism of the Japanese imperial military comparing its inhumane rules to other nations' more "humane" military systems. In *Escape at Dawn*, criticism of the Japanese military is explicitly contrasted to other militaries. When Mikami and Harumi are captured by the Chinese military, a Japanese-speaking Chinese officer talks to Mikami:

> In your country, they abhor soldiers becoming POWs because they are afraid that they will leak military secrets. They teach you to kill yourself rather than be captured. They also tell you that you will be executed if you come back. In your country's extremely strict military, they are afraid that soldiers will desert otherwise. However, in the United States and Europe, POWs are respected because it means that they bravely fought until they were captured. Which interpretation do you think is more humane? (My translation)[50]

Clearly, in their criticism of the Japanese imperial military, the U.S. and European militaries are depicted as more humane (possibly reflecting Allied censorship). While not explicitly compared, the kindness and peace loving nature of the Chinese military is also shown in stark contrast to the strict inhumane rules governing the Japanese imperial military. In a scene where Harumi washes clothes at a river together with young Chinese women after they were captured, the Chinese women ask innocently about their relationship and the Japanese military, accompanied by peaceful background music. One woman asks when Mikami and Harumi are getting married and Harumi answers: "Probably after the war is over." Asked why they wait, Harumi responds that Mikami was drafted. Asked about the draft system, Harumi answers that, in Japan, all men have to go to war whether they want to or not. The Chinese woman suggests that Harumi and Mikami should stay with the Chinese military and get married, pointing out that many Japanese POWs got married and are working to bring peace to both countries now.

The unfavorable comparison of the Japanese imperial military with other nations' militaries, especially the Chinese military, can also be found in the movie version of *Story of a Prostitute* although in a more subtle form. Just like in *Escape at Dawn* and the original novel, a Japanese-speaking Chinese officer talks to Mikami and Harumi when they are captured by the Chinese military. Though he does not compare the Japanese imperial military to other nations' militaries as he does in *Escape at Dawn*, he does emphasize the humane treatment practiced in the Chinese military. He sates: "We don't hate Japanese soldiers and, as a POW, you have rights under international law." When Uno, a Japanese soldier who deserted the Japanese military talks to Mikami, criticism of the empire becomes more direct:

> Mikami, just think. What are you trying to accomplish in China? Have you done any good? China will govern itself. Live with the Chinese for a while. It's a good experience. The Japanese are attacking again, so we're evacuating. Come with us and recover your strength. You will be killed by your own people if you go back. You swear your loyalty and that's how they repay you? Come. We'll go together. (English subtitles)[51]

In addition to Uno's statement, the Chinese military's humane treatment of POWs is underscored by Uno's content and healthy appearance.

Similarly, criticism of the Japanese imperial military regarding its aggressive occupation policies in China can be found. In the movie version of *Story of a Prostitute*, it is reflected in Uno's statement above, "What are you trying to accomplish in China? Have you done any good? China will govern itself." He makes it clear that what the Japanese military is doing is nothing more than the invasion of a foreign country. The statement can also be seen as a criticism of the "Greater East Asia Co-Prosperity Sphere," an ideology promoted by the Japanese government to justify its aggressive expansion policy. The Greater East Asia Co-Prosperity Sphere impressed upon the Japanese general public that Japan was fighting a sacred war to liberate Asia from Western colonial powers and create a Great East Asian empire led by Japan, an interpretation of history that is still found among Japanese nationalists today. In *Escape at Dawn* and *The Locust*, a passage/scene briefly describes the suffering of Chinese civilians as a result of Japan's invasion of China. For instance, in *Escape at Dawn*, one of the comfort singers notices that there are many empty houses in the town where a unit of the Japanese military is stationed. She says, "I wonder how those people who had to move out are living right now." Also, in *The Locust*, when Hiroko is injured, Harada looks for Chinese men who can carry her but cannot find anybody: "There were no men who appeared useful because they knew that they would be either killed or taken to carry heavy things if they were caught by Japanese soldiers."[52] This illustrates habitual cruel conduct of Japanese soldiers toward Chinese civilians with Harada, the main protagonist, presenting no exception because he himself was going to force Chinese men to carry "heavy things."

Collective Forgetting and Discursive Amnesia

This section discusses discursive amnesia in the memories of sexual slavery and considers what ideologies may have contributed to these omissions. First, the suffering and pain of the women are forgotten. For example, Yun Doo Ri, one of the survivors interviewed by Kim-Gibson, relates her painful experiences as follows:

> My vagina felt like it was rotting, and my waist, back, everything hurt. I felt a big clot on my lower back developed from wounds, from the gun stock. I touched it and pain went through my body like electricity, oozing from flesh starting to rot. Every time when they got on top of me and banged like animals, my back was crushed and the pain was so sharp . . . "Please stop. I am in pain." "Don't you worry, I will do all the work." My body was a small battlefield—on top, soldiers attacked, and my back and everything else that touched the mattress screamed with intense pain, gradually turning into rotting, blue flesh.[53]

Although, in the discussed artifacts, the heroines, "comfort women" or in the case of *Escape at Dawn*, a comfort singer, do not find a happy ending, the end is brought about by their own choices not by being forcibly or deceptively placed into "comfort" stations by the Japanese military (or in the case of *The Locust*, death is as a result of enemy attacks). The experiences of "comfort women" themselves are not depicted as unpleasant or painful. These texts are very different from actual survivors' testimonies. A patriarchal, masculinist ideology may have played a role in the collective absence of pain in these stories. A patriarchal, masculinist way of thinking about uncontrollable male sexual desires justified the creation of the "comfort" system in the first place—men need sex to function and they might force themselves on women if no other opportunity for sexual release is provided.[54] Former Japanese soldiers, possibly including Tamura and many of the readers of his novels and viewers of the film, had been with "comfort women" as "customers" based on this masculinist belief. If "comfort women" were to experience pain, this would make the "comfort" system less acceptable and former Japanese soldiers would feel more like perpetrators than customers. Orientalist beliefs about insatiable women, "lustful colonized natives," probably helped to ameliorate feelings of guilt and contributed to the construction of memories devoid of pain. Thus, this collective forgetting privileged former Japanese soldiers and a masculinist ideology.

In the case of *Escape at Dawn*, "comfort women" themselves have been forgotten and replaced with memories of "comfort singers." The film was produced during the Allied occupation, when prostitution was one of the antisocietal topics the GHQ attempted to suppress although prostitution provided for Allied soldiers was rampant in reality. Director Taniguchi wanted to create an antiwar film depicting the inhumane treatment of soldiers in the Japanese imperial military.[55] Taniguchi thought he could achieve this in part by presenting "women who suffered under Japan's imperial war." Although Taniguchi attempted to convince GHQ censorship officers that the only women who were near soldiers and could have had romantic relationships with soldiers during the war were "comfort women," GHQ censorship remained opposed to the idea of "comfort women" in the film, stating that "comfort women" represented an Eastern way of thinking and depicting them in a movie would only incite nostalgic feelings in the audience. The amnesia regarding the "comfort women" in the film inadvertently privileged the Japanese government by preventing a wartime transgresssion by the former Japanese military from receiving wide public attention. It also possibly privileged former Japanese soldiers by concealing their potential infidelity through intercourse with "comfort women."

While criticism of the Japanese imperial military is abundant in these artifacts, criticism of the "comfort" system itself is missing. Criticism of discrimination toward Koreans, especially Korean "comfort women," can be observed, albeit not as explicitly as criticism of the Japanese military. It is most obvious in the movie version of *Story of a Prostitute*, where a clearly Korean "comfort woman" complains that Korean "comfort women" are paid less than their Japanese counterparts. Furthermore, we see a number of soldiers lining up to sleep with Harumi and others while the Korean "comfort woman" has difficulty finding "customers." In addition, in the original novel of *Story of a Prostitute*[56] and in *The Locust*,[57] Japanese soldiers derogatorily refer to Korean "comfort women" as *pi* or *Chōsen pi*. This shows that the author was aware of discrimination against "comfort women," in particular Korean ones (who constituted the majority). However, Tamura could not bring himself to go beyond this criticism and disapprove of the "comfort" system itself. This is not surprising, considering his descriptions of the positive effects of the "comfort" stations on soldiers in *Story of a Prostitute* and in *The Locust*. Based on a masculinist ideology of uncontrollable male sexual urges, the "comfort" system itself was a necessity from Tamura's perspective. The "comfort" system's negative effects on women and the sexist and racist ideologies behind it are forgotten (i.e., women were simply objects to satisfy men's sexual desires and Korean women, colonial subjects, served this function). This absence of criticism of the "comfort" system again privileges the masculinist ideology that is based on men's uncontrollable sexual desires and implicitly condones sexist and racist ideologies.

Finally, the nationalities of the "comfort women" are forgotten in both films. As discussed earlier, in the case of *Escape at Dawn*, this is perhaps due to censorship by the Allied occupation forces because "Koreanness" could remind the viewers of the "Great East Asia Empire." In the case of *Story of a Prostitute*, it seems plausible that this happened because of prevailing racist ideologies—a romance between a Japanese and a Korean was not acceptable for the general Japanese public. In fact, the main reason the Japanese military selected Korean women as "comfort women" was racially motivated. As colonial subjects they were considered lesser beings, mere objects for soldiers' sexual satisfaction.

Wander discusses the Third Persona, as a negated audience. As opposed to the First Persona, a speaker and their intent (the "I"), and the Second Persona, the "you" or the intended audience, the Third Persona is "undesirable," "insignificant," and "the 'it' that is the summation of all that you and I are told to avoid becoming." They are negated through silence and in history.[58] Likewise, Drzewiecka argues public memory as "a discourse of exclusion" that sets the "imaginary horizon of the belonging of groups" in history.[59] Then who is negated and excluded here? "Comfort women," particularly Korean ones, who were discriminated and suffered from physical and psychological pain are negated and excluded through silence and in history. This negation and discursive amnesia regarding "Koreanness" further inadvertently allowed the Japanese public to collectively forget their colonialist past. Consequently, the discursive amnesia privileges the Japanese public by enabling them to further solidify their collective memory of their role in the Asia-Pacific War as "victims."

CONCLUSION

In summary, both in the novels and in the movies, "comfort women" and comfort singers are depicted in a romanticized way. The relationship between a "comfort woman" and a Japanese soldier is shown as forbidden love. "Comfort women" are remembered as common prostitutes who led this life for the usual reasons (debt). In addition, during this period, "comfort women" are portrayed very similarly to "Oriental" women in accounts of Western Orientalists—exotic, passionate, and lustful. On the other hand, their actual nationality is frequently suppressed and we do not learn about their pain, suffering, or the circumstances of their recruitment. The assumption that "comfort women" were paid prostitutes likens the "comfort" system to common prostitution. Prostitution in Japan was obviously also a form of sexual slavery but it was historically accepted and established in society. If the Japanese military only tapped into an existing system of social injustice, its practices would not differ from any other army and it would be difficult to view the "comfort" system as a war crime. Consequently, criticism of the "comfort" system and the military's role in operating it is practically absent in the examined sources.

Despite his Orientalist depictions of Korean "comfort women" as irrational, passionate, and sex driven, Tamura's overall stance toward them appears to be positive. For instance, in both of his stories, he lets Japanese soldiers refer to the women in derogatory terms such as *pi*; however, narration consistently addresses them in relatively neutral terms as *kanojo* [she/her], *kanojotachi* [they/their/them], or *onnatachi* [women]. If we assume an authorial voice in narration,[60] the neutral appellations reflect Tamura's positive feelings toward them, considering that there were really no positive terms to address "comfort women" at that time with the exception of euphemisms such as *shakufu* [alcohol pouring women]. In both *Story of a Prostitute* and *The Locust*, there are passages where narration describes Korean "comfort women" more positively than Japanese "comfort women" or points out how the women helped soldiers to feel human again. For instance, in *Story of a Prostitute*, the narration states:

> However, even on rare occasions when soldiers, on a mission, got to go to a bigger city where Japanese comfort women were stationed, soldiers were despised by Japanese women for their low rank and dusty clothes and they came back to Korean women, complaining about Japanese women. Korean women took those soldiers seriously. Soldiers were able to feel slightly alive by loving them and crying and arguing together with the women. (My translation)[61]

In another part of the same novel and the movie, narration states that "comfort" stations were cleansing places for soldiers to wash their bodies and souls. After coming to the "comfort" station, soldiers felt refreshed as if they were reborn.[62] While this idea of "comfort" stations as "soldiers' soul washing places" is problematic because the women are still objectified, it resonates with a romanticized Orientalist idea of the Orient as a place for spiritual regeneration for the

West as pointed out by Said,[63] the expression is much more positive than the more common appellations such as "public toilets."

In *The Locust*, the reader also encounters criticism of Japanese "comfort women" who were reserved for officers only and lived in nice rooms. While Japanese women were not willing to go to the frontlines by leaving a relatively safe town near the railroad, Korean women were at "comfort" stations located near the frontlines. Korean women wore Western-style clothes or even Japanese clothes on holidays, which made soldiers feel nostalgic toward their home country.[64] Also, narration points out the benefits for soldiers who were able to feel alive when sleeping with these women: "Because death may await them tomorrow, they wanted to gain satisfaction, which was able to make them feel as if they were extending the length of their lives, enjoying the feeling that they are still alive."[65] Although Tamura seems oblivious to the fact that Korean "comfort women" probably did not have much of a choice regarding where they were stationed, the passages still illustrate his nostalgic feelings toward them.

If Tamura had positive feelings toward Korean "comfort women," why did he depict them as irrational, lustful paid prostitutes? Growing up in the Japanese empire as an imperial subject, Tamura, like everybody else, was exposed to the paternalist and colonial ideologies that came with Japanese imperialism. Tamura's beliefs and thinking were shaped by the ideologies of his time and it seems likely that he either consciously or subconsciously internalized Orientalist ideologies toward Koreans and other colonial subjects.

The abundance of criticism of the Japanese imperial military in all artifacts analyzed is another interesting point. It shows that neither Tamura nor the directors, Taniguchi and Suzuki, were nationalists who would paint a more positive picture of the former military. Their overall views toward the military are comparable to those of Japanese progressive historians analyzed in later chapters. Yet, their memories of Korean "comfort women" are very similar to those promoted by Japanese nationalists from the 1990s and later. Therefore, while they held an overall progressive view toward history or at least as far as the Japanese military was concerned, the authors of these artifacts could not get away from the masculinist and colonial ideologies they had internalized in the Great Japanese Empire. The Orientalist memories of Korean "comfort women" constructed by Tamura and the movie directors have persisted in Japan until today, becoming more subtle in some ways while being appropriated with negative twists by Japanese nationalists in more recent years. Their Orientalist texts have created the very reality they purport to describe while keeping Orientals silent and maintaining them merely as objects of descriptions.[66]

What is interesting though is that, because of this mischaracterization, the analyzed texts give valuable insights on the "comfort women" issue, especially the role of the military in its operation. As a former Japanese soldier who served in China for seven years, Tamura's depictions of "comfort women," skewed and romanticized as they may be, are a form of testimony nonetheless. The novels were written decades before the discussion about the extent to which the Japanese imperial military was involved in the operation of the "comfort" system. The question whether this constitutes a war crime had not been asked. From Tamura's point of view, the "comfort" system was necessary and, if we believe his testimony as far as his own convictions are concerned, a legal form of prostitution. Consequently, he had no reason to fabricate accounts of the involvement of the Japanese military. Together with the films, the novels unequivocally document the Japanese military's involvement in operating the "comfort" system. In all novels and films, the military is responsible for transporting the women. For instance, in *The Locust*, Harada's mission is to transport urns and Korean "comfort women." When he reports to an officer that three of the five women died on their way, he is held accountable. Similarly, in the two versions of *Story of a Prostitute* and *Escape at Dawn*, Harumi is able to just walk around the commanding office of the military base. It is interesting to see there is no hesitance in depicting how integrated "comfort" stations were into army bases in these artifacts.

NOTES

1. One exception is a 1948 military tribunal held by the Netherlands in Batavia (current Jakarta) in Indonesia where nine Japanese officers and four Japanese proprietors were prosecuted for coercing Dutch women into sexual slavery after Japan occupied Indonesia. Eleven of them were convicted with one of them being executed.
2. Tamura, *Shunpūden*.
3. Tamura, *Inago*.
4. *Akatsuki no dassou* [Escape at Dawn], directed by Taniguchi Senkichi (1950; Tokyo: Shin Toho), film.
5. *Shunpūden* [Story of a Prostitute], directed by Suzuki Seijun (1965; Tokyo: Nikkatsu), film.
6. Marukawa, "The Representation of 'Asia,'" 276.
7. Hirano, *Tennō*, 144–149.
8. Jun Etō, *Tozasareta gengo kukan: Senryogun no kenetsu to sengo nihon* [The Closed Language Space: The Censorship of the Occupation Force and Postwar Japan] (Tokyo: Bungei Shuju, 1994), 237–245.
9. Lee and Wander, "On Discursive Amnesia," 152–154.
10. Although *Shunpū* in the original Japanese title, *Shunpū Den*, is translated into English as "Prostitute," the term is not common in Japan and most Japanese readers or viewers would not arrive at that meaning (春婦 or *Shunpū* literally means "Spring Woman").
11. Tamura, *Shunpūden*, 104.

12. Tamura, *Inago*, 164.
13. Ibid., 166–177.
14. *Shunpūden*, directed by Suzuki.
15. Ibid.
16. Said, *Orientalism*, 188.
17. Ueno, *Nashionarizumu, 127*. Ueno cites Suzuki Yukō here.
18. Yoshimi, *Jūgun*, 45–148.
19. Said, *Orientalism*, 39–40.
20. George Hicks, *The Comfort Women: Japan's Brutal Regime of Enforced Prostitution in the Second World War* (New York: W. W. Norton & Company, 1995), 27.
21. Yoshimi, *Jūgun*, 94.
22. Lee and Wander, "On Discursive Amnesia," 152–154.
23. Said, *Orientalism*, 152.
24. Tamura, *Shunpūden*, 144.
25. Paul Vitello, "Yoshiko Yamaguchi, 94, Actress in Propaganda Films: [Obituary (Obit); Biography]." *The New York Times*, September 23, 2014, Late Edition (East Coast). http://pitt.idm.oclc.org/login?url=https://www-proquest-com.pitt.idm.oclc.org/docview/1564106074?accountid=14709.
26. Marukawa, "The Representation of 'Asia,'" 277.
27. *Akatsuki*, directed by Taniguchi.
28. Hirano, *Tennō*, 145.
29. Tamura, *Shunpūden*, 104–105.
30. Said, *Orientalism*, 178.
31. Ibid., 247.
32. Ibid., 187–188.
33. *Shunpūden*, directed by Suzuki.
34. Ibid.
35. Tamura, *Inago*, 184–185.
36. Hirano, *Tennō*, 154–155.
37. Marukawa, "The Representation of 'Asia,'" 276.
38. Ibid., 276.
39. Said, *Orientalism*, 190.
40. Taijirō Tamura, *Nikutai no Mon* [Gate of Flesh] (Tokyo: Chikuma Shobō, 1947), 65–66.
41. Rumiko Nishino, *Jūgun Ianfu* [Military comfort women]. (Tokyo: Akashi Shoten, 1992), 115.
42. Ibid., 69.
43. Soh, *The Comfort Women*, 183–185.
44. Said, *Orientalism*, 160.
45. Ako Inuzuka, "A Dialectic between Nationalism and Multiculturalism: An Analysis of the Internationalization Discourse in Japan," in *Intercultural Communication in Japan: Theorizing Homogenizing Discourse*, eds. Satoshi Toyosaki and Shinsuke Eguchi (London: Routledge, 2017), 207–223.
46. Ryūji Tanabe, *Koizumi Yakumo* (Tokyo: Hokuseidō, 1980), 114–115.

47. Etsuko Fujimoto, "Japaneseness, Whiteness, and the "Other" in Japan's Internationalization," in *Transforming Communication about Culture: Critical New Directions*, ed. Mary Jane Collier (Thousand Oaks, CA: Sage, 2001), 2.
48. Wayne C. Booth, *The Rhetoric of Fiction* (Chicago: University of Chicago Press, 1961), 298.
49. Tamura, *Shunpūden*, 147
50. *Akatsuki*, directed by Taniguchi.
51. *Shunpūden*, directed by Suzuki.
52. Tamura, *Inago*, 194.
53. Kim-Gibson, *Silence Broken*, 187.
54. Soh, *The Comfort Women*,116.
55. Hirano, *Tennō*, 148–153.
56. Tamura, *Shunpūden*, 118.
57. Tamura, *Inago*, 167–168.
58. Philip Wander, "The Third Persona: An Ideological Turn in Rhetorical Theory," *Central States Speech Journal* 35 (1984): 209–210.
59. Drzewiecka, "Public Memories," 288.
60. Booth, *The Rhetoric of Fiction*, 298.
61. Tamura, *Shunpūden*, 114.
62. Ibid., 112–113.
63. Said, *Orientalism*, 113–115.
64. Tamura, *Inago*, 183–184.
65. Ibid., 215.
66. Said, *Orientalism*, 94.

Chapter 3

The Memories of Sexual Slavery in Japan from the 1970s to 1990

Japanese War Guilt, Victims, and Romanticized Memories

From the early 1970s to 1990, the perception of the "comfort women" changes and portrayals of the "comfort women" as victims emerge for the first time. After the radical period of the 1960s when people became active in various movements such as the anti-U.S.-Japan security treaty movement or the anti-Vietnam War movement, many Japanese people became more reflexive of their nation's past militarism. As a consequence, literature on the Japanese imperial military's atrocities became popular at the end of the 1960s. Motivated by this trend, some works during this period tend to focus on sensationalism, emphasizing the gruesome nature of the "comfort" system.

The texts I examine in this chapter are authored by Senda Kakō, Kawata Fumiko, Kim Il Myon, and Yoshida Seiji. Senda was a reporter for the *Mainichi Shimbun*, a major Japanese newspaper. I analyze two of his books: *Jūgun Ianfu: Seihen* [Military Comfort Women: Main Edition] (in 1973)[1] and *Jūgun Ianfu: Zokuhen* [Military Comfort Women: Sequel] (in 1978).[2] *Jūgun Ianfu: Seihen* is considered the first systematic report on sexual slavery in Japan where Senda interviewed Japanese survivors of sexual slavery and some former Japanese soldiers who used "comfort" stations. Senda's research also included official Japanese military documents. Kawata Fumiko is a nonfiction writer and activist. She is currently an officer for the *Nihon no Sensō Sekinin Shiryō Sentā* [the Center for Research and Documentation on Japan's War Responsibility], a Japanese NPO that supports redress for sexual slavery survivors, which was founded in 1993. Her book, *Akarenga no Ie: Chōsen kara Kita Jūgun Ianfu* [House with a Red Brick Roof: Military Comfort Women from Korea][3] (published in 1987), is analyzed in this chapter. For the book, she interviewed Pe Pongi, the first Korean survivor who came forward. Pe Pongi continued to live in Okinawa after the war and testified publicly to avoid deportation in 1975. When Pongi applied for welfare due to her deteriorating health, she faced deportation because she did not have a valid permit to live in Japan. By testifying to the circumstances under which she was brought to Okinawa, she avoided deportation. Based on her interviews with Pe Pongi, former Japanese soldiers who had met Korean "comfort women" in Okinawa, and Okinawan residents who had interactions with the women, Kawata describes Pe Pongi's life from childhood to recruitment into the "comfort" system and to her life in Okinawa after the war together with her life at the "comfort" stations in Okinawa and the lives of other Korean "comfort women."

Yoshida Seiji, a former Japanese solider, wrote about his experiences of "hunting" young Korean women on Jeju Island, an island off the coast of the southern part of Korea. His books are also cited in the Coomaraswamy report (see chapter 1) submitted to the United Nations in 1996. However, Yoshida's writings are considered fabrications by most experts today (see chapter 4). Two of his books are examined in this chapter: *Chōsenjin Ianfu to Nihonjin* [Korean Comfort Women and the Japanese] (published in 1977)[4] and *Watashi no Sensou Hanzai* [My War Crimes] (published in 1983).[5]

Kim Il Myon, a Korean nonfiction writer living in Japan, focused on the hardships Korean "comfort women" faced in the service of the Japanese military. Kim's *Tennō no Guntai to Chōsenjin Ianfu* [The Emperor's Forces and Korean Comfort Women][6] published in 1976 features direct quotes from Senda's writings with Senda's name appearing on the reference list at the end of the book, although specific passages from Senda are not referenced. There are also direct quotes from *Kuruwa* [Brothels],[7] a work of fiction by Nishiguchi Katsumi, in Kim's work, which are used as if they were actual events without clear reference. Likewise, Nishiguchi is listed as a source at the end of the book.

"Historical truth" is only one aspect of collective memory and it may be said that most collective memories are not historically accurate in one way or another, or that that historical accuracy lies in the eye of the beholder for that matter. It is interesting to ask though, what motivates authors to fabricate, plagiarize, or turn fiction into fact on a historically loaded topic such as "comfort women." Answering such questions may allow us to better understand societal pressures and motivations that led to the adoption of certain collective memories over others during certain time periods. As previously mentioned, Yoshida's books were cited in the 1996 Coomaraswamy report and were also widely mentioned in the *Asahi Shimbun* in the 1990s. Kim's *The Emperor's Forces and Korean Comfort Women* was also widely read and went through thirteen editions by 1992. Both authors' books undeniably had a wide audience in their time and numerous citations show their impact on public and scholarly perceptions regarding "comfort women" after the 1970s.

In all of these texts, "comfort women" are remembered as victims who were used as commodities to take care of Japanese soldiers' sexual needs. Both Japanese and Korean "comfort women" are portrayed as victims although the process of victimization differs between the two groups. Nevertheless, there are still some images of "comfort women" comparable to the "romantic" portrayals we have seen in the preceding decades.

Across the texts there are several recurring themes: (1) "comfort women" as victims; (2) Korean "comfort women" being more mistreated than their Japanese counterparts; (3) discrimination against Koreans in general; (4) romantic, idyllic memories of "comfort women"; (5) Orientalist, exotic, erotic depictions of Korean women; (6) pure, innocent Korean "comfort women"; (7) vulgar, greedy "comfort" station proprietors; and (8) the Japanese imperial military's responsibility. Although some of the themes such as discrimination against Koreans in general and vulgar, greedy "comfort" station proprietors are not directly related to memories of Korean "comfort women," I have decided to include those because they are relevant to the overall aim of providing a fuller understanding of the controversy surrounding the memories of "comfort women" in contemporary Japan. In addition, the theme of discrimination against Koreans in general is a prominent theme in all the texts examined in this chapter.

"COMFORT WOMEN" AS VICTIMS

The portrayal of "comfort women" as victims is most prominent in Kim's *The Emperor's Forces and Korean Comfort Women*. He describes the ways in which Korean virgins were taken forcefully or lured into "comfort" stations under false pretenses where they were forced to grueling sexual labor under unsanitary conditions. According to Kim, many of the women died as a result while others were killed by the military at the end of the war. For instance, under the heading, "Ianfu to Byōki" [Comfort women and Illness], Kim lists various types of ailments and diseases "comfort women" suffered from: swollen genitals, constipation, pain in the breasts, tuberculosis, STDs, and malaria.[8] The descriptions are so unusually graphic that, considering the indiscriminate use of partially fictional sources, they appear almost voyeuristic. For instance, he describes in grueling detail how the women's genitals were affected by frequent intercourse:

> Comfort women who were placed into cages at "comfort" stations had their vaginas and uteruses injured and they bled as a result of attacks of several dozen

penises a day. I hear there were many who became bedridden as a consequence. Even among those who were fortunate enough not to be injured, it was common that their vaginas were unusually swollen. Although they, of course, applied ointment, they were not given enough time to recover. When women grimaced in pain, soldiers thought they were being ecstatic and they attacked the part even more. Eventually, the genital area would swell up like a steamed bun which would obstruct the anus. As a result, the women became constipated. The more attractive a woman was, the faster these symptoms occurred. The swollen genitals became numb and they would not have felt pain even if they had been bitten by locusts or rats. (My translation)[9]

Kim also writes about other diseases. For example, he writes that while all "comfort women" were exposed to STDs, Korean women had an even higher risk to contract STDs because they looked younger and less like prostitutes and soldiers often had intercourse with Korean "comfort women" without condoms, assuming that the women must be disease free. Many women developed painful lumps in their breasts. As the soldiers continued to grab their breasts, this condition worsened and, according to Kim, caused those women to die (which seems implausible and may be another example of Kim's nonchalant approach to historical writing). He also mentions that some women developed tuberculosis. Whatever illnesses they contracted, Kim reports that they were treated inadequately and that treatment was often discontinued if there was no hope for recovery. He states that some proprietors even reduced the amount of food given to the sick to accelerate their decline. The remains of dead "comfort women" were then buried or cremated by their fellow "comfort women" rather than being shipped back to their families in Korea.[10]

While Kim depicts Japanese "comfort women" as aging prostitutes who volunteered and were generally treated better than Korean women, Senda's account shows them as victims nonetheless. For instance, Saitō Kiri, a former Japanese "comfort woman" in China, interviewed by Senda, reports that they were referred to as "public toilets" by some officers. She also commented on the negative effects that life as a "comfort woman" had on her body:

Many women lost all sexual sensation within three months because we were having intercourse with dozens of soldiers everyday. It happened to me, too.... During our periods, just like at brothels in Japan, we drank lots of salt water. Within six months, our periods became irregular and eventually stopped.... Then we became infertile. That was when our hope to be normal women disappeared and we became real comfort women. It was the beginning of a sad life with no return. (My translation)[11]

Infertility could also affect a woman's life after the war. Senda mentions a case of a former Japanese "comfort woman" who was divorced after the war because of her infertility. Senda also interviewed one Korean survivor of sexual slavery living in Japan. She claims that she had to attend to roughly 300 soldiers a day. Each soldier took about three minutes and she had to do this for up to seventeen hours a day. She ate during sex, often felt sick, and did not even have time to go to the bathroom, urinating there, sometimes during intercourse.[12] Senda also describes how "comfort women," both Japanese and Korean, were abandoned at the end of the war when Japanese soldiers withdrew and left them to fend for themselves. They had to flee from Allied attacks into the mountains and jungles of the Philippines and Myanmar without supplies and many died as a result. When soldiers died during the war, they were typically awarded a medal and their family received a pension. However, the deaths of "comfort women" remained unrecorded.[13]

One common theme among former soldiers' testimonies in Senda's books is how they objectified "comfort women." They were often remembered as "essential supplies." Senda quotes Itō Shōzō, a former Japanese soldier who served in China:

> They ["comfort women"] were called *Yachi* [wild chicken]. I don't know the origin but it meant that having sex with "comfort women" was simply discharge rather than sex. As soon as you ride them, it's over and it's the next person's turn. Possibly they imagined chickens' sex because of this. In fact, sex was miserable there. Barrack buildings are lined up and if you enter one, you'll see a mattress. Of course, it is dirty because it is a mattress that absorbed the sweat and grease of thousands of men. Women were lying on those mattresses wearing a chemise. Japanese "comfort women," Korean "comfort women," and Chinese "comfort women" were all like that. (My translation)[14]

The indifference for "comfort women" becomes obvious in the expression "wild chicken" with the women seen as mere objects for "discharge." Similarly, another former Japanese solider, Yamada Shōzō, is reported to have said that "comfort women" were derogatorily called, "Jaran pi," meaning "walking prostitutes" because they traveled with units of the Japanese military.

For the "comfort woman" Pongi, in Kawata Fumiko's *Akarenga no Ie*, the most miserable experiences came after the war. Pongi herself is quoted as saying that it was after the war when she was released from one of the camps operated by the Allied forces that she truly felt that she was abandoned in a foreign land to which she was brought by the Japanese military. Pongi's life as a prostitute in Okinawa after the war was harder than her life as a "comfort" woman during the war. While she had to have sex with a large number of men both during and after the war, at "comfort" stations, she did not have to worry about customers. After the war, however, she had to find her own customers and, without customers, there was no income. Her proprietors made her feel ashamed and worthless when she could not get enough customers. When talking about her life immediately after the war, she states that she walked all day in Okinawa and, at night, she went into one of the brothels and asked for a job. On the following morning, though still feeling tired, she left, lying to the proprietors that she had to go to pick up her belongings and walked all day again to another red light district. She continued to do the same thing for about a year because she felt, "restless." Although she eventually settled in one place and gained a job outside of the prostitution field as years passed, she could not fully support herself without selling her body until the 1970s.[15]

Kawata's description of Pongi's neuralgia clearly communicates the pain Pongi continued to suffer from, even decades after the war. Pongi says that she became neuralgic as a result of sleeping in a cold cave that was used as a temporary secret base by the unit of the Japanese military with which she was affiliated after the Allied forces landed on the island. However, Kawata wonders if neuralgia is related to her traumatic memories of being a "comfort woman" during the war and being a prostitute after the war because Pongi seems to suffer from especially severe pain when she recounts her past as a "comfort woman":

> Pongi curses when recollecting her life in which she had to sell her body. Pongi goes crazy, cursing. Pongi says, "That's why I go crazy. I often have a headache. I feel like stabbing my neck. Really. My eyes hurt. My head hurts. Neuralgia. There are days when I want to stab my neck with scissors when applying Salonpas [pain relieving patches]. It would be nice if I could die immediately, otherwise, that would be even more pathetic. I wouldn't be suffering if I had been killed by a shot during the war." (My translation)[16]

Kawata clearly establishes Pongi as a victim, connecting her continuous postwar suffering to potential PTSD caused by her wartime traumatic experience as a "comfort woman."

KOREAN "COMFORT WOMEN" BEING MORE MISTREATED THAN THEIR JAPANESE COUNTERPARTS

Senda, Kim, and Kawata are in agreement that Korean "comfort women" were more severely mistreated than their Japanese counterparts. Senda describes how Korean women were forcefully taken from small villages in contrast to Japanese "comfort women" who were usually volunteers. According to a Korean witness, interviewed by Senda, a Japanese police officer handed young girls a notice stating, "You are now a member of the Voluntary Service Corps," three days before they were transported. Girls who were considered a flight risk were incarcerated. Answering Senda's question on where those girls were gathered, the witness states:

> In front of the police station. From there, policemen took those girls to Seoul by train or truck, guarding them so they could not escape. Their families, especially mothers, cried holding onto their daughters. When policemen tried to separate them, the mothers begged them, "Return my daughter, please!" crying and holding onto the policemen, but they were kicked away. Where in the world are mothers pleased to have their daughters being raped by soldiers? (My translation)[17]

Senda also argues that the fact that the majority of "comfort women" were taken from the Korean peninsula is due to discriminatory feelings against the Koreans held among the Japanese military officials as well as the general Japanese public. While there were practical reasons as well—it was more feasible to quickly gather a great number of women from a colony and Korea's official language at the time was Japanese, Senda argues that the discriminatory feelings toward Koreans in Japanese society allowed them to dehumanize their victims and "use" Korean women as if they were "public toilets." While the Japanese empire was responsible for colonizing Korea, Senda argues that the government's discriminatory colonial policies were widely supported by the people of Japan.[18] As mentioned in chapter 1, Japan's modernization that began in the mid-nineteenth century was about Westernization. In the process of Westernizing the nation, other Asians especially Chinese and Koreans were despised and discriminatory feelings toward Chinese and Koreans developed among many Japanese. Recollections from former "comfort women" and Japanese soldiers support the notion that Korean "comfort women" had to work harder than Japanese "comfort women." For example, Japanese "comfort women" were given a day off after "working" for several days, while Korean "comfort women" had to work for a month before they had a day off. Senda also recorded examples of individual biases among Japanese soldiers. For instance, Kage Teruo is quoted as saying that Korean "comfort women" were disorderly and did not have good manners in comparison to Japanese nurses from the Red Cross when fleeing from the Allied forces in the Philippines. Kage reports that while the nurses maintained their dignity and kept their uniforms to wear on the final occasion (to die with dignity), Korean "comfort women" just threw away everything including the last toilet paper because they did not want to carry heavy baggage. Kage states that Korean "comfort women" were no comparison to Japanese nurses. In response to Kaga's criticism of Korean women, Senda wonders who took away that dignity from the Korean women by forcing them into prostitution.[19] Another example of discrimination recorded by Senda is an incident in Saitama, Japan immediately after the war. A former Korean "comfort woman" moved to Saitama with a former Japanese soldier to whom she was engaged. However, she was killed by the man one year later. Though it was obvious that he murdered her (e.g., her body was found under his house and there were strangulation marks on her neck), the police did not seriously investigate the case because she was Korean and the killer got away.[20]

Kim also details discrimination against Korean "comfort women" in comparison to Japanese "comfort women." Just like other authors, Kim describes how many common soldiers Korean women had to serve while Japanese women were frequently reserved for officers and had to attend to fewer men. According to Kim, the large number of men took a toll on their bodies which often made it difficult for Korean women to lead "normal" lives after the war. In contrast, some former Japanese "comfort women" were able to live happily after the war (according to Kim). Kim also argues many Korean "comfort women" did not survive until the end of the war or were unable to return to Korea because they were either abandoned or even killed by the Japanese military.[21] To illustrate this point Kim cites a story from Nishiguchi's fictional novel, *Kuruwa*, in which Japanese soldiers shoot a group of "comfort women" with machineguns. He contrasts Korean "comfort women's" misfortune with Japanese "comfort women" who were mostly helped by the military to return to Japan.[22] He also relates an incident where a Japanese military doctor discovered a Japanese virgin in a "comfort station" among Japanese prostitutes when examining the women. The doctor was enraged, scolded the proprietors who had brought her, and ordered them to send her back to Japan. Kim acknowledges the ethical behavior of the military doctor but notes that this would not have happened if the virgin had been Korean because Korean virgins were recommended as ideal "comfort women" by a military doctor.[23]

Kim's descriptions of the recruitment and treatment of Korean victims match the reports from other sources.[24] Most women were lured to "comfort" stations with false promises or simply abducted. They were then raped, mostly by officers, because of a superstition that one would not get wounded after intercourse with a virgin. Thereafter, they had to comfort dozens of soldiers a day which led many of them to contract diseases and suffer physical injuries. Insufficient rest and little medical treatment led to the death of many of them.

Kawata Fumiko's *House with a Red Brick Roof* also points out the inequality between Korean and Japanese "comfort women" though these passages are relatively short. Pongi's testimony occupies the majority of Kawata's book, but it does not go into detail regarding her life at the "comfort station" in Okinawa. Her stories' focus is on her childhood and adolescence in Korea, her life after she hid in a cave as a result of the Allied attack on the island, and her life in Okinawa after the war. So most of the inequalities described by Kawata focus on her life as a prostitute in postwar Okinawa. There are, however, two examples of Japanese "comfort women" in the book, which illustrate the point that Japanese "comfort women" were able to return to normal lives after the war, whereas Korean "comfort women" had to continue to sell their bodies to survive, sometimes for decades after.

The first Japanese "comfort woman" was Miyagi Tsuru (pseudonym). She was sold into prostitution in Naha, a major city on the Okinawa main island to pay for the medical bills of her sick grandfather. After Naha's red light district was destroyed by Allied air raids in October 1944, she became a "comfort woman" for the Japanese military at the age of nineteen. She only had to have intercourse with a limited number of officers but she became pregnant as a result and carried the baby to term. However, since she did not have enough breast milk, the baby died soon after birth. Several years after the war, she married an Okinawan man and had four children.[25] In Miyagi's story, we can see Japanese "comfort women" "treated better" during the war than their Korean counterparts, consistent with other sources.[26] The fate of the other Japanese "comfort women," Uwake Tamako reads more like the stories of Pongi and other Korean "comfort women." Yet, she seems to have led a relatively happy, peaceful life after the war. Uwake was a prostitute on the Japanese mainland before she went to Southeast Asia as a "comfort woman." After Japan lost the battle of Saipan in 1944, she was captured by the U.S. forces. After the war, she returned to Okinawa together with other captured Japanese. She made a living in postwar Okinawa as a prostitute where she met an Okinawan farmer to whom she got married several years later. Uwake's comparisons of life as a "comfort woman" during the war and that as a prostitute at private brothels after the war read similarly to that of Pongi:

> It was better with the army than at private brothels. At a private brothel, for example, if there are five women, they hang the women's name plates on the wall in the order of the number of customers they have had. If you are third or fourth, it's OK. But you don't want to be last. At "comfort" stations, soldiers just came and formed a long line every day. Yes, I was able to handle 50 or even 100 men without a problem. (My translation)[27]

The number of soldiers she had to serve shows that she did not receive the special treatment Miyagi and other Japanese "comfort women" may have received. The number is comparable to the numbers many Korean survivors report. Uwake's comparison between her life at a "comfort" station and at a private brothel sounds very similar to Pongi's comments. Both state that their lives at private brothels were more taxing than their lives as "comfort women," primarily because they did not have to compete for customers in the "comfort" system. Considering that, Uwaki's peaceful life afterward is in stark contrast with Pongi's lonely life suffering from neuralgia.

Since Kawata traced the postwar lives of only a few Korean and Japanese "comfort women," it is difficult to generalize from these reports. It is possible that there were many Korean "comfort women" who were able to return to "normal" lives, whereas a number of Japanese "comfort women" could not. For instance, Keiko, a former Japanese "comfort woman" interviewed by Senda for another book, *Jūgun Ianfu Keiko* [Military Comfort Woman Keiko], testifies that she continued to support herself as a prostitute after the war until 1956 when prostitution became illegal in Japan and the red light district where she worked closed down.[28] We can also assume that it must have been hard for both groups of women to return to a "normal" life, considering that many survivors became infertile, which is considered a crucial "deficit" in patriarchal societies, in addition to the loss of chastity, not to mention the psychological consequences of prolonged abuse. Getting married was the only way to lead a "normal life" for the majority of women at the time and it is not hard to imagine that former "comfort women" regardless of their nationality faced considerable obstacles in that regard. Nonetheless, Kawata contrasted the two Japanese survivors' positive postwar experiences with Pongi's and other Korean survivors' miserable lives after the war, which emphasizes the victimhood of Korean survivors. Kawata also describes the difficulties Pongi encountered when trying to find a non-prostitution job in postwar Okinawa. Pongi tells her story of trying to make a living by selling vegetables on the black market in postwar Okinawa. She states that she could not compete with other sellers because of her limited knowledge of the Japanese language.[29] In addition, considering discrimination against Koreans that is still prevalent in Japanese society today, it is easy to imagine how difficult life for Pongi and other Korean survivors must have been in postwar Japan.

I also wonder how the knowledge about "comfort women" among Okinawa residents affected the treatment of Korean women after the war. In mainland Japan, no "comfort" stations were operated by the military and, as a result, most Japanese except for former soldiers were oblivious to the existence of the "comfort" system as well as the origin of the majority of "comfort women." In Okinawa, however, residents had to know to some extent as there are examples of "comfort" stations created in residential areas. The knowledge that most "comfort women" were Korean must also have been widespread. The presence of Korean women in postwar Okinawa must have been associated with their former "profession" by Okinawans to some extent which surely influenced their interaction including employment opportunities and opinions about their fitness for marriage.

DISCRIMINATION AGAINST KOREANS IN GENERAL

In addition to the different standards of treatment reserved for Korean and Japanese "comfort women," discrimination against Koreans in general is a dominant theme found in reports of this period. In Kawata's writings, this mostly appears in the descriptions of the treatment of Korean laborers during the battle of Okinawa. During this battle, everybody including Japanese soldiers, Okinawan residents, and Korean "comfort women" was starving but Korean laborers suffered the most because their food was more strictly rationed. As a result, some laborers resorted to stealing. Pongi remembers an incident where laborers stole a few potatoes from a field owned by Okinawan residents for which they were beaten so severely that they could not get up for several days.[30] She also recalls that laborers were caught stealing food from a house of residents for which they were executed. Kawata also mentions that Japanese soldiers were openly taking food from Okinawans who themselves were a discriminated minority, without repercussions.[31] All Japanese soldiers had to do was "to ask for food" because Okinawans were afraid of them. Kawata also describes a case of desertion where twenty Korean laborers escaped together with a Japanese soldier. Failing to catch the deserters, the officer in charge of the unit consequently made up another desertion incident and ordered the execution of four Korean laborers as alleged deserters to save face and set an example for other soldiers and laborers.[32] While the Japanese military is infamous for a casual approach to their own soldiers' lives, Korean lives mattered even less.

Discrimination against Koreans is also reported in Yoshida's *My War Crimes*. It is ubiquitous especially when he describes the "hunting" of Korean men for slave labor. In the beginning, Yoshida explains the situation of Korean laborers in Japan as he was working for the office that was in charge of "recruiting" laborers and assigning them to various places such as coal mines and construction sites. He writes that Korean laborers' deaths were called *shomo* [wastage]. He recalls the day when he went to pick up the remains of a dead Korean laborer at an airbase construction site:

> After we were led to an office, a young lieutenant ordered me to find a replacement for the dead Korean laborer and take the urn that was casually placed on a desk. Once I handed the urn to my colleague I brought with me, we went to see a sergeant. After writing down the man's information like his name and where he was from, I asked about the circumstances under which he died. The

sergeant, while organizing documents on his desk, quickly said, "It was not an accidental death at work. On the previous day, he was punished by a soldier because he skipped work pretending to be sick. When we noticed that he had died in the evening, we quickly sent his body to a crematorium." The sergeant left the office, laughing. (My translation)[33]

Yoshida later elaborates that "punishment" by soldiers or supervisors, which involved severe beatings, was a common cause of death among Korean laborers together with suicide. Korean laborers' deaths were treated with no more concern than broken tools. Soldiers simply laughed it off and ordered replacements.

Kim also discusses discrimination against Koreans. In his opinion, the Japanese colonial government's policies of drafting young healthy Korean men as soldiers, forcing others to work in Japan as laborers, as well as forcing young Korean women into sexual servitude were a planned attempt at genocide because these policies led to the deaths of numerous Korean men and women. He also suggests that the Japanese government, by exploiting young Korean men and women, tried to prevent Koreans from organizing an independence movement in case of Japan's defeat in the war.[34] Kim further discusses other discriminatory colonial policies such as the law that forced Koreans to adopt Japanese names, which was humiliating to many Koreans. He relates a story of one Korean family that committed suicide because of this law.[35]

ROMANTIC, IDYLLIC MEMORIES OF "COMFORT WOMEN"

While "comfort women" are depicted as victims in all texts analyzed for this period, a contrary theme makes an appearance in some of the texts: "comfort women" as willing companions. In some cases "comfort women" are remembered in a rather romantic fashion. For instance, Mita Kazuo, a former Japanese soldier interviewed by Senda, relates his memories of "comfort women" as follows:

> It seems that soldiers began to feel as if the comfort women were their wives and soldiers did not desire them in a sexual way after they had lived together for some time. . . . Soldiers took good care of the comfort women. In response, on their days off, the comfort women visited soldiers with gifts, did laundry for soldiers, sat by soldiers who were cleaning machine guns, or gathered flowers. It was a peaceful time, hearing birds sing in the sky. . . . Of course, soldiers were better at doing laundry than those women in prostitution. Nonetheless, we were happy with their offer. (My translation)[36]

To Mita, "comfort women" were prostitutes, Japanese soldiers were nice to them, and, as a result, soldiers and women formed married-couple like relationships.

Another former Japanese soldier, Yoshikawa Masayoshi, interviewed by Senda has positive memories of "comfort women" as well. Yoshikawa spent some time with "comfort women" in China before he was sent to Papua New Guinea. He recalls that when his ship was departing, both Japanese and Korean "comfort women" saw them off while waving flags. He recalls that Korean "comfort women" gave him some sausage as a farewell gift and he was comforted by that memory when he was running from the enemy in the forests in Papua New Guinea. To him who was single and had no girlfriend, they were the only women and his soul mates.[37]

Kawata also introduces some of the "positive" memories of Korean "comfort women" shared by former Japanese soldiers. For instance, Inoue recollects Aiko, a Korean "comfort woman," as his favorite and states that he felt as if she was his younger sister. He also talks about a gift from Aiko, a handmade pillow made of Aiko's *obi*, a traditional wide belt. He states that the pillow was adorned with her name, Aiko, in elaborate stiches. Kawata explains that because Inoue supervised the "comfort" station, he had frequent contact with the women there. She presumes that the handmade pillow meant more than "a gift for a soldier who took care of her." Inoue also states that he heard from other soldiers that Aiko, severely injured during the Allies' air raids, wanted to see him.[38]

Similarly, Kim's book contains romanticized memories of Korean "comfort women" recalled by Japanese soldier Itō Keiichi who served in China:

> Every time soldiers came back to the base after battles late at night, being exhausted and feeling cold, as we reached the gate, the women were always there and waved to us, saying, "Welcome back," regardless of how late it was. They made efforts to verbally comfort us. This illustrates a unity and harmony between the troops and the women based on basic feelings. Soldiers used to say that they forgot all of the exhaustion from the battle as soon as they heard the women's voices. (My translation)[39]

Kim also talks about affection between Japanese soldiers and Korean "comfort women." He writes that, in most cases, Korean "comfort women" were hostile toward Japanese soldiers for obvious reasons but, in some situations, where they encountered friendly soldiers, they developed feelings for them. According to Kim, most "comfort women" had a soldier they were excited about and for whom they had special feelings. While there were many more cases where soldiers developed one-sided crushes on Korean "comfort women," cases where those feelings were mutual could even lead to desertion.[40] Itō is further quoted:

> Among women, there were some who liked to take care of a specific soldier just like wives who like to take care of their husbands. I'd like you to understand that military comfort women were not simply the objects for sexual release. Human relationships developed as well. As special feelings between a soldier and a woman developed, one experienced deep sadness when one of them left or died. There was even a woman who did not take any customers for a month after learning of the death of the soldier she liked. (My translation)[41]

While it seems doubtful that women were allowed not to take any customers for a month, Itō's recollection further underscores positive, romanticized memories of the women held by former soldiers.

Although Senda, Kawata, and Kim are sympathetic toward the predicaments of "comfort women" and highly critical of the former Japanese military, they report on individual Japanese soldiers who perpetuated the system having favorable recollections of "comfort women." The majority of the women's stories are narrated from soldiers' perspectives. While Senda attempted to interview former "comfort women," many of them refused which in itself hints at a less idyllic reality. These writers may be consciously or unconsciously distinguishing between the military and the empire as an institution and the soldiers as individuals. By depicting soldiers who had positive memories, the military, an institution, that created the inhumane system is consistently blamed (i.e., "individual soldiers were unaware that they were perpetrators in an inhumane system"), which must have been more appealing to a wider audience because most readers would feel more comfortable reading about the institution being blamed rather than their husbands, brothers, or fathers being depicted as perpetrators.

While there is no doubt the imperial military should be blamed for the inhumane "comfort" system, the problem of ambiguously blaming the military institution is that it becomes difficult to locate the party that should be held accountable, creating uncertainty regarding who in the military was in charge of this inhumane system. That is precisely the point of the 1996 Coomaraswamy report that demanded the Japanese government investigate the "comfort" system and prosecute those in charge (see chapter 1). Another issue is whether or not their lack of knowledge could really absolve individual soldiers of this inhumane treatment of women. In the end, without soldiers going to "comfort" stations, the "comfort" system would not have existed. Another question is whether the soldiers were truly unaware of the inhumane situations. Some of the soldiers interviewed by Nishino state that they heard Korean "comfort women" say that they had been deceived, which made them sympathize with the women but did not stop them from frequenting "comfort" stations.[42] Nonetheless, regardless of their awareness and knowledge of the inhumane system, the complicity of individual soldiers should be noted.

While romanticized memories of "comfort women" are mostly narrated by former soldiers, one notable exception is *House with a Red Brick Roof* by Kawata, which includes Pe Pongi's, a former Korean "comfort woman's," positive, idyllic memories of relationships between Japanese soldiers and Korean "comfort women." Kawata writes that Pongi felt close to a Japanese officer who was born and raised in Korea. He frequently visited the "house with the red brick roof" that was used as a "comfort" station and was friendly with the Korean women there. "He was a good-looking man. He used to come to see Micchan (another Korean woman) often. He was a well-built, kind man, and he died." (Pongi as quoted in Kawada.) Pongi also has fond memories of another Japanese soldier, Inoue. She starts her story, stating that Inoue was a very nice man. After the Allied forces landed on Okinawa, Japanese troops hid in a cave together with Korean "comfort women." Pongi and Kazuko, another Korean "comfort woman," were assigned to a cooking unit. One day, Inoue asked Pongi, Kazuko, and two Korean laborers to teach him Korean. As Inoue's pronunciation was funny, the five of them laughed a lot.[43] The story does not have a happy ending because Inoue and the Korean men were beaten by Inoue's superiors who heard their laughter, yet one gets a sense that this was a positive memory for Pongi.

Surprisingly, Pongi even told Kawata that she was sad when the Japanese lost the war. Kawata explains:

While being in the valley [to escape from air raids by the Allies], Pongi had believed that Japan would win [the war]. However, in mid August [1945], flyers calling for surrender were dropped over the island and she, together with Japanese soldiers, attended a disarmament ceremony. Pongi says that when she saw Japanese officers handing over their weapons to American officers, she cried because she was sad. Wasn't it the Japanese military that brought Pongi to Okinawa and destroyed her adult life? (My translation)[44]

There is also a passage describing Pongi's and Kawata's trip to Tokashiki Island, one of the islands in Okinawa where Pongi was stationed during the war (she lived on the main island of Okinawa after the war). Kawata states that when they visited the remains of the former Japanese military base in the mountains, Pongi prayed by the river near the base. Pongi recalled that many Japanese soldiers went on a sortie with poor equipment and came back severely injured. She used to wash their uniforms covered with dried blackish blood stains at the river. Pongi used to feel sorry for the soldiers, as if they were her relatives, when they came back injured after doing little harm to the U.S. military facing their superior weapons.[45]

Pongi's positive memories of Japanese soldiers seem to corroborate the claims of contemporary Japanese nationalists—that "comfort women" were not mistreated at "comfort" stations. Because Kawata wrote Pongi's story not Pongi herself, there is a chance that some stories may have been modified. However, Kawata's background makes it unlikely that she intentionally modified Pongi's testimony to fit the nationalist agenda. Kawata has been an active member of the Center for Research and Documentation on Japan's War Responsibility, a Japanese organization that supports the redress movement for survivors of sexual slavery. Pongi's "positive" memories and attachment to Japanese soldiers may be psychologically similar to Stockholm syndrome as she was held in captivity for years. But there might also be a connection to her unfortunate upbringing. According to Kawata's book, Pongi was born in an extremely poor family and grew up without her family (her father lived separately because he was a servant for a wealthy family and her mother left when she was a little girl). After two failed marriages, Pongi supported herself by working various jobs ranging from maid to factory worker.[46] Pongi did not know much happiness before the war, and the military environment with its comradery among soldiers and women alike, as well as the harsh but predictable living conditions may have inspired a sense of belonging where others would only feel despair. Either way, Pongi's experiences may be interpreted as supporting the claim that "comfort women's" experiences at "comfort" stations differed considerably depending on their backgrounds and the type and location of the "comfort" station.[47]

ORIENTALIST, EXOTIC, EROTIC DEPICTIONS OF KOREAN WOMEN

The next theme identified in the selected texts is a familiar one. Although not as prevalent as in the previous period from 1945 to the 1960s, there are erotic and exoticized depictions of Korean women that differ from the portrayals of Japanese women. For example, in Yoshida's *My War Crimes*, we can observe women on Jeju Island depicted as sexually open exotic women similar to the portrayals of Oriental women by Western Orientalists.[48] Oyster divers from the island are shown as "care-free" as they did not hide their breasts or thighs from Japanese men. Yoshida's recollections of "catching" women on the island are presented in a rather erotic manner:

> As the first boat approached the shore, Japanese soldiers jumped into the water and went ashore on a rocky area. The end of the area was blocked by a high cliff. As the women tried to escape toward the right side, soldiers from the second boat who had been hiding jumped out and the women's screams echoed. Soldiers from the first boat now also approached the women until they were completely surrounded by naked Japanese men.

Lieutenant Tani and I, avoiding the rocky area, swam and approached the women from the ocean. The women were all well-built, exposing large breasts. Although they were covering their bellies with black or white, handmade bathing suits, those were soaking wet and stuck to their glistening bodies. (My translation)[49]

In this passage, Korean women seem to fulfill Japanese men's sexual fantasy just like Western Orientalists associated the Orient with the "escapism of sexual fantasy."[50]

Kim also depicts Korean "comfort women" and their experiences rather erotically. Some of the expressions he uses are different from those used by other writers from this and other periods. For instance, Kim calls soldiers' penises, *hinotama* [fire balls][51] or "comfort women" *seiki no drei* [slaves of genitals].[52] Kim's sometimes strangely erotic depictions appear most prominently under the header "Tokushu Ryokan he Tsurekomi Irojigoku no 'Tokkun' wo" [Bringing women in a special inn and training them for "sex hell"]. Here he details the fate of five Korean women who were recruited as "comfort women" under the pretense of enlisting them in the *Aikoku Houshi Tai* [Patriotic Service Corp]. Kim describes how Tamako, a female proprietor, carefully washed the five girls in the bathroom. As Tamako gently washed their breasts and scrubbed their pelvic regions, "the girls' skin glistened and their breasts looked as if they were two clear jewels."[53] Here is my translation of a scene narrated in the same section where one girl is raped for the first time:

As I entered the room, the man [Kanazawa] ordered me while standing by the pillows.
"Hey, undress me."
His eyes were sharp like a leopard's though he was drunk. I took off his military jacket, belt, trousers, and shirt. . . . Kanazawa was standing only wearing underwear.
"Take this off, too!"
He said, remaining standing. My hands shivered.
"Hurry up!"
He said in a low, intimidating voice. As I unraveled the thin string, it fell on the tatami mattress. I will never forget the thing I saw for the first time in my life. It was a shocking, scary thing. I stared while holding my breath.
Kanazawa said,
"Well, you seem to fall in love with me. But you shouldn't be surprised at this. There are others who have a much better one in my unit. Now it's your turn to get naked. Why don't you take off everything in front of my eyes."

Kanazawa sat on the floor. I was so scared that I couldn't look away from it. He again said, staring at me.

"Hurry up!"

I stood up in front of him and took off the belt of my *yukata* [a Japanese summer dress]. I recalled the faces of my parents—my father who looked sad to see me off and my mother crying that morning.

"Father, Mother, please forgive me. Getting naked and becoming a toy of a man is a duty of the Patriotic Dedication Corp."

As I apologized to my parents in my mind, I took off my *yukata*. I stood naked in front of the man. I covered my breasts with one hand and my lower abdomen with the other. Then I quickly sat down. But Kanazawa yelled at me.

"Stand up! And you must show me everything. You're now a part of the unit."

I stood up but I kept covering my breasts and lower abdomen.

"Hey, take your hands away. Put your hands behind your head"

I hesitantly put my hands behind my head.

"Straighten your back! Yes, like that. Turn a few times! Yes, you have quite a nice body. You will be able to comfort many soldiers in the unit with a body like that. You look healthy and it looks like you can work hard. Come here."

Kanazawa touched my back with his hairy hand.

"You have very smooth skin. You cannot enjoy this firmness with a *naichi onna* ['inside land women' referring to Japanese women]"

Soon he kissed me with his bearded mouth and my body was pushed down and forced to open. I cannot speak of the suffering at that time in detail. Tears of sadness, pain, and humiliation poured one after another. It was four hours later when everything was over. During this time, this man forced young me to do various embarrassing deeds and sought my body over and over again. (My translation)[54]

Since the women were raped, it is not surprising to encounter explicit passages. However, many of these passages are narrated from a male perspective and even those narrated by women, in Kim's case, contain a level of detail, a choice of words that add a flavor of voyeurism. Although the above passage is a quote from *Kin Haruko: Chōsenjin Ianfu no Shuki* [Kim Chun-ja: A Korean Comfort Woman's Story], its credibility remains questionable. Published in 1965, the book is believed to be either fictional or highly embellished if based on a true story.[55] In cases where similar situations are narrated from a reliable source the reports are strikingly different.

Survivors' testimonies in Dai Sil Kim-Gibson illustrate that point. For instance, Yun Doo Ri, a survivor interviewed by Kim-Gibson relates the memory of her first rape as follows:

> When my cuts and bruises [from her successful attempt at escape from rape a few days prior] had healed slightly, they put me back into the same room. Another officer was waiting for me. They must have warned him about me. He did not wait and did not give me a moment even to think of protesting. He swiftly knocked me down, and started pushing his thing inside of me. It happened all so fast. I found myself bleeding. I wasn't even sure where the blood was coming from. I only felt pain. Something in my body was torn apart. I put my teeth into his cheek. Now we were both bleeding, he from his face and I, somewhere below. . . I was fifteen.
> My bottom, vagina and uterus, everything felt like they were torn in shreds.[56]

Yoshida's depictions of Korean women containing erotic, Orientalist descriptions are not surprising, considering that a Japanese man, a former colonizer, fabricated "memories" of the formerly colonized women. However, Kim, a Korean man living in Japan, also seems to share the erotic, Orientalist depictions of Korean "comfort women" to some extent. Although he is not a former colonizer, during his time in Japan he may have unconsciously internalized some of these views. Alternatively, the portrayals may reflect the effort of the writer to appeal to his Japanese audience who held Orientalist views of Korean women since colonial times.

Korean women are also depicted differently from Japanese women. For instance, in Yoshida's *My War Crimes*, he recalls seeing "comfort" stations in China. He writes that many Japanese soldiers lined up at the "comfort" stations especially before important battles when soldiers received a few days off. He quotes a military contractor: "I hear the [Korean] women are made to have sex with 50 soldiers on a day like this. Korean women are tough, aren't they?" (my translation).[57] Although this contractor was clearly aware that it was not the Korean women's choice, the difference between Korean women and Japanese women is underscored in this statement. Similarly, Senda, in *Jūgun Ianfu: Seihen*, quotes a former Japanese soldier who had heard that if "comfort women" served about fifty soldiers a day, the length during which the women could continue to work without a day off was one week for Japanese women, one month for Korean women, and three months for Chinese women. According to this former Japanese soldier, there were differences in physical strength among women of various nationalities. Senda refutes this theory of differences by citing a gynecologist.[58] Of course, it could be simply an attempt to justify the exploitation of Korean women and women of other nationalities because, this way, soldiers could feel less guilty about Korean and other women's predicaments. Nonetheless, these types of comments made by former soldiers about Korean women's toughness appear in their testimonies, underscoring perceived differences between Korean and Japanese women.

Likewise, when describing "comfort" stations for officers in Nanjing, Yoshida explains that most "comfort women" there were Japanese, with only a few Korean women who were young, beautiful, and spoke Japanese well serving at the "officers only" "comfort" stations. He continues that those Korean "comfort women" who were selected for officers looked like Japanese when wearing *kimonos* [traditional Japanese dresses].[59] This brief statement implies that Korean women look different from Japanese women and that it is better to look like a Japanese woman, similar to Orientals being seen as different from "superior" Westerners and "destined to bear its foreignness" as Said mentions.[60]

PURE, INNOCENT KOREAN "COMFORT WOMEN"

The somewhat erotic depictions of Korean women in Yoshida and Kim's books are consistent with Orientalist depictions of Oriental women as carnal creatures. However, the sixth theme, especially emphasized in Kim's book, and seemingly in contrast to the above, underlines the innocence and pureness of Korean "comfort women" in comparison to Japanese "comfort women." It is emphasized that Korean "comfort women" were "recruited" against their will while most Japanese "comfort women" had already been prostitutes in Japan before they agreed to work at "comfort" stations. While this theme emerges in all texts examined in this chapter, the Korean expat Kim especially emphasizes the youth and purity of Korean "comfort women," compared to old, experienced, greedy, and lazy Japanese "comfort women" who had been prostitutes previously. For instance, Kim explains that whereas Japanese "comfort women" volunteered to work at military "comfort stations," which was a much higher paying job than working at brothels within Japan, Korean "comfort women" were virgins who were deceitfully or forcefully taken. Also, citing Asō, a military doctor who examined "comfort women" in Shanghai and was interviewed by Senda, Kim writes that most Japanese "comfort women" had STDs and were used to going through STD examinations while Korean "comfort women" frequently cried and refused to go through the examinations because they were virgins and had never done that.[61] When emphasizing the pureness and innocence of Korean "comfort women," Kim even discusses the superiority of the Korean women over the Japanese women as "comfort women":

> There were even many officers who went to Korean comfort women because they were tighter, saying, "I prefer Koreans as far as women go." They avoided

Japanese "comfort women" who were "sluts" and whose bodies made them feel as if they became "burdock roots in the Pacific." Soldiers also preferred Korean comfort women and said,

"I like Korean *pi* because you don't catch a disease. Officers go to Japanese prostitutes and Korean *pi* are for us. Yet, they sneak into our territory."

There are two reasons. One of them is that Japanese *pi* were so arrogant that they looked down on soldiers. Another reason is that Korean *pi* tried harder to prove they were better than Japanese women. Besides, they had better bodies and were pure because they were young. (My translation)[62]

Similarly, in another section, Kim argues that Japanese "comfort women" were professionals with better technique in bed who often faked orgasms, while Korean girls were pure and honest, which made them popular among Japanese soldiers. On their days off, while Japanese "comfort women" spent their free time, lying around, doing nothing, because their physical strength deteriorated to the point that they could not even carry a bag as a result of their lazy lives as prostitutes for years, Korean "comfort women" spent their free time more actively, starting their days with doing laundry because they were young and grew up helping in fields in their hometowns.[63] While Kim's intention in these comparisons may be simply to emphasize the youth and innocence of Korean women who were forced and deceived, he seems to have forgotten that Japanese "comfort women" were also forced into prostitution, albeit not by the "comfort" system. Most of them also came from poor families mostly from agricultural areas and many also grew up, helping in the fields. The emphasis on the pureness and innocence of Korean "comfort women" underscores the women's victimhood and is similar to an approach adopted by the leading South Korean support organization for survivors, the Korean Council.

Some of the examples from Kim's book in the previous paragraph draw on Senda's writings such as Asō's observation of Korean "comfort women" and Japanese "comfort women" making soldiers feel as if they were burdock roots in the Pacific, and Japanese "comfort women" faking orgasms. However, while describing Japanese "comfort women" as experienced prostitutes who volunteered for this "job" at "comfort" stations, Senda also depicts them as women who were driven by patriotism. Interviewing several former Japanese "comfort women," he quotes them saying that they had been happy to be able to contribute to their "honorable country" [*okuni no tameni*] and that they had believed that it was their duty to their honorable country and emperor to satisfy soldiers' sexual desires, although they realized after the war that they had been deceived.[64] Likewise, Senda, citing some of the former Japanese soldiers he interviewed, describes some of the battles in Burma (Myanmar) where Japanese "comfort women" chose to die with Japanese soldiers while encouraging Korean "comfort women" to flee and surrender to the enemy.⁶⁵ Therefore, while Senda depicts Japanese "comfort women" as willing prostitutes as Kim does, Senda's presentations of them are overall more positive.

Senda also depicts Korean "comfort women" as young, kind, and vital women. Citing Kage Teruo, a former Japanese soldier, he writes that Korean "comfort women" were energetic and composed even in difficult situations. Kage recollects his experiences of fleeing together with Korean "comfort women" from the enemy in the Philippines at the end of the war. When everyone was starving, the Korean women were able to catch small crabs in rivers and find edible plants in the mountains. Senda attributes this to the fact that Koreans were exploited and were often forced to find food in the wilderness under Japan's colonial rule. Kage also explains that Korean women often shared the food they found with Japanese nurses and Japanese "comfort women" and, one time, one of them even shared potatoes with a Japanese mother and children whom they ran into.⁶⁶

VULGAR AND GREEDY "COMFORT" STATION PROPRIETORS

Another interesting theme, especially prominent in Kim's *Tennō no Guntai to Chōsenjin Ianfu*, is an emphasis on the role of private proprietors who were greedy and vulgar and took an active role in the forceful and deceitful recruitment and mistreatment of Korean women. This is similar to one of the points made by Park Yu-Ha in her controversial book, *Teikoku no Ianfu* [Comfort Women of the Empire], in which she argues that the responsibility of the proprietors should be investigated because of their role in the recruitment and mistreatment of Korean women, according to the testimonies of a number of survivors.⁶⁷

There are similarities to contemporary Japanese nationalists who also blame proprietors for the women's misfortune. However, Kim suggests that most proprietors were Japanese from the Kansai or Kyushu regions whereas Japanese nationalists argue that proprietors were mostly Koreans. Kim writes that Japanese proprietors were complicit with Japanese officers bribing them with money and virgins. In return, proprietors received the rights to operate military "comfort" stations. According to Kim, after promising innocent Korean women factory jobs, recruiters would pay the women's parents 10 yen before they were taking them to Manchuria. Then, they would add fees such as train tickets and food along with interest. By the time they arrived in Manchuria the women would owe 50 or 100 yen. The recruiters would then disappear and proprietors would show up in their place claiming that the women now owed 300–500 yen. As the women realized what was happening, the proprietors would threaten to hand them over to the Japanese authorities unless they could "pay back" the money. Then, Kim argues, the tone would soften:

> Taking care of parents is important in Korea, isn't it? If you work here, pay back your debt, and send some money to your parents, it would be good for your parents. Besides, this is Manchuria, it is thousands of kilometers away from your country and we're surrounded by brutal Manchurian bandits. Here we are protected by Japanese soldiers day and night. If you comfort soldiers with your body, it is "for the sake of your honorable country" while making money. This would also mean taking care of your parents in your hometown. There is no better job than this. (My translation)[68]

Kim's "comfort" station proprietors take advantage of young women's sense of filial devotion instilled in them since they were little girls.

Eventually the women gave in and began to work at "comfort" stations. Kim further describes in some detail the ways in which proprietors ran the "comfort" stations to maximize their profits. They collected 60% of the women's earnings. Further fees for clothes and food were deducted from the remaining 40%. In addition, proprietors misled the women about the number of soldiers they served as it was difficult for them to keep track accurately. This is contrasted to Japanese "comfort women" who knew how greedy their proprietors were and would count soldiers by scratch marks on a bed post or wall[69]—a description taken from Nishiguchi's fictional novel.

According to Kim, proprietors were quick to flee when it became clear that Japan was going to lose the war.[70] They left with the money, bribing military officers while abandoning their "comfort women" in the battlefields. Once Japan lost the war and the Allied occupation started in Japan, proprietors quickly gathered Japanese women—prostitutes, war widows, and other women with financial problems and opened "comfort" stations for the Allied occupation troops, continuing to earn money.[71]

In August 1945, immediately after Japan's surrender, the Japanese government created the Recreation and Amusement Association (RAA) "comfort" stations for Allied soldiers, throughout the nation, to prevent Allied soldiers from raping Japanese women as Japanese soldiers had done in China and other occupied areas in Asia. According to Senda, over 50,000 Japanese women, who were mostly war widows and others who had no other options, worked as "comfort women" until March 1946 when the RAA was ordered to close its "comfort" stations because of the spread of STDs.[72] These "comfort" stations for Allied soldiers were another example of women's human rights being ignored based on the masculinist ideology of uncontrollable men's sexual urges. Classism in the system should be noted as well—impoverished women were sacrificed, though Senda contends that Korean women would have been targeted if Korea had not gained independence. Although the government provided funds and facilities, "comfort" stations were operated by civilians. Kim mentions that those civilian proprietors were former "comfort" station proprietors who prevailed like rats, whatever happened, calling them "Ningen to shite saitei" (the worst human beings).[73]

THE JAPANESE IMPERIAL MILITARY'S RESPONSIBILITY

Similar to the previous period from 1945 to the 1960s, the involvement of the Japanese imperial military in the operation of "comfort" stations is obvious in all texts examined in this chapter. The involvement of the Japanese imperial military in the recruitment of "comfort women," however, is absent in earlier texts. Recruitment became an important topic in the 1990s because of the details of recruitment have ramifications for the nation's accountability, especially according to Japanese nationalists. In the texts from 1970 to 1990, no one seems to contest the military's role in both the recruitment of women and the operation of the "comfort" system; however, only two texts, Yoshida's and Senda's explicitly address the issue of recruitment.

Yoshida in his fabricated accounts unmistakably follows military orders, when "hunting" Korean women on Jeju Island and Korean women living in Shimonoseki, Japan. Senda details how the idea of a "comfort" system was promoted by military officials to prevent soldiers from contracting STDs and raping local women in late 1937 after the Nanjing Massacre where thousands of Chinese women were raped and hundreds of thousands of Chinese residents and prisoners of war were massacred. Japanese military officials in China *ordered* Japanese civilians working for the military to gather women and the military provided advance payments for the recruited women. Senda describes that the first military comfort station was established near Shanghai in early 1938 using facilities provided by the military and one of the military doctors, Asō, was ordered to examine the women for STDs. Senda also quotes regulations set by the military for the first "comfort" station such as the use of condoms and the amount of time allocated to soldiers. However, as the station was unpopular among soldiers and the military was worried about the appearance of "the emperor's military running brothels," the operation of "comfort" stations was turned over to civilian proprietors and the military maintained indirect control by providing necessities (e.g., facilities, food, transportation) and setting regulations (e.g., military doctors' regular examinations of women, time schedules for soldiers). Most "comfort women" were assigned to units of the military and moved together with the units.⁷⁴ Senda also quotes Kamiya Shigeo, a former Japanese soldier who was in charge of military supplies for one unit in Burma, stating that Kamiya's duties included providing supplies to "comfort" stations.⁷⁵ According to Kamiya, after important strategy meetings, banquets were held at "comfort" stations reserved only for high-ranking officers. Kamiya was responsible for the banquets and assigning "comfort women" to each officer after the banquets. Senda unequivocally depicts the involvement of the military in the operation of "comfort" stations with the Japanese military's involvement in the recruitment of "comfort women" also clearly presented.

Initially, private recruiters who were ordered or requested by the military recruited Japanese prostitutes from brothels in Japan and deceived Korean women living in Japan by offering them "a well-paid job, doing laundry and cooking for soldiers." However, as the war expanded, an increasing number of women were needed. The military began to focus on the Korean peninsula as their main location for gathering young healthy women in large numbers in a short period of time and ordered the Korean colonial government to recruit women. The order was passed down to the local governments of Korea and many women were deceived or threatened into compliance. As the war went on, recruitment practices became increasingly aggressive as illustrated by Senda's description of the confinement of women in Seoul.⁷⁶ Although Senda does not state that the Japanese government is liable for the "comfort" system as contemporary scholars argue, the involvement of the Japanese imperial military in the recruitment of women and the operation of the "comfort" system is unequivocally depicted.

CONCLUSION

During the period from 1970 to 1990, "comfort women" are remembered as victims of the "comfort" system whose bodies were destroyed in the process of "comforting" soldiers. They are shown as women who suffered from both physical and psychological trauma during and after the war. Korean women were treated worse than Japanese women. However, from the perspectives of former Japanese soldiers, "comfort women" were still frequently remembered in a positive, romantic light, similar to Tamura's novel and its movie adaptation from the preceding time period. Likewise, similar to the immediate postwar memories, Korean "comfort women" are remembered in an erotic, exotic manner as Oriental women were remembered by Western Orientalists. The involvement of the Japanese imperial military in the operation of "comfort" stations and the forceful recruitment of women is plainly depicted as well as the roles of recruiters, most of them Japanese. Although memories of the victim role of "comfort women" make their first appearance during this period and the involvement of the Japanese imperial military is stated as plain fact, the "comfort" system is not viewed in the context of war crimes, a connection that was not made until 1991 when Kim Hak-sun and two other Korean survivors took legal action against the Japanese government as will be discussed in the following chapters.

The emergence of the memories of "comfort women" and Korean men and women in general as victims during this period may have been precipitated by developments in the late 1960s when the Japanese public became "conscious" of Japan's colonial past and crimes of war. After the radical era of the 1960s when campaigns against the U.S.-Japan security treaty took place and failed (the security treaty was first renewed in 1960 and, for the second time, in 1970), the Japanese government's militaristic and authoritarian stances may have reminded the public of the empire during the war. In addition, the renewal of the U.S.-Japan security treaty at the height of pacifist and antinuclear movements may have fueled the public's fear of a return to militarism. As a consequence of the U.S.-Japan security treaty, Japan could have been drawn into conflicts of the United States including the Vietnam War. This may have contributed to a public tendency to become more reflexive and critical of their nation's past militarism. During this time, a number of writings depicting the atrocities of the Japanese imperial military surfaced. For instance, in the 1970s, the journalist Honda Katsuichi, published a series of articles titled, "Chūgoku no Tabi" [Travels in China], for the *Asahi Shimbun*. In this series, Honda examined military documents and interviewed survivors of the atrocities committed in China by the Japanese imperial military during the war, including the Nanjing Massacre of 1937. The articles were compiled and published as a book in 1972. Ōe Kenzaburō, a Nobel Prize laureate, published *Okinawa Nōto* [Okinawa Notes] in 1970 in which he describes the mass suicides of Okinawan residents forced by the Japanese imperial army during the battle of Okinawa in 1945. In this context, Ienaga Saburō, a Japanese history textbook writer who sued the Japanese Education Ministry/Government for unconstitutional textbook screening, won one of his three lawsuits against the government, although he lost the other two. The memories of "comfort women," especially Korean ones, as victims along with memories of discrimination against Koreans in general may have become a prominent theme during this time because of this societal trend. As a number of collective memory scholars argue (e.g., Blair, Dickinson, and Ott;[77] Gronbeck[78]), collective memories are influenced by today's concerns.

NOTES

1. Kakō Senda, *Jūgun Ianfu: Seihen* [Military Comfort Women: Main Edition] (Tokyo: Sanichi Shobō, 1973).
2. Senda, *Jūgun Ianfu: Zokuhen*.
3. Fumiko Kawata, *Akarenga no Ie: Chōsen kara Kita Jūgun Ianfu* [House with a Red Brick Roof: Military Comfort Women from Korea] (Tokyo: Chikuma Shōbō, 1987).
4. Seiji Yoshida, *Chōsenjin Ianfu to Nihonjin* [Korean Confort Women and Japanese] (Tokyo: Shinjinbutsu Ōraisha, 1977).
5. Seiji Yoshida, *Watashino Sensō Hanzai: Chōsenjin Kyosei Renko* [My War Crime: Forced Recruitment of Koreans] (Tokyo: Sanichi Shobō, 1983).
6. Kim, *Tennō*.
7. Katsumi Nishiguchi, *Kuruwa* [Brothels] (Tokyo: Tōhō Shuppansha, 1969).
8. Kim, *Tennō*, 159.
9. Ibid., 159.
10. Ibid., 160–162.
11. Senda, *Jūgun Ianfu Seihen*, 90–91.
12. Senda, *Jūgun ianfu: Zokuhen*, 128–129.
13. Senda, *Jugūn Ianfu Seihen*, 154–166.
14. Ibid., 169.
15. Kawata, *Akarenga*, 94–111.
16. Ibid., 111.
17. Senda, *Jugūn Ianfu Seihen*, 117.
18. Ibid., 65.
19. Senda, *Jūgun ianfu: Zokuhen*, 109.
20. Ibid., 122–126.
21. Kim, *Tennō*, 21.
22. Ibid., 271.
23. Ibid., 222.
24. For example, Takagi Kenichi, *Jūgun Ianfu to Sengo Hoshō* [Military Comfort Women and Postwar Compensation] (Tokyo: Sanichi Shobō, 1992), 21; Dai Sil Kim-Gibson, *Silence Broken: Korean Comfort Women* (Parkersburg, IA: Mid-Prairie Books, 1999), 41.
25. Kawata, *Akarenga*, 262–263.
26. For example, Senda, *Jugūn Ianfu Seihen*, 93–97; Nishino, *Jūgun*, 168–170.
27. Kawata, *Akarenga*, 263.
28. Kakō Senda, *Jūgun Ianfu Keiko* [Military Comfort Woman Keiko] (Tokyo: Kōbunsha, 1981), 276.
29. Kawata, *Akarenga*, 106–107.
30. Ibid., 92.
31. Okinawa was a separate kingdom until the early seventeenth century when Shimazu, a Japanese federal lord, conquered and made it a Japanese colony. Although

Okinawa was officially incorporated in Japan as a prefecture in the late nineteenth century, Okinawans were a discriminated minority.

32. Kawata, *Akarenga*, 150–168.
33. Yoshida, *Watashino*, 16.
34. Kim, *Tennō*, 14–17.
35. Ibid., 62.
36. Senda, *Jugūn Ianfu Seihen*, 73–74.
37. Ibid., 178–178.
38. Kawata, *Akarenga*, 80–81.
39. Itō as cited in Kim, *Tennō*, 36.
40. Kim, *Tennō*, 146.
41. Ibid., 147.
42. Nishino, *Jūgun*, 169–170.
43. Kawata, *Akarenga*, 90–92.
44. Ibid., 118.
45. Ibid., 117–118.
46. Ibid., 13–39.
47. Soh, *The Comfort Women*, 47.
48. Said, *Orientalism*, 187.
49. Yoshida, *Watashino*, 141–142.
50. Said, *Orientalism*, 190.
51. Kim, *Tennō*, 112.
52. Ibid., 113.
53. Ibid., 70.
54. Ibid., 73–74.
55. Kan Kimura, "Nihon niokeru Ianfu Ninshiki: 1970 nendai Izen no Jyōkyō wo Chūshin ni" [Perceptions of Comfort Women in Japan: Focusing on the Situations before the 1970s], *The Journal of International Cooperation Studies* 25, no. 1 (July 2017): 30.
56. Kim-Gibson, *Silence Broken*, 189.
57. Yoshida, *Watashino*, 25.
58. Senda, *Jūgun ianfu: Zokuhen*, 148–149.
59. Yoshida, *Watashino*, 23.
60. Said, *Orientalism*, 244.
61. Kim, *Tennō*, 131.
62. Ibid., 156.
63. Ibid., 150.
64. Senda, *Jugūn Ianfu: Zokuhen*, 11.
65. Senda, *Jugūn Ianfu Seihen*, 138.
66. Senda, *Jugūn Ianfu: Zokuhen*, 108–112.
67. Yuha Park, *Teikoku no Ianfu* [Comfort Women of the Empire] (Tokyo: Asahi Shimbun Shuppan, 2017), 23–34.
68. Kim, *Tennō*, 31.
69. Ibid., 143.
70. Ibid., 248.

71. Ibid., 260.
72. Senda, *Jugūn Ianfu Seihen*, 213–216.
73. Kim, *Tennō*, 32.
74. Senda, *Jugūn Ianfu Seihen*, 13–43.
75. Senda, *Jūgun ianfu: Zokuhen*, 65–78.
76. Senda, *Jugūn Ianfu Seihen*, 103–109.
77. Blair et al., "Introduction," 6–7.
78. Gronbeck, "The Rhetorics," 56.

Chapter 4

The Memories of Sexual Slavery from 1991 to 2015
Nationalist Memories

The year 1991 marks a turning point in the "comfort women" issue when Kim Hak-sun and two other Korean survivors of sexual slavery during World War II came forward and sued the Japanese government, demanding compensation for victims. This gave the issue much public attention in Japan, South Korea, and other countries. In Japan, in particular, the issue sharply divided public opinion. While "comfort women" are remembered as victims of rape and sexual slavery and the "comfort" system as a war crime and a violation of international laws among progressives, nationalists remember them in drastically different ways. They remember "comfort women" as prostitutes who knowingly accepted "the job" for money and believe that former "comfort women" came forward because they were financially motivated.

This chapter focuses on the memories created and promoted by nationalist writers, while the next chapter discusses memories held by progressives. Since 1991, both sides have published a number of books because of the widespread interest in this topic. The books examined in this chapter are *Ianfu to Senjō no Sei* [Comfort Women and Sex in Battlefields] (published in 1999) by Hata Ikuhiko,[1] a professor at Chiba University; *Shin Gōmanism Sengen: Dai 3 Kan* [New Gomanism Declaration: Volume 3] (in 1997)[2] by Kobayashi Yoshinori, a cartoonist; *Yokuwakaru Ianfu Mondai* [Understanding the Comfort Women Issue] (published in 2007)[3] by Nishioka Tsutomu, a professor at Tokyo Christian University; and *Rekishi Kyōkasho Tono 15nen Sensō* [A 15-Year War with History Textbooks] (published in 1997),[4] an anthology containing chapters by Nishio Kanji, a professor at Denki Tsūshin University, Kobayashi Yoshinori, Fujioka Nobukatsu, a professor at Takushoku University, and Takahashi Shirō, a professor at Myōjō University. This chapter also considers the *"Jūgun Ianfu": Asahi Shimbun vs. Bungei Shunjū* ["Military Comfort Women": Asahi Newspaper vs. Bungei Shunjū] edited by the editorial office of *Bungei Shunjū*, a literary magazine (in 2014),[5] which includes essays from Nishioka Tsutomu, Hata Ikuhiko, writer Kamisaka Fuyuko, historian Hosaka Masayasu, journalist Sakurai Yoshiko, former assistant cabinet secretary Ishihara Nobuo, writer Shiono Nanami, and novelist Itō Keiichi.

ANALYSIS

Through my analysis, the following themes have emerged: (1) "comfort women" as prostitutes who knowingly accepted the "high risk, high reward" job and their lives at the "comfort stations" were "not too bad"; (2) irrational and unreliable Korean "comfort women"; (3) "war is tragic," as war victimized soldiers; (4) the "comfort" system being a common practice among militaries worldwide; (5) denial of the officially sanctioned and coerced recruitment of Korean women into the "comfort" system; (6) the "comfort women" issue as a Japanese-made issue; (7) antiforeignism, especially anti-Korean sentiment; and (8) criticism of progressives. As we can see, some of these themes concern the memories of sexual slavery and their survivors/victims, whereas others simply concern the criticisms of progressives and other nations. Since Japanese progressives and other nations have attempted to create and promote memories of sexual slavery that are contradictory to the memory of nationalists, disputing and sometimes even attacking progressives and other nations have emerged as major themes. Thus, the "memory war" began after 1991.

"Comfort Women" as Prostitutes

With regard to the first theme, among nationalist writers "comfort women" are remembered as prostitutes who became "comfort women" for money. They insist that the women's lives at "comfort" stations were "not too bad," contradicting the Japanese contemporary progressive circle's widely remembered memory of "comfort women" being treated as sex slaves. This idea is promoted to challenge the memory of "comfort women" as sex slaves. For instance, nationalist scholars such as Nishioka Tsutomu argue that the term "sex slaves," used to refer to "comfort women," was first used by Takagi Kenichi, a Japanese lawyer who represented Kim Hak-sun and two other Korean survivors of sexual slavery in the 1991 trial against the Japanese government. Nishioka explains that Takagi adopted the term "sex slaves" simply to draw attention to the issue overseas, though he opines that the term was far from reality. Nishioka states that the term continued to be used by Radhika Coomaraswamy in her 1996 report to the United Nations. To refute the claim that the experiences of "comfort women" were similar to those of sex slaves, nationalist writers argue that the lives of most "comfort women" were "not too bad."

For instance, Hata Ikuhiko cites an article in *CBS Round Up* in 1944 in which five "comfort women" captured by the U.S. military in Burma were interviewed. According to the article, one of them was Japanese while the others were Koreans who came to Burma for financial gain.[6] In response to the women who state that they were deceitfully or forcibly taken, nationalist writers emphasize the role of the evil and deceitful, often Korean, contractors who lied to the women and took them to "comfort" stations without the knowledge of the military. For instance, in the case of the testimony of Kim Hak-sun, one of the three women who first sued the Japanese government, her mother sold her to a foster father who sent her to a *kisen* school. Hata explains that a *kisen* is like a Japanese *geisha* and is only one step away from prostitution. It was common in Korea for poor parents to sell their daughters to brothel contractors who "adopted" them as their stepdaughters, and thus, Hata claims that at least her mother and "foster father" knew that she was going to become a "comfort woman."[7] Thereby, it was her mother and "foster father," who deceitfully took her to the "comfort" stations, not the Japanese military.

In addition, by comparing the life of a "comfort woman" to that of a prostitute, other women in battlefields such as military nurses, and Japanese soldiers at that time, Hata argues that most "comfort women's" lives were "not too bad." By comparing them to prostitutes, he states that, in most cases, the number of customers the women had to serve per day was about the same (around five per day), although the number wildly varied between days. Moreover, there might have been days when they had to have intercourse with a few dozen soldiers. Hata explains that as their incomes directly correlated with the number of soldiers served, most women wanted to serve many soldiers. Citing former military doctor Nagasawa Kenichi, Hata introduces a story where Nagasawa ordered the temporary closure of "comfort" stations in a city in China the day after a large unit of soldiers arrived in town, as many women had swollen vaginas. Nagasawa had stated that the women protested the closure because it was a good opportunity for them to earn extra income. Hata explains that the ratio of money divided between the women and proprietors at "comfort" stations was more advantageous, with an average of 50% at "comfort" stations compared to 25–40% in brothels in Japan. He introduces a few Korean "comfort women" who managed to save a lot of money, such as Mun Ok-chu, who saved 26,000 yen in three years (which Nishioka suggests was the amount for five houses in Tokyo at that time), and sent 5,000 yen to her family in Korea. While he acknowledges that there were cases where proprietors did not pay the women, he simply concludes that the money must have become mere pieces of paper after Japan lost the war (soldiers were paying with a special military currency that was issued in Japan's occupied areas),[8] although the fact that the women did not receive money has nothing to do with the proprietors being unable to keep the money. In addition, considering that the lives of prostitutes in Japanese brothels before the war were akin to those of sex slaves (also considering how exploited they were by receiving only 25–40% of their earnings as Hata mentions), as feminist scholars such as Ueno argue, it seems that "comfort women" were not well-off, even if their lives were better than those of Japanese prostitutes.[9] Hata concludes that "comfort women" made more money than prostitutes in Japan, Japanese soldiers, and military nurses, and, therefore, their lives were not too bad.

In other aspects, the lives of "comfort women" are remembered as being "not too restricted" in comparison to those engaged in other occupations during the war. For example, Hata cites Mun who stated that in some areas in Burma "comfort women" were able to go shopping in town for a few days a month, though there were restrictions in terms of how often or where they were able to go, similar to other people in occupied areas during wartime, such as soldiers and military nurses.[10] Similarly, Kobayashi quotes passages from a report prepared by the U.S. military that interviewed captured Korean "comfort women" in 1944 to argue that "comfort women" were well off:

> The women's lives in Myitkyina were rather luxurious compared to other places. . . . Although food and other necessities were not heavily rationed, the women's lives were good because they received enough money to buy what they needed. In addition to gifts they received from soldiers, they were also able to buy clothes, shoes, cigarettes, and make-up. During their stay in Burma, the women enjoyed themselves by participating in sporting events with soldiers, and went on picnics and attended plays and dinner parties. They owned a gramophone and were allowed to go shopping in cities. (My translation)[11]

Kobayashi asserts that "it is impossible to believe that they were sex slaves if they were treated this well."[12] While Kobayashi takes the position that the survivors' testimonies are not reliable because they could be lying or hiding something they are ashamed of, or there may be something that they themselves are unaware of (e.g., their parents may have secretly agreed to sell their daughters to the "comfort" system and received money), he seems to believe the report that was based on testimonies written by a Japanese American soldier who interviewed the women, because he states that a report written by "the enemy" must be neutral (the American soldier had no reason to defend or justify the Japanese military's "comfort" system) and therefore credible. Progressives from the same period, or later, point out the bias held against

Korean "comfort women" by the author of the report, Alex Yorichi (chapter 6). However, the report continues to be cited as evidence by nationalists to deny the position of "comfort women" as sex slaves, as explained in chapter 6. Moreover, it should be noted that there is a possibility that the women may have lied (e.g., they could have been threatened by their proprietors). It should also be pointed out that this report notes that the "comfort" station described was an exception ("rather luxurious *compared to other places*"). Even if the luxurious lives depicted in this report were true, it does not mean that they were representative.

In addition, while Hata acknowledges that the women's experiences must have varied depending on when and where they were sent, he writes that there are always people who focus only on positive memories, whereas some focus only on negative memories, implying that the former "comfort women" who related their negative experiences belong to the latter group.[13] Of course, nationalist writers such as Hata, Takahashi, and Kobayashi tend to only "remember" those who narrated more positive experiences. Hata mentions that since people from that time used to start working and get married at a much younger age, we cannot judge these women's lives using today's standards. He concludes that "it is rude to label 'comfort women' as sex slaves by only referring to extreme examples when, in reality, there were occasions of friendly interactions between soldiers and comfort women" (my translation).[14] He dismisses the testimonies of negative experiences. By engaging in discursive amnesia[15] on the majority of survivors who had negative experiences, nationalist writers vindicate former Japanese soldiers because, in that way, they can remain "customers" and "lovers" rather than perpetrators.

In a similar vein, nationalist writers emphasize that the majority of Korean "comfort women" were able to return to Korea after paying off their debts or after the war, although there were some unfortunate cases in which women were inadvertently involved in *gyokusai*, mass suicides to avoid the dishonor of being captured. Nationalist writers do so to refute the idea that most Korean "comfort women" were either killed or abandoned in battlefields at the end of the war. For instance, Hata details that "comfort women" were able to go home once they had made enough money to pay back their debts, which in most cases happened within several months after their arrival at "comfort" stations. However, toward the end of the war, despite the Japanese military's policy of sending women home, many chose to stay because they were fearful of their lives due to the frequent bombing of Japanese ships by the Allies. As a result, many unfortunately died after being involved in battles and mass suicides.[16] Still, Hata concludes that the majority of Korean "comfort women" survived the war by surrendering to the Allies and went back to Korea before the Japanese were able to go home. The women were no longer Japanese citizens and received better treatment while the Japanese women were raped and forced to serve the sexual needs of the Allies, such as the Soviet and British soldiers (citing testimonies of Japanese witnesses including Tamura Seitaro, a former Japanese soldier).[17] These reports of rape by Allied soldiers resonate with a later theme of "comfort" stations as universal military practices, implying that it was not only the Japanese military that had the "comfort" system. Therefore, Japan should not be criticized for it. It also emphasizes the victimhood of the Japanese as explained in more detail in the later theme of "war is tragic."

Some nationalist writers go beyond this idea of "comfort women's" lives not being "too bad" and they provide romanticized memories similar to those promoted during the postwar period between 1945 and the 1960s and, to a certain extent, the period between 1970 and 1990 as well. Hosaka Masayasu writes that there were cases of romance between Japanese soldiers and Korean "comfort women," their suicides together, and their disparate desertions together. In addition, by citing a former Japanese military officer, Hosaka writes that he heard that there were many cases in which Japanese soldiers and Korean "comfort women" fled to a southern nation and lived happily together. Hosaka argues that soldiers and "comfort women" shared *seihonnou* [life instinct] through intercourse. He explains that soldiers could not choose their fate of being sent to the battlefields just as "comfort women" could not choose their fate of being sold to comfort stations. Thus, Hosaka argues that soldiers and "comfort women" shared a tragic fate and comforted each other, developing an affection toward each other.[18] Happy endings in the relationships between Japanese soldiers and "comfort women" also appear in the essay by Tokiura Ken included in Kobayashi's *Shin Gōmanism Sengen*.[19] Similarly, Itō Keiichi, a writer who served in the war and whose testimony also appears in Kim's *The Emperor's Military and Korean Comfort Women* from the previous period, provides romanticized memories of the relationships between Japanese soldiers and "comfort women." He recalls Korean "comfort women" as Japanese soldiers' important comrades. Itō writes that it was common for soldiers and "comfort women" to feel respect and affection for each other. It was the "comfort women" who shared both pleasure and sadness with soldiers who were ill fated to die soon. Itō even states that there was a legend that prostitutes were reincarnations of the Buddha, which soldiers in the battlefields believed.[20] Itō's memories of "comfort women" drastically differ from those discussed in other sources from other periods, or from progressive writers from the same period (e.g., "public toilets" and "sex slaves"). Of course, if the "comfort women" were truly perceived as noble beings by soldiers as Itō recollects, we must ask ourselves why there have not been any former "comfort women" who have been open about their past.

Irrational and Unreliable Korean "Comfort Women"

For nationalist writers, some of the former Korean "comfort women" had low intellects and, therefore, were seen as "irrational" and they were financially motivated to come forward, which suggests that their testimonies were unreliable. In this theme, Orientalist depictions of Korean survivors appear most prominently as the Orientals were seen "irrational, depraved (fallen), childlike, 'different'" by Western Orientalists according to Said.[21] Hata, for instance, summarizes the characteristics of the former "comfort women" who came forward as follows:

(1) Their lives as comfort women seemed to have been tougher than those of the average comfort women.
(2) They led unfortunate lives after the war.
(3) They did not have family members to stop them from coming forward.
(4) Their intellectual level was low, and they were easily influenced by comments from others. (My translation)[22]

The first point suggests that the average comfort woman's life was not that terrible, and the women who came forward represent a small minority (that was mistreated). Similarly, since they were both financially and personally unhappy after the war, they were motivated to lie for financial gain (points 2 and 3). The fourth point suggests that, since they lack intelligence, their memories are unreliable. As they can be easily influenced by others, they may have been affected by their support organizations. In the same vein, Hata dismisses some of the testimonies of the former Korean and Chinese "comfort women" as irrational and contradictory. For example, in the case of two Chinese women who testified that they were kidnapped, gang raped, and confined, he disagrees with their testimonies, quoting three former Japanese soldiers who were stationed in the same area. In interviews, these soldiers stated that such acts would have been impossible under their strict commanding officers. However, they offered the surprising alternative explanation that "it must have been Chinese soldiers who were disguised as Japanese soldiers."[23] Throughout his book, Hata attempts to discredit the testimonies of the former "comfort women" by taking the word of former Japanese soldiers over that of the women because their "intellectual levels are low," and thus their testimonies are "irrational." Compared to irrational Orientals, Western men were considered more intelligent, "rational, virtuous, mature, [and] 'normal'" beings by Western Orientalists;[24] similarly, Japanese men (soldiers) are seen as more intelligent and reliable.

Likewise, nationalist writers such as Nishioka and Kobayashi point out that some survivors changed their testimonies. For instance, when she first came forward Kim Hak-sun said that she had been sold to a *kisen* by her mother at the age of fourteen and taken to a comfort station in China by her "stepfather" at the age of seventeen. However, when the Korean Council for the Women Drafted for Military Sexual Slavery by Japan interviewed her later, she stated that she had been forcibly taken by a group of Japanese soldiers in Beijing.[25] Nishioka states that another survivor, Mun, said that she had been forcefully taken by the *kenpei* [Japanese special police] when interviewed by the Korean Council; however, when she previously sued the Japanese government she stated that she had been deceived by a Korean recruiter. Similarly, Nishioka disputes some of the other survivors' testimonies as "unreliable" and "illogical." Additionally, by praising An Byeong-jik, a South Korean professor who interviewed some of the survivors and said that there were cases where he felt that some were lying, Nishioka attempts to establish the unreliability of Korean survivors' testimonies. Similarly, Hata dismisses Chong Ok-sun's testimony. He explains that, although she testified that she had been taken to a "comfort" station in Korea, there was no such station in Korea; however, there had been civilian brothels because Korea did not become a battlefield. In addition, by responding to Chong's claim of witnessing a Korean "comfort woman" who protested against being killed, Hata argues that the "comfort women" were valuable commodities, therefore, it would not make sense to kill them for such minor reasons.[26] Further, Hata cites another survivor, Song, who was interviewed by the Japanese newspaper *Asahi Shimbun*, to validate his point of Korean survivors being irrational. He explains that Song stated that she hated Koreans because they warred among themselves, and that she had sued the Japanese government just for fun.[27] In another article based on a discussion between Hata and Kamisaka Fuyuko, Hata states that the testimonies of former "comfort women" are usually ambiguous, and that the locations of "comfort stations" are often described as "southern islands with palm trees."[28] While it is widely known that victims of sexual assault tend to have inconsistent memories due to their traumatic experiences as, nationalist writers are oblivious of the fact and are quick to point out some inconsistencies to claim that the survivors' stories are all unreliable. In terms of their ambiguity regarding the locations of the "comfort" stations, we should not forget about the language barrier. Most Korean "comfort women" had limited knowledge of the Japanese language and might have had difficulty comprehending where they were when explained in Japanese.

Shiono Nanami and Hata further detail the unreliability of survivors' testimonies, implying the irrational and temperamental nature of Korean survivors like Orientals depicted by Western Orientalists as discussed by Said.[29] Shiono states:

Humans tend to insist that they are forced to do so when they feel ashamed of their past deeds. After a while, they even start to believe the lie as they continue to repeat it. . . . Therefore, asking survivors repeatedly would not have made a difference. Reporters would simply have been screamed at. (My translation)[30]

Hata compares the testimonies of the "comfort women" to *"joro no minoue banashi"* [prostitute's life stories], meaning that those stories are interesting, emotional, and dramatic, and can incite much sympathy from the listeners. Yet these stories are mostly fictional and unreliable. Hata mentions that when he was young, he himself used to believe in *"hosutesu no minoue banashi"* [escorts' life stories].[31] Here, again, Orientalist depictions of the "comfort women" as irrational and untrustworthy because of Orientals' "habits of inaccuracy"[32] are emphasized.

This theme of the irrationality of Korean "comfort women" also expands to other Koreans in general in these writings by nationalist writers. For instance, Nishioka writes that South Korean president Lee Myung-bak (2008–2013) initially stated that the South Korean government would not seek apologies from Japan and invited the Japanese emperor and empress to South Korea in 2008. However, he suddenly changed his attitude in 2011. Lee landed on the Liancourt Rocks islets (*Takeshima* in Japanese/*Dokdo* in Korean), whose territorial rights are disputed by the two nations, and demanded the Japanese emperor's apology to Korean independence movement activists. While speculating that the reason for his change in attitude was the 2011 South Korean court's decision, ruling it as unconstitutional for the South Korean government not to seek individual compensation from the Japanese government, Nishioka criticizes Lee for his rudeness. Here we can see Orientalist depictions of South Korean politics being "capricious."[33]

In the same way, based on a discussion with Hata, Kamisaka discusses South Korea's illogical demand for compensation from Japan. She questions whether a new country occupying only the southern half of the Korean peninsula could demand compensation from Japan for an incident that had happened even before the nation was founded.[34]

Thus, Koreans, especially Korean survivors, have become the Third Persona[35] in Japanese nationalist circles. Korean survivors were negated in history when they were forced to remain silent for a half-century; when they finally spoke up, they were "being negated" along with their testimonies.

"War is Tragic," as War Victimized Many People Including Soldiers

While nationalist writers tend to remember that the lives of "comfort women" were "not too bad," they also acknowledge that the women suffered to a certain extent. However, they dismiss the women's victimhood by arguing that everybody, including Japanese soldiers, suffered during the war because war is tragic. This theme is illustrated by emphasizing the victimhood of various groups of Japanese during the war, and is similar to the idea of Japanese victimhood promoted through peace education and the pacifist movement in Japan. The war is attributed as the cause of suffering for the "comfort women" and others such as Japanese soldiers and civilians. For instance, as illustrated in the later theme of "comfort systems as universal practices," Kobayashi discusses Soviet soldiers' rapes of Japanese women in Manchuria and Korea after Japan's defeat in August 1945. While many people suffered during the war, nationalist writers argue that, in the end, Japanese soldiers suffered the most.

Kobayashi, for example, asserts that the former Japanese soldiers who have been silenced are the real victims in the "comfort women" issue:

> Soldiers fought and died for their nation, families, and descendants. The public was excited [about the war] and the newspapers incited public fever [during the war]. Everybody was excited and everybody enthusiastically sent soldiers to the battlefields. However, once the nation lost the war, soldiers were wrongfully accused as invaders, killers, and rapists by their countrymen and descendants. Now those grandfathers are about to end their lives. Are they not the victims? (My translation)[36]

Additionally, Kobayashi cites a book written by a former soldier regarding a description of his and his comrades' experiences of using "comfort" stations before battles, thinking that it may be their last intercourse in their lives. He calls those who criticize soldiers as rapists "*onichikusho*" [demons and beasts].[37] Nishio Kanji also argues that Japanese soldiers were victims of the "comfort" system because they were expediently forced to take care of their sexual needs in the battlefields instead of having sex with somebody they love. He opines that it was a tragedy for men during the war.[38]

By introducing *Minami no Shima ni Yuki ga Furu* [It Snowed on a Southern Island] published in 1961, a book written by actor Kato Daisuke, based on his war experience in New Guinea, Kobayashi also argues that Japanese soldiers are the victims and he swears to fight to defend their honor. The book is not about "comfort women" but about Kato's experience of performing plays with several other soldiers for other Japanese soldiers. One scene featured snow on the stage by using pieces of white paper and hundreds of Japanese soldiers from the northern part of Japan cried because it reminded them of home.[39] Kobayashi explains that his grandfather was one of the soldiers who performed with Kato, and declares:

I have to fight to defend grandfathers. I also have to defend the comrades of grandfathers who died thinking of their country and looking at paper snow on a southern island. The media, left-wing journalists, civic organizations, lawyers, and others consider that war is bad and, therefore, as a lesson, or to set an example never to have war, they should accuse our grandfathers of all kinds of crimes and have them despised all over the world.

I am going to fight against them! (My translation)[40]

Kobayashi's enthusiasm for this issue is manifested through his personal ties, as his grandfather was a Japanese soldier who may have potentially used "comfort" stations. He argues that soldiers were victims because they had to fight and die for their nation, families, and descendants. When they had to take care of their sexual needs in battlefields, they simply thought they were buying prostitutes, which was legal in Japan until the 1950s. Even then, they had to spend much money for short, miserable sexual encounters because, as Kobayashi claims, soldiers were not even allowed to take off their shoes so that "comfort women" could make more money in a short period of time. After the war, those soldiers' descendants (i.e., the Japanese people today) accuse them as rapists.[41]

Kobayashi and other nationalist writers argue that the soldiers are the "real victims" because they were forced to sacrifice themselves during the war and are now blamed for the "comfort" system. While I agree that many Japanese soldiers were victims themselves, this does not diminish the victimhood of others. Victims can still be abusers and, in this case, the "comfort women" were at the very bottom of the power hierarchy.

Moreover, Fujioka Nobukatsu states that "there were so many who had misfortunate experiences during the war, and many of the Japanese soldiers who had intercourse with comfort women died as well," and opines that "it is unfair to provide special treatment only to comfort women."[42] Similarly, while Itō acknowledges that "comfort women" had to live unreasonable lives, he also proposes that soldiers led even worse lives:

> Soldiers worked quietly, most of them died quietly, and they will not come back. Comfort women lived tragic, unreasonable lives, and soldiers lived even more unreasonable lives, and they had to die. That is why soldiers and comfort women at times understood each other, and some soldiers died thinking of their fond memories with comfort women. (My translation)[43]

While it may be true that the fatality among soldiers was higher than that of "comfort women," and it can never be ascertained whose lives were more "unreasonable" and "tragic," there is a large difference between the lives of soldiers and those of "comfort women" after the war. Soldiers who died in the war were considered to have an "honorable death," and their families received a pension. Surviving soldiers were able to get together with their former comrades after the war. However, we have no information about the "comfort women" who died in battlefields because the military did not even create lists of the women who were sent to the battlefields as "comfort women." After the war, the surviving comfort women lived their lives, hiding their Pasts. Another issue is whether it should matter if there are people who suffered more. The claim that the women had to live inhumane, unreasonable lives should be enough to affirm their victimhood. In the end, by settling on the common pacifist argument in Japan that "war is tragic" and many including Japanese soldiers suffered, the women's suffering is minimized. An abstract entity such as "war" is blamed for the "comfort women's" suffering instead of specific people or the government and, thus, nobody is held accountable in the discourse.

The "Comfort" System Being a Common Practice among Militaries Worldwide

The "comfort" system is also remembered as a commodity that may be an anachronism today but was commonplace in most militaries around the world. Therefore, other countries have no right to condemn Japan for its past. This theme is based on a masculinist ideology, "men's uncontrollable sexual desires," similar to the idea discussed by Soh as mentioned in chapter 1.[44]

According to Hata and Hosaka, soldiers/men need to have a place for sexual release, otherwise, soldiers either rape local women or go to buy local prostitutes. To prevent this, the military needed to provide "safe" women as explained in chapter 1. Hata[45] and Hosaka[46] argue that the Imperial Japanese Army would not have needed comfort stations if it had had as many resources as the United States Armed Forces. They discuss that the U.S. military was able to provide breaks to its solders between battles, who were able to rest and satisfy their sexual needs in places such as Australia. They also suggest that female soldiers functioned as "comfort women" under the guise of romantic relationships within the U.S. military. Similarly, Kobayashi argues that men tend to have more sexual desires under extreme stress such as the fear of death because of their instinct to have children.[47] Itō also discusses an episode of Colonel Hishida Motoshiro founding a "comfort" station in China because Hishida had an understanding about soldiers' sexual desires. Although Hishida's proposal to create a "comfort" station was met with opposition from the *kenpei*, he insisted on the need to take care of his soldiers' sexual desires.[48] While Japanese nationalists at times reiterate that they believe that it was tragic that some women had to become "comfort women," which was a human rights violation, they seem to justify it as a "necessary evil." The same patriarchal ideology used by the Imperial Japanese Army is suggested by these nationalist writers.

Due to this "uncontrollable men's sexual desires," Hata argues that countries such as Germany, the United States, and France had similar "comfort" systems used to prevent the spread of STDs among soldiers. In the case of Germany during World War II, Hata, citing the German scholar Franz Seidler, discusses that the military gained control of preexisting brothels. In the occupied eastern territories, such as the former Soviet Union, they created their own comfort stations by forcibly gathering local women.[49] In the case of the United States, Hata discusses official military brothels called "recreation centers" during the Vietnam War. Vietnamese women worked at these recreation centers and had weekly medical examinations (for STDs) conducted by military doctors.[50] Hata also explains various cases in which the Japanese military's "comfort" stations were used with locally recruited "comfort women" by the Allied soldiers after the Japanese military and Japanese and Korean "comfort women" fled.[51] Additionally, most of these writers state that the soldiers from the former Soviet Union raped many Japanese women, created their own comfort stations, and demanded Japanese women as "comfort women" when the former Soviet Union sent troops to Manchuria and Korea in August 1945.[52] Hata argues that other nations had a "comfort" system very similar to that of Japan, concluding that Japan as a nation is no more guilty than other nations. It may be true that other militaries have similarly violated the human rights of women by using them as mere objects of soldiers' sexual release. However, the question that should be asked is whether it matters. Just because other countries are guilty of violating human rights, it does not make the Japanese imperial military less guilty. It should be about respect and social justice for women.

In addition, some nationalist writers such as Nishio give details of Japanese "comfort women" being provided to the U.S. military in occupied Japan after the war. For instance, Nishio opines that if the Japanese government was to pay compensation to former Korean "comfort women" for the Imperial Japanese Army's actions, Japan should also demand compensation from the United States. He alludes that there were approximately 200,000 Japanese "comfort women" for the U.S. army, and most were those who had no other option to support their families, such as war widows. Nishio states that the RAA comfort stations were created because of requests from U.S. occupation forces. The Japanese women who worked as "comfort women" must be currently in their seventies or eighties, yet nobody has come forward. He predicts that none of the Japanese women will ever come forward because they are not shameless.[53] By idealizing that former Japanese "comfort women" have maintained their past as a secret, Nishio reinforces the societal bias against prostitutes. In addition, by creating a dichotomy between former non-Japanese "comfort women," who are "shameless" to admit they were "comfort women," and former Japanese "comfort women," who have remained silent, Nishio is silencing those who may hope for redress by coming forward.

Denial of the Officially Sanctioned and Coerced Recruitment of Korean Women

The next theme found among nationalist writers is their denial of the forced recruitment of Korean women by the Japanese authorities; however, they no longer deny the involvement of the Japanese military in the operation of "comfort" stations. Among nationalists, the recruitment of Korean women is mostly remembered as acts of deception and coercion by private recruiters who are almost always Koreans. For instance, Hata, quoting from *The Dong-A Ilbo*, a South Korean newspaper, states that Japanese officials ordered Korean recruiters to gather many impoverished Korean prostitutes and took them to China to make them work at military "comfort" stations. According to the same article, recruiters working for the Japanese military came to Korea and deceived women, promising an "easy job that could enable them to earn a lot of money," together with police officers and the heads of villages.[54] Hata also argues that the testimonies of survivors proved that many of the former Korean "comfort women" who grew up in an impoverished family were deceived by their close acquaintances (implying that they were Korean), and there are no cases of the Japanese military forcibly taking women. By citing a Korean reporter, Nishioka opines that in colonial Korea, it was impossible for Japanese private recruiters to go into small Korean villages to recruit women, and therefore it must have been Korean recruiters who deceived them. Likewise, Hata in his discussion with Kamisaka states that there were almost no Japanese people who spoke Korean well enough to deceive Korean women.[55]

While the Japanese military's coerced recruitment of Korean women is denied, their involvement in the operation of "comfort" stations is clearly depicted. When the issue of "comfort women" began to attract public attention in June 1990, Shimizu Norio, a Japanese labor secretary, stated that "comfort women" were prostitutes who were employed and supervised by civilian proprietors and, therefore, the issue had nothing to do with the Japanese government. The comment drew international and domestic criticism, but the Japanese government had to admit the military's involvement when Yoshimi's discovery of documents proving the military's involvement was reported in the *Asahi Shimbun* in January 1992. Since then, nationalist writers do not seem to deny the military's involvement. Hata explains by citing memoirs written by former Japanese soldiers such as Admiral Okabe Naosaburō, which show how deeply the military was involved in the operation of the first military "comfort" station in Shanghai. Hata states that the military requested the Nagasaki governor to send a group of "comfort women," as the navy previously did. Hata also details the operation rules for the "comfort" station as set by the military, such as who can use the facilities, the use of condoms, the opening hours, and admission fees. In addition, Hata cites Asō Tetsuo, a military doctor, to explain that military doctors examined the women for STDs.[56]

Although the nationalist writers have admitted to the Japanese military's involvement, they tend to argue that this was about protecting women from evil, exploitive Korean recruiters, and proprietors. Kobayashi emphasizes that the involvement of the Imperial Japanese Army was due to *"yoi kainyū"* [good interventions] that were meant to protect the rights of the "comfort women" because private recruiters or proprietors, who were usually Korean, tended to exploit the women. For instance, by citing the documents reported by the *Asahi Shimbun* in January 1992 as evidence of the involvement of the Japanese military, Kobayashi argues that this proved the military's "good interventions" because the Japanese officials attempted to prosecute private recruiters who conducted unlawful recruitment.[57] For instance, Hata cites Nagasawa, a military doctor, to explain that when around thirty women, led by two Korean proprietors, arrived in 1944, one of them began to cry saying that she had been deceived as she had been promised another job. Thereby, she was assigned to another job.[58]

Tokiura Ken, Kobayashi's assistant, argues by citing a book written by Nagasawa, the aforementioned former military doctor, that military officials made efforts to protect "comfort women" from private proprietor's unlawful exploitation (Tokiura's essay appears in Kobayashi's comic). For instance, in brothels in Japan, it was common for proprietors to add overpriced "living expenses" to a woman's debt to exploit her as much as possible. However, Tokiura explains that Fujisawa, a military doctor, created a rule stipulating that military officials had to approve when proprietors wanted to add debt. Tokiura argues that Korean proprietors were even more vicious. As a result, many Korean "comfort women" did not have a written contract, and Korean proprietors bought women from extremely poor families and treated them as though they were slaves. Although the women had no hope to be free for the rest of their lives, they seemed to be unaware of their circumstances. To correct this, Fujisawa enforced the proprietors to make contracts and created a system in which the women would be free once they paid back their debts.[59] Hata makes it clear that Korean "comfort women" were not forced or deceived, at least by the Japanese military, who actually tried to protect them from evil Korean recruiters. Here we can see that paternalistic ideologies were used to justify colonization, suggesting the need of the colonized public to be saved by their evil oppressors.

Similarly, Kobayashi, citing documents in which military officials were stipulating the cleanliness of "comfort" stations, argues that the Japanese military officials were the ones who made efforts to improve the living conditions of the "comfort women," because the proprietors were not concerned about their well-being. In addition, by referring to incidents in which Dutch women were forced to become "comfort women" in Indonesia, Kobayashi argues that it was simply an isolated case in which a group of Japanese soldiers who ignored military rules committed a crime. Citing the fact that those comfort stations were ordered to close after two months, Kobayashi argues that the Japanese imperial military's policy was not to force women into the "comfort" system.[60]

This denial surrounding the coerced recruitment of women among Japanese nationalist scholars is understandable considering their dismissal of "comfort women" as "mere prostitutes." However, their acceptance of the military's involvement in the operation is interesting. This may have much to do with their dismissal of the documents that proved the Japanese military's involvement in the "comfort" system as discovered by Yoshimi Yoshiaki in 1992. Nationalist scholars argue that the Japanese military's involvement had been known because how else could private brothel proprietors have traveled to the frontlines without military transport? Of course, the military was involved but that does not mean that the military as an organization coerced Korean women to work at military brothels. It seems to be in their interests to dismiss Yoshimi's discovery. In a similar vein, the documents found are discussed as "proof that the Japanese military was not involved in the coercive recruitment" among these nationalist writers, who argue that there has been no documental evidence that proves the involvement of the Imperial Japanese Army in the coerced recruitment of women. They argue that if there is no evidence that the military itself forced women into prostitution, there is no reason for the Japanese government to compensate the former "comfort women."

Some nationalist writers argue that if the women were not forcibly recruited by Japanese authorities, they were not sex slaves but simply prostitutes; the Imperial Japanese Army's "comfort" system was not different from the similar "comfort" stations operated by other nations' militaries. Therefore, the Japanese government is not liable for the "comfort" system. Their definition of "slaves" is defined rather narrowly. To Nishioka, if women were not "hunted" as slaves were hunted in Africa in the past, they were not slaves. Therefore, by refuting the claim that women were forcibly taken by Japanese authorities because of the absence of documental evidence, they argue that the women were not sex slaves. What they seem to not be aware of is that, to most people in the world, Japanese progressives included, the definition of slaves hinges on how the people are being treated (such as how they are confined or harsh labor environments without compensation). If being hunted is the only definition of slaves, most of the slaves in the nineteenth-century United States who were born as children of slaves would not have been considered slaves. Similarly, some slaves in ancient Rome who became slaves because of debt would not have been slaves, either. While some of them (e.g., Kobayashi) argue that the "comfort women" were not sex slaves in terms of the treatment they received (which was "not bad"), whether the women were "hunted" by Japanese officials occupies a large part of the discussion.

The "Comfort Women" Issue as a Japanese-Made Issue

Similar to the theme of "Criticism of Progressives" as discussed later is that the issue of "comfort women" is a Japanese-made issue that Koreans did not initially care for. In arguing so, nationalist scholars attack progressive Japanese activists, writers, and media. One of the activists who were attacked is Aoyagi Atsuko, a homemaker from Oita, Japan; she is presented as the person who "created" the "comfort women" issue. For instance, based on his interview with Aoyagi, Nishioka explains that she worked under Soh, a Korean antidiscrimination activist living in Japan. From the late 1970s to the 1980s, Soh attempted to sue the Japanese government for Koreans left in Sakhalin after the war.[61] Nishioka states, however, that Soh's trials did not go well because he did not hire a lawyer. Takagi Kenichi, a human rights lawyer, took over the trials, and the issue was settled because of the Japanese government's compromise on humanitarian grounds. Nishioka argues that because the trials were taken over by Takagi, Soh and Aoyagi were looking for Koreans who could become plaintiffs to sue the Japanese government. Therefore, Aoyagi went to South Korea in November 1989 to recruit plaintiffs. Although she could not find any during her visit, the Association for the Pacific War Victims, an association based in South Korea, contacted her afterward and offered to become plaintiffs. She returned to Seoul in March 1990 and met with around 1,000 members of the association in a building near the Japanese Embassy. She gave a speech stating that Japan had done terrible things in Korea in the past and that the association, together with Aoyagi, should sue the Japanese government and demand an official apology and compensation. Nishioka explains that Aoyagi told them that she and Soh had accumulated 4 million yen (about $35,000) for the lawsuits, and that they needed ten plaintiffs. Afterward, they organized a demonstration in front of the Japanese Embassy to demand compensation, and Nishioka argues that it was the first of such demonstrations and it was actually initiated by a Japanese person. Nishioka writes that the demonstrations were taken over by "comfort women's" support groups and are still being carried out in front of the Japanese Embassy every Wednesday. Nishioka argues that after the governments of South Korea and Japan settled on reparations in 1965, the former distributed compensation paid by the latter to the bereaved families of those who had died as a result of forced labor or from serving in the Imperial Japanese Army. He writes that the Association for the Pacific War Victims was founded to negotiate terms such as the amount of individual compensation from the South Korean government and did not dream of receiving more money from the Japanese government. According to Nishioka, however, from the association's perspective, there was no reason not to demand more money when Aoyagi, a Japanese person, suggested suing the Japanese government together, and even had money prepared for it. Although this trial by Aoyagi did not go well because of a lack of attorneys, Nishioka argues that Aoyagi's move inspired the Association for the Pacific War Victims and led them to sue the Japanese government again together with Kim Hak-sun and two other survivors in December 1991.

Takagi Kenichi, a Japanese lawyer who represented Kim Hak-sun and two other Korean survivors in the 1991 trial, is also criticized by nationalist writers as another person who "created" this "comfort women" issue. For instance, Hata introduces an episode where he met Takagi to assert his point that Takagi's reason for suing the Japanese government was simply to criticize Japan, rather than for the well-being of the survivors. Hata points out that Takagi sued the Japanese government knowing that they were not going to win. Hata did not think that the cases of Kim Hak-sun and the two survivors were very strong because Kim Hak-sun was sold to a *kisen* and the other survivors' stories were "not very convincing." Hata asked Takagi whether there were any other "comfort women" with more convincing testimonies; Takagi responded that he had found stronger cases in South Korea as he thought that the cases of the initial three women were not strong enough. Hata then opines that the additional ones were not strong, either.[62]

Nishioka also denounces Takagi for "criticizing the Japanese government by making false accusations" without actually caring for the well-being of former comfort women.[63] Nishioka writes that Takagi should have told Kim that her past as a *kisen* would not be a good fit for the trial and that she would be humiliated by making her past public. Although he and other nationalist scholars are the ones who humiliated Kim by dismissing her testimony as a plaintiff and victim simply because of her past as a *kisen*, Nishioka asserts that he cannot forgive Takagi. Also, Hata states that, by responding to the *Nichibenren*'s [Japan Federation of Bar Associations (JFBA); an organization to which Takagi belongs] support of the Coomaraswamy report, especially regarding the prosecution of those responsible for the "comfort" system, it was shocking that the lawyers who supposedly advocate human rights were willing to sacrifice the human rights of those who were involved in the system. Hata calls the association "hypocritical."[64] To him, the human rights of those who were involved in the "comfort" system are so important that they cannot be prosecuted regardless of what they did.

Likewise, Nishioka claims that as anti-Japan Japanese forces were losing in the discussion of the forced recruitment of Korean women within Japan, they began to spread the lie overseas that the "comfort women" had been forcibly mobilized. He elaborates on this claim, explicating that when Japanese politicians make comments on the "comfort women" issue, Japanese anti-Japan media sources report on it widely, causing foreign governments such as South Korea to criticize the Japanese government. Alternatively, Japanese reporters spread the news overseas by interviewing Koreans regarding the inappropriate comments made by Japanese politicians on the "comfort women" issue. According to them, it is anti-Japan Japanese who have incited South Koreans. To nationalist writers, without some Japanese instigating Koreans and creating the "comfort women" issue, there would have been no diplomatic controversy, no lawsuits, and no negative international public relations and anti-Japan sentiment. The Japanese, including the Japanese government and those who oversaw the "comfort" system, could have lived peacefully.

Antiforeign, Especially, Anti-Korean Sentiment

Nationalist writers also attack other countries such as both North and South Koreas, China, and the United States. One major idea among some of these books is "anti-Koreanism," which is similar to the Korean survivors being depicted as "irrational." Koreans in general are depicted as temperamental and violent and the governments of North and South Korea are presented as being sneaky and using the "comfort women" issue for their political agendas, similar to Orientalist depictions of Orientals as barbaric,[65] bloodthirst,[66] driven by passions and instincts,[67] and untrustworthy.[68] Those countries are depicted as unlawfully intervening in Japan's domestic affairs.

Regarding Koreans being presented as temperamental and violent people, Nishioka discusses his and other Japanese people's fear of being beaten by Koreans. When Nishioka points out the ties between Uemura, an *Asahi* reporter, and the Association for the Pacific War Victims, a South Korean organization, Nishioka explains that the editorial office from *Bungei Shunjū*, a literary magazine that was going to publish Nishioka's research, suggested that one of their writers should accompany him as a bodyguard because the editors were worried that he might be attacked by bereaved families or activists in South Korea. Nishioka declined the offer simply because he considered it a burden to take somebody who did not speak Korean (Nishioka is fluent in Korean). Similarly, prior to meeting several Koreans from the support organizations for Pacific War victims and their Japanese supporters after he published an article stating that the forced recruitment of Korean "comfort women" by Japanese authorities was not proven, he writes that "I wondered if I might be beaten."[69] In the end, it seems that he has never experienced violence from Koreans but his and others' unfounded fear of Korean violence, which has nothing to do with his main thesis, makes it to his book.

In addition, the irrationality of Koreans is presented by depicting the irrationality of South Korean media. Nishioka writes that, in South Korea, the media do not have to check for accuracy in the cases of anti-Japan reports. By learning of the "irrational" and "manipulative" South Korean media, according to Nishioka, a number of Japanese people developed anti-Korean sentiments:

> Many elderly Japanese people who actually experienced Japan's colonization of Korea say that there was no coerced recruitment of comfort women by Japanese authorities. However, these stories never make it to the South Korean media, and, as a result, anti-Korea sentiments spread rapidly among a certain group of Japanese people . . .
> We received many phone calls and letters in the editorial office of *Current Korea* [a Japanese magazine he edits], stating that they want to beat Koreans, or that they want to kick Koreans out of Japan, or that Japan should terminate diplomatic relationships with South Korea. (My translation)[70]

Interestingly, it is the Japanese people who want to beat the Koreans, unlike Nishioka's concern that Koreans might beat him. In his 1992 article (published in *Military Comfort Women: Asahi Shumbun vs. Bungei Shunjū*), Nishioka writes that he "is worried about anti-Korean sentiment spreading among Japanese" because of the "comfort women" issue. He explicates that right-wing activists protest against South Korea in front of the South Korean Embassy in Tokyo and branch offices of the South Korean media located in Japan are receiving threatening phone calls.[71] It seems that Japanese people are the ones being temperamental and violent instead of Koreans. However, in the same article, Nishioka praises how Taiwan sought individual compensation for those who suffered under Japan's colonization, because they "never showed anti-Japan sentiment" unlike South Koreans. According to Nishioka, South Korean anti-Japan attitudes caused anti-Korean attitudes among Japanese nationalists as if there had been no anti-Korean sentiment in Japan previously and anti-Korean messages promoted by Japanese nationalist writers like himself have nothing to do with the rise of anti-Korean sentiment in Japan.

Moreover, other foreign governments, especially North Korea, have been depicted as using the "comfort women" issue for their political agendas. For instance, Nishioka's book even has a chapter titled "*Ri Meihaku no Hannichi Pafoumansu to Haigo ni Ugomeku Kitachōsen no Kousaku*" [Lee Myung-bak's Anti-Japan Performance and North Korea's Manipulation Behind Him] and he repeatedly argues that the diplomatic conflict over the "comfort women" issue between South Korea and Japan has been manipulated by the communist governments of North Korea and China because they do not hope for a close tie between the two democratic nations. For instance, Nishioka claims that the Korean Council for the Women Drafted for Military Sexual Slavery by Japan (currently the Korean Council for Justice and Remembrance), the major support organization for survivors, has promoted anti-Japan movements together with secret agents of North Korea. Nishioka claims that "the real goal of the Korean Council is not to find out what actually happened and to solve this issue, but to worsen the South Korea–Japan relationship."[72] Nishioka opines that this is the reason the Korean Council was strongly opposed to the settlement of the issue after the Kōno Statement. Nishioka states that, when the Japanese government admitted the coerced recruitment of women and apologized through the Kōno Statement, the South Korean government was willing to settle on the issue and began to provide financial aid to survivors. Nishioka argues, however, that the Korean Council was strongly opposed to it, and that they even criticized the Asian Women's Fund simply because the settlement of the issue was not their goal.

Nishioka elaborates on this issue and argues that the ultimate goal of the North Korean government is to weaken the relationships between Japan, South Korea, and the United States. They may be doing that, according to Nishioka, by spreading the "lie" of coerced recruitment overseas, which he argues led the U.S. Congress to adopt a resolution in 2007 seeking the Japanese government to unequivocally admit and apologize for Japan's wrongdoings in the "comfort" system, which caused the relationship between Japan and the United States to become strained. Nishioka also argues that North Korean secret agents successfully created a dichotomy between the "corrupt" pro-Japanese and "truly Korean" anti-Japanese in South Korea. In this dichotomy, some of the South Korean politicians such as Park Chung-hee, who signed the Japan-South Korea normalization treaty of 1965, are remembered as being "tainted" pro-Japanese (he was educated in the Japanese system during colonization and served in the Imperial Japanese Army), while North Korea's first leader, Kim Il-sung was an independence movement activist in colonial Korea, and therefore, a "pure" Korean. Nishioka argues that North Korean secret agents have succeeded in creating this dichotomy between "pure" Koreans who are supportive of North Korea and "tainted" Koreans who are pro-Japan and pro-United States. For this purpose, Nishioka opines that North Korea, aided by China, uses the "comfort women" issue for their political agenda.

Fujioka also shares his conspiracy theory of North Korea's secret agendas behind the "comfort women" issue. By citing an anonymous South Korean professor, Fujioka argues that South Korea's movements in support of the "comfort women" are being carried out either by North Korean sympathizers or by those actually connected to North Korea. He argues that the true purpose of the movement is to gain as much money from Japan as possible for the Kim Dynasty. He uses the fact that *Chōsen Jihō*, a newspaper published for North Koreans living in Japan, has many articles on the "comfort women" issue, and has criticized Fujioka's views on the "comfort women" issue. Fujioka even discusses his opinion that the anti-U.S. military base movement in Okinawa is connected to North Korea. He points out that Hisakawa Seiichi, one of the consultants for the former Okinawan governor Ōta Masahide, is the Chair of a group that studies North Korean thought. Fujioka further argues that the true purpose of the anti-U.S. military base movement in Okinawa is to make Japan fall under the control of China or North Korea because Japan cannot protect itself without the U.S. military if a conflict is to break out on the Korean peninsula.[73] Fujioka's thinking is consistent with the wartime thought, "Okinawa should be sacrificed to protect the main islands of Japan." Just like the battle of Okinawa between April and June in 1945 was considered by Japanese military officials as a strategy to buy time to prepare for the protection of the mainland, regarding Okinawa as "Sute ishi" [abandoned stones] for the mainland, Fujioka seems to believe that Okinawans should be sacrificed for the "greater good" to protect the Japanese on the main islands. Although Okinawa prefecture occupies only 0.6% of Japan's homeland, 70.27% of the U.S. military bases in Japan are in Okinawa.[74] Many Okinawan farmers lost their land at the end of the war because their land was confiscated by the U.S. military to construct their bases. Accidents during the U.S. military's training such as a helicopter crash on the Okinawa International University campus in 2004 and crimes such as sexual assaults committed against Okinawan civilians by U.S. service personnel[75] have been rampant. Overall, Fujioka concludes that "the 'comfort women' issue was discovered by those who believed in socialism to attack Japan, and has been used by other nations that are hostile to Japan including the United States" (My translation).[76]

North Korea's accusation of Japan for the "comfort women" issue is, according to Nishioka, simply a distraction from the issue of its abduction of Japanese citizens. Nishioka argues that the communist regimes of China and North Korea are committing serious human rights violations. Thus, Nishioka's chapter ends with a strong condemnation of North Korea and China:

> At this time, women who escaped from North Korea are being sold to become "sex slaves" in farming villages in China. There are even some whose legs are

chained so that they cannot escape. This is an unforgivable human rights violation committed by the dictatorship countries of North Korea and China. We have to know who the real enemy is, and who is behind the forces that spread lies. (My translation)[77]

Kobayashi also states, without providing sources, that hundreds of women go missing in South Korea and China every year, and are sold in brothels.[78] Although it may be true that there are some human rights violations in China as well as both North and South Korea, it should not distract people from the "comfort women" issue. This is similar to the theme of "the comfort system as a universal practice" where nationalists justify Japan's "comfort" system on the grounds of "others having done it, too."

Further, other governments such as both North and South Korea as well as China are presented as unlawfully intervening in Japan's domestic affairs. For instance, Nishioka writes that the governments of South Korea and China always complain about the Japanese government's treatment of the past. As a result, Japanese politicians censor their speeches in Parliament so as not to invite criticism from those countries and Nishioka argues this constitutes those countries' intervention in Japan's domestic affairs. Nishioka suggests that China's and both Koreas' protests against certain history textbooks used in Japanese schools are another example of their intervention in Japan's domestic affairs. Nishioka explicates that this trend was created in the 1980s when the textbook issue occurred.[79] Since then, the governments of China and South Korea have constantly protested against certain Japanese history textbooks; yet, the textbooks to be used should be a concern for Japan's domestic affairs. He calls China's and South Korea's protests against certain Japanese textbooks *"naisei kansho no kiwami"* [the most extreme domestic affairs intervention]. (My translation)[80]

As the book *History Textbooks and the Fifteen Year Old War* that includes Fujioka's chapter was published in 1997, only a few years after the Cold War ended, it is understandable to see this conspiracy theory in which "communist nations are behind in order to destroy our democratic nation." However, it is interesting to see this conspiracy theory in Nishioka's book, which was published in 2012. It may be rooted in a deeply and widely held anti-Asian sentiment among many Japanese people, especially targeting Chinese and Koreans.

Criticism of Progressives

The final theme is the nationalist writers' criticism of progressives, including redress movement activists, progressive media, and scholars. The memories promoted by progressives are in sharp contrast to those created by nationalists. Their especially strong criticism is targeted toward: (1) Yoshida Seiji, (2) the *Asahi Shimbun*, (3) the Kōno Statement, and (4) the Coomaraswamy report.

Criticism of Yoshida Seiji

A fierce attack on Yoshida Seiji's confessional books is dominant within nationalist circles. As stated in chapter 1, Yoshida's books have been officially regarded as fabrications since the *Asahi Shimbun* retracted some of its articles citing Yoshida's books in 2014. Most of the books examined in this chapter were written before that, and we can see nationalist writers making an effort to disprove Yoshida's confessional books. For instance, Hata details his own experience of conducting research on Yoshida's books by interviewing Yoshida and going to Jeju Island, where Yoshida claimed to have hunted young Korean women for the "comfort" system in 1943. Hata points out the discrepancies and contradictions between the two books and Yoshida's unconvincing answers. For example, Hata states that he asked Yoshida about the order he received in 1943 that required him to go to Jeju Island to mobilize 200 Korean women. Hata pointed out to Yoshida that, although he wrote in his second book that his wife had written down the order in her diary, his first book states that he got married in 1944. Yoshida responded that they officially got married in 1944, but had lived as a married couple even before that, possibly starting in 1941. Hata pointed out that Yoshida wrote in his first book that he was in prison between 1940 and 1942 because he had unknowingly helped a Korean independence movement activist. When asked if he got married while in prison, Yoshida answered that he could not confirm it because his wife had already passed away. Hata asked for the names of Yoshida's former colleagues but Yoshida refused, claiming that they wished to remain anonymous. Feeling skeptical, Hata went to Jeju Island to look for witnesses of the forced recruitment of Korean women Yoshida had described in one of his books. In his second book, he describes that he along with others hunted sixteen women from a shell button factory. Hata then went to the area and talked to several elderly people who used to work in the shell button factories in the area, but nobody could confirm this. Hata also found an article from a local newspaper in 1989 when Yoshida's books were translated into Korean. In the article, a reporter interviewed residents of the island but could not find anybody who could confirm Yoshida's story. The article quoted an elderly local woman who stated that it would have been a big incident if fifteen women had been taken from a small village of 250 families, but she had never heard of anything like this. The article also quoted a Korean historian who criticized the books as a product stemming from financial motivation, and demonstrating Japanese greediness. Hata repeatedly calls Yoshida a *shokugyōteki sagishi* [professional liar], which is repeated by other nationalist writers such as Kobayashi.[81]

Criticism of the Asahi Shimbun

The *Asahi Shimbun* was also strongly criticized for "intentionally fabricating and spreading false anti-Japan messages." In particular, the anthology, *Jūgun Ianfu: Asahi Shimbun vs. Bungei Shunjū* [Military Comfort Women: Asahi Shimbun vs. Bungei Shunjū], as the title suggests, is dedicated to criticism of the *Asahi Shimbun*, though there are a few essays that do not touch on the topic. Nishioka who has also been especially vocal against the newspaper discusses an article reported in the *Asahi* in August 1991 in which Kim Hak-sun had come forward for the first time to reveal her past as a "comfort woman." He further argues that the newspaper intentionally hid the fact that her mother sold Kim to a *kisen* three years before her "stepfather" took her to a "comfort" station in China. Nishioka argues that the newspaper hid this fact to claim that "comfort women" were forcefully taken by Japanese authorities. For Nishioka, just like other nationalist writers, Kim's past as a *kisen* drastically changes the credibility of her testimony.[82]

Nishioka additionally condemns that Uemura Takashi, an *Asahi* reporter who mostly wrote articles on the "comfort women" issue, including the above-mentioned article from August 1991, is married to a daughter of Yang Sun-im, who heads the Association for the Pacific War Victims, the Korean organization that sued the Japanese government together with sexual slavery survivors in 1991. Nishioka states that "the viciousness of the *Asahi Shimbun* is distinct here" (my translation).[83] Nishioka traveled to Seoul to meet Yang, the president, just to confirm that Uemura is indeed her son-in-law. Nishioka accuses Uemura of intentionally writing false articles that would benefit his mother-in-law for her lawsuit. By mentioning that Uemura's article from August 1991 broke the news on Kim Hak-sun earlier than Korean or any other newspapers in the world, Nishioka suspects that Uemura must have gained the information from his family source. Nishioka states that, though he has repeatedly criticized the *Asahi Shimbun* and Uemura since 1992, the *Asahi Shimbun* has not responded at all. The newspaper has not refuted Nishioka's accusations, issued corrigenda to its articles, apologized, or punished Uemura. Instead, the newspaper continued to send Uemura to Seoul to have him write articles on Korean issues, leading Nishioka to assert that he "can never forgive their unapologetic attitudes."[84] Nishioka writes that the *Asahi*'s intention is simply to expose Japan's past, and they do not want a positive relationship between South Korea and Japan. For Nishioka, a positive relationship between the two nations implies being silent about Japan's past deeds.

Fujioka criticizes the *Asahi* for "creating the impression of Japanese authorities' forceful recruitment by using the documents banning forceful recruitment" (referring to the documents discovered by Yoshimi) and calls the *Asahi* a con artist as well as a criminal.[85] Kobayashi also criticizes the *Asahi* for not reporting on opposing opinions to their own. Kobayashi states that neither his own opinions nor those of other nationalists such as Fujioka make it to the newspaper.[86] Shiono argues that the *Asahi* knew by 1997 that Yoshida's confessional books were fabricated; however, the newspaper did not retract its articles citing Yoshida until 2014, and blames the newspaper for spreading anti-Japanese sentiments in other countries.[87]

Nishio discusses his anti-*Asahi* stance in relation to anti-Japanese sentiments held among Westerners. He argues that there has been a strong anti-Japan trend in the United States and Europe. He states that because of a trend from the Meiji era (1868–1912), when Japan's modernization and Westernization began, some Japanese people believe that having similar ideas to Westerners is a characteristic of intellectuals, and the *Asahi Shimbun* represents this trend.[88]

Criticism of the Kōno Statement

In addition, among nationalist writers, the Kōno Statement is criticized as being a carelessly issued statement based on diplomatic compromise and a "big mistake" made by the Japanese government. As explained in chapter 1, the Kōno Statement of 1993 officially admitted the involvement of the Imperial Japanese Army in the "comfort" system along with the coercive recruitment of women. It was issued by Chief Cabinet Secretary Yōhei Kōno. Hata explains that because the *Asahi Shimbun*'s report on the discovery of the documents indicating the Japanese military's involvement in the operation of the "comfort" system was published in January 1992, a few weeks before Japanese prime minister Miyazawa Kiichi's scheduled visit to South Korea, Miyazawa apologized several times during his visit without having thorough knowledge about the issue.[89] Nationalist scholars such as Hata argue that since Miyazawa apologized, he is now considered to have admitted to the nation's wrongdoing. They suggest that, although Miyazawa ordered thorough research to find documents that proved that Japanese officials (such as military personnel or police officers) were involved in the coerced recruitment of Korean women, they could not find any. In the meantime, there was pressure from the South Korean government who demanded that the Japanese government admit to Japanese officials' coercive recruitment and issue an official apology as anti-Japan sentiment had drastically increased among the South Korean public. The South Korean government considered that it would restore the women's honor. Citing an article from the *Yomiuri Shimbun*, a Japanese newspaper, Hata writes that the South Korean president Kim Young-sam announced in March 1993 that the important thing was for the Japanese government to make the truth public, and financial compensation was not necessary. Nationalist writers such as Hata and Sakurai Yoshiko[90] assume that it must have appeared to be a good deal to the Japanese government. In the meantime, the Japanese government's attempt to find documental evidence for coerced recruitment by Japanese authorities was failing. In a desperate attempt to find evidence, the Japanese government decided to interview sixteen Korean survivors. As some of the sixteen survivors claimed that they were forcefully recruited by Japanese officials, those nationalist scholars argue that the Japanese government decided to admit coerced recruitment by Japanese officials without validating their testimonies. They, including Hata, opine that it had already been decided that they would be admitting to Japanese officials' coerced recruitment when they decided to conduct the interviews. In fact, the Kōno Statement was issued only five days after the interviews were completed. Hata argues that they rushed because the Miyazawa administration was about to be replaced by the Hosokawa administration two days later and Prime Minister Miyazawa simply wanted to settle on the "comfort women" issue before he left office. Hata argues that it was a big mistake because the Coomaraswamy report cites the Kōno Statement as proof of the coerced recruitment of women; in any case, the Japanese and South Korean redress movement began to seek legal reparations from the Japanese government after the Kōno Statement. After interviewing some of the former Japanese officials involved in drafting the Kōno Statement, Sakurai argues that there were secret negotiations between the Japanese and South Korean governments. Additionally, Nishioka criticizes the Kōno Statement's broad definition of "forcefulness." Nishioka argues that, despite not finding any documental evidence of coerced recruitment, the Japanese government had to admit it to maintain a harmonious relationship with South Korea. Nishioka states that, as a result, the Kōno Statement came up with a "broad definition of the authorities' coerced recruitment," that "the women were recruited against their will." Nishioka criticizes this broad definition, arguing that it was simply based on a "subjective opinion." He writes that they would all become examples of "coerced recruitment" as long as the women stated that they did not wish to become "comfort women." Nishioka trivializes this broad definition of coercion by providing the following analogy: "Office employees would be 'coerced' if their wives or mothers forced them to get up in the morning when they did not want to."[91] Of course, this is an irrelevant comparison. If the situations were the same, office employees would be deceitfully recruited, confined with no freedom to leave, and made to work under harsh conditions.

Criticism of the Coomaraswamy Report

Similarly, nationalists have severely denounced the 1996 report by Radhika Coomaraswamy, a United Nations special rapporteur. As explained in chapter 1, Coomaraswamy's report, as submitted to the United Nations Human Rights Committee (UNHRC), had several demands for the Japanese government. Hata interacted with Coomaraswamy when she came to Tokyo for her research. Hata criticizes her report for containing many factual errors because she misquoted or inadequately cited others. For instance, Hata criticizes Coomaraswamy for mostly relying on only one book written by George Hicks, an Australian journalist, for the section explaining the "comfort" system. Hata points out many mistakes in Hick's book because Hicks cannot read Japanese and had to rely on a translator. For example, Hata discusses that Hick's book states that Lieutenant General Okamura requested the Nagasaki governor to send a group of Korean women to Shanghai, and that this was the first group of comfort women; however, Japanese women were sent to Shanghai instead. Hata read the two books Hicks cites about the passage, but neither of them makes the mistake. Hata assumes that the error must have occurred during the process of translation of the two books, and this erroneous statement made it into Coomaraswamy's report. Hata also criticizes her report for her heavy reliance on Yoshida's confessional books when discussing the case of the coerced recruitment of Korean women, despite Hata himself having established by then that Yoshida's books were fabrications. Nonetheless, the Coomaraswamy report was welcomed by a number of Japanese progressives including the *Asahi Shimbun* and the JFBA to which Takagi and Totsuka belong.[92]

Overall, progressive activists and media are severely criticized among nationalist writers. Among these writers, progressives are referred to by different names such as *jigyaku ha* [masochist faction] or *hannichi* [anti-Japan], or *hannichi undōka* [anti-Japan activist]. Nishioka proudly advocates that he coined the phrase *hannichi nihonjin* [anti-Japan Japanese], and he calls Yoshimi Yoshiaki, a progressive historian, a *shokugyōteki hannichi sendenya* [professional anti-Japan campaigner].[93] Progressives are depicted as those who hate and criticize Japan for no logical reasons. For instance, Nishioka writes that the only goal for an anti-Japan Japanese person is to criticize Japan because they do not care for the truth. Nishioka accuses the anti-Japan Japanese of "dedicating themselves to carrying out anti-Japan campaigns by selecting only the 'evidence' and 'witnesses' that can fit their goal of exposing Japan's 'evildoings,' and including lies such as the Labor Corps being the same as comfort women."[94] To Nishioka, progressives are willing to lie for the sake of criticizing Japan. It should be noted that the idea that the members of the Labor Corps were akin to "comfort women" has been a widely held misperception among the South Korean public until recently.[95] This misperception was shared among many Japanese people in the 1990s when the "comfort women" issue first received much public attention; however, there had not been much research conducted on the topic.

Some nationalist writers even propose a conspiracy theory in which left-wing anti-Japan forces are attempting to destroy Japan using the "comfort women" issue. For instance, Kobayashi suspects that it may be left-wing forces with an anti-Japanese ideology disguised as humanism that insists on an apology from the Japanese government. He argues that they have already influenced politicians from most parties and have created a public opinion that Japan is evil and, therefore, must apologize repeatedly. Kobayashi asserts that because he loves the country, he is going to fight against the forces that are attempting to destroy it. Kobayashi further suggests not to be "deceived by left-wing ghosts and anti-Japan groups that are selling out the nation, who are active behind the scene in the world."[96] For whatever reasons, Japanese left wingers and other countries are so anti-Japan that they are attempting to destroy Japan. Their criticism of progressives continued to the twenty-first century and became increasingly fierce as discussed in chapter 6.

CONCLUSION

Overall, after 1991, nationalist writers remember sexual slavery simply as an officially sanctioned prostitution system that was legal in Japan at that time. Although daughters from impoverished families, mostly from colonial Korea, were sold into "comfort" stations and it was a tragedy to the women, it was a common practice in poor areas in Japan at that time as many Japanese women from impoverished families were also being sold to brothels in Japan. In some cases, women were deceived or coerced by private recruiters who were usually Korean, and not by Japanese authorities. The women made much money and their lives were not that bad, and, as a result, some women went willingly. Although it may have been a tragic experience for some, many people, including Japanese soldiers, suffered a lot more because of the war. Moreover, even if it appears to be a tragic experience, we cannot judge the past by today's standards. Back then, many young men and women experienced difficulties in life. Additionally, there is no documental evidence of the coerced recruitment of "comfort women." The only evidence is the survivors' unreliable testimony. The "comfort women" issue was simply created by anti-Japan progressives; therefore, the Japanese government is not liable for the "comfort" system.

Interestingly, as nationalists became more vocal, they seem to have received more support in Japan. The description of "comfort women" appeared in junior high school students' textbooks in 1997 after the Coomaraswamy report but disappeared by 2012. Manabisha, a new publisher, began to include a brief description of "comfort women" in their textbooks in 2016, and it remains the only junior high school history textbook that includes such a description. Nationalist writers, such as Fujioka, Kobayashi, and Nishio, formed the *Atarashii Rekishi Kyōkasho wo Tsukurukai* [Japanese Society for History Textbook Reform] in 1996 to teach children a more "positive" history of the nation. The association also campaigned to have descriptions of "comfort women" removed from textbooks, which was successful. They even published their first textbook in 2001, a second in 2005, a third in 2009, and a fourth in 2011, respectively. Although the percentage of schools that have adopted the textbook is still small (0.4% in 2005, 1.7% in 2009, 3.8% in 2011, and over 6% in 2015, Kil Yon-hyon, 2015), the increase is alarming and it may reflect a trend of leaning toward conservatism and nationalism in Japan.

NOTES

1. Hata, *Ianfu*.
2. Yoshinori Kobayashi, *Shin Gōmanism Sengen: Dai 3 Kan* [New Gomanism Declaration: Volume 3] (Tokyo: Shōgakkan, 1997).
3. Tsutomu Nishioka, *Yokuwakaru Ianfu Mondai* [Understanding the Comfort Women Issue] (Tokyo: Sōshisha, 2007).
4. Kanji Nishio, Yoshinori Kobayashi, Nobutatsu Fujioka, and Shiro Takahashi, eds., *Rekishi Kyōkasho Tono 15nen Sensō* [A 15-Year War with History Textbooks] (Tokyo: PHP Kenkyūsho, 1997).
5. Bungei Shunjū ed., *"Jūgun Ianfu": Asahi Shimbun vs. Bungei Shunjū* ["Military Comfort Women": Asahi Newspaper vs. Bungei Shunjū] (Tokyo: Bungei Shunjū, 2014), Kindle.
6. Hata, *Ianfu*, 123–124.
7. Ibid., 180.
8. Ibid., 391–394.
9. Ueno, *Nashionarizumu*, 127.
10. Hata, *Ianfu*, 276.
11. Kobayashi, *Shin Gōmanism Sengen*, 180
12. Ibid., 181.
13. Hata, *Ianfu*, 276.
14. Ibid., 393
15. Lee and Wander, "On Discursive Amnesia."
16. Hata, *Ianfu*, 192–195.
17. Ibid., 138–142.

18. Masayasu Hosaka, "Jūgun Ianfu Mondai wo 50 Nengo ni Danzai Suruna" [Do not Prosecute People for the Comfort Women Issue 50 Years Later], in *"Jūgun Ianfu": Asahi Shimbun vs. Bungei Shunjū* ["Military Comfort Women": Asahi Newspaper vs. Bungei Shunjū], ed. *Bungei Shunjū* (Tokyo: Bungei Shunjū, 2014), chap. 6, Kindle.

19. Ken Tokiura, "Heishi Taikenki, 'Shazaiha' Shōgenshu kara Yomu Ianfutachi no Jisseikatsu Daikenshō" [An Examination of the Lives of Comfort Women by Reading Soldiers' Memoirs, "Apology Faction'" Testimonials], in *Shin Gōmanism Sengen: Dai 3 Kan* [New Gomanism Declaration: Volume 3] (Tokyo: Shōgakkan, 1997), 102–103.

20. Keiichi Itō, "Kedakaki Ianfu tachi" [Proud Comfort Women], in *"Jūgun Ianfu": Asahi Shimbun vs. Bungei Shunjū* ["Military Comfort Women": Asahi Newspaper vs. Bungei Shunjū], ed. Bungei Shunjū (Tokyo: Bungei Shunjū, 2014), chap. 11, Kindle.

21. Said, *Orientalism*, 40.
22. Hata, *Ianfu*, 178.
23. Ibid., 202.
24. Said, *Orientalism*, 40.
25. Kobayashi, *Shin Gōmanism Sengen*, 177.
26. Hata, *Ianfu*, 273–274.
27. Ibid., 274.

28. Fuyuko Kamisaka and Ikuhiko Hata, "Hashimoto Souri ha Dare ni Nani wo Abiruto Iunoka" [To Whom is Prime Minister Hashimoto Apologizing for What?], in *"Jūgun Ianfu": Asahi Shimbun vs. Bungei Shunjū* ["Military Comfort Women": Asahi Newspaper vs. Bungei Shunjū], ed. Bungei Shunjū (Tokyo: Bungei Shunjū, 2014), chap. 5, Kindle.

29. Said, *Orientalism*, 317.

30. Nanami Shiono, "Asahi Shimbun no 'Kokuhaku' wo Koete" [Beyond the Asahi Shimbun's Confessions], in *"Jūgun Ianfu": Asahi Shimbun vs. Bungei Shunjū* ["Military Comfort Women": Asahi Newspaper vs. Bungei Shunjū], ed. *Bungei Shunjū* (Tokyo: Bungei Shunjū, 2014), chap. 10, Kindle.

31. Hata, *Ianfu*, 177.
32. Said, *Orientalism*, 205.
33. Ibid., 178.
34. Kamisaka and Hata, "Hashimoto Souri," chap. 5
35. Wander, "The Third Persona," 210.
36. Kobayashi, *Shin Gōmanism Sengen*, 88.
37. Ibid., 89.

38. Kanji Nishio, "Douka Gokai Shinaide Hoshii" [Please Don't Misunderstand the Issue], in *Rekishi Kyōkasho tono 15 Nen Sensō*, eds. Kanji Nishio, Yoshinori Kobayashi, Nobutatsu Fujioka, and Shirō Takahashi (Tokyo: PHP Kenkyūsho, 1997), 144.

39. Kobayashi, *Shin Gōmanism Sengen*, 130–133.
40. Ibid., 134.
41. Ibid., 80–81.

42. Nobukatsu Fujioka, "Rekishi Kyōkasho no Hanzai" [Crimes of History Textbooks], in *Rekishi Kyōkasho tono 15 Nen Sensō*, eds. Kanji Nishio, Yoshinori Kobayashi, Nobutatsu Fujioka, and Shirō Takahashi (Tokyo: PHP Kenkyūsho, 1997), 64.

43. Keiichi Itō, "Kedakai Ianfu tachi" [Proud Comfort Women], in *"Jūgun Ianfu": Asahi Shimbun vs. Bungei Shunjū* ["Military Comfort Women": Asahi Newspaper vs. Bungei Shunjū], ed. *Bungei Shunjū* (Tokyo: Bungei Shunjū), chap. 11, Kindle.

44. Soh, *The Comfort Women*, 116.

45. Hata, *Ianfu*, 163–164.

46. Hosaka, "Jūgun Ianfu Mondai," chap. 6.

47. Kobayashi, *Shin Gōmanism Sengen*, 79.

48. Itō, "Kedakai," chap. 11.

49. Hata, *Ianfu*, 149–152.

50. Ibid., 171–172.

51. Ibid., 141.

52. For example, Hata, *Ianfu*, 153–154.

53. Kanji Nishio, "Gaikoku karano Gokai ya Bujoku niha Tadachini Hangeki seyo" [Immediately Strike back against Misunderstandings and Insults from Foreign Countries], in *Rekishi Kyōkasho Tono 15nen Sensō* [A 15-Year War with History Textbooks], eds.,Kanji Nishio, Yoshinori Kobayashi, Nobutatsu Fujioka, and Shirō Takahashi (Tokyo: PHP Kenkyūsho,1997), 102–104.

54. Hata, *Ianfu*, 18.

55. Kamisaka and Hata, "Hashimoto Souri," chap. 5.

56. Hata, *Ianfu*, 63–75.

57. Kobayashi, *Shin Gōmanism Sengen*, 163–167.

58. Hata, *Ianfu*, 93.

59. Tokiura, "Heishi Taikenki," 91–106.

60. Kobayashi, *Shin Gōmanism Sengen*, 171–172.

61. A number of Koreans were brought to work in the mines in the southern part of Sakhalin during the war as it was within the Japanese territory at that time. After the war, most Japanese residents and some Koreans from the northern part of Korea were repatriated to their homelands, but Koreans from the southern part of Korea were not allowed to leave because the former Soviet Union and South Korea did not share a diplomatic relationship.

62. Hata, *Ianfu*, 180.

63. Nishioka, *Yokuwakaru*, 55.

64. Hata, *Ianfu*, 264.

65. Said, *Orientalism*, 150.

66. Said, *Culture*, 121.

67. Ibid, 317.

68. Ibid., 321.

69. Nishioka, *Yokuwakaru*, 84.

70. Ibid., 68.

71. Tsutomu Nishioka, "'Ianfu Mondai' toha Nandattanoka" [What was the 'Comfort Women' issue?], in *"Jūgun Ianfu": Asahi Shimbun vs. Bungei Shunjū*

["Military Comfort Women": Asahi Newspaper vs. Bungei Shunjū], ed. *Bungei Shunjū* (Tokyo: Bungei Shunjū, 2014), chap. 2, Kindle.
72. Nishioka, *Yokuwakaru*, 270.
73. Nobukatsu Fujioka, "'Ianfu Mondai' ha Nikkan Kankei wo Warukusurudake" ["The Comfort Women Issue" only Worsens the Japanese-South Korean Relationship], in *Rekishi Kyōkasho Tono 15nen Sensō* [A 15-Year War with History Textbooks], eds. Kanji Nishio, Yoshinori Kobayashi, Nobutatsu Fujioka, and Shirō Takahashi (Tokyo: PHP Kenkyūsho,1997), 134–138.
74. "U.S. Military Bases," Okinawa Prefectural Government Washington, D.C. Office, accessed June 26, 2020, https://dc-office.org/wp-content/uploads/2018/03/E07.pdf
75. One of the incidents that especially caused anger among Okinawans was a case of gang rape of a twelve-year-old girl by several U.S. service men in 1995 (Cameron W. Bar, "US rushes to placate Japanese, angered by rape in Okinawa," *Christian Science Monitor*, September 22, 1995, 6
76. Fujioka, "'Ianfu Mondai,'" 138.
77. Nishioka, *Yokuwakaru*, 274.
78. Kobayashi, *Shin Gōmanism Sengen*, 186.
79. In 1982, Japanese newspapers reported that the Japanese Ministry of Education made history textbook writers replace the word, *shinryaku* [invasion] with the less direct *shinshutsu* [advancement], referring to the Imperial Japanese Army's action in Asia during the war. As the governments of China and South Korea protested against this, it developed into a diplomatic conflict (chapter 1).
80. Nishioka, *Yokuwakaru*, 154.
81. Hata, *Ianfu*, 229–248.
82. Tsutomu Nishioka, "Asahi 'Ianfu Hōdō' 22 Nengo no Sajutsu" [Asahi's Tricks, 22 Years after "Comfort Women Reports"], in *"Jūgun Ianfu": Asahi Shimbun vs. Bungei Shunjū* ["Military Comfort Women": Asahi Newspaper vs. Bungei Shunjū], ed. Bungei Shunjū (Tokyo: Bungei Shunjū, 2014), chap. 1, Kindle.
83. Nishioka, *Yokuwakaru*, 39.
84. Ibid.,48.
85. Fujioka, "Rekishi Kyōkasho," 59.
86. Yoshinori Kobayashi, "'Jinken Shinri Kyō' ni Dokusareru Nihon no Masukomi" [Japanese Media that is Poisoned by "Human Rights Veneration"], in *Rekishi Kyōkasho Tono 15nen Sensō* [A 15-Year War with History Textbooks], eds. Kanji Nishio, Yoshinori Kobayashi, Nobutatsu Fujioka, and Shirō Takahashi (Tokyo: PHP Kenkyūsho,1997), 74–75.
87. Shiono, "Asahi Shimbun," chap. 10.
88. Nishio, "Gaikoku," 94–95.
89. Ikuhiko Hata, "Yugamerareta Watashi no Ronshi" [My Falsely Modified Point], in *"Jūgun Ianfu": Asahi Shimbun vs. Bungei Shunjū* ["Military Comfort Women": Asahi Newspaper vs. Bungei Shunjū], ed. Bungei Shunjū (Tokyo: Bungei Shunjū, 2014), chap. 4, Kindle.
90. Yoshiko Sakurai, "Mitsuyaku Gaikō no Daishō" [Price of Secret Diplomacy], in *"Jūgun Ianfu": Asahi Shimbun vs. Bungei Shunjū* ["Military Comfort Women":

Asahi Newspaper vs. Bungei Shunjū], ed. *Bungei Shunjū* (Tokyo: Bungei Shunjū, 2014), chap. 8, Kindle.
 91. Nishioka, *Yokuwakaru*, 112.
 92. Hata, *Ianfu*, 259–272.
 93. Nishioka, *Yokuwakaru*, 139.
 94. Ibid., 125.
 95. Soh, *The Comfort Women*, 18–20.
 96. Kobayashi, *Shin Gōmanism Sengen*, 187.

Chapter 5

The Memories of Sexual Slavery from 1991 to 2015
Progressive Memories

As mentioned in chapter 4, following the 1991 lawsuit initiated by Kim Hak-sun and two other Korean sexual slavery survivors, the issue of sexual slavery began to draw the attention of scholars, journalists, and the general public, generating controversy between progressives who support survivors' efforts at gaining redress and nationalists who have a more positive view of the Japanese government and military's role in the "comfort" system. In this chapter, I analyze progressives' memories of the issue by examining *Jūgun Ianfu* [Military Comfort Women] published in 1995[1] by Yoshimi Yoshiaki, professor emeritus at Chūo University; *Nashonarizumu to Jendā* [Nationalism and Gender][2] published in 1998 by Ueno Chizuko, professor emeritus at Tokyo University; *Jūgun Ianfu: Motoheishitachi no Shōgen* [Military Comfort Women: Testimonies of Former Soldiers][3] published in 1992 by Nishino Rumiko, a journalist; *Jūgun Ianfu to Rekishi Ninshiki* [Military Comfort Women and History Understanding] (in 1997)[4] edited by Arai Shinichi, late professor emeritus at Ibaragi University, Nishino Rumiko, and Maeda Akira, a professor at Tokyo Zōkei University; *"Ianfu" Mondai ga Toutekitakoto* [What the "Comfort Women" Issue has Led us to Question] (in 2010)[5] edited by Oomori Noriko, a lawyer who represented Chinese survivors who sued the Japanese government in 1995, and Kawata Fumiko, a journalist and writer who wrote a book about Pae Pong-gi, which was analyzed in chapter 3; and *Jūgun Ianfu to Sengo Hoshō* [Military Comfort Women and Postwar Compensation] (in 1992)[6] by Takagi Kenichi, a lawyer who represented Kim Hak-sun and two other survivors in the 1991 lawsuit. Many of these writers, including Yoshimi, Nishino, Arai, and Kawata have been officers and active members of *Nihon no Sensō Sekinin Shiryō Sentā* [The Center for Research and Documentation on Japan's War Responsibility], an NPO that conducts research on Japan's war crimes and responsibility.

ANALYSIS

Among progressives, the "comfort" system is considered a war crime for which the nation is responsible, and the "comfort women" are remembered as victims of rape and sexual slavery. Themes that emerged from the artifacts examined for this chapter include: (1) "comfort women" as victims of sexual slavery, (2) romanticized memories of "comfort women" and soldiers' gratitude to the women, (3) the violation of international laws, (4) the Japanese imperial military's involvement in the "comfort" system, (5) how women were recruited, (6) the South Korean origin of the "comfort women" issue, (7) criticism of nationalist writers, and (8) discrimination against Koreans in general. Just as nationalist writers fiercely criticize progressives as shown in chapter 4, progressives, in turn, criticize nationalist writers.

"Comfort Women" as Victims

The first theme, "comfort women" as victims of rape and sexual slavery, is the most dominant one, possibly because of progressives' efforts to counter nationalist writers' assertion that "comfort women" were paid prostitutes whose lives were not "so bad." To establish that "comfort women" were sex slaves, progressive writers emphasize the terrible reality of their lives. For instance, Yoshimi quotes the testimony of Kim Hak-sun, one of the 1991 lawsuit's three plaintiffs, regarding her rape by a Japanese officer on her first night at a "comfort" station. Also, citing a rule book regarding the operation of "comfort" stations issued by the military, he argues that "comfort women" were confined and kept under surveillance by the military and "comfort" station managers. Similarly, he details the terrible conditions in which the women lived, citing survivors' testimony and military records that documented several incidents in which soldiers beat "comfort women" for refusing to serve them. Military records have also revealed that "comfort women" typically had only one or two days off per month, at most.[7]

Progressive writers also point out that most of the women did not receive payment, although most soldiers did pay. Yoshimi notes that the women often did not receive payment because most of it was kept by their proprietors "to pay back their debts." He writes that the women's debt enslaved them, making their plight inescapable. As in Japan's brothels, proprietors added various "costs" to the women's debt, including overpriced daily necessities such as clothes and makeup products, charged interest on their debt, and penalized them for "losses" resulting from days off because of illness. Even those who managed to save money lost it, because those from Japan's former colonies lost access to their accounts after the war. Also, most were paid in a special military currency that became worthless after Japan's defeat.[8]

Yoshimi also details cases in which "comfort women" became addicted to morphine and other drugs that they used to alleviate their physical and psychological pain. He quotes testimony of a former soldier who knew of a Korean "comfort woman" who became addicted to drugs. The soldier related her experience as follows:

> I was deceived by a recruiter in Korea, being told that all I would have to do was to comfort soldiers by singing and dancing so I came to China. In China, I was told to "take customers" [Kyaku wo tore]. Without knowing what "taking customers" meant, I went to a customer and I was raped. After that, I gave up on my life and took many customers; I had to take many customers because soldiers kept coming one after another. When I was busy, I just lay down leaving my legs open while eating rice balls. Soldiers came, rode me, and left one after another. The painful stage had already passed and the lower part of my body was swollen and became numb. Soon, it became hard to get up and my lower belly became swollen, felt heavy and was plagued by dull pain all day long. I knew that I would feel better if I could rest for a few days but could not because customers kept coming one after another. It was a living hell. (Kawasaki, as quoted in Yoshimi) (my translation)[9]

This description of the situation leading to the development of her drug habit clearly depicts her painful experience.

The authors further show how severely the women were punished when they resisted or attempted to escape. In an interview with the Korean Council (cited in Nishino), a former Korean "comfort woman," who was taken to Truk Island when she was seventeen, testified that another woman attempted to escape but was caught. She was hung upside down naked in front of the others, her breasts were cut off, and her belly was cut open so that her organs could be pulled out; a soldier then threw them at the rest of the women, saying that the same fate would befall them if they attempted to escape. The woman who testified was so scared that she tried to escape but was caught and hung upside down and her back was branded as she passed out after being forced to drink too much water.[10] Kawata also cites the story of Song Sin-do, a former Korean "comfort woman" living in Japan, who sued the Japanese government. Kawata reports that Song had a 10-cm-long scar on her belly and another scar on her thigh from being stabbed by soldiers; furthermore, she was deaf in her right ear from being beaten by soldiers and her proprietors when she resisted them. Although Song attempted to flee several times, she was caught each time, resulting in her proprietors dragging her by her hair and severely beating her, telling her to pay off her "debt" if she wanted to leave. Song testified that she did not receive any money when she was deceptively recruited for a "job in the battlefields for the sake of the honorable country." The proprietor simply charged her for the cost for transportation, lodging, food, and clothes as her "debt." Kawata adds that it was impossible for Korean and Taiwanese "comfort women" to escape because they did not have money and were taken to China and other Asian countries where they did not understand the language and were unfamiliar with the surroundings.[11] Nishino additionally cites survivors' descriptions of the violence they experienced when they resisted their captors. For instance, a former Chinese "comfort woman" who sued the Japanese government testified that her face was severely beaten when she resisted, causing bone fractures and blindness. A Filipino survivor testified that she was struck every time she resisted even a little, describing how her eyes and head were severely beaten with a stick and a belt. Nishino argues that the fear of violence kept the women from resisting and wonders whether Japanese soldiers noticed the physical and mental pain that "comfort women" were enduring.[12] This statement contains an implicit criticism of nationalist writers who argue that the "comfort women" were willing prostitutes who were merely motivated by money, and former Japanese soldiers who maintained idyllic memories of the "comfort women." That "comfort women" rarely resisted, and, from former soldiers' perspectives, appeared happy, cannot be considered proof that they were actually content with their "profession" or lives.

Nishino quotes testimony from Shirota Suzuko, a former Japanese "comfort woman," which aired on the radio in 1986 to illustrate her terrible experiences:

> It has been 40 years since the end of the war but no words about the "military comfort women" have been brought up in Japan or anywhere else, although the deaths of soldiers and civilians are commemorated everywhere. Women were forced to sexually serve soldiers in China, Southeast Asia, the Pacific Islands, and the Aleutian Islands and they were abandoned when they became a burden at the end of the war. They wandered in the wilderness, starved in frozen lands, became food for wild dogs and wolves, became just bones, and became part of the earth.
>
> Soldiers lined up with a ticket of 1.5 or 1 yen and the women suffered from excruciating pain from being forced to serve them without even having time to wash themselves. I cannot remember how many times I thought about strangling the soldiers. I was going half crazy. If you died, you would be thrown into a pit in the jungle and there was no way to contact your parents. I saw it. I saw hell with my own eyes. (My translation)[13]

Although Japanese "comfort women" were thought to have been treated better than "comfort women" from other nations, Shirota's testimony shows that Japanese "comfort women's" lives were not always better.

The number of soldiers whom "comfort women" had to serve is further evidence of their plight as victims rather than willing workers. In an interview with Nishino, Matsubara Shuji, a former Japanese soldier who stayed in the Philippines, recalled that, on their days off, many soldiers with nothing better to do went to nearby "comfort" stations. He estimated that each woman must have had to serve approximately fifty soldiers per day. Another former soldier, interviewed by Nishino, reported that a Korean comfort woman told him that she had to serve 40–45 soldiers per day, but another woman served about 60 per day. He was sympathetic to their situation, saying that he heard that their bodies became exhausted and numb (although it seems that his sympathy did not stop him from visiting the "comfort" stations).[14] As a result of serving so many soldiers every day and contracting STDs, many women became infertile. Some former soldiers interviewed in Nishino's book expressed guilt over the "comfort women's" situation. Yuasa Ken, a military doctor interviewed by Nishino, testified that he had heard of a "comfort woman" who had died after serving thirty soldiers. He was also sympathetic toward "comfort women" because they could not refuse customers and were required to be pleasant regardless of how tough their situations were. He mentioned that women who refused to serve or were unfriendly were beaten, which explains why some soldiers remember only friendly "comfort women."[15] Some survivors cited by Takagi stated that they intentionally refrained from cleaning themselves during menstruation in the hopes of deterring soldiers from coming to them, but it did not help—the soldiers kept coming anyway.[16] This account differs from nationalist writers' memories of the "comfort women," which assert that the women wanted to serve many soldiers because it meant more income.

Contracting STDs was another terrible experience "comfort women" endured. Although military doctors regularly examined them for STDs, most of them had not been trained in gynecology; consequently, their examinations were not thorough. Yoshimi cites a military doctor who said that even when women passed STD examinations, they were not necessarily free from STDs, and women with mild symptoms were made to work under the condition that they use condoms, because there were few "comfort women" who had not contracted STDs. Yoshimi writes that there were also many soldiers who were unconcerned about contracting STDs because they realized that they could die at any time.[17] Nishino also explains that "comfort women" who contracted STDs often remained untreated, citing the story of Sim Mi-ja, a Korean survivor, who testified that she and others caught diseases such as syphilis and gonorrhea and had to ask soldiers for medicine because military doctors did not provide it. When she could not get medication, she washed her vagina with salt water or applied homemade herbal remedies made from dandelions or fish herbs.[18] She also testified that about 70% of the women at her "comfort" station were infected with syphilis.[19] Hwang Kum-ju cited by Nishino, vividly describes her and her peers' experiences with contracting STDs:

> In the meantime, I caught gonorrhea and syphilis and received 606 shots [Salvarsan-based syphilis medication]. I don't know if I ever got pregnant because 606 shots cause miscarriages. If you catch an STD, it is painful and your face and entire body become swollen. When it happened, those women were moved to a separate room and treated. Once they became a little better, they had to begin having sex with soldiers again. There was a woman who repeated the cycle about three times and she disappeared after a while. If women died, couldn't work due to illness, or were moved to the frontlines, new girls were brought in.
>
> I had to have sex with 50 to 60 soldiers on a normal day and 70 to 80 soldiers on their days off. In the end, I caught an STD and began to bleed and discharge pus. When I told a soldier that intercourse was unbearably painful, he told me to lick his penis instead. When I refused, he slapped my face, went ahead, and inserted his penis into my mouth. I am not a dog but someone's daughter! (My translation)[20]

The testimony shows that "comfort women" were made to serve soldiers even after contracting STDs, and when their conditions became too severe, they mysteriously disappeared.

Scott Stern explains that the Salvarsan-based syphilis medication was ineffective and caused serious side effects such as pain at the injection site and kidney damage.[21] However, until penicillin became widely available in the 1940s, it was the only modern medication for syphilis in the West as well.[22] Some of the testimonies indicate that even this ineffective, dangerous medication was considered "too valuable" for Korean "comfort women" in some cases, which further underscores their victimhood. According to Nakazato Chiyo, a former Japanese military nurse whose testimony was published in Arai, Nishino, and Maeda's anthology, Korean "comfort women" were not given even the Salvarsan-based syphilis medication at the hospital where she worked during the war because a military doctor thought STD medication was too valuable to use on Korean "comfort women"; it was reserved for Japanese soldiers who had contracted STDs. Additionally, the military doctor barely examined the Korean "comfort women" and when they were obviously infected with STDs, he simply ordered nurses to apply antiseptic solution. She recalls a Korean "comfort woman" who was about nineteen or twenty years old and had an advanced case of syphilis that left her vagina red and deformed. When Nakazato applied antiseptic solution to her vagina, the "comfort woman" cried. Nakazato thought the "comfort woman" was going to say that she was in pain but, instead, she said that she was sad. Nakazato recalls that this "comfort woman" came back a few more times as her condition continued to worsen. Nakazato later heard that Korean "comfort women" had to serve twenty to thirty soldiers per day even when they were in terrible condition from STDs; otherwise, they were beaten.[23]

Yoshimi writes that many "comfort women" died of such diseases or killed themselves. He reveals military records documenting that women were also forced to commit suicide along with soldiers who became desperate about their fate. Nishino interviewed a former soldier who was in Manchuria near the border with the former Soviet Union and recalled a Korean "comfort woman" he felt close to who possibly died there. He stated that she disappeared from her room one day, and a new woman told him that the woman he had asked for was sick. Later, he came across an area, in the mountains, that was used as a cemetery for "comfort women." He described rows of small wooden markers with Korean characters and believed that many "comfort women" must have died because they lived in such a cold area and their work was so strenuous.[24]

Under the theme of "comfort women" as victims, there are also accounts of them being abandoned. Nishino interviewed Shimada Kiyoshi, a former soldier who described seeing a ship that was transporting Korean "comfort women" being targeted by U.S. bombers when he was working on Okinoshima, a sacred island in southern Japan that is affiliated with a nearby Shinto shrine. The soldiers could not allow the women onto the island because women were not permitted there. The ship attempted to evade the attackers but, in the end, it was bombed and sank. No one was rescued.[25] Likewise, Araki Kanichi, a civilian working for the military during the war, is cited in Arai, Nishino, and Maeda's anthology as saying that he was ordered not to rescue Korean "comfort women" from a sinking ship. He recalls being in a fleet traveling to Thailand and Vietnam that was attacked by U.S. submarines; some of the ships sank. Since his ship was unharmed, they returned to rescue the survivors and he heard some Korean "comfort women" screaming for help but his superior ordered them to rescue soldiers first and laborers second. The superior said that they did not need to rescue Korean *pi* because they could find as many Korean *pi* as they wanted in Korea.[26] Hwang Kum-ju, a Korean survivor also testifies that when the war was over, soldiers simply fled and she and other Korean "comfort women" were abandoned. Some were too sick to flee but she managed to flee by on her own.[27] These descriptions show that the "comfort women" were treated as expendable "military supplies."

Being a "comfort woman" and Korean may have been a deadly combination when resources were scarce and only a limited number of people could be saved. Of course, this does not mean that Japanese "comfort women" and other groups of people were not also at risk of abandonment. As Keiko, a former Japanese "comfort woman" interviewed by Senda Kakō in the 1970s testifies, she along with other Japanese and Korean "comfort women" was almost abandoned immediately after the war in Burma when former Japanese officers thought that it would be shameful if the Allies found out that the Japanese imperial military was taking "comfort women" along.[28] Also, as we can see in a later paragraph, "comfort women," regardless of their nationalities, were assigned to the bottom of the vessel, the place where they would have been least likely to survive if the ships sank. Japanese "comfort women" were equally despised and seen as expendable. Once they "fell" from grace, regardless of their circumstances, Japan's patriarchal society that valued women's chastity made "comfort women" into easily replaceable military supplies. In addition, when people are experiencing life-or-death situations, their only concerns are their own survival. They may also be forced to make difficult decisions regarding whom to save. Considering the racist and patriarchal ideologies internalized by many Japanese at the time and the fact that the testimonies regarding abandoned "comfort women" tend to concern Koreans (in the case of the testimony by Araki Kanichi, he was specifically instructed not to rescue Korean "comfort women" because "there are many Korean *pi* anyway"), I cannot help wondering if Japanese "comfort women" might have had a better chance of being saved or if Japanese women who were not "comfort women" might have had an even better chance of being saved in such situations. In the case of the testimony by Shimada Kiyoshi, I cannot help wondering whether they would have been as strict about the religious stricture against allowing women onto the island if the women had not been Korean, "comfort women" or both. As mentioned in chapter 4, although nationalist writers claim that everyone suffered during the war and Korean "comfort women" were not an exception (e.g., Fujioka[29]), the above cited testimonies and similar ones alike suggest that Korean "comfort women" were more easily abandoned than their Japanese counterparts.

Nishino also reveals that Japanese soldiers referred to "comfort women" as "public toilets," asserting that she heard several former Japanese soldiers use that term, which also appeared in a 1939 report written by Asō Tetsuo, a military doctor who examined "comfort women" in China in 1937, and wrote that military "comfort" stations were "sanitary public toilets" [eiseiteki naru kyōdō benjo]. Nishino writes that, while there were many young soldiers who fell in love with "comfort women" and deny that the women were merely "public toilets," there are many others who confirmed that the "comfort" stations were indeed seen as "public toilets." Nishino further cites former Japanese soldiers who testified that each soldier had only 5–10 minutes with a woman who then switched to another soldier one after another as soon as they were "done with their business" [yō wo tasu]. She extends this "public toilet" concept and argues that the women were merely seen as "military supplies" [gunju busshi], suggesting that this viewpoint of "comfort women" as military supplies was evident in the ways the women were transported. Citing Senda's book, Nishino writes that since there was no category for women in the military transportation rules, the "comfort women" were categorized as "transported supplies." Citing Tomioka, a former Japanese soldier, Nishino writes that the "comfort women" rode along with weapons and cargo on trains, and on ships, they were assigned to the bottom of the vessel, where they would be least likely to survive if the ship sank.[30]

Yoshimi describes how "comfort women's" tragic experiences extended beyond the war, describing how most of them continued to suffer physically and psychologically after the war ended. The long-term physical effects of constant abuse included lingering STDs, damaged uteruses, and infertility. Many survivors also suffered from PTSD, developing depression and language problems.[31] Nishino recounts that when Kim Hak-sun came to Japan in 1991 to testify, she reported feeling nervous about standing in front of the Japanese, that the sight of tatami mattresses made her anxious, and that she was tortured by her memories of being forced to serve Japanese soldiers' sexual needs—evidence that Kim was possibly suffering from PTSD.[32] Kawata interviewed Pae Pong-gi from the 1970s to the 1980s and describes how Pae suffered from a severe chronic headache that worsened when she related her past experiences, suggesting that the problem may have been caused by PTSD. Kawata also describes the harsh life that Pae endured immediately after the war, a further example of the negative outcomes that "comfort women" suffered after the war ended. As Kawata wrote in *The House with a Red Brick Roof*, for a long time after the war, Pae engaged in prostitution to survive.[33] Yoshiike writes that former Chinese "comfort women" also suffered from PTSD, experiencing extreme symptoms, such as loss of consciousness when relating their past experiences. Yoshiike argues that PTSD, in conjunction with their countries' patriarchal ideology shaming victims of sexual assault, may account for why the survivors did not come forward for half a century.[34] In making this statement, Yoshiike implicitly refutes nationalist writers' argument that the women did not come forward sooner because they were paid prostitutes and were simply lying in recent times for financial gain. Yoshimi[35] and Takagi assert that many survivors also suffered from discrimination and were ostracized from their communities and even by their relatives; therefore, they lived their lives without revealing their pasts. Many report failed relationships because of their past as "comfort women" and the resulting infertility. Takagi also suggests that many survivors lived alone without relatives to rely on because of a Confucian belief held by many South Koreans that women who were sexually "violated" cannot live "normal" lives. Since they are now elderly and cannot work, many live on welfare.[36] Hwang Kum-ju, quoted by Takagi, states that she has lived thinking only of taking revenge on Japan. She further states that, even now, people are unkind to former "Volunteer Corps" members, although the discrimination was worse previously when they were not even regarded as human. She did not marry and had to have her uterus removed, leaving her with a body that had been destroyed without the ability to have children.[37] Yoshimi relates former "comfort women's" continued suffering to the Japanese government's denial of their legal responsibility. In citing some of the survivors, Yoshimi asserts that finally coming forward and relating their pasts provided them with some relief, yet hearing Japanese officials deny the government's responsibility caused them to suffer more, as it robbed them of their dignity.

The "comfort women's" young age was further evidence of their status as victims. It is especially emphasized in Nishino's book that most Korean "comfort women" were teenagers, many between fifteen and sixteen years old with some as young as twelve or thirteen. Ozawa Kazuhiko, who served in the imperial navy stated:

> There were many Korean comfort women who had little pubic hair. I initially thought it was their lifestyle and their preference for spicy foods like kimchi, but this was not the case. They were still children and they felt inferior [to the Japanese women] because of it. (My translation)[38]

A Korean man who was forcibly taken to Japan in 1942 to work in construction is cited in Nishino's book as saying that he remembers seeing young Korean girls wearing bloomers walking back and forth the aisles when he was made to ride a train to Busan on his way to Japan. He wonders if those young girls, who still looked like children, were made to become "comfort women."[39] That many "comfort women" were actually children underscores the inhumane nature of the "comfort" system.

Romanticized Memories of "Comfort Women" and Soldiers' Gratitude for the Women

While Korean "comfort women" as victims of sexual slavery have been a strong theme in progressive circles since the early 1990s, in the next theme, Korean "comfort women" are also romanticized in ways similar to the memories of Korean "comfort women" during previous periods as Western Orientalists romantically reconstructed the Orient.[40] This is strongly evident in Nishino's book in which she recounts interviews with many former Japanese soldiers, such as Motoyama Toshimi, who related his positive memories of a Korean "comfort woman" in China. When he was twenty-one years old, an older soldier took him and another soldier to a "comfort" station. Motoyama and the other soldier happened to pick the same woman and decided to let her choose:

> As a result, she chose me. Actually, she was my first and I fell in love with her. I began to go only to her. She was my first love and I kept all the sweets I received in the military and took them to her. There were a few times I took her out after bribing the proprietor. One time we went on a hike.
>
> I tried to look nice when I went to see her. I pressed my pants by placing them under my mattress the night before I was going to see her and wore a greenbelt I made on my own.
>
> There were soldiers who called the women "public toilets," but I wanted to interact with them in a humane way even during short periods of time. To me, comfort women were not merely for taking care of sexual needs. I felt as if I could regain my humanity when I went to see them. It was proof that I was still alive. (My translation)[41]

Other soldiers interviewed by Nishino recall that some Korean "comfort women" seemed to have an unwritten rule that once a soldier began visiting a specific woman, he could not visit another. Soldiers were often refused because they were someone else's customer. Ozawa Kazuhiko, another former soldier Nishino interviewed, said that, as a result, soldiers felt as if they were in relationships with the "comfort women." Ozawa also mentions that some soldiers gave the women gifts, such as necklaces, so the women would like them, and the women gave soldiers gifts in return. Ozawa recalls that he received gifts, such as watches and handmade dolls, and the "comfort women" were like girlfriends and mothers to him.[42] Similarly, Nakayama Mitsuyoshi, a former military doctor interviewed by Nishino, recalls that where he was stationed in Manchuria, the military held an annual athletic event to which "comfort women" were invited, and some of the women even competed with soldiers.[43]

Other former Japanese soldiers also recall receiving affection from Korean "comfort women." Nishino interviewed a former soldier who recalled that when he was stationed in Manchuria, there were some "Korean *pi*" who wanted to marry Japanese soldiers, stating that they could still have children despite their line of work.[44] Other former soldiers recalled incidents in which Japanese soldiers and Korean "comfort women" committed suicide together.[45] A couple in a forbidden relationship committing suicide together [*shinjū*] is a romantic theme in Japanese literature, as mentioned in chapter 2. In reading the testimony, Japanese readers may imagine that soldiers and "comfort women" who committed suicide together were in consensual relationships under tragic circumstances, but we cannot know how many of these cases involved desperate soldiers forcing "comfort women" to die with them. Some survivors testified that they were scared of the soldiers who wanted to die with them.[46] As we can see, even more recently, some soldiers have romanticized memories of Korean "comfort women."

While these "romantic memories" of Korean "comfort women" that were held by former soldiers may suggest that at least some of the soldiers had good intentions and that potentially humane relationships developed between some soldiers and the women, it should be noted that such discourse can also conveniently encourage discursive amnesia regarding soldiers' complicity by differentiating individual soldiers from the evil institution—the military—as suggested in chapter 3. At least some of the soldiers appear to have been unaware that they were supporting an inhumane "comfort" system. Also, when examining their testimonies, we can see that there was only a fine line between such romanticized memories and a justification of the "comfort" system: In tragic situations during the war, the "comfort women" helped soldiers to regain humanity and made soldiers feel that they were alive; therefore, they were grateful for the "comfort women." For instance, there is clearly a tie between soldiers' gratitude toward "comfort women" and their justification of the "comfort" system in a comment made by another former Japanese soldier whom Nishino interviewed:

> Why are you making only comfort women such a big issue now? We, the Japanese soldiers, were forced to go to war as well. We didn't want to go and we didn't want to kill people, either. Many of our comrades also died. In the military without regard for human rights, we could not live like humans under the name of 'for the sake of the honorable country.' The comfort stations were the only places where soldiers who had been robbed off their humanity could regain it. I am grateful for them. (My translation)[47]

Nishino writes that this soldier was trying to justify the "comfort" system by "thanking" "comfort women." She criticizes the soldier for being unaware that he and his fellow soldiers destroyed the women's and their country's dignity. This appreciation for the "comfort women" as a justification for the "comfort" system is a common theme among former soldiers. Another former soldier interviewed by Nishino states the following:

> I really appreciate the comfort women for comforting so many soldiers. I did a lot of bad things. It was a war. I couldn't help it because it was a war. I cannot change my past now. I couldn't help it. War is like that.[48]

The fact that such things happened during wartime is used to justify soldiers' use of "comfort" stations and other wrongdoing. Nakayama Mitsuyoshi, a military doctor interviewed by Nishino, defends Japanese soldiers, stating that "everything was really crazy then":

> It was not a time when soldiers could live as humans. I have no intention of blaming soldiers. They were in an extremely stressful situation in which they could die at any time. (My translation)[49]

That soldiers were entrenched in a stressful life-or-death situation has also been used to justify the "comfort women's" suffering.

The seemingly innocuous romanticized memories of Korean "comfort women" held by former Japanese soldiers and soldiers' gratitude to the "comfort women" seem to justify the "comfort" system and have been used as a rationale for exonerating individual soldiers. These ideas have led to the assumption that the "comfort" system was simply another tragic event that occurred during the war, just like many other tragic events that can occur in such a context. This parallels thoughts of the nationalists of the same period, who believe that Korean "comfort women" suffered during the war but that many others also did, including Japanese soldiers and women.

The Violation of International Laws

This is also the period when, for the first time, the "comfort" system was considered a violation of international laws, in other words, a war crime, in progressive circles. Progressive writers such as Yoshimi[50] and Oomori[51] argue that by the end of the 1920s Japan had ratified an international treaty that banned recruiting women younger than twenty-one to prostitution, even if they consented. Japan had ratified another international treaty that banned forcibly or deceitfully recruiting women of any age to prostitution. Yoshimi and Oomori argue that the "comfort" system was a violation of multiple international treaties, including the Haag treaty of 1907 that banned rape and forced prostitution during war (ratified by Japan in 1911).

Yoshimi elaborates on some of the international laws' loopholes that Japan used and Japan's potential violation of international laws, stating that the Japanese government used a loophole excluding colonies to sidestep the international laws that banned recruiting women younger than twenty-one to prostitution and prohibited coercion or deception in recruiting women of any age into prostitution. He argues that this is another reason that mostly Korean and Taiwanese women were targeted as potential "comfort women," in conjunction with the discriminatory feelings held toward them by many Japanese. Although some nationalist writers argue that Japan did not violate any international laws because of the loophole excluding colonies, Yoshimi contends that international laws were violated, because, citing Abe Kōji, an international law scholar, ships and trains used to transport Korean and Taiwanese "comfort women" would have been legally regarded as "Japanese soil"; therefore, international laws should have applied to them. He also asserts that the International Court of Justice's (ICJ) interpretations of the laws are more strict and the ICJ states that colonies were made exempt in 1921 because of the custom of paying dowries in some colonies, and that the intent of the exemption was not to condone recruiting women from colonies into prostitution.[52] Yoshimi[53] and Oomori[54] also state that the International Labour Organization announced in 1996 that the "comfort women" were sex slaves and the "comfort" system was a violation of an international labor law banning forced labor.

Furthermore, Oomori details that Gay McDougall, a UN special rapporteur on violence against women, submitted a report in 1998 stating that the "comfort" system was a modern form of slavery. According to McDougall, even if it did not meet the conventional definition of slavery under international laws, it involved sex crimes during war, which were also a violation of international laws, and it met the definition of a "crime against humanity." As Oomori explains, McDougall argued that the Japanese government must prosecute those who were responsible for establishing and operating the "comfort" system and make efforts to restore the dignity of the victims. Oomori further explains that the UN human rights committee reported in 2008 that the Japanese government had not accepted legal responsibility for its violation of international laws regarding the "comfort" system. It had not prosecuted those who were responsible for the "comfort" system, paid official reparations to the victims, apologized to the victims in an unequivocal way to restore their dignity, or sufficiently taught schoolchildren about the "comfort" system. The UN committee further contended that some politicians and the media were continuing to harm the victims by denying the issue. Progressive writers strongly argue that the "comfort" system was a violation of international laws even according to wartime standards.[55]

In his later writing, published in Arai, Nishino, and Maeda's anthology, Yoshimi (1997) elaborates on international law violation arguments and provides counterarguments to nationalist writers' assertion that no international laws were violated. Regarding the international law banning the recruitment of minors to prostitution, while nationalist writers cite an interview record by the U.S. military in Burma stating that most "comfort women" were adults, Yoshimi argues that, according to the same U.S. military record, more than half of the captured Korean "comfort women" were minors when recruited, although they were adults when interviewed. He criticizes nationalist writers who frequently cite this document to bolster their argument but overlook this "inconvenient" fact. Yoshimi also argues that although Sakurai Yoshiko, a nationalist journalist, suggests that this law was enforced in Korea and Taiwan as well as in Japan, her statement is based on mere speculation. Similarly, Yoshimi criticizes Kobayashi Yoshinori, a nationalist cartoonist, for completely misreading a military document that ordered the *kenpei* to control vicious recruitment. According to Yoshimi, Kobayashi argues that the order targeted Japanese military personnel in China, which means that the order was issued to protect potential Chinese "comfort women," although it was actually issued to prevent unlawful recruitment within Japan. Yoshimi points out that an international treaty ratified by Japan stipulating that even women older than twenty-one could not be coerced into prostitution was clearly not followed, as is evident in the survivors' testimonies.[56]

The Japanese Imperial Military's Involvement in the "Comfort" System

The next theme encompasses the Japanese imperial military's deep involvement in both the "comfort" system's operation and recruitment of women. Progressives write about the Japanese military's involvement in response to a Japanese official's June 1990 statement in Parliament, in which he denied the involvement of the Japanese authorities. Yoshimi attempts to prove that the former Japanese military was involved in the "comfort" system by citing documents, such as diaries of former soldiers who were ordered to set up "comfort" stations, and letters written by former officers, in which they ordered soldiers to place "comfort" stations under their control. In one section, Yoshimi quotes Kanai Nobutaka, a former soldier who testified that he was taught how to run "comfort" stations when he attended a military accounting school during the war, learning about women's endurance, locations for finding women, and how much time soldiers of various ranks should be allotted for sex at "comfort" stations. Kanai claimed that there was even a book with guidelines for setting up "comfort" stations. Yoshimi also discusses examples of the military running "comfort" stations and recruiting local women in occupied areas, citing another former soldier, Suzuki Takushiro, who recalls witnessing Japanese officers ordering Chinese leaders to gather women in exchange for materials.[57]

Ichikawa Ichiro, a former *kenpei* interviewed by Nishino, states that his responsibilities in Manchuria included supervising "comfort women." Ichikawa unequivocally testifies that it was a lie that "the military was not involved."[58] Yuasa Ken, a former military doctor also interviewed by Nishino, discusses the military's involvement in the "comfort" system, describing his role as a military doctor, examining the women for STDs and performing abortions on "comfort women." He also states that he was involved in running "comfort stations" in China by developing schedules for soldiers and determining fees. He asserts that, although proprietors may have managed "comfort" stations in most cases, the military made most of the management decisions.[59] Nishino echoes Ichikawa's and Yuasa's testimonies, reporting that even when civilian proprietors ran "comfort" stations, the military and proprietors were not independent of each other; the latter were required to report to the former. The "comfort women" had to obtain permission from the military to travel outside of their stations. Nishino asserts that the Japanese government is responsible for the "comfort" system because the military was in charge of it, not simply present. The military held the power to issue orders to proprietors and had the authority to close "comfort" stations. Nishino condemns the military for not closing down "comfort" stations until the war ended, destroying related documents at the end of the war, and failing to return "comfort women" to their homelands after the war.[60]

Takagi argues that, since the military was so deeply involved in the operation of "comfort" stations, "comfort women" should be given the status of *gunzoku*, or civilians who worked for the military, such as laborers and nurses. Since *gunzoku* received pensions after the war, Takagi argues that "comfort women," whose work was under contract with the military (because the military had authority over them even when "comfort stations" were operated by civilian proprietors), should also receive pensions.[61]

How Women Were Recruited

The next theme concerns how women were recruited. As progressive writers report, recruitment practices were both forceful and deceptive, although nationalist writers have reached a different conclusion, denying that Japanese officials' involvement in deceptive or forceful recruitment. In contrast, some progressive writers argue that the Japanese imperial military was directly involved in the coerced recruitment of women. Although this is widely depicted by progressive writers as having occurred in Japan's occupied areas, studies on forced recruitment conducted by Japanese authorities in Korea and Taiwan are still limited. For Korea and Taiwan, progressive writers mostly focus on deceptive recruitment.

Citing books written by former Japanese soldiers, Yoshimi writes about several cases of the forced recruitment of Indonesian women by the Japanese authorities, including military personnel and police officers. Referring to a work by Nogi Harumichi, who served in the Japanese imperial navy in Indonesia, Yoshimi writes that on Ambon Island, Japanese "comfort women" were sent back to safer areas and "comfort stations" staffed with local women were closed in 1944 as the fighting intensified between Japan and the Allied forces. However, as Japanese soldiers' unlawful activities increased, the commanding officers on the island decided to reopen "comfort" stations under their supervision, creating a list of potential "comfort women" that included former "comfort women" and women who were rumored to have been prostitutes. Although the Japanese military initially attempted to negotiate with the women, in the end, that navy officials decided that they had no choice but to force women to become "comfort women" because there were not enough volunteers. When police officers were ordered by the navy to coerce women to board a ship, the area's residents gathered at the port and protested, shouting, "Return our daughters." In another example, Yoshimi cites Itabe Kosei, a naval officer who heard young Indonesian women crying at a "comfort" station on Ambon Island on several occasions after establishing "comfort" stations using local women who were brought by force.[62] Yoshimi also writes that a Japanese military officer ordered the leader of local residents to recruit women, citing an article by Hirofumi Hayashi, a historian. According to Hayashi, in Kwabira on the Malay Peninsula, the leader, a Chinese Malaysian, gathered eighteen women out of fear for his own life because there had been occasions when Chinese residents in Malaysia were massacred by the Japanese military. The gathered women were crying and begging to be returned home. Yoshimi asserts "this is nothing but coercion."[63]

According to Yoshimi, the Japanese military's involvement in coerced recruitment occurred through ordering local authorities to recruit women in Japan's occupied areas. Hirahara Kazuo, an officer stationed in China, recalls that his predecessors demanded women from Chinese local authorities. Yoshimi reports that, to prevent the transmission of sexual diseases, the military preferred women who had not been prostitutes and local authorities could not refuse the military's demand, so there were cases in which women were forcibly recruited. Yoshimi also cites a diary written by a former military doctor stationed in China, which describes a village near the Yangtze River where local women who had not been prostitutes were brought to become "comfort women." Yoshimi directly quotes the doctor's description of these women's STD examinations:

> As the STD examination was about to begin, she [the Chinese woman] became more and more embarrassed and she was reluctant to take off her pants. The translator and the president of the local safety maintenance committee yelled at her and she finally took off her pants. As I made her lie down on her back and tried to examine her vagina, she resisted and scratched my hand. She was crying and she continued to cry even after she left the room.
>
> The next girl was the same and that also made me want to cry. It was probably their first time experiencing such an embarrassing thing and it was natural for them to feel humiliated because of the purpose. I wonder if they reluctantly agreed to come after the president of the safety maintenance committee persuaded them to do so for the sake of the safety of their village. (My translation)[64]

Yoshimi asserts that this passage clearly indicates what kind of women were recruited. Although this military doctor writes that there was no coercion by the military and the military simply requested women from local communities, Yoshimi argues that the "requests" from the Japanese military must have been perceived as "orders" by the residents of occupied areas, asserting that it is natural to assume that the Japanese military must have known that those women were being forcefully recruited by local safety maintenance committees.[65]

Matsui also describes the violent, forced recruitment and rapes of women in Japan's occupied areas. She cites Tomokiyo Takashi, a former soldier, who wrote that he and others were led to an open area one night in the Philippines and ordered to rape and kill the women who had been gathered there. Matsui also explains that, in the Philippines, the Japanese imperial military adopted the strategy of massacring all the villagers when anti-Japan guerrilla activities occurred in a village; however, the military kept young women alive and they were raped at military bases every day. She further explains that in other cases, soldiers raided houses and took women at gunpoint, sometimes killing the rest of the family who begged them not to take the women. When the Allied troops approached, Matsui explains, that Japanese soldiers killed the women because they had to flee and the women would become a burden to them. Matsui states that she has met many Filipino "comfort women" with scars from Japanese swords.[66] Kawata introduces similar testimony of survivors from Japan's occupied areas regarding their experiences of forced recruitment by Japanese soldiers. Kawata describes the testimony of Rosita Bakarto Nashino, a Filipino survivor, in which she states that she was captured by Japanese soldiers on her way to her grandmother's house. She was stabbed in the thigh, confined, and gang raped every day for a month. Another survivor, Suhana from Bandon, Indonesia, testifies that she was kidnapped by Japanese soldiers when she was sixteen and released one and a half years later after contracting an STD. When she returned home, she discovered that her father had been killed by Japanese soldiers when he went to the Japanese military base to beg them for her return. Her mother died of desperation following the loss of her daughter and husband. Kawata tells another story of an Indonesian woman from Jogjakarta who was forced to become the second wife of a Japanese officer. As his "second wife," she was actually confined to their house and her "husband" once became outraged and cut her clothes with a sword when she went into the yard to see a festival.[67] Although Indonesian "lovers" and "second wives" are often romanticized in the memories of former Japanese soldiers, this testimony refutes such an image and reveals that from the perspectives of the "lovers" or "second wives," such relationships amounted to nothing more than confinement and repeated rape.

Citing soldiers' testimonies, Nishino writes that most Korean "comfort women" were recruited under false pretenses, while some were forcibly taken. Nakayama Mitsuyoshi, a former military doctor interviewed by Nishino, states that when he asked Korean "comfort women" why they came all the way to the frontlines, he learned that most had been deceived by somebody offering a job as a military nurse or caretaker for soldiers. Nakayama also heard from a gynecologist that there were many virgins among Korean "comfort women."[68] Takagi quotes several survivors' testimonies in which they state that they were deceived. For instance, Mun Ok-chu testifies that her acquaintance told her that she could make much money working at a restaurant although she would have to travel far away.[69] Another survivor testifies that a middle-age Korean man came to her village and stated that she could earn much money if she went to Shanghai, although he did not say what exactly she would have to do there.[70]

The coerced recruitment of Korean women is also described in some progressive writers' works, such as Takagi's book that includes a description of No Ching-ja's experience of walking alone at the age of sixteen and being caught by a group of Japanese soldiers, hit in the face and thrown into a truck.[71] Similarly, No Ok-sil was kidnapped at age eighteen when she was taking a nap and three soldiers came into her house with guns and swords and forced her into a truck. Her father begged the soldiers not to take her but they kicked him.[72] Takagi's book, which was published before Yoshida's confessional books were suspected of being fabrications, also cites Yoshida's testimony regarding his experience of the forceful mobilization of Korean women. Matsubara Shunji, a former soldier whose testimony is published in Nishino's book, states that his older brother was a military officer and he once delivered a letter to the family of a Korean "comfort woman" in Seoul. From her family, Matsubara's brother learned that she had suddenly disappeared when she had gone shopping. The next day, a *kenpei* came and told her parents that their daughter was going to work for the military and the parents needed to sign a consent form. As the *kenpei* did not say anything further, the parents had no idea what exactly their daughter was going to do.[73] This testimony indicates that she was taken under coercion.

Yoshimi emphasizes the role and cooperation of Japanese officials, such as Japan's colonial governments in Korea and Taiwan or the Japanese imperial military, even when women appear to have been deceitfully recruited by civilians. Yoshimi writes that in 1941, when Japanese military officials were preparing for a potential war against the former Soviet Union, they gathered over 740,000 troops in Manchuria near the border under the guise of conducting a "military exercise." Yoshimi also writes, citing Senda, that for the soldiers who were sent there, the military requested 20,000 women from the Japanese colonial government in Korea and 8,000 "comfort women" were actually recruited in the end. He argues that to recruit that many women in such a short period of time, the cooperation of the colonial government must have been indispensable.[74] In another example Yoshimi cites the testimony of Keiko, a Japanese "comfort woman" interviewed by Senda, who states that, although she agreed to become a "comfort woman" when she was a twenty-one-year-old prostitute in Japan and received 1,000 yen in advance, there were Korean women living in Japan who had been deceitfully recruited. Both Keiko and the Korean women were recruited by a Japanese civilian recruiter ordered by the Japanese imperial military.[75] Yoshimi also cites the case of the Kitamuras, Japanese proprietors, who were captured by the U.S. military in Burma. He states that, according to interview records conducted by the U.S. military, the couple originally owned a restaurant in Seoul, but after business dried up, they decided to become proprietors and recruited twenty-two Korean women. According to the record, they prepaid the women from 300 to 1,000 yen each. Yoshimi asks how they obtained so much money when their business was not doing well (estimating that they would have needed about a total of 11,000 yen assuming they paid 500 yen on average) and implies that the military must have provided them with the money.[76] Yoshimi further argues that, because the Japanese police issued permits for women to work overseas, it was reasonable to assume that Japanese officials were involved in the forceful or deceitful recruitment of women even when private recruiters actually conducted the recruiting. Yoshimi concludes that Japanese officials were directly involved in the recruitment of Korean women by ordering private recruiters to gather women, providing them with money, or simply granting them permission to operate their "businesses" overseas.[77]

Ueno indicates that she did not believe that Japanese authorities publicly engaged in the forceful recruitment of women for the "comfort" system in the same way that they forcibly mobilized Korean men as laborers. She is more concerned that the women were in "coerced labor conditions" under surveillance. Ueno describes the "comfort" system as "military sexual slavery" and criticizes the framework that dichotomizes victims into "model victims" (forced or deceived virgins who tried to escape or kill themselves) and those who had not been virgins and/or received money. Women who were not "model victims," just like many Japanese "comfort women" who had previously been prostitutes and volunteered to become "comfort women," are frequently dismissed as not being "real victims" in the sexual slavery discourse.[78] Ueno argues that the prostitution system in Japan before and during the war was already a system of "sexual slavery" criticizing nationalist writers who dismiss the issue as "mere prostitution" by arguing that women possessed free will. She clarifies that the women are a commodity in prostitution, business transactions between customers and proprietors. In addition, she believes that the distinction between "model victims" and "non-model victims" made it more difficult for "non-model victims" to come forward. To Ueno, regardless of whether women were forcefully recruited or knowingly accepted the offer, the fact that they were treated like slaves at "comfort stations" is a more important issue. By focusing on "model victims," "non-model victims" may have become the Third Persona, those negated through silence and in history[79] in the memories held by progressives. Discursive amnesia[80] of "non-model" victims also tends to privilege a patriarchal ideology that values women's chastity.

The South Korean Origin of the "Comfort Women" Issue

As discussed in the previous chapter, Japanese nationalist writers argue that the "comfort women" issue was created by progressive anti-Japan Japanese, which resonates with an Orientalist characterization[81] of Koreans by patronizingly assuming that "Koreans could not have started the movement on their own." To challenge this view, progressive writers attribute the development of the "comfort women" issue to South Korean activists, such as the Korean Council for the Women Drafted for Military Sexual Slavery by Japan. Yoshimi and Ueno write that the existence of "comfort women" had long been known in Japan among both former Japanese soldiers and the public, because many books had been written about them, such as *Story of a Prostitute* by Tamura and *Military Comfort Women* by Senda.[82] Yoshimi and Ueno suggest, however, that societal concern had been muted until South Korean women's activist groups raised awareness.[83] Matsui Yayoi, a journalist whose chapter appears in Arai, Nishino, and Maeda's anthology, writes that, although Japanese women's activist groups had information about Korean "comfort women," they could not do anything because South Korea was under a militaristic authoritarian regime at that time.[84]

Until 1988, South Korea was ruled by an autocratic militaristic regime under Syngman Rhee (president 1948–1960), Park Chung Hee (1961–1979), and Chun Doo Hwan (1980–1988). Peterson explains that their rule had been broken by brief periods of democratic reform but real democratization of the country did not occur until the late 1980s.[85] Peterson discusses that due to the popularity of democracy in the modern world and South Korea's heavy reliance on the United States for foreign aid, the South Korean government had to uphold the pretense of having a democratic government, holding elections but dissidents were policed and prosecuted. It was only after the democratization movement in the 1980s and Chun stepping down from his position that the nation's autocracy ended.

Ueno traces the beginning of the redress movement to South Korea's movements in the 1970s and the 1980s preceding the Korean Council.[86] Ueno and Matsui[87] argue that South Korean women's criticism of Japanese men's *kisen* tourism (sex tourism) in the 1970s eventually led them to the "comfort women" issue. Citing the Asia Josei Shiryō Center [Asia-Japan Women's Resource Center], Ueno states that it was South Korean women's groups that likened Japanese men who bought Korean *kisen* women in the 1970s to those who mobilized Korean women to serve as "comfort women" during the war. Matsui also explains that the South Korean women's movement of the 1970s condemned female leaders who had cooperated with the Japanese government during colonial times. She suggests that the women's movement activities in South Korea were the basis for today's South Korean redress movement for the "comfort women."

Similarly, Matsui explains how exactly the redress movement began in South Korea and the Philippines in the 1980s and 1990s, respectively. Matsui reports that some Japanese journalists had written about two Korean "comfort women"—Kawata reporting on Pae Pong-gi in Okinawa and Matsui on No Su-bok in Thailand. Yun Chong-ok, who later cofounded the Korean Council, met with Matsui in 1988 to ask her about No Su-bok. Yun went to Thailand to meet No and published her story in a South Korean newspaper, which gained much public attention. Around the same time, South Korean women's activist groups held a press conference, demanding, from the Japanese government, investigations, an apology, reparations, and education for Japanese children on the issue. Matsui further argues that Korean women founded the Korean Council later and that the redress movement arose from the South Korean women's movement. She condemns those who claimed that the South Korean redress movement for "comfort women" was created by the Japanese, alleging that they are biased against Korean women as they patronizingly assume that South Korean women could not have begun the movement on their own. Matsui further argues that the redress movement in the Philippines was initiated by Filipino women's activists inspired by the South Korean redress movement. She writes that in December 1990, the Asian Women's Human Rights Council based in Manila held a conference to discuss ways to end human trafficking. The South Korean representatives discussed the issue of "comfort women," which inspired women from other Asian countries, including the Philippines, which already had a strong women's movement, to create their country's first redress movement. She argues that there is no way that the Japanese traveled to those countries to begin redress movements.[88]

Ueno further argues that there was a paradigm shift in South Koreans' understanding of sexual assault in the 1980s, under the influence of the democratization movement, which contributed to fostering an increased awareness of women's rights, ultimately leading to the creation of the redress movement for "comfort women." She explains that sexual assault had previously been considered shameful for the victims but people's perception of the issue shifted, and the public began to consider it a crime. Ueno reports that a sexual assault incident during the South Korean militarist regime played an influential role in changing the paradigm. Kon Im-Suk, an activist in the democratization movement, came forward as a victim of sexual assault and accused the regime of using sexual assault as a means of torture. It was a shocking incident to many yet she received much support from women's activist groups.[89]

Takagi criticizes Satō Katsumi, a nationalist writer and critic, for insulting former "comfort women" by arguing that, when coming forward, the survivors were simply following the directions of Japanese activists. Takagi quotes Sato's statement:

> Regarding the three former "military comfort women" who sued the Japanese government seeking compensation, it was a Japanese lawyer and Japanese from so-called "well-intentioned" civic groups who gave them the idea and made them sue the government. In addition to the "military comfort women" issue, there are cases in which Japan has been sued regarding its past actions but in many cases, Japanese nationals have encouraged Koreans to sue. Of course, such Japanese must regard themselves just by taking the side of the oppressed. (My translation)[90]

Takagi is aware that the "Japanese lawyer" in this passage referred to him. He criticizes Satō and other nationalist writers for their patronizing assumption. Takagi explains that Kim Hak-sun was indignant at the Japanese government's statement that the military was not involved and, as a result, she came forward. He states that Kim had decided to sue the Japanese government before she met Takagi and other Japanese. Takagi further argues that Satō and others are ignoring the initiatives taken by the survivors.

Criticism of Nationalist Writers

As nationalist writers oppose the arguments of progressive writers, progressive writers oppose the arguments of nationalist writers, which is the basis of the next theme that will be discussed. Ueno refutes some of the points made by nationalist writers who dismiss the "comfort women" issue. She summarizes nationalist writers' ideas as follows: "Western nations have committed similarly evil acts yet have not apologized and, therefore, there is no reason for Japan not to act like Western nations."[91] The first point Ueno refutes is nationalists' argument that there is no documented evidence supporting the claim regarding the coerced recruitment of "comfort women" by Japanese authorities. Ueno illustrates the absurdity of this argument by comparing it to the argument made by neo-Nazis that the Holocaust did not happen because there is no document signed by Hitler ordering the mass murder of Jewish people. She points out that it is common for defeated countries to destroy "inconvenient" documents.[92]

The second point Ueno criticizes is nationalists' dismissal of victims' testimonies because there is no documented evidence to support them. Ueno claims that crimes could be concealed by killing or silencing witnesses. Again, by comparing the issue to the Holocaust, Ueno explains that no victims ever returned alive from the gas chamber; therefore, there are no eye witnesses to testify what happened within any of them. A lack of testimony, therefore, cannot be considered proof that an event did not happen. In the case of the "comfort women" issue, the victims were silenced for a long time and hence there had been no "witnesses," allowing the "comfort" system to remain concealed for half a century. Ueno, together with other progressive writers such as Matsui,[93] criticizes nationalists for dismissing the women's testimonies as "untrustworthy" when the victims finally came forward because the dismissal significantly damaged the survivors' dignity.[94]

A third point Ueno refutes is the claim that it is inappropriate to teach middle school students about the dark side of sex. She states that this idea is based on a belief that middle school students today are sexually innocent. She points out the hypocrisy of shielding middle schoolers from information on the "comfort" system while exposing them to information on sex through the media.[95] Arai, in his chapter in Arai, Nishino, and Maeda's anthology, discusses that deleting the passage on "comfort women" from middle school textbooks contravenes worldwide efforts to combat sexual assault and protect women's rights.[96]

The final point Ueno criticizes is the "recovery of national pride" proposed by nationalists. She challenges nationalists' attempt to create the correct version of history [seishi] that would enable the Japanese people to feel proud of their country by abandoning a "masochistic historical viewpoint" [jikoku jigyaku shikan].[97] She argues that the notion of "the correct version of history" negates the diversity and conflicts among people and criticizes nationalists for calling themselves patriots and labeling progressives "anti-Japan." She further argues that the competition to be viewed as "more patriotic" is dangerous because it encourages the creation of a division between "the people" [kokumin] and "those against the people" [hi kokumin], which could lead to the persecution of the latter, just as those who opposed national policies were persecuted as *hi kokumin* before and during the war.[98]

Another idea promoted by nationalist writers and criticized by progressive writers is that the "comfort women" were not sex slaves because their lives were not "so bad." Yoshimi, writing in Arai, Nishino, and Maeda's anthology, refutes the report by Alex Yorichi, a Japanese American soldier who interviewed captured Korean "comfort women" and their proprietor in Burma. As mentioned in chapter 4, the report states that "comfort women" participated in athletic events, banquets, and picnics along with soldiers and were permitted to go shopping. Based on the report, nationalists such as Kobayashi Yoshinori argue that they were not sex slaves. However, Yoshimi is skeptical of the report's validity. Pointing to other parts of the report in which Yorichi described the Korean "comfort women," he argues that Yorichi was biased against the women.[99] Yorichi stated that average Korean comfort women were uneducated, childish, whimsical, selfish, and self-centered, wanting to talk only about themselves; they were not attractive by Japanese or Caucasian standards, and they exhibited female cunning. Yoshimi points out that another report written by another American soldier describes the lives of the "comfort women" more negatively. Yoshimi, together with Maeda,[100] whose work appears in the same anthology, asserts that it is ridiculous to assume that slaves must have had no "freedom" at all or they must have spent every day crying because most people attempt to adapt to situations to ensure their own survival. Yoshimi further argues that some women may have attempted to become soldiers' or officers' "girlfriends" to survive. He also asserts that when "comfort women" knew their lives would be at risk if they resisted, most stopped resisting. Responding to nationalists' claim that the "comfort women" were not sex slaves because they could go for a walk and attend banquets, Maeda compares their situations to those of slaves in the United States and argues that American slaves also had some "freedom" and many could go for a walk under certain conditions, but they were still not free because they remained the property of others.

In addition, Oomori criticizes former Japanese prime minister Abe Shinzō, a nationalist politician, for his 2007 comment denying the direct involvement of Japanese officials in the coerced recruitment of women. As described in chapter 1, responding to the 2007 resolution that was passed by the U.S. Congress, calling for an unequivocal apology by the Japanese government, Abe stated that there was no evidence of the Japanese military's involvement in the forced recruitment of women. Oomori responds as follows:

> In the international community, regardless of whether women were forcefully or deceitfully recruited, if they were made to serve soldiers against their will, it would be, of course, a serious human rights violation; therefore, the Japanese military (government) that created the "comfort" sytem is liable. However, Prime Minister Abe, the representative of the Japanese government, denied the nation's responsibility, asserting that the military did not forcefully recruit women, which caused the international community to view the Japanese government even more negatively. (My translation)[101]

Kawata also criticizes nationalist politicians, scholars, and writers for lobbying against including "comfort women" in middle and high school history textbooks. She explains that, after the history textbook controversy in the 1980s (i.e., the education ministry ordering textbook authors to replace *shinryaku* [invasion] with *shinshutsu* [advancement]), a *kinrin shokoku jōkō* [neighboring countries clause] was added to the textbook screening rules, which suggests that references to neighboring countries should promote international understanding and cooperation. As a result, in 1994, nineteen of the twenty Japanese high school history textbooks included descriptions of "comfort women," and by 1997, all seven middle school history textbooks included descriptions of them, which meant that all children in compulsory education had an opportunity to learn about the "comfort women" issue (compulsory education ends upon completion of middle school in Japan). Responding to the inclusion of the history of "comfort women" in middle school textbooks, Kawata explains that various nationalist groups began lobbying against it, including *Nihon no Zento to Rekishi Kyōiku wo Kangaeru Wakate Giin no Kai* [Association for Young Parliament Members who are Worried about Japan's Future and History Education] founded by nationalist politicians such as Abe Shinzō and *Atarashii Rekishi Kyōkasho wo Tsukurukai* [Japanese Society for History Textbook Reform] founded by many of the nationalist writers mentioned in chapter 4, such as Fujioka and Kobayashi. Kawata condemns them for arguing that the "comfort women" were mere prostitutes who chose their "occupation," and for insulting the survivors by implying that they were liars. Kawata calls these groups' insults to the survivors a "second rape," similar to Ueno's labeling of such insults as a "third crime" after the first crime of actual rape and the second crime of forcing the survivors to remain silent for half a century. In addition, Kawata suggests that, in 2002, only three textbooks included descriptions of the "comfort women" and that the number decreased to two by 2006, possibly in response to a comment made by Machimura Nobutaka, the nationalist education minister, who stated in 1998 that textbooks were biased and they were considering forcing publishers to make changes before they even submitted their textbooks for screening. Kawata laments that the spirit of the Kōno statement, "never to repeat the same mistake by forever engraving such issues in our memories through the study and teaching of history," was only reflected in middle school history textbooks for ten years, and had only been sufficiently covered for the first few of them.[102]

The debate continues as nationalist writers criticize progressive writers, and the latter criticize specific nationalist writers. In Arai, Nishioka, and Maeda's anthology, Matsui criticizes Sakurai Yoshiko, a nationalist journalist, for simply repeating Fujioka's and Hata's arguments without investigating exactly what happened.[103] Ueno also criticizes Sakurai for taking the side of those in power, referring to Sakurai's skepticism of survivors' testimonies. Sakurai bases her skepticism on a lack of official documents proving Japanese officials' direct involvement in the coercive recruitment of women. Ueno points out that "official documents" tend to be written by those in power.[104] In addition, Nishino criticizes Kobayashi by calling his claim that the military's involvement was a positive intervention, "vicious" (although Nishino does not specifically name Kobayashi, it is assumed that the criticism was directed at Kobayashi because such claims were mainly made by him).[105]

General Discrimination against Koreans

Another theme that emerged in progressive circles is discrimination against Koreans, including both Korean "comfort women" and Koreans in general. In her book, *Military Comfort Women*, Nishino extensively discusses the issue of Korean laborers who were forcibly brought to Japan during the war. She began her book with the testimony of a Korean man who was forcibly brought to Japan as a laborer and tortured when he attempted to escape. In a later chapter, she describes her participation in a trip, "Kyōsei Renkō wo Tadoru Tabi" [Trip to trace sites related to forced mobilization], in which she and others went to sites related to the forced mobilization of Korean men, such as former Japanese coal mines where Korean men were forced to work under harsh conditions and a Korean village where the villagers were massacred because of their anti-Japan protests during colonial times.[106] For Nishino, the Korean "comfort women" issue is one of colonization as well as sexism and racism. Therefore, she argues that the discrimination and hardships experienced by Korean "comfort women" should be discussed alongside the suffering inflicted on Korean men and women under Japan's colonization.[107] Nishino illustrates how Japanese soldiers' treatment of Korean "comfort women" was influenced by what Japanese children were taught about Koreans and other Asians during colonial times. For instance, Nishino interviewed Kojima Takao, a former Japanese soldier, and Yuasa Ken, a military doctor whose testimony appears in Arai, Nishino, and Maeda's anthology, and reports that during the war, Japanese children grew up looking down on other Asians including the Chinese and Koreans. Yuasa also relates his own bias against Koreans, which he held during the war:

> I didn't go to the comfort stations for about half a year. When I saw the "comfort women" in the meantime, it was when I taught them, alongside female Japanese residents, how to treat injured people. When I saw Korean "comfort women," I felt a sense of superiority, thinking that "even Koreans can do something like this." In addition, I thought that Koreans must feel fortunate

to be under the rule of the same emperor. One of the reasons why I didn't go to comfort stations for half a year was that I felt Koreans were dirty. (My translation)[108]

Progressive writers such as Takagi argue that because of discrimination and feelings of superiority over Koreans, the Japanese did not hesitate to mobilize Korean and other Asian women as "comfort women."[109]

Nishino further illustrates that Korean "comfort women" were discriminated against at "comfort" stations, citing former Japanese soldiers' testimony that they heard Korean "comfort women" say, "Don't make fun of us by calling us *Chōsen, Chōsen*.[110] We are children of the same emperor." She explains that Korean "comfort women" used to say that when they were being insulted by Japanese soldiers. It was a clever way to defend themselves because the Japanese empire taught that Koreans and Taiwanese were also imperial subjects (*koumin*) and children of the Japanese Emperor, which stipulated (at least in theory) that Koreans and Taiwanese were equal to and had the same rights as the Japanese. Matsubara Shunji, a former Japanese soldier interviewed by Nishino, asserts that such an argument must have been the only way for Korean "comfort women" to defend themselves.[111] Nishino explains that discrimination existed even among the "comfort women," with Japanese "comfort women" at the top of the hierarchy and Korean "comfort women" below them. She argues that Korean women were supposed to shield Japanese soldiers from STDs.[112]

Nishino argues that the *Kouminka Seisaku*, the Imperial Subjects Policy, a Japanese colonial policy, prompted Koreans and Taiwanese to Japanize themselves and become imperial subjects equal to the Japanese by relinquishing their own languages and cultures, yet this "equality" came with obligations, such as engaging in forced labor and becoming "gifts to the emperor's troops." In this sense, Nishino believes that the forced labor issue and the "comfort women" one are related and should be discussed together.[113]

Thus, under the theme of discrimination against Koreans, the issue of Korean forced laborers ubiquitously appears in Nishino's opening chapter, in which Chon Jun-mo, a Korean forcibly brought to Japan during the war relates his experience of being tortured by the *kenpei*:

> They stuck an awl between my fingernails and fingers and kept pushing it. It was far being painful. It felt as if my body was on fire. (My translation)[114]

He vividly narrates his experience of being brought to a coal mine in Japan and his subsequent escape. He also helped other Korean laborers escape, which led the *kenpei* to arrest and torture him. Although his friends died, he managed to survive. Chong also narrates the story of 200 Korean laborers who constructed secret military headquarters in Japan's mountains and mysteriously disappeared at the end of the war—they were presumably killed to keep the secret. In her book, Nishino discusses the issue of Korean laborers who were abandoned in Sakhalin at the end of the war. Nishino interviewed Im Pan-ge, a Korean living in Sakhalin, who relates his experience of being forced to work in a coal mine in Sakhalin and of being abandoned there after the war:

> We were made to work all day long without breaks with a small amount of food. While the Japanese managers were eating rice, we were only given beans as if we were horses. There were no meal breaks either and we had to eat beans along with water dripping from the ceiling while working in the mine. We, of course, did not have enough energy but we were whipped if we stopped working for even a short period of time. (My translation)[115]

He further recalls that he was finally able to return home forty-eight years after the war but his parents had already passed away and his relatives were gone. The land that should have been his had become someone else's.

Takagi discusses how Korean men were forcibly taken to the frontlines as laborers because Japan experienced a labor shortage during the war. Because Korean laborers were not trusted, they were not given weapons and were forced to expose themselves to enemy attacks while working.

CONCLUSION

Ueno argues that, in the early 1990s, a paradigm change occurred, allowing the "comfort women" issue to become viewed as a war crime rather than a shameful incident in the victims' pasts. She claims that the "comfort women's" existence was known and had not been hidden, and many former soldiers had written about their experiences with "comfort women" without any sense of guilt or shame. However, the perception of the issue has changed; the "comfort" system that no one, including the perpetrators, had previously considered a crime has been reconstructed as sexual assault by women identifying themselves as victims. In other words, the belief that "comfort women" were a necessity of war and not victims of a crime, which had been perpetuated by the victims' silence, has been overturned by their efforts to construct another reality. Kawata also suggests that Japanese society first began to pay attention to the "comfort women" issue after South Korean women's groups brought it to light in the late 1980s, which brought the subject to the attention of scholars, journalists, and the general public.[116]

As discussed in the previous chapter and this one, progressives' and nationalists' memories of the "comfort" system and the survivors of sexual slavery differ dramatically. Nationalists remember the survivors as mere prostitutes who became "comfort women" for financial reasons, whose experiences were not that bad. To them, former "comfort women" are deceitful and, thus, falsely accuse the Japanese government of crimes to benefit even more. Conversely, progressives remember "comfort women" as victims of sexual slavery who were forced to undergo unspeakable experiences and then remained silent for half a century. These differing memories have led nationalists and progressives to severely attack each other. To nationalists, progressives are anti-Japan Japanese who created the "comfort women" issue by instigating South Koreans. To progressives, nationalists are revisionists, destroying the dignity of the survivors by dismissing the issue and calling survivors "liars."

As Japanese progressives' main concern is redress for the survivors, they tend to emphasize their victimhood. At the same time, the discursive amnesia in their memories of sexual slavery may be the survivors who remember their experiences in less gruesome ways although romanticized memories held by former soldiers have been reported as illustrated earlier. Although few in number, some survivors' testimonies reveal idyllic memories (e.g., Bae Jok Gan fondly recalls a nice Japanese soldier who wanted to marry her in Kim's book,[117] Pae Pon-gi in Kawata's book from the previous period[118]). Although it is likely that their "positive memories" stem from Stockholm Syndrome, some women did relate positive memories of their experiences. Forgetting such memories could lead to the silencing of those who were not so-called model victims, those who had not been virgins when forcibly or deceitfully recruited and had not tried to kill themselves or escape or did receive compensation.[119] Thus, such oversight could support a patriarchal ideology that values women's chastity and ostracizes "promiscuous" women. Women are expected to be "perfect victims" to claim their victimhood. For the same reason, most of the Japanese "comfort women" who did not fit the model victim role seem to have been mostly forgotten.

This memory war between nationalists and progressives went beyond scholarly debate and resulted in a live discussion on national television, *Asamade Namaterebi* [Live TV Show Until the Morning], in the 1990s, revealing the extent of both public and scholarly interest in the topic. Although the intensity of the debate declined after the 1990s, scholars and the public remained interested in the issue through the 2000s. In 1998, progressive activists such as the late Matsui Yayoi founded the VAWW RAC, a Japanese NPO, to facilitate redress for survivors of sexual slavery. In 2000, the VAWW RAC, together with the Korean Council and other groups, held the Women's International War Crimes Tribunal on Japan's Military Sexual Slavery, a hypothetical trial, in Tokyo. In 2005, the VAWW RAC opened the Women's Active Museum on War and Peace in Tokyo, Japan's first museum commemorating the victims of sexual slavery. Meanwhile, nationalists continued their fight to have passages about "comfort women" removed from middle school textbooks and finally succeeded in the early 2000s, when most textbook publishers removed descriptions of "comfort women." Although they seemed to become relatively inactive after their success in textbook censorship, their movement was reenergized after the Korean Council erected a "comfort woman" statue in front of the Japanese Embassy in Seoul in 2011. Subsequently, Koreans living abroad began to install similar statues in other countries, including the United States. In 2014, the *Asahi Shimbun* retracted its articles citing Yoshida Seiji and in 2015, Japanese prime minister Abe Shinzō and South Korean president Park Geun-hye reached the "final, irreversible" agreement on the "comfort women" issue. Since then, the memory war between nationalists and progressives over the "comfort women" issue has been rekindled.

NOTES

1. Yoshimi, *Jūgun Ianfu*.
2. Ueno, *Nashonarizumu*.
3. Nishino, *Jūgun*.
4. Shinichi Arai, Rumiko Nishino, and Akira Maeda, eds., *Jūgun Ianfu and Rekishi Ninshiki* [Military Comfort Women and History Interpretation] (Tokyo: Shinkō Shuppan sha, 1997).
5. Noriko Oomori and Fumiko Kawata, eds., *"Ianfu" Mondai ga Toutekitakoto* [What the "Comfort Women" Issue has Led us to Question] (Tokyo: Iwanami Shoten, 2010).
6. Takagi, *Jūgun*.
7. Yoshimi, *Jūgun Ianfu*, 130–151.
8. Ibid., 145–148.
9. Ibid., 153.
10. Nishino, *Jūgun*, 224.
11. Fumiko Kawata, "'Ianfu' Mondai no Kiten" [The Origin of the "Comfort Women" Issue], in *"Ianfu" Mondai ga Toutekitakoto* [What the "Comfort Women" Issue has Led us to Question], eds. Noriko Oomori and Fumiko Kawata (Tokyo: Iwanami Shoten, 2010), 18–20.
12. Rumiko Nishino, "Shōgen to Shijitsu kara Ukiagaru Nihongun 'Ianfu'" [Japanese Military "Comfort Women" from Testimonies and Historical Facts], in *Jūgun Ianfu and Rekishi Ninshiki* [Military Comfort Women and History

Interpretation], eds. Shinichi Arai, Rumiko Nishino, and Akira Maeda (Tokyo: Shinkō Shuppan sha, 1997), 81–82.
 13. Nishino, *Jūgun* 109.
 14. Nishino, *Jūgun*, 106.
 15. "Senjichū Ianfu ni Atta 4 Nin no Shōgen" [Testimonials of 4 People Who Met Comfort Women during the War], in *Jūgun Ianfu and Rekishi Ninshiki* [Military Comfort Women and History Interpretation], eds. Shinichi Arai, Rumiko Nishino, and Akira Maeda (Tokyo: Shinkō Shuppan sha, 1997), 66.
 16. Takagi, *Jūgun*, 44.
 17. Yoshimi, *Jūgun Ianfu*, 155.
 18. Nishino, *Jūgun*, 119.
 19. Takagi, *Jūgun*, 66.
 20. Nishino, *Jūgun*, 121–122.
 21. Stern, *The Trials of Nina McCall*, 25.
 22. Ibid., 239–240.
 23. "Senjichū," 53–54.
 24. Nishino, *Jūgun*, 106–107.
 25. Ibid., 101.
 26. Nishino, "Shōgen," 47–48.
 27. Nishino, *Jūgun*, 122–123.
 28. Senda, *Jūgun Ianfu Keiko*, 271–272.
 29. Fujioka, "Rekishi Kyōkasho," 64.
 30. Nishino, *Jūgun*, 42–52.
 31. Yoshimi, *Jūgun Ianfu*, 213–217.
 32. Nishino, *Jūgun*, 112–113.
 33. Fumiko Kawata, "Maegaki" [Introduction], in *"Ianfu" Mondai ga Toutekitakoto* [What the "Comfort Women" Issue has Led us to Question], eds. Noriko Oomori and Fumiko Kawata (Tokyo: Iwanami Shoten, 2010), 2–4.
 34. Toshiko Yoshiike, "'Ianfu Mondai' no Jūgyō Tenkai" [Development of the "Comfort Women Issue"], in *Jūgun Ianfu and Rekishi Ninshiki* [Military Comfort Women and History Interpretation], eds. Shinichi Arai, Rumiko Nishino, and Akira Maeda (Tokyo: Shinkō Shuppan sha, 1997), 113–116.
 35. Yoshimi, *Jūgun Ianfu*, 217–218.
 36. Takagi, *Jūgun*, 111–112.
 37. Ibid., 48.
 38. Nishino, *Jūgun*, 50–51.
 39. Ibid., 139–140.
 40. Said, *Orientalism*, 158.
 41. Nishino, *Jūgun*, 48.
 42. Ibid., 56.
 43. Ibid., 94.
 44. Ibid., 108.
 45. Ibid., 94.
 46. Yoshimi, *Jūgun Ianfu*, 159.
 47. Nishino, *Jūgun*, 22.

48. Ibid., 18–19.
49. Ibid., 94.
50. Yoshimi, *Jūgun Ianfu*, 166–172.
51. Noriko Oomori, "Sabakareta Nihongun Seidoreisei" [The Japanese Military Sex Slavery System being Prosecuted], in *"Ianfu" Mondai ga Toutekitakoto* [What the "Comfort Women" Issue has Led us to Question], eds. Noriko Oomori and Fumiko Kawata (Tokyo: Iwanami Shoten, 2010), 35–36.
52. Yoshimi, *Jūgun Ianfu*, 165–169.
53. Ibid., 169–170.
54. Noriko Oomori, "Kokusai Shakai karano Kankoku" [Warning from the International Community], in *"Ianfu" Mondai ga Toutekitakoto* [What the "Comfort Women" Issue has Led us to Question], eds. Noriko Oomori and Fumiko Kawata (Tokyo: Iwanami Shoten, 2010), 44.
55. Ibid., 43–44.
56. Yoshimi Yoshiaki, "'Jūgun Ianfu' no Rekishiteki Jijitsu" ["Comfort Women's" Historical Facts], in *Jūgun Ianfu and Rekishi Ninshiki* [Military Comfort Women and History Interpretation], eds. Shinichi Arai, Rumiko Nishino, and Akira Maeda (Tokyo: Shinkō Shuppan sha, 1997), 24–25.
57. Yoshimi, *Jūgun Ianfu*, 113.
58. "Senjichū," 44.
59. Ibid., 67–68.
60. Nishino, "Shōgen," 84–86.
61. Takagi, *Jūgun*, 99–100.
62. Yoshimi, *Jūgun Ianfu*, 125–217.
63. Ibid., 123.
64. Ibid., 116.
65. Ibid., 117.
66. Yayori Matsui, "'Jūgun Ianfu' to Josei no Jinken, Media no Yakuwari" ["Comfort Women" and Women's Human Rights, Roles of the Media], in *Jūgun Ianfu and Rekishi Ninshiki* [Military Comfort Women and History Interpretation], eds. Shinichi Arai, Rumiko Nishino, and Akira Maeda (Tokyo: Shinkō Shuppan sha, 1997), 101–102.
67. Fumiko, Kawata, "'Ianfu' Seido toha Nannde attaka" [What was the "Comfort" System], in *"Ianfu" Mondai ga Toutekitakoto* [What the "Comfort Women" Issue has Led us to Question], eds. Noriko Oomori and Fumiko Kawata (Tokyo: Iwanami Shoten, 2010), 24–26.
68. Nishino, *Jūgun*, 94.
69. Takagi, *Jūgun*, 35.
70. Ibid., 26–27.
71. Ibid., 43.
72. Ibid., 49–50.
73. Nishino, *Jūgun*, 170.
74. Yoshimi, *Jūgun Ianfu*, 32–33.
75. Ibid., 91.
76. Ibid., 99–100.

77. Ibid., 104–106.
78. Ueno, *Nashionarisumu*, 125–126.
79. Wander, "The Third Persona," 209–210.
80. Lee and Wander, "On Discursive Amnesia," 152–154.
81. Said, *Orientalism*, 204.
82. Yoshimi, *Jūgun Ianfu*, 2–3; Ueno, *Nashionarisumu*, 100.
83. Ueno, *Nashionarisumu*, 102–103; Yoshimi, *Jūgun Ianfu*, 2–3.
84. Matsui, "'*Jūgun*,'" 92.
85. Mark Peterson, A Brief History of Korea (Facts of File, 2009), http://pitt.idm.oclc.org/login?url=https://search.credoreference.com/content/entry/fofbk/south_korea_s_long_road_to_democracy_1953_2009/0?institutionId=1425
86. Ueno, *Nashionarisumu*, 102–104.
87. Matsui, "'*Jūgun*,'" 92–96.
88. Ibid., 92–96.
89. Ueno, *Nasionarisumu*, 101–104.
90. Takagi, *Jūgun*, 153–154.
91. Ueno, *Nashionarisumu*, 148.
92. Ibid., 148.
93. Matsui, "'*Jūgun*,'" 91.
94. Ueno, *Nashionarisumu*, 148–149.
95. Ibid., 149–150.
96. Shinichi Arai, "Rekishi wo Mitsumerukoto no Imi" [The Meanings of Reflecting on History], in *"Ianfu" Mondai ga Toutekitakoto* [What the "Comfort Women" Issue has Led us to Question], eds. Noriko Oomori and Fumiko Kawata (Tokyo: Iwanami Shoten, 2010), 13.
97. "Jigyaku shikan" means "a masochistic history viewpoint." Nationalists use the term to refer to a history viewpoint promoted by progressive historians because they believe that progressive historians focus on the negative aspects of Japan's history.
98. Ueno, *Nashionarisumu*, 150–151.
99. Yoshimi, "'Jūgun,'" 20–23.
100. Akira Maeda, "Seidorei toha Nanika" [What are Sex Slaves?], in *"Ianfu" Mondai ga Toutekitakoto* [What the "Comfort Women" Issue has Led us to Question], eds. Noriko Oomori and Fumiko Kawata (Tokyo: Iwanami Shoten, 2010), 138–140.
101. Oomori, "Kokusai," 45.
102. Fumiko Kawata, "Kyokasho Mondai" [The Textbook Issue], in *"Ianfu" Mondai ga Toutekitakoto* [What the "Comfort Women" Issue has Led us to Question], eds. Noriko Oomori and Fumiko Kawata (Tokyo: Iwanami Shoten, 2010), 27–31.
103. Matsui, "'*Jūgun*,'" 89.
104. Ueno, *Nashionarizumu*, 156.
105. Nishino, "Shōgen," 77.
106. Nishino, *Jūgun*, 183–217.
107. Ibid., 220–221.
108. "Senjichū," 64.
109. Takagi, *Jūgun*, 79.

110. A derogatory term referring to Koreans.
111. Nishino, *Jūgun*, 168–169.
112. Ibid., 227–228.
113. Ibid., 229–230.
114. Ibid., 1.
115. Ibid., 190.
116. Kawata, "'Ianfu' Mondai," 6–8.
117. Kim-Gibson, *Silence Broken*, 91–94.
118. Kawata, *Akarenga*.
119. Ueno, *Nashionarisumu*, 125.

Chapter 6

The Memories of Sexual Slavery in Japan from 2015 to the Present
The 2015 Bilateral Agreement and "Comfort Women" Statues

Chapter 6 discusses the memories of sexual slavery since 2015 when the governments of South Korea and Japan agreed on the bilateral treaty. While public attention to the issue is not as strong now as it was in the 1990s, many developments related to the issue of "comfort women" occurred around 2015, which reenergized activists and scholars from across the political spectrum. For instance, statues commemorating "comfort women," which were initially erected only in South Korea were being erected outside South Korea by 2015. This prompted the nationalist movement in Japan to push for the removal of these statues. In 2011, the Korean Council for the Women Drafted for Military Sexual Slavery by Japan erected its first statue symbolizing "comfort women" in front of the Japanese Embassy in Seoul. Within a few years, Korean and Chinese groups began to install similar statues, both within and outside South Korea, including Australia, Canada, China, Germany, and the United States. The emergence of these statues caused nationalist writers and activists to launch movements to prevent the erection of further statues. The first such statue outside South Korea was installed in Glendale, California, in 2013. It was controversial: the area's Japanese residents argued that its presence was likely to foster anti-Japanese sentiments, hatred, and discrimination. When another statue was erected and donated to the city of San Francisco in 2017, then-mayor of Osaka Yoshimura Hirofumi announced the termination of the sister city relationship between Osaka and San Francisco, which had been in place since 1957. In 2013, Park Yu-ha, a South Korean professor of Japanese literature, published her book *Comfort Women of the Empire* (a Japanese version was published in 2014). Whereas her book was positively received in Japan and won several awards there, it was negatively received within South Korea. She was sued for defamation by some South Korean survivors. In 2014, the *Asahi Shimbun*, a Japanese progressive newspaper that has been supportive of the redress movement, admitted that the late Yoshida Seiji's confessions about "hunting" Korean women on Jeju Island were fabricated, and retracted all its articles citing Yoshida's testimony. As the 1996 Coomaraswamy report cites Yoshida's testimony as proof of the forced mobilization of women, then-Japanese prime minister Abe Shinzō sent Satō Kuni, Japan's ambassador in charge of human rights issues, to ask Radhika Coomaraswamy to modify her report. She refused on the grounds that Yoshida's testimony was only a small portion of the evidence she used for her report. In December 2015, Abe and South Korean president Park Geun-hye reached a "final and irreversible" agreement on the sexual slavery issue.[1] Abe was to issue another apology, the Japanese government was to pay about $8.3 million dedicated to the care of survivors, and the South Korean government was to refrain from making any future claims on the subject. Some survivors were not pleased with this resolution because they had no voice in its negotiation and the resolution itself did not include an admission of Japan's legal responsibility.[2] Reports that the Japanese government demanded that the South Korean government remove a statue symbolizing "comfort women" in Seoul further angered many Koreans.[3] A year later, in December 2016, the Korean Council erected another "comfort women" statue in front of the Japanese Consulate in Busan, South Korea. The Japanese government demanded its immediate removal, but this demand was not met by the new South Korean government. The Japanese government considered this a violation of the 2015 agreement, and this issue has since strained the diplomatic relationship between both countries.[4]

This period has, in short, been "busy" in connection with the issue of sexual slavery. This chapter covers both nationalist and progressive memories of this issue since 2015. To address nationalist memories, I analyze *Kokuren ga Sekai ni Hirometa "Ianfu = Seidorei" no Uso: Junēbu Kokuren Hakendan Hōkoku* [A Lie Spread All Over the World Through the United Nations, "Comfort Women = Sex Slaves": Reports by a Team that was Sent to Geneva for the United Nations' Meetings][5] edited by Fujioka Nobukatsu and published in 2016; *Ianfu Mondai no Kessan* [Settlement of the Comfort Women Issue][6] by Hata Ikuhiko, published in the same year; and articles from the newspaper *Sankei Shimbun*. Both Fujioka and Hata are historians, and I analyze their work in chapter 4 as well. In addressing progressive memories, I analyze *Q & A Chōsenjin "Ianfu" to Shokuminchi Shihai Sekinin: Anatano Gimon ni Kotaemasu* [Q & A Korean "Comfort Women" and the Responsibility for Colonization: We Will Answer Your Questions][7] edited by Kim Puja, a professor at Tokyo Gaikokugo Daigaku [Tokyo University of Foreign Studies], and Ryūta Itagaki, a sociology professor at Doshisha University (in 2015); articles from the newspaper *Asahi Shimbun*; exhibits at the Active Museum:

Onnatachi no Sensōto Heiwa Shiryōkan [Women's Active Museum on War and Peace] in Tokyo; and the 2018 documentary film *Shusenjō: The Main Battleground of the Comfort Women Issue*,[8] directed by Japanese-American filmmaker Miki Dezaki. The WAM was opened in Tokyo in 2005 by the nonprofit organization *Sensō to Josei he no Bōryoku: Research Action Center* [Violence against Women in War Research Action Center] (VAWW RAC). It is a small museum (measuring 1,238 square feet). Museum director Nishino Rumiko states that it was originally founded to preserve the memory of the Women's International Tribunal on Japan's Military Sexual Slavery, a hypothetical trial held in Tokyo in 2000 to prosecute those who were responsible for sexual slavery. The museum was founded to honor survivors of sexual slavery and "to establish a base for peace and human rights activism in order to wipe out wartime violence against women."[9] In making *Shusenjō*, Dezaki interviewed various writers and activists from across the political spectrum, including Fujioka and Yoshimi Yoshiaki, a progressive historian. *Shusenjō* received public attention in 2019 when some nationalist activists interviewed for the film sued Dezaki for not informing them of the film's commercial release (they claim that he told them that the film was a graduate project) and for misrepresenting their viewpoints, which Dezaki denied.

As this chapter covers a relatively short period, I assess works by both nationalists and progressives in detail below. The first half of the chapter covers works by nationalists, and the second half covers works by progressives. Before moving to my analysis, I briefly discuss the controversial "comfort women" statues.

"COMFORT WOMEN" STATUES

Abousnnouga and Machin argue that objects of art such as paintings and sculptures can "communicate discourses, or motivated versions of events, comprising kinds of identities, values, assessments of events."[10] The "comfort women" statues that have caused controversy all over the world need to be examined regarding the values, motivations, and assessments of events they promote.

The "Statue of Peace" or so-called "comfort women" statue was first installed in front of the Japanese Embassy in Seoul on December 11, 2011, to mark the 1000th Wednesday demonstration. The statue was created by Kim Seo-kyung and Kim Eun-sung, South Korean sculptors, and installed by the Korean Council. The same or similar statues have been erected both in and outside South Korea. The Japanese government has demanded that those near the Japanese Embassy in Seoul and the Japanese Consulate in Busan be removed as mentioned earlier. Also, as discussed later in more detail, nationalist Japanese groups and politicians have made efforts to prevent more statues from being erected outside South Korea. In some cases, these Japanese groups have failed (e.g., San Francisco, Glendale) while, in other cases, they have succeeded (e.g., Stratford, Australia).

I argue that the statues promote identification with the viewers by suggesting the ubiquity and everydayness of survivors: Anybody could have fallen victim to sexual slavery, your daughter, wife, sister, niece, friend, or even you. The statues in Seoul and Busan are life-size, approximately 160 centimeters. According to Abousnnouga and Machin, the size of statues is related to significance and power.[11] They suggest that vastly larger than life statues tend to be connected to dictatorship where "the idea is to create an imposing image."[12] By erecting a large, oversized statue, one can communicate significance yet, as Abousnnouga and Machin suggest, it can also communicate militarism at the same time. Likewise, Abousnnouga and Machin explain that elevated statues communicate loftiness.[13] The life-sized "Statue of Peace" that is not elevated may then communicate everydayness. She is just like us and among us. The statue has short unevenly cut hair though Korean women during colonial times had long hair and wore their hair braided. Kim Seo-kyung, one of the creators of the statues, explains that it signifies that her hair was forcefully cut by Japanese soldiers and that "her ties with her family and her country were severed with the sexual enslavement."[14] I also argue that her short hair promotes identification with the viewers as the statues' short bob gives off an impression of contemporariness. Today, long-braided hair is less common. With her hairstyle, she becomes one of "us."

Although the statues have features signifying the past, they seem to effectively connect the past to the present, inviting viewers to participate in their fight for redress. Abousnnouga and Machin argue that bronze signifies tradition and timelessness.[15] The bronze "comfort women" statues may be communicating the issue's timelessness—events may have occurred decades ago but the issue is timeless, violence against women during wartime. The girl wears *hanbok*, traditional Korean clothes commonly worn by women at the time, and there is an empty chair next to her. Kim Seo-kyung also explains that the empty chair is an invitation for others to sit next to her, for "comfort women" who have already passed away and anyone who wants to fight together with the survivors. Kim is quoted in Park, stating "Anyone who passes by this statue can sit on the chair and ponder what makes the old women continue their fight for over 20 years."[16] Sexual slavery occurred in the past as seen in her clothes, many survivors have already passed away, yet the issue has not been settled and it is also contemporary as seen in her hairstyle. The statues invite more people today to participate in the fight.

The statue in Seoul stares at the Japanese Embassy. Together with her clenched fists, Kim Seo-kyung also explains that it symbolizes the survivors' "determination that they will not give up until they have an apology."[17] In addition, as the statue is life size, it feels as though she is looking at us, the viewers. Abousnnouga and Machin suggest that when statues look at us, it is a form of address.[18] Just like in social interaction, when statues look at the viewers, we feel that we are acknowledged and our response is necessary. Abousnnouga and Machin argue that the kind of response required depends on "factors such as facial expression, posture and setting."[19] Considering the statue's determined facial expression and setting, in front of the Japanese Embassy where the Wednesday demonstrations take place in the case of the one in Seoul or near the Japanese Consulate in Busan, the response that the statues demand becomes obvious—participation in the fight.

The statues seem to symbolize a bridge between the past and the present: the survivors' youth and sexual slavery that happened in the past, its unsettledness and their continuing determination to continue to fight, inviting people to participate in their fight even today. The features of the statues emphasizing the everydayness of the survivors can also promote identification in observers. An examination of these seemingly innocuous statues reveals that many of the ideas symbolized by the statues are at odds with the ideas promoted by Japanese nationalists. As explained in chapter 4, Japanese nationalists deny the forceful recruitment of Korean "comfort women" by the Japanese military, they argue that "comfort women" were prostitutes as opposed to forcefully or deceitfully recruited everyday girls, and they consider the "comfort women" issue settled as a result of the 1965 bilateral agreement, and, therefore, argue that no fight for redress is necessary. Consequently, to nationalists, "comfort women" statues are "vulgar" (Hata)[20] and should not be erected especially in the West.

ANALYSIS OF CONSERVATIVE MEMORIES

By examining the works of nationalist scholars and activists, several themes have emerged: (1) antiprogressive arguments, (2) arguments on how the "comfort women" issue and Japan are presented in the international community, (3) denial of "comfort women" as sex slaves, (4) anti-Korean and anti-Chinese sentiments, (5) mixed evaluations of the 2015 bilateral agreement, and (6) opposition to the Kōno Statement of 1993. Below, I address each of these in turn. Most of these works simply critique certain memories of sexual slavery or how those memories have been constructed and promoted rather than constructing or promoting particular memories of their own. As a result, the "comfort women" issue has developed into an intense memory war between progressives and nationalists.

Antiprogressive Arguments

As the first theme, antiprogressive arguments dominate the nationalist commentary on the "comfort women" issue. Nationalists are against the progressive movement in general, and call progressives "hannichi sayoku" [anti-Japanese left wingers] (e.g., Fujiki).[21] They specifically target certain progressive figures and media outlets, such as lawyer Totsuka Etsurō, historian Yoshimi Yoshiaki, and the newspaper *Asahi Shimbun*. There are several subthemes under the general theme of antiprogressive arguments: (1) general antiprogressive sentiments, and attacks on (2) Totsuka Etsurō, (3) Yoshimi Yoshiaki, and (4) the *Asahi Shimbun*.

General Antiprogressive Sentiments

General antiprogressive sentiments are prevalent among Japanese nationalists. For instance, in Fujioka's edited anthology *Kokuren ga Sekai ni Hirometa "Ianfu = Seidorei" no Uso: Junēbu Kokuren Hakendan Hōkoku*, Fujioka and others argue that the "lie" that "comfort women" were sex slaves has been spread all over the world by anti-Japan Japanese left wingers' NGOs. This is similar to what we saw in a previous chapter when nationalists argued that anti-Japan Japanese left wingers created the "comfort women" issue. In writing about attending the meetings of the UNHRC for the first time from 2015 to 2016, these nationalist writers argue that Japanese left-wing NGOs have continuously submitted proposals, for the last twenty years, that the UNHRC recognize "comfort women" as sex slaves. They further state that most members of the UNHRC are not familiar with the "comfort women" issue and that they therefore believe everything proposed by these left wingers.[22]

For example, nationalist activist Fujiki's chapter in Fujioka's anthology states that he met a Japanese employee of the UN at one of the UNHRC meetings who lamented the presence of Japanese left wingers. According to Fujiki, this person stated:

> The origin of the misunderstanding of the comfort women issue is the result of false information disseminated by anti-Japanese left wingers. I really appreciate your organization coming to the United Nations to counter-argue. (My translation)[23]

Fujiki concludes that nationalists should continue to attend these UNHRC meetings in order to prevent anti-Japan left wingers from spreading their lies and fabrications. Like other nationalists, Fujiki refers to progressives as *hannichi sayoku* (anti-Japan left wingers). At the same time, he denies the charge that nationalists are "rekishi shusei shugisha," or historical revisionists as progressives refer to them, saying:

> First, we should insist that it was the left-wingers, not us, who revised history. To this end, we should disseminate the truth about the comfort women issue by submitting our documents to the [human rights] committee. (My translation)[24]

To Fujiki, progressives' framing of the "comfort women issue" is nothing more than fabrication. Yamamoto Yumiko, the president of the NGO *Nadeshiko Akushon* [Japanese Women for Justice and Peace], also attended these UNHRC meetings. She suggests in the same anthology that the "comfort women" issue became an issue of global concern because of anti-Japan Japanese left wingers. She explains that Japanese progressive NGOs submit proposals to the UNHRC requesting an inquiry into the government's handling of the "comfort women" issue, and that these proposals usually cite the *Asahi Shimbun*. These proposals spark an inquiry that, although disputed by the Japanese government, results in the committee setting several recommendations for the Japanese government to follow. This result is widely reported by the *Asahi Shimbun*. She argues that the entire issue has been fabricated by an alliance of progressive publications and activists.[25]

Attacks on Totsuka Etsurō

Nationalists have also criticized Japanese lawyer Totsuka Etsurō's reference to "comfort women" as sex slaves at UNHRC meetings. Nationalists see Totsuka as the originator of the idea that "comfort women" were sex slaves. Fujioka points out that from 1984 onward, Totsuka attended UNHRC meetings and submitted various proposals on human rights issues in Japan, but his proposals received no attention. However, Fujioka explains that members of the UNHRC suddenly paid attention to Totsuka when he used the term "sex slaves."[26] Similarly, Fujiki harshly criticizes Totsuka while recalling a conversation he had with him in Geneva in which the latter was "pushing his one-sided argument and changing subjects, which is typical of left-wingers."[27] However, in the chapter's rendering of that conversation, it does not appear as though Totsuka changed the subject, and he seemed to have answered all of Fujiki's questions. Instead, it seems as though Fujiki is seeking an argument and is trying to make it personal. For example, Fujiki criticizes Totsuka for saying, "I like human rights" by saying that it seems that every political question is a matter of personal preference to Totsuka. Furthermore, he asked Totsuka whether he thought slavery by white people was acceptable but slavery by Japanese people was unacceptable, which Totsuka denied. Fujiki continued, asserting that Japan was the only country that insisted on the abolition of slavery (which is false), and Totsuka denied this as well. In response to Totsuka stating that individual abolitionist efforts were, historically, more important than nations' abolitionist efforts and Totsuka adding that he liked the fact that Roosevelt coined the term "human rights," Fujiki mentions that Totsuka believed that Japan was evil and that white people were morally superior,[28] which was a clear and intentional misunderstanding of what Totsuka said in this conversation.

Attacks on Yoshimi Yoshiaki

Nationalist writers also criticize historian Yoshimi Yoshiaki, whose work is analyzed in the previous chapter. For instance, Hata argues that Yoshimi initially claimed that Korean women were forcibly mobilized by Japanese officials, but has since shifted his position to argue that these women lived as sex slaves at comfort stations because there is no documentary evidence of forced mobilization. Hata also relates an anecdote in which he asked Yoshimi whether he thought that "comfort women" were actually sex slaves in light of the reports of Alex Yorichi, a Japanese-American soldier who interviewed captured Korean comfort women and their Japanese proprietors in Burma in 1944. Yorichi's report indicated that "comfort women" had luxurious lives and were able to attend various events together with soldiers. Hata states that Yoshimi simply affirmed without providing evidence or reasoning. In response, Hata asserts that Yoshimi must have already made up his mind before seeking evidence (or a lack thereof), and that there is no room in Yoshimi's mind for argument.[29]

Attacks on the Asahi Shimbun

Nationalists also express antipathy toward the *Asahi Shimbun* on this issue. They argue that the newspaper spreads "the lie" that comfort women were sex slaves in tandem with the anti-Japan left wingers mentioned above. For instance, many authors from Fujioka's anthology and Hata's work criticize the newspaper's 1992 report on Yoshimi's discovery of documents that proved the involvement of the Japanese imperial military in the "comfort" system. Both Fujioka and Hata assert that the existence of the documents had been known to researchers before 1992, and that the documents actually proved the military's "good involvement" in the system. They argue that military officials ordered Japanese officials in China not to select vicious recruiters who would kidnap women, whereas Yoshimi argues that the order was intended for recruitment in Japan. They argue, nonetheless, that the newspaper reported the findings so that readers would think that the documents and the government's actions had been hidden from the public. Fujioka and

Hata also suspect that the documents' "discovery" must have been carefully planned because they were made public with perfect timing: three Korean former "comfort women" sued the Japanese government in December 1991, the newspaper reported that the documents had been found in January 1992, and then-Japanese prime minister Miyazawa Kiichi was scheduled to visit South Korea during the same month. This chain of events resulted in Miyazawa offering repeated apologies to the South Korean people during his visit.[30]

Similarly, in Takahashi Shinrō's chapter in Fujioka's anthology, he accuses the *Asahi Shimbun* of citing now-discredited books by Seiji Yoshida to incorrectly report that the Japanese military forcibly mobilized 80,000–200,000 Korean women under the pretense of the labor corps.[31] Likewise, Kawaguchi Mann Emi, a journalist who also contributed to Fujioka's anthology, blames the *Asahi Shimbun*, and the Western, South Korean, and Chinese media for spreading anti-Japanese messages.[32] In light of the *Asahi Shimbun*'s reporting on the UNHRC's recommendations to the Japanese government regarding the "comfort women" issue, many nationalists argue that Japanese who trust the UN are being brainwashed into believing that "comfort women" were indeed sex slaves, although these recommendations are unduly influenced by anti-Japan Japanese left wingers such as the editors of *Asahi Shimbun*.[33] Member of Japan's Liberal Democratic Party, Sugita Mio and Fujii Mitsuhiko, a nationalist activist, argue in the same anthology that the *Asahi Shimbun* has defamed Japan in the international community with false reports and has consequently violated the human rights of the Japanese people.[34] Likewise, when commenting on how the *Asahi Shimbun* retracted its articles that cited Yoshida, Hata criticizes the newspaper's continued emphasis on the Japanese government's "coerciveness" and "the involvement of the military" by citing some isolated cases of individual war crimes that occurred in China and Indonesia.[35]

Similarly, the nationalist newspaper *Sankei Shimbun* criticizes the *Asahi Shimbun* for spreading the "lie" that "comfort women" were sex slaves, citing Yoshida's now-discredited testimony.[36] In an October 13, 2018, article in the *Sankei Shimbun*, Yamaoka Tesshū, a nationalist activist who leads the Australian-Japan Community Network (AJCN), criticizes the *Asahi Shimbun* severely for preventing their English-language articles that correct the newspaper's confusion around "comfort women" with the Labor Corps from appearing on Internet search engines.[37] Yamaoka and American lawyer Kent Gilbert coauthored another article for the newspaper on August 12, 2018, which details their experience of going to the *Asahi Shimbun*'s headquarters to file a complaint. They criticize the *Asahi Shimbun*'s coverage of the "comfort women" issue in its English-language articles, for example, the newspaper's description of "comfort women" as those "who were forced to provide sex to Japanese soldiers before and during World War II." They argue that the newspaper's coverage contradicts itself because the *Asahi Shimbun* had admitted that the evidence it used (i.e., Yoshida's books) to make these assertions was fabricated. They add that although they repeatedly requested that the paper modify its coverage, the *Asahi Shimbun* refused, contending that it did not state that the military kidnapped women and made them sex slaves. However, Yamaoka and Gilbert counterargue that English speakers would assume that the military actually kidnapped women and made them sex slaves if they read the passage. Their specific requests for the newspaper are as follows:

1) Not to use the phrase, "forced to provide sex," from now on;
2) Run an additional article explaining that Yoshida's books was fabrications and that the newspaper retracted its articles citing Yoshida's testimony;
3) If the *Asahi Shimbun* insists that the above expression does not mean the military's forceful mobilization or sexual slavery, they should clearly explain what exactly they mean; and
4) If the *Asahi Shimbun* adds a description of comfort women, it should be "Comfort women who worked in brothels regulated by the military authorities." (My translation)[38]

Yamaoka and Gilbert see the assertion that "comfort women" were forcefully mobilized by the Japanese military and made into sex slaves as a lie that should be corrected. This contradicts progressives' perspective that a lack of official documents that reveal the military's role in forceful mobilization does not mean that it never happened. Indeed, progressives argue that even if women were deceitfully recruited into the system, it should be still considered "coercion" because they were forced to have sex with soldiers against their will. To nationalists, progressives who are anti-Japan left wingers have created the myth of the "comfort women" as sex slaves and nationalists have made efforts to stop them.

How the "Comfort Women" Issue and Japan Are Presented in the International Community

The next theme concerns how the "comfort women" issue and Japan are presented in the international community, especially in Western countries. This theme seems to have become more important to nationalists lately, possibly because of various events surrounding the issue outside Japan, which threaten nationalist writers, including the U.S. Congress's 2007 resolution that calls on the Japanese government to make an unequivocal apology and the erection of "comfort women" statues around the world since 2013. As these events attract international attention to the "comfort women" issue and its history, the issue's relation to perceptions of Japan has become an important bone of contention for Japanese nationalists. Here, it is important to note that nationalist writers see "the international community" as synonymous with "the West"—they are more concerned with Western perceptions of the issue and of Japan than, for example, Chinese or Thai perceptions. Consciously or unconsciously, these nationalist commentators reinforce Western hegemony by adopting these positions.

For instance, Hata sees that the international community believes that Japanese authorities forcibly mobilized Korean women as "comfort women," and that "comfort women" were sex slaves. Hata and other nationalists seem to consider the spread of this so-called misunderstanding of the "comfort women" issue a result of South Korea's (and, for some, China's) aggressive efforts to spread this "lie" (Hata calls this South Korea's "tsugeguchi gaiko" or "tattletale diplomacy").[39] Hata summarizes South Korea's public relations efforts as follows:

1) Appeals to the U.S. Congress, as well as other local and national governments in the United States and Europe to pass resolutions to criticize Japan,
2) The erection of "comfort women" statues with a description of Japan forcibly mobilizing 200,000 Korean women for sexual slavery in various places in the world such as in Glendale in the United States,
3) Publication of testimonies of comfort women in English, and
4) Application for the inclusion of comfort women narratives in the UNESCO's Memory of the World Register. (My translation)[40]

The spread of the view that "comfort women" were sex slaves across the world is seen by Japanese nationalists as a "Korean and Chinese conspiracy" in collaboration with Japanese left-wing activists.

Nationalist writers often cite the erection of "comfort women" statues as evidence of this conspiracy. Yamaoka and Mera Koichi each contributed chapters to Fujioka's anthology, addressing the issue of such statues in the United States and Australia. Hata argues that Japanese embassies around the world should take *preventative* action as soon as they discover any plans to erect such "vulgar" statues as "comfort women" statues since it would be too late to suggest that such statues not be erected after a local government has already voted to do so.[41]

This theme of international perceptions of the "comfort women" issue and Japan also manifests in the form of anti-UN sentiments. Some nationalists argue that the UN should take some responsibility for spreading the "lie" that "comfort women" were sex slaves to the international community. For proof, we need to look no further than the title of Fujioka's anthology. Many of the anthology's contributors depict the UN as an incompetent organization controlled by the former Allied countries. These authors argue that the members of the UNHRC mostly come from Third World countries where human rights violations occur far more frequently than in Japan, and that these committee members are unfamiliar with Japanese history and society and are thus easily influenced by anti-Japan left-wing Japanese activists.[42] Hisae Kennedy writes in Fujioka's anthology that although Japan pays the second-highest amount of money to the UN, it has comparatively little influence over UN matters. Kennedy argues that the UN continues to criticize Japan by connecting the "comfort women" issue to human rights issues, and states that she does not believe that there are human rights violations in Japan that would require intervention by the UN.[43] Fujioka even calls these UN committees "Sayoku no Soukutsu" [Dens of Left-Wingers] and uses this term as a heading in one of his chapters: "Kokuren Iinkai ha Sayoku no Soukutsu" [The UN Committees are Dens of Left-Wingers].[44]

Hata also agrees that the UN has played an important role in spreading the "lie" about "comfort women" as sex slaves. He states that Japanese and South Korean groups have succeeded in spreading "lies" about "forceful mobilization" and "sex slaves" in the international community by persistently placing these ideas before the UNHRC. Hata argues that the UN has been exploited by Koreans and Japanese left wingers.

Denial of "Comfort Women" as Sex Slaves

As they did during the previous period between 1991 and 2014, nationalists have lately denied that "comfort women" were sex slaves and have argued that "comfort women" were prostitutes and that the survivors who came forward were lying for financial gain. However, nationalists' messages seem to have been toned down in comparison to the earlier period. This may be because, as some of the contributors to Fujioka's anthology suggest, they believe that there is no documentary evidence of the forced mobilization of "comfort women" and, therefore, women were not sex slaves, and that this idea is already established within Japan as seen in a lack of descriptions of "comfort women" in Japanese history textbooks. Nonetheless, nationalists argue that survivors are lying, citing inconsistencies and mistakes in some of their testimonies. (As discussed later, progressive writers criticize nationalists for their tendency to deny the entire issue by pointing out some of the inconsistencies in these testimonials.)

For instance, Fujioka denies the testimony of Chong Ok-sun, a North Korean survivor who was quoted in the 1996 Coomaraswamy report. Chong stated that she was taken to a military base in Korea with over 5,000 soldiers, and recalled that there were about 400 "comfort women" at the base. She was also quoted as stating that when one of the Korean "comfort women" questioned why they had to serve forty soldiers every day, she was stripped naked and killed by being rolled over a nail board. Chong also testified that some "comfort women" were thrown into pools filled with snakes and were also buried alive. Citing Hata, Fujioka indicates that there were no military "comfort" stations in Korea during the war because Korea was not a war zone. However, he points out that there were civilian brothels in Korea at the time. Fujioka suggests that these testimonies were fabricated by North Korean agents and that they had made a fatal mistake by exaggerating the means of torture and death that was supposedly witnessed at the base. He states that both stories, being killed on a nail board and in a pond with snakes, are not realistic but, especially being killed in a pond with snakes sounds absurd. Fujioka states that it does not make sense at all and he questions whether the Japanese military had that much time and money. He points out that members of the Asian Women Fund who quoted Chong's testimony from the Coomaraswamy report dropped her witness account of "comfort women" being killed in pools of snakes. Citing the nationalist journalist Sakurai Yoshiko, Fujioka suggests that even progressives thought that Chong's testimony was ridiculous and must have dropped it to maintain the seeming credibility of the Coomaraswamy report. Fujioka further argues that the Asian Women Fund was funded by taxpayer money, yet that those who were operating the fund had deliberately tried to hide the fact that Chong was lying from the general public.[45]

Likewise, Hata cites the testimony of Sim Mi-ja and criticizes it for being illogical. According to her, as a twelve-year-old in the northern part of the Korean Peninsula she was taken to a police station and raped and tortured there. She lost consciousness and found herself in a comfort station in Fukuoka, Japan when she awoke. Hata finds her testimony suspicious, stating that it is unlikely that she was unconscious during her long journey from northern Korea to the southern port town of Busan by train, then to Shimonoseki, Japan by ship, then to Moji, Japan by ship, and then to Fukuoka by train. He argues that it would have been easier if they had simply waited until she woke up. Hata also discusses the case of Lee Yong-soo, whom he brands as a liar. According to Hata, while testifying in front of the U.S. Congress in 2007 she claimed that she had been deceitfully recruited by civilian recruiters. However, two weeks later, she claimed at a press conference in Japan that she had been forcefully taken by soldiers who came into her house in the middle of the night. He claims that she changed her story back again after someone seated next to her whispered something in her ear.[46]

Nationalist writers also deny that "comfort women" were sex slaves, arguing that these women were not treated badly. As in the previous period, they cite Yorichi's interviews with captured Korean "comfort women" in Burma.

Hata presents some additional arguments to support the idea that "comfort women" were not sex slaves. He argues that these women earned about seventy times more than average Japanese soldiers did—even more than the commanding officer in Burma. He also argues that the women's lives were not that bad because the military had banned drinking, eating, and violence at "comfort" stations and improved the women's salaries in the hopes of improving their services to soldiers. He also states that these women were able to leave the comfort stations and return home once they repaid their debts, and that there was no forceful mobilization (except for a few isolated cases) on the grounds that he found old newspaper advertisements recruiting "comfort women" for high salaries.[47] Thus, he argues, it is evident that the Japanese military did not have to forcibly recruit women—being a "comfort woman" was, in his view, more like a job than a hardship. He also cites another U.S. report that states that "comfort women" were "nothing more than prostitutes" to support his argument. The underlying idea in these works by nationalists resonates with Western Orientalists' idea of Orientals as untrustworthy liars.[48]

Anti-Korean and Anti-Chinese Sentiments

The next theme that emerged from nationalist writers is their anti-Chinese and anti-Korean sentiments as observed among nationalists during the previous period. Nationalist writers tend to argue that Koreans and Chinese are connected to anti-Japanese left wingers within Japan who are active in the redress movement. Recently, nationalists cited the erection of statues commemorating "comfort women" within South Korea and abroad as evidence of a Chinese and South and North Korean conspiracy. According to these authors, authorities from these countries—especially China and North Korea—have undertaken this conspiracy to advance their ultimate agenda of severing the ties among Japan, South Korea, and the United States. We can ubiquitously see Orientalist ideas in nationalists' anti-Korean and anti-Chinese descriptions.

Kennedy suggests that although the 2015 bilateral treaty between Japan and South Korea was positively received in the West, the Chinese government was dissatisfied by the treaty. She argues that the treaty represented a drawback for Beijing, which has always attempted to foster distrust between Japan and South Korea as a means of eventually severing ties between Japan and the United States.[49] Fujioka also cites a report by the AJCN led by Yamaoka, who successfully prevented the erection of a statue symbolizing "comfort women" in Stratford, Australia in 2015. The report calls upon the U.S. and Australian governments to refrain from provoking anti-Japan sentiments, fearing that such sentiments in South Korea will be exploited by China. According to Fujioka, China is attempting to expand its influence in the Asia-Pacific region by fomenting anti-Japanese sentiments in South Korea and attempting to disrupt the ties among South Korea, Japan, the United States, and Australia.[50] Fujiki argues that anti-Japanese sentiments were not very strong in South Korea until the late 1980s, and that these feelings were fostered by the actions of the North Korean government.[51] We can observe an Orientalist paternalistic view[52] of South Koreans in which they assume that South Koreans are manipulated to hate the Japanese by the communist governments of China and North Korea.

In addition, these writers unequivocally depict Chinese and Koreans as shameless, vulgar people with anti-Japanese views. For instance, Yamaoka labels Chinese and Koreans as "sneaky," emotional, anti-Japanese peoples when writing about his experience of preventing the erection of a "comfort women" statue in Stratford, Australia. He explains that the vice-mayor of the city, who was Korean Australian, submitted a proposal to erect the statue on March 25, 2014, and that a city council meeting on the topic was scheduled for April 1. The timing of the meeting strikes Yamaoka as unusually sudden, and he concludes that Korean and Chinese interests had motivated the decision to erect the statue made in advance. When describing the city council meeting itself, Yamaoka states that Chinese and Korean speakers gave speeches in broken English, showed no manners, and reports that their speeches were merely emotional and aggressive. He describes the activities of Chinese and Korean groups as fueled by "flames of uncontrollable hate" [yokusei dekinai zouo no honoo],[53] in contrast to himself and other Japanese delegates whom he describes as civilized, polite, and calm.[54] This dichotomy between emotional, irrational Koreans and Chinese and calm, civilized Japanese is reminiscent of the distinction between an "advanced" West and a "backward" East by Western imperialists."[55]

Similarly, a *Sankei Shimbun* article from May 6, 2018, quotes a South Korean woman to illustrate how South Koreans are simple-minded, irrational people. The article explains that the woman, while watching a demonstration in South Korea on television, reported that North Korea must have been behind the demonstration because South Koreans are incapable of acting with unity and cooperation. In contrast, she stated that North Koreans are conditioned to such behavior, having lived under a totalitarian regime for a long time. She refers to a popular saying which states that in a fight between a Japanese and a Korean, the Korean will win because they are physically larger people; however, in a fight between two Japanese and two Koreans, the Japanese will win because the two Koreans would fight with each other instead of as a team.[56] The passage resonates with Orientalist representations of Orientals as being incapable of cooperation and coordination among themselves.[57] Again, in these Orientalist descriptions, irrational, emotional, simple-minded, and aggressive Koreans are contrasted with rational and calm Japanese.

The *Sankei Shimbun* also patronizes South Korea by describing it as a democratically underdeveloped nation, which corresponds with Western Orientalists' perceptions of the Orient as "lamentably under-humanized, antidemocratic, backward, [and] barbaric."[58] A January 19, 2019, article authored by Kurota describes how South Korea's criminal justice system is based on appeals to emotion rather than rigorous and rational legal institutions. The article explains the South Korean practice of photo-lining, wherein suspects in criminal cases are forced to answer questions from the media. These press conferences are often attended by rowdy members of the general public, which makes for a "very Korean scenery." Kurota argues that South Korean criminal justice focuses on humiliating suspects, not on prosecuting them under the law; it is a public spectacle, and not a reliable measure of justice. Kurota is bothered by this practice because, in his view, it influences Japan's diplomatic relationship with South Korea. Kurota describes that he wishes that South Korea would rethink its "hannichi aikoku muzai" [being anti-Japan equals patriotism rather than guilt] based on emotionalism. Kurota notes that South Korea is simply accusing Japan because it is more easily swayed by emotions rather than actually following the law and logic.[59] Kurota's example also depicts South Koreans as a perverse, bizarre people with a strange practice as Orientals were depicted by Western Orientalists.[60]

The Sankei Shimbun also presents the South Korean government and Korean people abroad as erecting statues of "comfort women" simply to promote their anti-Japanese agenda. For instance, an article from November 22, 2018, states that the "comfort women" statue in front of the Japanese Embassy in Seoul is symbolic of the anti-Japanese movement.[61] Likewise, another article from October 14, 2018, strongly criticizes those statues abroad as anti-Japanese. The article argues that those statues were erected in order to rouse anti-Japanese public opinion and harm Japan's relationships with its allies.[62] In another article, Mera Koichi, a conservative activist whose chapter also appears in Fujioka's anthology, recalls the unveiling ceremony for one of these statues in New Jersey: "At the opening ceremony, Korean drums were played, speeches criticizing Japan were delivered, and it was an anti-Japan event." He calls the speeches at the event "hate speech." He also indicates that a Korean organization is to perform a musical titled, "Comfort Women," and speculates that the content must be anti-Japanese.[63] In short, for Mera, the event was Korean anti-Japanese propaganda. His view is echoed among nationalists in general, who see Koreans as essentially anti-Japan and believe that promoting anti-Japan messages in the world is their utmost agenda, which is similar to Orientalists' depictions of Muslims as maintaining unrelenting hatred toward Christians and Jews.[64]

However, this is not all: these authors also assert that South Korea is a deceitful country that pursues the "comfort women" issue for financial gain. Fujioka states that, just as North Korea will never give up its nuclear weapon program, South Korea will never let the "comfort women" issue go because it is a useful way to pressure Japan for money—Fujioka calls this the "victim business" [higaisha bizinesu]. Similarly, journalist Ōtaka Miki writes in the *Sankei Shimbun* that South Korea brings up historical issues whenever it asks Japan for economic assistance and loans. For instance, when the history textbook issue happened in 1982 (i.e., the Japanese Education Ministry ordering textbook authors to replace "invasion" with "advancement" regarding the former Japanese military's actions in Asia), Japanese prime minister Nakasone Yasuhiro announced that Japan would lend South Korea $400 million. She concludes her article expressing her suspicion that President Moon may attempt to use the "comfort women" issue to squeeze more money from Japan.[65]

Nationalists also depict Koreans and Chinese as corrupt people who bribe corrupt local politicians in the United States to facilitate the installation of "comfort women" statues. Regarding the statue in Glendale, California, Kennedy explains that a Korean businessman living in Los Angeles invited Glendale's mayor and four city council members to South Korea. The mayor turned down the offer, but the others went along. "We only have to imagine how they were entertained in South Korea,"[66] says Kennedy, but afterward, two former "comfort women" suddenly visited Glendale and narrated their stories in tears, surprising the mayor. Several weeks later, the Korean businessman suddenly introduced the idea of erecting a "comfort women" statue in Glendale. Immediately afterward, the council members decided to sign on to sister city agreements with two South Korean cities. Kennedy adds that the city had already ordered the statue even before the city council voted on whether to build it, which indicates that they were very confident that the proposal would pass. She states that the city's mayor was the only city official who was opposed to the idea.[67] In short, Kennedy implies that the four council members who went to South Korea were bribed, and only the mayor was not corrupt and could therefore make the "right" judgment to not support the erection of the statue.

When discussing a statue symbolizing "comfort women" in Union City, New Jersey, Kennedy argues that Korean officials intentionally target American cities where local officials are corrupt:

> If you look at other local cities, they are very similar. One reason may be that they want votes from Korean Americans. By pretending to seriously work on the issue of women's rights from 70 years ago, city council members seem to be attempting to distract from their own corruption. It seems that communists

in China, South Korea, and Japan are targeting these corrupt politicians. (My translation)[68]

In Kennedy's mind, only corrupt U.S. officials support the erection of "comfort women" statues and uncorrupt politicians do not. She argues that the so-called anti-Japanese agenda represented by the statues is pushed by communists from Japan, China, and Korea; she ties most anti-Japanese statements or anybody who criticizes Japan for the "comfort women" issue to communism. She describes former U.S. president Barack Obama as a communist because he called on Japan to reflect on its history, including the "comfort women" issue.[69]

We can see Hata's anti-Korean sentiments in his description of the South Korean government's treatment of South Korea's past sex crimes. He asserts that throughout the 2010s, knowledge of various past sex crimes committed by the South Korean military was made public, for example, the existence of government-organized comfort stations around U.S. military bases in South Korea, and the fact that South Korean "comfort women" were forced to serve American soldiers. Although prostitution has been illegal in South Korea since 1946, the South Korean government encouraged these women to work in the comfort stations to earn foreign currency. As a result, as Hata writes, 122 former "comfort women" sued the South Korean government, seeking apologies and compensation. He also indicates that the South Korean military had similar comfort stations involving Korean women during the Korean War, and that it also maintained comfort stations in Vietnam during the Vietnam War, using Vietnamese women. He states that this was and remains largely unreported by the South Korean media. For Hata, this is an issue of hypocrisy: whereas former "comfort women" who served the Japanese military are now considered sacred in South Korean society and receive financial support from the government, former "comfort women" for the U.S. military are still seen as dirty and are ignored by society.[70] This is similar to the theme of the "comfort" system as a universal practice from the previous period, which was used to justify Japan's "comfort" system. The issue is about women's well-being, dignity, and rights. Other nations committing similar crimes should not exonerate Japan.

Hata and the *Sankei Shimbun* criticize not only the South Korean government but also the major Korean support organization for survivors of sexual slavery, namely, the Korean Council for the Women Drafted for Sexual Slavery by Japan (the Korean Council for Justice and Remembrance since 2016). For instance, Hata argues that survivors' testimonies relayed to the public by the Korean Council tend to be more dramatic than truthful because the Korean Council seeks to stir anti-Japanese emotions. Furthermore, he argues that the Korean Council avoids being questioned about inconsistencies in testimonials and that they introduce testimonies without key details, including who deceitfully recruited these women. He also argues that it is unnatural that there are no testimonies stating that these women were deceived by Koreans, because very few Japanese spoke Korean well enough to deceive Koreans during the colonial period. Hata argues that survivors' testimonies tend to be rather ambiguous and unconvincing. Hata also argues that the Korean Council is tied to and acts in the interests of North Korea. He states that the husband and a sister-in law of the Korean Council's current president were arrested for being North Korean spies in 1993, and that, therefore, it is no surprise that the Korean Council and other similar organizations are anti-Japanese and anti-American.[71] The *Sankei Shimbun* echoes similar sentiments. In articles dated February 17 and March 21, 2018, Ōtaka describes the Korean Council as a secret North Korean agency that is attempting to disrupt South Korean–Japanese relations by fostering anti-Japanese sentiments around the world. She also argues that the Korean Council suppresses freedom of speech by suing people who attempt to reveal the true nature of the "comfort women" issue.[72] Hata also criticizes the Korean Council's hypocrisy in despising the former "comfort women" who served the U.S. military and differentiating them from the heroic "comfort women" who served the Japanese imperial military.[73] As we will see in the latter part of this chapter, this is not the case.

Not only is South Korea presented as an "irrational, emotional, underdeveloped country," but Japan is also presented as rational in comparison. For instance, an article dated February 1, 2018, from the *Sankei Shimbun* describes Japan as dealing with the Moon administration's handling of the 2015 bilateral agreement calmly, like an adult, and describes South Korea as acting like a child by not keeping its promises. The same article also praises Prime Minister Abe's statement in response to President Moon's criticism of the bilateral agreement: "An agreement is a promise between nations and maintaining it is an international principle." The article asserts that South Korean demands for apologies should have ended after the bilateral agreement.[74] These authors use an Orientalist framework to describe Japan as a country of sincere, reasonable people who are continually and unfairly forced to apologize, and South Korea as a country of deceitful and sneaky people who unjustly demand further apologies. Just as a comparison between Orientals and Occidentals led to inequality between the two as discussed by Said,[75] the comparison between Japan and South Korea affirms Japan's superiority over South Korea.

Mixed Evaluations of the 2015 Bilateral Agreement

The next theme is nationalists' mixed responses to the bilateral agreement of 2015. As mentioned earlier, some survivors opposed the 2015 bilateral resolution because they felt that their voices were not heard in the agreement. The fact that the Japanese government wanted the "comfort women" statue in Seoul to be removed caused even more opposition. Interestingly, the 2015 resolution was not welcomed by some of the Japanese nationalists. Some saw the resolution as a big mistake and asserted that the Japanese government had conceded too much unnecessarily.

Fujioka severely criticizes the resolution in his anthology. His first problem with the resolution is that then-Japanese foreign minister Kishida Fumio admitted, when announcing the resolution on December 28, 2015, in his statement, that the "comfort" system was operated under "the involvement of the military" [gun no kanyo]. Fujioka senses malicious intent behind this phrase because the *Asahi Shimbun* used the same phrase to "fabricate" the "comfort women" issue when it reported on the discovery of official documents that prove the military's involvement in 1992. Fujioka further argues that the Kōno Statement of 1993 also used the phrase. Fujioka indignantly claims that, when the Kōno Statement was issued, the majority of the Japanese were still "deceived" as to the truth of the "comfort women" issue. However, by the time Kishida made his statement, the use of "the involvement of the military" was inexcusable because the *Asahi Shimbun* had admitted that its source (Yoshida's confessions) was unreliable. As mentioned above, Fujioka and other nationalists argue that, because Yoshida's confessions were proven to be fabricated, the military was not involved in the forceful mobilization of "comfort women." He argues that the military *was* involved in the "comfort" system for practical reasons—the "comfort women's" proprietors could not have operated "comfort" stations without the military's permission—but that it did not actively manage the stations. He argues that the military's involvement was "good" because they regulated the stations' operations, prices, and sanitation to protect the women from exploitation. Yet, unlike "what actually happened," Fujioka argues that this "involvement" created a negative impression.[76]

Fujioka also criticizes Kishida's statement that this issue "deeply damaged the honor and dignity of women." In response, Fujioka asks, "What about the honor of Japanese soldiers who died for their country?."[77] He opines that Japanese soldiers, the ancestors of contemporary Japanese citizens, have been wrongfully accused of being rapists, perverts, and serial killers. He argues that, if the honor and dignity of these women were damaged, it was a result of their being engaged in prostitution, and that by that same logic, the Japanese government should apologize to former Japanese prostitutes who worked under Japan's legal prostitution system at the time.

Fujioka also criticizes the Japanese government's promise to pay 100 million yen (about $8.3 million) from taxpayer funds. Fujioka points out that the Japanese government had long considered the reparations issue settled by the 1965 bilateral treaty between both nations and laments that the Japanese government itself reneged on this understanding. He argues that if the Japanese government paid even a small amount, it would have admitted its wrongdoing to the international community. Fujioka states that "South Korea cannot be trusted to keep a promise and, by treating the country as an equal, Japan has become a second-class country that cannot keep an international treaty itself."[78] Here again, we see an Orientalist depiction of South Korea as Orientals were considered deceitful[79] and untrustworthy[80] by Western Orientalists.

Fujioka also states that the resolution is supposed to be "final and irreversible," but because Japan reneged on the 1965 treaty, South Korea will continue to bring up the issue expecting Japan to pay every time. He even predicts that South Korea will never let the "comfort women" issue go because it is profitable for them.[81]

Fujioka's final criticisms are that South Korea promised to "make an effort" to remove the statues of the "comfort women," and that the two nations agreed that they would not criticize each other at the UN or at other international meetings. He argues that while the 2015 treaty does not bind Korean redress organizations that criticize Japan, because they are civilian organizations, it makes it difficult for the Japanese government to refute these "misunderstandings."[82]

In contrast, Hata reacts positively to the 2015 resolution. He considers it a good deal for Japan, but expresses negative views toward South Korea. In a chapter from his book, he recounts a conversation he had with *Sankei Shimbun* journalist Abiru Rui. Abiru considered the resolution a Japanese victory, because Japan did not have to include the word "kyōseirenkō" [forceful mobilization], in the statement, which South Korea had long insisted upon. Abiru also considers the resolution a win because it has the potential to stop South Korea from continuing its so-called tattletale diplomacy. Hata and Abiru also voice suspicions that the United States may have pressured Japan and South Korea to arrive at an agreement to settle regional security concerns.[83] Throughout their dialogue, Hata and Abiru make derogatory remarks about South Korea: "Japan is like a big brother of South Korea," "South Korea is never consistent,"[84] "Korean leaders stated, upon Japan's annexation of Korea, that Koreans could not govern on their own,"[85] and "[i]t is impossible for South Korea to have democracy."[86] Although Fujioka, Hata, and Abiru have different opinions on the resolution, they share an anti-Korean view. Their patronizing view of Korea is consistent with an Orientalist view of Orientals, "Orientals have never understood the meaning of self-government the way 'we' do,"[87] which justified Western colonization of the Orient.

Opposition to the Kōno Statement of 1993

Another theme that emerged from nationalist circles most recently is opposition to the 1993 Kōno Statement. This opposition was reenergized by a 2013 *Sankei* report that described the Japanese government's "not-so-thorough" research in preparation for the Kōno Statement and examined the statement's drafting in 2014.

Hata criticizes the Kōno Statement severely for relying solely on unreliable survivor testimonies because the Japanese government could not find documentary evidence of military-ordered forced mobilization. He explains that Japanese government officials interviewed sixteen Korean survivors who were introduced by the Association for the Pacific War Victims in South Korea but that they could not even confirm some of the women's names or birth dates. The officials only had about three hours to interview each survivor—Hata estimates that in reality they must have had a little over an hour, considering the time required for translation. He relates that the interviews were conducted in the presence of the survivors' supporters who made it impossible to ask follow-up questions. As a result, he argues, many of these testimonies do not make sense: for instance, three of the sixteen survivors testified that they were sent to "comfort" stations within Japan. He argues that these women must have actually been sent to civilian brothels and were merely confused about their situation. Furthermore, four of the survivors seemed to have been sent to civilian brothels, which would not make them "military" comfort women. He also points out that some of the survivors gave inconsistent testimonies, especially with respect to their recruitment. In sum, he criticizes Kōno Yohei and other Japanese government officials who helped Kōno draft the 1993 statement for relying on unreliable testimonies.[88]

Hata also argues that the content of the Kōno Statement was negotiated in advance. According to him, the South Korean government assured the Japanese government that they would not seek monetary compensation, but insisted that the word "kyōseirenkō" [forceful mobilization] be included in the statement. Although the Japanese government initially refused to include the word, in the end, they decided to compromise by including an ambiguous statement on women being recruited against their will.[89] Overall, Hata is critical of the Kōno Statement because in his mind, it formed the basis for other countries to argue that the Japanese government had admitted to wrongdoing.

In summary, six themes emerged from the nationalist discourse on the "comfort women" issue. Some of these (antiprogressivism, denial of "comfort women" as sex slaves, and anti-Korean and anti-Chinese sentiments) were already found in the previous period, but others (the issue's impact on the international perception of Japan, mixed evaluations of the 2015 bilateral agreement, and opposition to the 1993 Kono Statement) are new to the recent period. However, all of these themes are related: Because of anti-Japan leftwingers (i.e., Japanese progressives) and anti-Japan, irrational Koreans and Chinese, the "lie" of "comfort women" as sex slaves has spread all over the world and the Japanese government was tricked by deceitful Koreans for the 2015 agreement and for the 1993 Kōno Statement. Racist, Orientalist depictions of Korean survivors in particular and Koreans and Chinese in general dominate nationalist commentaries on this issue.

PROGRESSIVE WRITERS

As with the nationalist writers I just analyzed, some of the themes that emerged from progressive discussions about the "comfort women" issue originated earlier, and some originated more recently. Overall, six themes characterize progressive writing on this issue: (1) survivors as victims, (2) Japanese colonization of Korea as the cause of the "comfort" system and postcolonial *kisen* tourism, (3) contributions of the redress movement, (4) criticism of the 2015 bilateral agreement, (5) criticism of nationalist writers, and (6) criticism of Park Yu-ha's book.

Survivors as Victims

This first theme, survivors as victims, originally appeared in the 1970s, but is still a dominant theme among progressives. For instance, the documentary film *Shusenjō* features progressive writers and activists who refute the idea that "comfort women" were prostitutes and argue instead that they were sex slaves. In the film, nationalists (including Fujioka) claim that the women were not sex slaves because they earned a lot of money—one woman, Mun Ok-chu, made the equivalent of five houses in Tokyo.[90] In response to this claim, progressive scholars such as Yoshimi Yoshiaki and Hayashi Hirofumi assert that the inflation rate in Burma at the time was so high that the amount Mun Ok-chu saved was actually quite low. The same idea is supported by Yoshimi and Hayashi in Kim Puja and Itagaki Ryuta's anthology[91] and by Kitano Ryūichi and Hakoda Tetsuya in an article dated May 17, 2016, in the *Asahi Shimbun*.[92] Similarly, Watanabe Mina from the WAM states, in the film, that she believes that the women were sex slaves regardless of the money they received because they were made to serve men against their will.

The film features nationalist writers claiming that "comfort women" were simply prostitutes, quoting a report from the U.S. military. However, Dezaki has progressive activists refute this claim by arguing that this statement is simply the opinion of the report's author. Nationalists' claim that "comfort women" were allowed to leave "comfort" stations and attend various events is refuted by the assertion that it is wrong to assume that slaves have absolutely no freedom. In the film, progressives argue that enslaved people in the United States were "allowed" to leave the confines of their plantations and "permitted" to gather under certain circumstances, but this does not mean that they were not enslaved.[93] In addition, Kitano and Hakoda cite Yoshimi's testimony that most women did not have the right to refuse customers, quit, or go outside.[94] Furthermore, Dezaki refutes the nationalist claim that survivors' testimonies are inconsistent, by stating that such testimonies are often inconsistent because of the trauma of sexual assault.[95]

Song Eoun-ok, a professor at Aoyama Gakuin University in Tokyo, refutes, in a chapter in Kim and Itagai's anthology, that Kim Hak-sun, a Korean survivor who sued the Japanese government, was originally a *kisen* and, therefore, was a prostitute rather than a victim of sexual slavery. *Kisen* were women who were specially trained to perform songs and dances—some *kisen* even became professional singers and actors. Although nationalists often suggest that Kim was sold into prostitution by her impoverished single mother because she received 40 yen from the man who adopted Kim and sent her to a *kisen* school, Song explains that 40 yen was about ten times less than the usual price for selling a daughter into prostitution at that time. Thus, Song argues that Kim should not be considered a prostitute.[96] The film also debunks the idea that the newspaper advertisement for "comfort women" could serve as evidence that "comfort women" were mere prostitutes. It argues that the advertisement was geared toward potential proprietors because they were written in Japanese, which many young Korean women from poor families could not read. In addition, the advertisement would have been in contravention of international law because it sought women as young as seventeen years.[97] Cofounder of the Korean Council Yun Chung-ok states, in a chapter in Kim and Itagaki's anthology, that most Koreans, at the time, had no idea what "comfort women" were, anyway, so even if women had volunteered on their own, they would not have known what they were entering.[98]

Progressive works also describe survivors' terrible experiences at "comfort" stations although less frequently than works from the previous period. Kitano and Hakoda assert that "comfort women" had to serve twenty to thirty soldiers per day, that those who resisted were beaten, and that some killed themselves. They also cite former soldiers' testimonies and assert that many "comfort women" were abandoned at the end of the war and died while fleeing.[99] Kim Puja states that victims were supervised by their proprietors or Japanese soldiers and that they were deprived of their freedom. She further suggests that the "comfort" system was indeed sexual slavery under international law and that Japan is the only country that has denied this fact.[100] Although Dezaki clearly takes the position that "comfort women" were sex slaves, he is also cautious about overemphasizing their victimhood. At the end of his film, he cautions progressive activists against exaggerating the situation of the "comfort women" so that nationalists will not have a basis to attack these exaggerations.[101]

Progressives have also discussed various ways in which Korean women were deceitfully and forcefully recruited into the "comfort" system. Kim Puja cites testimonies of survivors and former Japanese soldiers who claim that Korean women were often recruited under false pretenses.[102] Yun Chung-ok, in a chapter in the same anthology, indicates that, toward the end of the war, soldiers even began to kidnap Korean women in the streets.[103] Likewise, Kitano and Hakoda explain, in their article in the *Asahi Shimbun*, that Korean and Taiwanese women were deceitfully recruited by recruiters ordered by the military and were transported by the military.[104] Similarly, the 2019 special exhibit at the WAM—"Chōsenjin 'Ianfu' no Koe wo Kiku" [Listen to the voices of Korean "comfort women"] begins with 183 survivors' testimonies and photos. In each testimony, visitors can see survivors' stories of forceful or deceitful recruitment and of the terrible treatment they received at "comfort" stations.

Japanese Colonization as the Cause of the "Comfort" System and Postcolonial *Kisen* Tourism

Progressives argue that Japan's colonization was the cause of the "comfort" system during the war and postcolonial *kisen* tourism, which eventually caused the formation of the redress movement for "comfort women" in South Korea. Like the previous period, progressives from this most recent period argue that the colonial mentality of the Japanese meant that the Japanese military did not hesitate to recruit Korean women into the "comfort" system. For instance, citing Yoshimi's research from 1995, Kim Puja argues that the Japanese imperial military's discriminatory attitudes toward Koreans facilitated the recruitment of a large number of young women who had no prior experience in prostitution.[105] Likewise, on November 30, 2016, in the *Asahi Shimbun*, Kitano Ryūichi and Nakano Akira cite Professor Tonomura Masaru's contention that Japanese soldiers and police officers did not directly mobilize Korean women, but that the system of colonial rule ensured that Koreans, rather than Japanese, recruited Korean women.[106] Kim discusses how Korean "comfort women" were treated worse at "comfort" stations than Japanese "comfort women" as has been discussed by many.[107] Some of the chapters in Kim's anthology discuss the discrimination faced by Koreans during colonial occupation (e.g., by enforcing corporal punishment).

Some WAM artifacts also illustrate how Japan's colonial government transformed Korea's sex industry into a system similar to the Japanese official prostitution system. The WAM's 2019 special exhibit, "Listen to the

Voices of Korean 'Comfort Women,'" discusses how *kisen* were initially not prostitutes in precolonial Korea. It also suggests that Japan's colonial influence over Korea continues through *kisen* tourism—a form of sex tourism that was especially popular among Japanese men in the 1970s and the 1980s. The transformation of Korea's sex industry and *kisen* under Japan's colonial rule and *kisen* tourism in postcolonial Korea are discussed in connection with Korean "comfort women" under the Japanese imperial military as we can see from the exhibit title.

This connection between the "comfort" system during the war and postcolonial *kisen* tourism was also made explicit on July 7, 2019, when the WAM hosted a public lecture by Yamaguchi Akiko who has been an activist against *kisen* tourism since the 1970s. Yamaguchi emphasized that her group was inspired by and cooperated with Korean women's groups, which originated in South Korea's democratization movement. As a consequence, Yamaguchi's group came to consider the "comfort women" issue their issue as well. She argued that sex tourism, including *kisen* tourism, is about sexism and political economy where men from wealthier nations can travel to poorer nations to buy women. In addition, the WAM's 2019 special exhibit features a subsection titled "Kankoku no Minshūka Undō to 'Ianfu' Mondai Zenshi" [South Korea's Democratization Movement and a Prior History to the "Comfort Women" Issue], which describes how the South Korean democratization movement of the 1970s and 1980s worked together with a Korean Christian organization to end *kisen* tourism, which attracted about 500,000 Japanese men annually. According to the exhibit, the organization brought Korean and Japanese women's groups together to work toward this goal, which became the foundation of the redress movement for "comfort women."

Progressives argue that the redress movement for "comfort women" can be traced back to the Korean movement against *kisen* tourism and the democratization movement in South Korea in the 1970s and the 1980s. Thus, it originated in South Korea. In the previous period, progressives voiced a similar idea: that the redress movement originated in South Korea rather than being the creation of Japanese citizens. In response to nationalist allegations that Japanese progressives "created" the "comfort women" issue, more and more progressives have been detailing the origins of the redress movement. Whereas progressives from this period also trace the redress movement back to South Korean movements for democratization in the 1970s and the 1980s, they have also begun to relate the redress movement to the movement against *kisen* tourism.

Contributions of the Redress Movement

The next theme among progressives is an emphasis on the contributions of the redress movement. This theme is not surprising given that progressives themselves have been active in the redress movement. However, these progressives tend to focus on the activities of the Korean Council and other Korean groups. This theme emerged in response to fierce nationalist attacks on the redress movement, that it is anti-Japanese or supported by communists from North Korea or China. Generally, progressives attempt to promote a more favorable view of the redress movement.

Activist Yang Ching-ja states, in one of her chapters in Kim and Itagaki's anthology, that the presence of support organizations such as the Korean Council has enabled victims to come forward with their testimonies. She further explains that providing support for victims has been the main activity of the Korean Council. She states that the Korean Council periodically visits victims, attempts to understand the lives and well-being of victims, and operates a shared house for victims. She also details that the Korean Council has won various social security benefits for victims, including monthly living stipends and free medical support, by demanding that the South Korean government take responsibility for not supporting these victims for half a century. Yang argues that the Korean Council treats the "comfort women" issue as one about violence against women during wartime, and not as one involving an anti-Japanese sentiment. Therefore, the Korean Council condemns all nations that have exploited women sexually, including South Korea. These criticisms revolve around the "comfort" system that was in place for the South Korean military during the Korean War, a similar system that was in place for American soldiers during the Korean War, and yet another system that used Vietnamese women for the pleasure of South Korean soldiers during the Vietnam War.[108]

Yang Ching-ja's above-mentioned essay and the WAM's exhibits explain how *halmŏni* have transformed from "victims of sexual assault" to human rights activists with the support of the Korean Council. They detail that two *halmŏni* learned of the "comfort" system for the U.S. military and wanted to establish an organized means by which they could help women who suffered from sexual violence during wartime. As a result, the Korean Council created a fund in 2013 to help victims of sexual violence during wartime and began to support Vietnamese victims who had faced sexual violence at the hands of South Korean soldiers. Although nationalists such as Hata criticize the South Korean media, government, and activist groups for hypocritically overlooking these transgressions while still criticizing Japan's "comfort" system,[109] progressive activists argue that these charges of hypocrisy are unfounded, as redress for those issues is also important for Korean activist groups.

Progressives depict the erection of statues commemorating "comfort women" as a meaningful element of redress. For instance, the *Asahi Shimbun* depicts the erection of these statues in the West as a symbol of human rights. Articles in the *Asahi Shimbun* by Nakai Daisuke, Hirayama

Ari, and Miyaji Yū[110] and Tokutome Kinuyo[111] present the erection of these statues in the United States as something that was made possible by the unified efforts of various Asian Americans, including Korean, Chinese, and Japanese Americans. These articles state that such a statue was erected in San Francisco with the support of a group that fought for redress regarding Japanese Americans' internment during World War II. When the city of San Francisco decided to erect a statue symbolizing "comfort women," the city council declared that it is not enough to only criticize Japan and that their combined efforts should go toward education that may stop human trafficking all over the world.[112] The chairperson of the San Francisco City Council stated that he hoped that the statue would restore the survivors' dignity and promote peace, unification, and healing.[113] In New Jersey, the county chair stated that the statue was erected as a means of remembrance, and not of blame.[114] While nationalists perceive these statues and the redress movement as anti-Japanese, progressives see them as symbols of human rights and the redress movement as a fight against sexual violence against women during wartime in general.

Criticism of the 2015 Bilateral Agreement

As some nationalists do, progressives also criticize the 2015 bilateral agreement. At the beginning of *Shusenjō*, a survivor accuses South Korean foreign minister Yun Byung-se for signing the 2015 agreement without soliciting input from survivors. We also see a Wednesday demonstration in front of the Japanese Embassy in Seoul where participants are chanting, "Repeal, repeal!."[115]

Itagaki criticizes the resolution for not soliciting survivors' input and criticizes the Japanese government's attitude toward it. He introduces criticism from international organizations such as the UN's Committee on the Elimination of Discrimination against Women (UNCEDAW) that argues that the bilateral resolution is not victim centered and does not provide effective rescue plans for victims. He also criticizes the Abe administration for ignoring these comments from international organizations and Itagaki suggests that Abe wanted to simply end the public discussion of the issue. As a result, when Abe was asked by the South Korean foundation that was created to distribute the funds from the Japanese government to survivors to write a letter of apology, he refused and made it clear that he considered the resolution the state's final apology. Itagaki also criticizes the Abe administration for continuing to demand that the South Korean government remove the statue in Seoul. When another statue was erected in front of the Japanese Consulate in Busan, the Japanese government was indignant and recalled its ambassador in protest, rendering Abe's statement on "feeling responsible" insincere.[116]

Okamoto Yuka, an activist whose chapter also appears in the anthology, criticizes the coverage of the resolution in Japan's major newspapers. She examines five major newspapers: *Yomiuri Shimbun*, *Asahi Shimbun*, *Nihon Keizai Shimbun*, *Mainichi Shimbun*, and *Sankei Shimbun*. She states that all of them, including the liberal *Asahi Shimbun*, welcomed the resolution. This universal support for the resolution explains, to her, why the South Koreans and Japanese viewed the resolution differently: each newspaper focused on survivors who welcomed the resolution rather than dissenting views. She demonstrates that when South Korea announced the results of its investigation into the process of arriving at the 2015 resolution, all five newspapers simply advocated keeping the resolution. Although the Moon administration has put forward a victim-centered approach to the issue since 2017, none of these major Japanese newspapers reported on this approach or the UNCEDAW's support for South Korea's new approach. In short, she criticizes the Japanese media for not critically examining the Japanese government's position.[117]

Despite Okamoto's criticism, the *Asahi Shimbun* introduces dissenting opinions on the 2015 resolution, although the newspaper itself does not directly address its own position on the resolution. On February 10, 2018, the paper published South Korean president Moon's comments on the 2015 resolution, in which he states that the content of the resolution is not accepted by victims and the South Korean public. Moon states that the "comfort women" issue will be considered settled when the victims' honor and dignity are restored. According to the newspaper, Moon argues that the survivors' pain will not heal as a result of negotiations between governments[118]—a direct response to Abe's comments. Historian Yoshizawa Fumitoshi is interviewed for an article in the *Asahi Shimbun*. Yoshizawa criticizes the resolution and calls for more dialogue with victims. He states thus:

> What victims are seeking most is sincerity not money. Japan needs to communicate with the victims clearly and directly regarding what exactly the nation is responsible for. If he is taking this issue seriously, Prime Minister Abe should visit South Korea and apologize to the victims using his own words rather than having somebody else read his apology aloud although there is still a possibility of criticism that this is merely a performance. (My translation)[119]

While the *Asahi Shimbun* introduced the opinion that the 2015 resolution was not victim centered, it also stated, multiple times, that many survivors have requested or received money from the Japanese government. *Asahi* reporter Takeda Hajime details how most survivors and bereaved families requested money but because President Moon closed down the foundation that distributed the money, many of these requests remain unfulfilled. Takeda introduces several such stories of bereaved families who requested money because they believed that the money had been set aside for the restoration of the survivors' honor and dignity. He states,

> If the organization is closed now, not only will the support money remain undistributed, but it will also be concluded that the organization did not contribute to the resolution of the issue at all. That is not the case. I wonder if both governments could listen to the voices of survivors carefully and find a way to utilize the resolution for the future. (My translation)[120]

To the newspaper, the South Korean government and the Japanese government are not victim centered and victims' voices should be heard more.

Criticism of Nationalist Writers

As progressives are criticized by nationalists, nationalists are also strongly criticized by progressives. Although this theme also emerged earlier, it seems that the memory war over the "comfort women" issue has intensified in recent years. This trend is not surprising, considering that it has been decades since the issue became controversial in Japan and both sides have had time to fully develop their arguments.

Progressives' criticisms are especially strong in *Shusenjō*, where they critique nationalists' racist attitudes toward Korean and Chinese people. In the film, Sugita, a nationalist politician, and Fujiki, a nationalist activist, argue that Japanese children are taught since childhood that they should never lie, whereas Koreans are taught not to be deceived because they assume that everybody lies. As discussed earlier, this is part of the nationalists' general Orientalist attitude toward Koreans as being deceitful just like colonized people are seen as "incapable of telling the truth or even of seeing it" by Western Orientalists.[121] To refute these arguments, Dezaki interviews South Koreans and asks them whether it is more important not to lie or not to be deceived. His interviewees unanimously answer that not lying is more important. Later, Sugita and American YouTuber Tony Marano (a.k.a. "Texas Oyaji," or Texas Daddy), who works with Japanese nationalist activists, discuss that the "comfort women" issue is really a Chinese conspiracy meant to destroy the relations between Japan, South Korea, and the United States. Dezaki summarizes that these nationalist activists tend to be racist.[122]

Criticism of Prime Minister Abe emerges as a subtheme, here. Nishino Rumiko whose chapter appears in the anthology criticizes Abe for claiming that women were simply sold into the "comfort" system by their parents as many Japanese women from poor families were sold into prostitution around that time. Abe's statement therefore pins responsibility for the "comfort women" issue on these women's parents, and not on the Japanese military.

Nishino further argues that through Abe's claim that "comfort women" were sold into human trafficking by their parents and civilian proprietors, he admitted that the "comfort" system operated in violation of international law because human trafficking was already banned under international law at the time.[123]

Shusenjō criticizes Abe's narrow definition of forced mobilization and his denial of the Japanese military's involvement in recruiting "comfort women." In the film, progressives such as Totsuka argue that forced mobilization means being taken against one's will, which includes deceptive recruitment. Even if civilian recruiters, rather than the Japanese military, deceitfully recruited these women, the Japanese military was still liable because they did not punish unlawful recruiters. Progressives in the film also refute the nationalist charge that there is no documentary evidence for forced mobilization by suggesting that documentary evidence is not the sole bearer of truth and that the Japanese military destroyed many documents at the end of the war.[124]

Similarly, Itagaki criticizes Abe's 2015 statement on the seventieth anniversary of the war's end for not addressing Japan's responsibility for colonizing Korea and Taiwan and its responsibility for the "comfort women" issue. Itagaki explains that although Abe vaguely apologized for "Japan's actions during the previous war," there were no specific apologies for colonization. He did not offer an apology for the "comfort women" issue—he only made vague statements such as "During the war, the dignity and honor of many women were significantly destroyed" and "the twenty-first century should be a century when women's dignity will be respected."[125] These statements were written in passive voice, rendering responsibility unclear. Itagaki criticizes Abe for being a revisionist ever since he was a young member of Parliament.

Progressive writers also criticize former Osaka mayor Yoshimura Hirofumi (between 2015 and 2019; the current Osaka Prefecture governor since 2019) for his decision to terminate the sister city contract with San Francisco in 2017 over San Francisco's decision to erect a "comfort women" statue. While nationalists commended Yoshimura's decision, progressive publications such as the *Asahi Shimbun* considered it a hasty decision that "should have been separated from politics." An article in the *Asahi Shimbun* criticizes Yoshimura for his decision, arguing that sister city contracts should be about cultural exchange rather than relations between national governments. The article further argues that a mayor alone should not have the power to terminate a sister city relationship.[126] Similarly, an *Asahi* article by Handa Naoko and Yoshikawa Takashi states that Yoshimura sent five letters to the city of San Francisco criticizing the erection of the statue and bringing up the possibility of terminating the sister city relationship. The article reports that a former Osaka city council person found Yoshimura's behavior strange and that this person believed that Yoshimura simply could not let the issue go at that time.¹²⁷ Professor Yamaguchi Kazuo encapsulates many progressives' views on this incident when stating in the *Asahi Shimbun* that the "comfort women" issue is about human rights and that these statues are erected from a desire to not repeat this grisly history. He argues that Yoshimura should not think of these statues as anti-Japanese.¹²⁸

Criticism of Park Yu-Ha's Book

Park Yu-ha's controversial book, *Teikoku no Ianfu* [Comfort Women of the Empire], has also been severely criticized by progressive writers. As mentioned earlier, this book was so controversial in South Korea that the author was sued for defamation by some survivors.

Park's book is criticized by most authors in Kim and Itagaki's anthology. These authors mostly criticize Park's argument that Japanese soldiers and Korean "comfort women" developed comradely relationships. Kim criticizes this idea, stating that Korean "comfort women" were discriminated against and were treated worse than their Japanese counterparts, and that even when they did develop affection or relationships with Japanese soldiers, these were probably cases of Stockholm syndrome. She also criticizes Park for confusing Korean and Japanese "comfort women" and for overlooking the differences in how each group of women were treated. She also criticizes Park for not considering the Japanese military's responsibility for the "comfort" system and Japan's responsibility for Korea's colonization.¹²⁹ In short, she argues that Korean "comfort women" were simply "comfort women of a colony" who were exploited to satisfy soldiers' sexual desires in support of Japan's invasive war.¹³⁰ Similarly, Han Hong-goo, a history professor at Sungkonghoe University in South Korea, states, in his chapter in the same anthology, that just because some Korean women may have internalized their Japanization education more thoroughly and cooperated with Japan's war effort, describing their relationships with Japanese men as comradely is an overstatement.¹³¹

Progressive writers also criticize Park's idea that civilian proprietors unlawfully recruited women and, therefore, proprietors, not the Japanese military, should be held accountable. Nishino argues that the military should be held liable because proprietors were under the military's direction and supervision.¹³² Han argues, by analogy, that during the Holocaust, it would be absurd to claim that those who actually captured the Jews should be held accountable over Adolf Hitler and other Nazi officials.¹³³ Chong Young-hwan, a professor at Meiji Gakuin University, criticizes Park in the anthology saying that she is an opportunist who projected the self-imagery that Japanese society desired and presented a narrative about "comfort women" which Japanese people and the state wanted to hear.¹³⁴

While Park's book has similar ideas to those of Japanese nationalists, it provides far fewer derogatory views of Korean "comfort women" than Japanese nationalists. However, the fact that it caused far more controversy in South Korea is worth noting. Of course, works by Japanese nationalists written in Japanese may not be as accessible to the South Korean public as Park's book written in Korean. However, it may be Park's national identity as South Korean that made the book controversial. As she is South Korean, her work depicting the relationships between Japanese soldiers and Korean "comfort women" positively can be exploited by Japanese nationalists who could use her book as a credible source to argue for humane relationships between Japanese soldiers and Korean "comfort women" simply because she is a South Korean (Hata categorizes Park as being on the same side as Japanese nationalists regarding the "comfort women" issue while placing Yoshimi on the opposite side[135]). I also wonder if she may be expected to promote the South Korean dominant memory of "comfort women" because of her nationality: "Comfort women were forcibly recruited and placed in slave-live conditions."

CONCLUSION

On the progressive side, completely different themes have emerged. Just like on the nationalist side, some of the themes on the progressive side have also persisted from before and new themes have emerged in recent times such as the 2015 bilateral agreement or Park Yu-ha's book. The main themes are "comfort women" as victims of sexual slavery as a result of Japan's colonization of Korea; the redress movement for sexual slavery that originated in South Korea's democratization movement and the movement against *kisen* tourism now fighting against any sexual violence during wartime; in the meantime, Japanese nationalists, the 2015 bilateral agreement, and Park Yu-ha's book continue to dishonor the survivors.

Since the 1990s, when the "comfort women" issue received increasing public and scholarly attention, "meta-memory" has become a large part of the public discourse around this issue. Nationalists and progressives have debated the memories of sexual slavery and its survivors and have fiercely attacked each other's attempts to construct and promote particular memories surrounding sexual slavery. Efforts on both sides to promote their versions of the memories have influenced the collective memory of sexual slavery in Japanese society. Nationalists' efforts led to changes in middle school history textbooks, creating a generation of Japanese who "have no memory" of "comfort women." Their denial of "comfort women" as sex slaves is repeated by even Japanese politicians such as Prime Minister Abe, and this particular memory is gaining more and more currency among many Japanese. At the same time, progressives' memory of "comfort women" as sex slaves has spread outside East Asia, which has also begun to create memories among those who "previously had no memory" of sexual slavery.

NOTES

1. Fifield, "An Early Roadblock for Landmark."
2. Soble and Hang-Sun, "'Comfort Women.'"
3. McCurry, "Former Sex Slaves Reject Japan."
4. "Impasse over Busan Statue Drags on."
5. Nobukatsu Fujioka, ed., *Kokuren ga Sekai ni Hirometa "Ianfu = Seidorei" no Uso: Junēbu Kokuren Hakendan Hōkoku* [A Lie Spread All Over the World Through the United Nations, "Comfort Women = Sex Slaves": Reports by a Team that was Sent to Geneva for the United Nations' Meetings] (Tokyo: Jiyūsha, 2016).
6. Ikuhiko Hata, *Ianfu Mondai no Kessan* [Settlement of the Comfort Women Issue] (Tokyo: PHP Kenkyūsho, 2016).
7. Puja Kim and Ryūta Itagaki, *Q & A Chōsenjin "Ianfu" to Shokuminchi Shihai Sekinin: Anatano Gimon ni Kotaemasu* [Q & A Korean "Comfort Women" and the Responsibility for Colonization: We Will Answer Your Questions] (Tokyo: Ochanomizu Shobō, 2018).
8. *Shusenjō: The Main Battleground of the Comfort Women Issue*. Directed by Miki Dezaki. Wyoming: No Man Productions LLC, 2018.
9. Rumiko Nishino, "The Women's Active Museum on War and Peace: Its Role in Public Education," *The Asia-Pacific Journal | Japan Focus* 12, no. 5 (December 2007): 1–3.
10. Gill Abousnnouga and David Machin, "Analysing the Language of War Monuments," *Visual Communication* 9, no. 2 (2010): 139.
11. Abousnnouga and Machin, "Analysing," 144.
12. Ibid.
13. Ibid., 145.
14. Lee Woo-young, "[Herald Interview] 'Comfort women' statues magnet for Koreans," *Korean Herald*, March 3, 2016, http://kpopherald.koreaherald.com/view.php?ud=20160303171935265707_2#:~:text=Sculptors%20Kim%20Seo%2Dkyung%20and,comfort%20women%2C%E2%80%9D%20since%202011.
15. Abousnnouga and Machin, "Analysing," 145.
16. Park Boram, "Deciphering Symbolism of Girl Statue," *The Korean Times*, September 6, 2016, https://en.yna.co.kr/view/AEN20160906000200315#:~:text=%22The%20allusion%20is%20that%20the,Kim%2C%20the%20sculptor%2C%20said.&text=Loaded%20with%20such%20heavy%20symbolism,way%20to%20rebuild%20the%20embassy.
17. Ibid.
18. Abousnnouga and Machin, "Analysing," 144.
19. Ibid., 144.
20. Hata, *Ianfu Mondai*, 32.

21. Shunichi Fujiki, "Kokuren de Nihon no Makikaeshi ga Hajimatta!" [Japan's Counterattack Started at the United Nations!], in *Kokuren ga Sekai ni Hirometa "Ianfu = Seidorei" no Uso: Junēbu Kokuren Hakendan Hōkoku* [A Lie Spread All Over the World Through the United Nations, "Comfort Women = Sex Slaves": Reports by a Team that was Sent to Geneva for the United Nations' Meetings], ed. Nobukatsu Fujioka (Tokyo: Jiyūsha, 2016), 286.

22. Nobukatsu Fujioka, Kiyoshi Hosoya, Yumiko Yamamoto, Shunichi Fujiki, Mitsuhiko Fujii, and Michio Sekino, "Itte Wakatta Kokuren Riyou no Karakuri" [Tricks of Utilizing the United Nations We Found Out by Attending], in *Kokuren ga Sekai ni Hirometa "Ianfu = Seidorei" no Uso: Junēbu Kokuren Hakendan Hōkoku* [A Lie Spread All Over the World Through the United Nations, "Comfort Women = Sex Slaves": Reports by a Team that was Sent to Geneva for the United Nations' Meetings], ed. Nobukatsu Fujioka (Tokyo: Jiyūsha, 2016), 198–228.

23. Shunichi Fujiki, "Kokuren Jinken Rijikai ni Norikonde Wakatta koto" [What I Found out by Attending UNHRC meetings], in *Kokuren ga Sekai ni Hirometa "Ianfu = Seidorei" no Uso: Junēbu Kokuren Hakendan Hōkoku* [A Lie Spread All Over the World Through the United Nations, "Comfort Women = Sex Slaves": Reports by a Team that was Sent to Geneva for the United Nations' Meetings], ed. Nobukatsu Fujioka (Tokyo: Jiyūsha, 2016), 290.

24. Ibid., 374.

25. Fujioka et al., "Itte Wakatta," 206–207.

26. Nobukatsu Fujioka, "'Ianfu = Seidorei' Setsu Netsuzō to Kakusan" [Fabrication and Promotion of the Theory, "Comfort Women = Sex Slaves"], in *Kokuren ga Sekai ni Hirometa "Ianfu = Seidorei" no Uso: Junēbu Kokuren Hakendan Hōkoku* [A Lie Spread All Over the World Through the United Nations, "Comfort Women = Sex Slaves": Reports by a Team that was Sent to Geneva for the United Nations' Meetings], ed. Nobukatsu Fujioka (Tokyo: Jiyūsha, 2016), 12–18.

27. Shunichi Fujiki, "Totsuka Etsurō shi tono Sougū to Taiwa" [Encounter and Conversation with Mr. Etsurō Totsuka], in *Kokuren ga Sekai ni Hirometa "Ianfu = Seidorei" no Uso: Junēbu Kokuren Hakendan Hōkoku* [A Lie Spread All Over the World Through the United Nations, "Comfort Women = Sex Slaves": Reports by a Team that was Sent to Geneva for the United Nations' Meetings], ed. Nobukatsu Fujioka (Tokyo: Jiyūsha, 2016), 254.

28. Ibid., 257–258.

29. Hata, *Ianfu Mondai*, 27–29.

30. Ibid., 140–141; Fujioka, "'Ianfu,'" 18–20.

31. Shirō Takahashi, "Beigikai Ketsugi no Konkyo tosareta 'Tanaka Yuki' shi no Chosho" [The Book by Mr. Yuki Tanaka that became the basis of the US Congress's Resolution], in *Kokuren ga Sekai ni Hirometa "Ianfu = Seidorei" no Uso: Junēbu Kokuren Hakendan Hōkoku* [A Lie Spread All Over the World Through the United Nations, "Comfort Women = Sex Slaves": Reports by a Team that was Sent to Geneva for the United Nations' Meetings], ed. Nobukatsu Fujioka (Tokyo: Jiyūsha, 2016), 116–121.

32. Emi Kawaguchi Mann, "Doitsu niokeru Ianfu Hōdō no Ronchō" [The Tone of Media Reports on Comfort Women in Germany], in *Kokuren ga Sekai ni Hirometa*

"*Ianfu = Seidorei*" *no Uso: Junēbu Kokuren Hakendan Hōkoku* [A Lie Spread All Over the World Through the United Nations, "Comfort Women = Sex Slaves": Reports by a Team that was Sent to Geneva for the United Nations' Meetings], ed. Nobukatsu Fujioka (Tokyo: Jiyūsha, 2016), 168–182.

33. Fujioka et al., "Itte Wakatta," 201–205.

34. Mio Sugita, "Furansugo de Kinchou no Supiichi" [French Speech Given Feeling Nervous], in *Kokuren ga Sekai ni Hirometa "Ianfu = Seidorei" no Uso: Junēbu Kokuren Hakendan Hōkoku* [A Lie Spread All Over the World Through the United Nations, "Comfort Women = Sex Slaves": Reports by a Team that was Sent to Geneva for the United Nations' Meetings], ed. Nobukatsu Fujioka (Tokyo: Jiyūsha, 2016), 302; Fujioka et al., "Itte Wakatta," 244.

35. Hata, *Ianfu Mondai*, 119–120.

36. "Ianfu Mondai no Genten 'Saharin Saiban' Chōsenjingari Shōgen shita Yoshida Seiji" [The Origin of the Comfort Women Issue, "Sakhalin Trials," and Seiji Yoshida who Confessed to "Hunting Koreans"], *Sankei Shimbun*, October 27, 2018, https://www.sankei.com/life/news/181027/lif1810270021-n1.html.

37. Tesshū Yamaoka, "Asahi Shimbun san Ianfu Teisei Kakusu tsumorija naiyone" [Asahi Shimbun, You are not Planning to Hide your Corrections regarding Comfort Women, are you?], *Sankei Shimbun*, October 13, 2018, https://www.sankei.com/entertainments/news/181013/ent1810130002-n3.html

38. Kent Gilbert and Tesshū Yamaoka, "Kent Gilbert Asahi Shimbun he 'Kougi' Houmonki" [Kent Gilbert's visit to the Asahi Shimbun for "protests"], *Sankei Shimbun*, August 12, 2018, https://www.sankei.com/premium/news/180812/prm1808120003-n3.html.

39. Hata, *Ianfu Mondai*, 99.

40. Ibid., 53.

41. Ibid., 32.

42. Fujioka et al., "Itte Wakatta," 224–225.

43. Hisae Kennedy, "2007 Nen Beigikai Ianfu Ketsugi kara Zenbei ni Fukyū" [Spreading all over the United States from the 2007 US Congress Resolution on Comfort Women], in *Kokuren ga Sekai ni Hirometa "Ianfu = Seidorei" no Uso: Junēbu Kokuren Hakendan Hōkoku* [A Lie Spread All Over the World Through the United Nations, "Comfort Women = Sex Slaves": Reports by a Team that was Sent to Geneva for the United Nations' Meetings], ed. Nobukatsu Fujioka (Tokyo: Jiyūsha, 2016), 103–104.

44. Fujioka, Hosoya, Yamamoto, Fujiki, Fujii, and Sekino, "Itte Wakatta," 217.

45. Fujioka, "'Ianfu,'" 39–44.

46. Hata, *Ianfu Mondai*, 42.

47. Ibid., 26–18.

48. Said, *Orientalism*, 39.

49. Kennedy, "2007 Nen," 102.

50. Nobukatsu Fujioka, "Ianfu 'Nikkan Gōi' to Sonogo" ["The Japan-South Korean Agreement" on Comfort Women and Afterward], in *Kokuren ga Sekai ni Hirometa "Ianfu = Seidorei" no Uso: Junēbu Kokuren Hakendan Hōkoku* [A Lie Spread All Over the World Through the United Nations, "Comfort Women =

Sex Slaves": Reports by a Team that was Sent to Geneva for the United Nations' Meetings], ed. Nobukatsu Fujioka (Tokyo: Jiyūsha, 2016), 345–346.

51. Fujiki, "Totsuka Etsurō shi," 274–275.
52. Said, *Orientalism*, 204.
53. Tesshū Yamaoka, "Glendale shi Ianfuzō Tekkyo Saiban no Tenkai to Mitōshi" [Development and Prospect of the Trial for Comfort Women Statue Removal in the City of Glendale], in *Kokuren ga Sekai ni Hirometa "Ianfu = Seidorei" no Uso: Junēbu Kokuren Hakendan Hōkoku* [A Lie Spread All Over the World Through the United Nations, "Comfort Women = Sex Slaves": Reports by a Team that was Sent to Geneva for the United Nations' Meetings], ed. Nobukatsu Fujioka (Tokyo: Jiyūsha, 2016), 162.
54. Ibid., 139–141.
55. Said, *Orientalism*, 206.
56. "Kankoku Saijo 'Shinnichi wo Semeru Kuni Bakabakashii' 'Yoshida Shōgen noyouna Kotoga Attara Chōsen no Otoko ha Damatte Miteinai" [South Korean Intelligent Woman "It is a Ridiculous Country where being Pro-Japan is Stigmatized,' 'Korean Men would have Intervened if Something like what Yoshida confessed Had Happened], *Sankei Shimbun*, May 6, 2018, https://www.sankei.com/west/news/18 0506/wst1805060005-n3.html.
57. Said, *Orientalism*, 309–310.
58. Ibid., 150.
59. Katsuhiro Kurota, "Jōcho Jūshi koso Sekiheki Miseshime Bunka ha Tainichi Kankei nimo Oyobu" [Tired of Emotionalism, South Korea's Focus on Setting an Example Can Influence Japan-South Korean Relationships], *Sankei Shimbun*, January 19, 2019. https://www.sankei.com/world/news/190119/wor1901190011-n1.html.
60. Said, *Orientalism*, 184.
61. "Ianfu Zaidan no Kaisan Yakusoku Yaburu Kuni toha Tsukiaenu" [The End of the Comfort Women Foundation, We should not have Diplomatic Relations with a Country that Breaks Promises], Sankei Shimbun, November 22, 2018, https://www.sankei.com/politics/news/181122/plt1811220001-n1.html.
62. "Shimai Toshi Kaishō Ianfuzō de Dakyō ha Fuyō da" [Termination of a Sister City Contract, No Compromise is Necessary for a Comfort Women Statue], *Sankei Shimbun*, October 14, 2018, https://www.sankei.com/column/news/181014/clm1810140002-n1.html
63. Kōichi Mera, "Nanboku Sekkin no Beikoku de Gekika suru 'Rekishisen'" [Heated "History War" in the United States where North and South Korea Become Closer to Each Other], *Sankei Shimbun*, June 27, 2018, https://www.sankei.com/wo rld/news/180627/wor1806270004-n1.htm.
64. Said, *Orientalism*, 317.
65. Miki Ōtaka, "Kankoku ha Itsumade Kyogi no Hi ni Sugaritsukunoka" [How long will South Korea Cling to Statues based on Lies?], *Sankei Shimbun*, March 21, 2018, https://www.sankei.com/west/news/180321/wst1803210020-n1.html.
66. Kennedy, "2007 Nen," 93.
67. Ibid., 92–94.
68. Ibid., 100.

69. Ibid., 102.
70. Hata, *Ianfu Mondai*, 72–91.
71. Ibid., 78.
72. Miki Ōtaka, "Ianfu Mondai de Nihon wo Hihan shitekita Kankoku ga Uso Shazaihi wo Fukkatsu saseta Hontō no Riyuu" [The Real Reason why South Korea that Continued to Criticize Japan Restored the Apology Monument based on Lies], *Sankei Shimbun*, February 17, 2018, https://www.sankei.com/politics/news/180217/plt1802170001-n1.html; Ōtaka, "Kankoku."
73. Hata, *Ianfu Mondai*, 81–84.
74. "Korega Kankoku da" [This is South Korea], *Sankei Shimbun*, February 1, 2018, https://www.sankei.com/premium/news/180201/prm1802010004-n1.html.
75. Said, *Orientalism*, 150–152.
76. Fujioka, "Ianfu 'Nikkan Gōi,'" 326–328.
77. Ibid., 330.
78. Ibid., 333.
79. Said, *Orientalism*, 49.
80. Ibid., 321.
81. Fujioka, "Ianfu 'Nikkan Gōi,'" 233–234.
82. Ibid., 335–336.
83. Hata, *Ianfu Mondai*, 97–100.
84. Ibid., 94.
85. Ibid., 94.
86. Ibid., 96.
87. Said, *Orientalism*, 107.
88. Hata, *Ianfu Mondai*, 37–38.
89. Ibid., 34.
90. *Shusenjō*.
91. Hiroshi Hayashi and Yoshimi Yoshiaki, "Mun Ok-chu sanha Biruma de Ooganemochi ni natta? [Did Mun Ok-chu Become Rich in Burma?], in *Q & A Chōsenjin "Ianfu" to Shokuminchi Shihai Sekinin: Anatano Gimon ni Kotaemasu* [Q & A Korean "Comfort Women" and the Responsibility for Colonization: We Will Answer Your Questions], eds. Puja Kim and Ryūta Itagaki (Tokyo: Ochanomizu Shobō, 2018), 43–46.
92. Ryūichi Kitano and Tetsuya Hakoda, "Iansho no Seikatsu Tadoru. Ko Mun Ok-chu san no Baai" [Trace the Lives of Comfort Women at Comfort Stations. The Case of the Late Mun Ok-chu], *Asahi Shimbun*, May 17, 2016, https://digital.asahi.com/articles/DA3S12360443.html?iref=pc_ss_date.
93. *Shusenjō*.
94. Kitano and Hakoda, "Iansho."
95. *Shusenjō*.
96. Song Eoun-ok, "Kim Hak-sun san ha Kisen Gakkou Shusshin dakara Higaisha deha nai?" [Since Kim Hak-sun is from a Kisen School, is it not True that She was a Victim?], in *Q & A Chōsenjin "Ianfu" to Shokuminchi Shihai Sekinin: Anatano Gimon ni Kotaemasu* [Q & A Korean "Comfort Women" and the Responsibility for

Colonization: We Will Answer Your Questions], eds. Puja Kim and Ryūta Itagaki (Tokyo: Ochanomizu Shobō, 2018), 37–41.
  97. *Shusenjō.*
  98. Yun Chung-ok, "Yun Chung-ok san ni Kiku" [Asking Yun Chung-ok], in *Q & A Chōsenjin "Ianfu" to Shokuminchi Shihai Sekinin: Anatano Gimon ni Kotaemasu* [Q & A Korean "Comfort Women" and the Responsibility for Colonization: We Will Answer Your Questions], eds. Puja Kim and Ryūta Itagaki (Tokyo: Ochanomizu Shobō, 2018), 28.
  99. Kitano and Hakoda, "Iansho."
  100. Kim Puja, "Chōsenjin 'Ianfu' ha Seidorei dehanaku 'Teikoku no Ianfu' datta?" [Korean "Comfort Women" were not Sex Slaves but "Comfort Women of the Empire"?], in *Q & A Chōsenjin "Ianfu" to Shokuminchi Shihai Sekinin: Anatano Gimon ni Kotaemasu* [Q & A Korean "Comfort Women" and the Responsibility for Colonization: We Will Answer Your Questions], eds. Puja Kim and Ryūta Itagaki (Tokyo: Ochanomizu Shobō, 2018), 54–55.
  101. *Shusenjō.*
  102. Kim Puja, "Shokuminchi Chōsen deha Teishintai to 'Ianfu' wo Kondou?" [In Colonial Korea, Was the Women's Labor Corps Confused with "Comfort Women"?], in *Q & A Chōsenjin "Ianfu" to Shokuminchi Shihai Sekinin: Anatano Gimon ni Kotaemasu* [Q & A Korean "Comfort Women" and the Responsibility for Colonization: We Will Answer Your Questions], eds. Puja Kim and Ryūta Itagaki (Tokyo: Ochanomizu Shobō, 2018), 24–26.
  103. Yun, "Yun Chung-ok," 29.
  104. Kitano and Hakoda, "Iansho."
  105. Kim Puja, "Chōsenjin 'Ianufu' ni Shōjo ha Sukunakatta?" [Were there few "Comfort Women" Who were Girls?], in *Q & A Chōsenjin "Ianfu" to Shokuminchi Shihai Sekinin: Anatano Gimon ni Kotaemasu* [Q & A Korean "Comfort Women" and the Responsibility for Colonization: We Will Answer Your Questions], eds. Puja Kim and Ryūta Itagaki (Tokyo: Ochanomizu Shobō, 2018), 49–51.
  106. Ryūichi Kitano and Akira Nakano, "Shokuminchi 'Sōdōin' no Shitade" [Colonies under "Moblization"], *Asahi Shimbun*, November 30, 2016, https://digital.asahi.com/articles/DA3S12682484.html?iref=pc_ss_date.
  107. Kim, "Chōsenjin 'Ianfu' ha Seidorei dehanaku," 56–57.
  108. Yang Ching-ja, "Kankoku no 'Ianfu' Mondai Kaiketsu Undō ha 'Hannichi' nano?" [Is the South Korean "Comfort Women" Redress Movement "Anti-Japan"?], in *Q & A Chōsenjin "Ianfu" to Shokuminchi Shihai Sekinin: Anatano Gimon ni Kotaemasu* [Q & A Korean "Comfort Women" and Responsibility for Colonization: We Will Answer Your Questions], eds. Puja Kim and the Ryūta Itagaki (Tokyo: Ochanomizu Shobō, 2018), 136–140.
  109. Hata, *Ianfu Mondai*, 82.
  110. Daisuke Nakai, Ari Hirayama, and Yū Miyaji, "Ianfu no Hi Zō Bei no Jijō ha" [Comfort Women Memorials and Statues, What are the Situations in the United States?], *Asahi Shimbun*, November 18, 2015, https://digital.asahi.com/articles/DA3S12072838.html?iref=pc_ss_date.

111. Kinuyo Tokutome, "San Francisco no Ianfu Kinenhi ga Setsuritsu sareta Riyū" [The Reasons why the Comfort Women Memorial was Erected in San Francisco], *Asahi Shimbun*, December 14, 2017, https://webronza.asahi.com/politics/articles/2017121400006.html?iref=pc_ss_date.

112. Nakai et al., "Ianfu."

113. Tokutome, "San Francisco."

114. Nakai et al., "Ianfu."

115. *Shusenjō.*

116. Ryūta Itagaki, "Nikkan 'Gōi' ha '1miri' mo Ugokasu bekidenai?" [Shouldn't the Japan-South Korea Resolution be Changed even a Little?], in *Q & A Chōsenjin "Ianfu" to Shokuminchi Shihai Sekinin: Anatano Gimon ni Kotaemasu* [Q & A Korean "Comfort Women" and the Responsibility for Colonization: We Will Answer Your Questions], eds. Puja Kim and Ryūta Itagaki (Tokyo: Ochanomizu Shobō, 2018), 185–188.

117. Yuka Okamoto, "Nikkan 'Gōi' wo meguru Nihon no Masukomi Hōdō ha Koredeiino?" [Are Japan's Media Reports on the Japan-South Korea "Resolution" Acceptable?], in *Q & A Chōsenjin "Ianfu" to Shokuminchi Shihai Sekinin: Anatano Gimon ni Kotaemasu* [Q & A Korean "Comfort Women" and the Responsibility for Colonization: We Will Answer Your Questions], eds. Puja Kim and Ryūta Itagaki (Tokyo: Ochanomizu Shobō, 2018), 191–195.

118. "Nikkan Shunō Kaidan" [Japan-South Korea Summit Meeting], *Asahi Shimbun*, February 10, 2018, https://digital.asahi.com/articles/DA3S13353327.html?iref=pc_ss_date.

119. Tetsu Kobayashi, Yoshihiro Makino, and Hajime Takeda, "Ianfu Mondai Gōi Shikisha ha Dou Miru? Nichi Bei Kan no 3 nin ni Kiku" [What do Experts Think about the Comfort Women Issue Resolution? Asking 3 Experts from Japan, South Korea, and the United States], *Asahi Shimbun*, December 31, 2015, https://digital.asahi.com/articles/ASHD003SKHDZUHBI028.html?iref=pc_ss_date.

120. Hajime Takeda, "Ianfu Gōi Hontōni 'Shissei' ka Shienkin Motomeru Moto Ianfu mo" [Is the Comfort Women Resolution Truly a "Failure"? Some Former Comfort Women Ask for the Support Money], *Asahi Shimbun*, July 7, 2019, https://digital.asahi.com/articles/ASM6J7QVLM6JUHBI019.html?iref=pc_rellink.

121. Said, *Orientalism*, 318.

122. *Shusenjō.*

123. Rumiko Nishino, "Gyōsha ga 'Jinshin Baibai' de Chōshū Renkō shitakara Nihongun ni Sekinin ha nai?" [As Proprietors "Human Trafficked" the Women, wasn't the Japanese Military Liable?], in *Q & A Chōsenjin "Ianfu" to Shokuminchi Shihai Sekinin: Anatano Gimon ni Kotaemasu* [Q & A Korean "Comfort Women" and the Responsibility for Colonization: We Will Answer Your Questions], eds. Puja Kim and Ryūta Itagaki (Tokyo: Ochanomizu Shobō, 2018), 31–33.

124. *Shusenjō.*

125. Ryūta Itagaki, "Abe Danwa ha Nani ga Mondai?" [What is the Problem about the Abe Statement?], in *Q & A Chōsenjin "Ianfu" to Shokuminchi Shihai Sekinin: Anatano Gimon ni Kotaemasu* [Q & A Korean "Comfort Women" and the

Responsibility for Colonization: We Will Answer Your Questions], eds. Puja Kim and Ryūta Itagaki (Tokyo: Ochanomizu Shobō, 2018), 175.

126. "Shimaitoshi Shimin Kōryū wo Tsuzuketekoso" [Sister Cities, It is Important to Maintain Interactions between Residents], *Asahi Shimbun*, November 19, 2017, https://digital.asahi.com/articles/DA3S13234938.html?iref=pc_ss_date/.

127. Naoko Handa and Takashi Yoshikawa, "Shimai Toshi Kaishō Kodawaru Wake ha Osaka Shichō no 'Orosenu Kobushi'?" [The Reason Why the Osaka Mayor Insists on the Termination of the Sister City Contract is his Criticism that Cannot be Taken back?], *Asahi Shimbun*, November 24, 2017, https://digital.asahi.com/articles/ASKCR4V6BKCRPTIL00L.html?iref=pc_ss_date.

128. Masako Kinkōzan, "Shimai Toshi Fukkatsu no Hitsuyō Saido Toku" [Arguing for the Need to Sign the Sister City Contract Again], *Asahi Shimbun*, December 12, 2017, https://digital.asahi.com/articles/DA3S13268830.html?iref=pc_ss_date.

129. Kim, "Chōsenjin 'Ianfu,'" 55–57.

130. Ibid., 57.

131. Han Hong-goo, "Jikoku no Kagai no Rekishi to Mukiau" [Confront Your Country's History of Aggression], in *Q & A Chōsenjin "Ianfu" to Shokuminchi Shihai Sekinin: Anatano Gimon ni Kotaemasu* [Q & A Korean "Comfort Women" and the Responsibility for Colonization: We Will Answer Your Questions], eds. Puja Kim and Ryūta Itagaki (Tokyo: Ochanomizu Shobō, 2018), 177.

132. Nishino, "Gyōsha," 35–36.

133. Han, "Jikoku," 177.

134. Chong Young-hwan, "'Sengo Nihon' Kōtei no Yokubou to 'Teikoku no Ianfu'" [Desire to Positively View "Postwar Japan" and "Comfort Women of the Empire"], in *Q & A Chōsenjin "Ianfu" to Shokuminchi Shihai Sekinin: Anatano Gimon ni Kotaemasu* [Q & A Korean "Comfort Women" and the Responsibility for Colonization: We Will Answer Your Questions], eds. Puja Kim and Ryūta Itagaki (Tokyo: Ochanomizu Shobō, 2018), 67.

135. Hata, *Ianfu Mondai*, 380.

Chapter 7

Reflections on the Memories of Sexual Slavery in Japan and South Korea

The memories of sexual slavery have greatly changed over the past seventy years. In the years following the war, victims of sexual slavery were remembered as prostitutes in a romanticized way. Tamura's *Shunpūden*, published in the 1940s, and the movie under the same title in the 1960s tell a story of forbidden love between a soldier and a beautiful "comfort woman." Especially Korean "comfort women" were remembered as exotic creatures: passionate, emotional, irrational, and lustful in the way Oriental women were remembered by Western Orientalists. The memories of former Japanese soldiers contributed to this romanticization.

In the 1970s, the memories of sexual slavery changed dramatically. The women were now remembered as victims of the "comfort" system who were exploited to satisfy soldiers' sexual needs. Many of them, especially Korean women, were viewed as forcibly and deceitfully recruited, forced to serve dozens of soldiers a day, and often abandoned at the end of the war. Though they were mostly seen as victims of an inhumane military system who should be sympathized with, their fate did not give rise to a public or political discourse, despite the commercial success of Senda's books.[1] Romanticized, Orientalist memories of Korean "comfort women" were, however, still present in the testimonies of former Japanese soldiers.

This changed during the sexual slavery trial in the early 1990s, the first attempt to hold the former military and, consequently, the Japanese nation accountable for the suffering of the victims. The legal undertaking combined with international interest ignited a political and public controversy in Japan, sparking a "memory war" involving scholars, journalists, politicians, and activists. Nationalists promoted memories of the "comfort women" as prostitutes, who mostly chose to become "comfort women" for financial gain, but could have been sold by their Korean parents, or taken by Korean recruiters also, rather than being illicitly taken by the Japanese imperial military. Moreover, they claimed that a 1944 U.S. military report indicated that "comfort women" led luxurious lives at "comfort" stations.

On the other hand, progressives promote memories depicting "comfort women" as victims of an organized, governmentally sanctioned system of sexual slavery operated by the Japanese imperial military. This is viewed as a war crime for which Japan should be held responsible. Korean women in particular are seen as deceitfully and forcefully recruited and held under slave-like conditions. They were forced into prostitution and were physically abused if they refused. They were held captive and led lives under strict supervision, which made escape nearly impossible. Many of them died of diseases, were killed by the Japanese military, or died after being abandoned at the end of the war. Those who survived underwent even more suffering from long-term effects of abuse, physical injury, STDs, and societal backlash.

Since the 1990s, the two groups have also fiercely debated about the ways in which the other side has created and promoted certain memories. According to nationalists, "anti-Japan left-wingers" (i.e., progressives) spread the "lie" of comfort women as sex slaves despite a lack of documented evidence of the forceful mobilization of Korean women by Japanese authorities. To progressives, on the other hand, revisionists (i.e., nationalists) such as Prime Minister Abe try to whitewash the role of the imperial military in the "comfort" system by discrediting the testimonies of survivors in an effort to evade legal and financial responsibilities.

As collective memory scholars such as Blair, Dickinson, and Ott suggest, collective memory is constructed based on present concerns.[2] In light of this, which concerns in each period influenced the changing memories of the "comfort women"? In the period from 1945 to the 1960s, the stories of "comfort women" were mostly narrated by and to former Japanese soldiers. These men had real interactions with the women, and they could have, consciously or subconsciously, been in denial about the nature of these interactions or the circumstances under which they took place. One must also bear in mind that many of these soldiers were young and sexually inexperienced. Altogether, these factors could explain why so many of these "relationships" were remembered as consensual, forbidden love. This changed in the 1970s when the Japanese became conscious and reflexive of Japan's wartime atrocities, and it became popular to expose the inhumane and brutal nature of the Japanese imperial military apparatus, especially crimes committed against marginalized groups such as Koreans, Chinese, Okinawans, and fellow Asians. After the sexual slavery trial in 1991, while progressive Japanese maintained their reflexive stance and were inspired by the trial (e.g., Yoshimi[3]), others adopted a reactive approach and became more nationalistic. Hidaka suggests that such nationalistic undercurrents have been present since the end of the war,[4] but were possibly energized due to the highly publicized controversies sparked by the spirit of the times and other seminal events. Remembering the textbook controversy of 1982, when it was reported that the Japanese Education Ministry had ordered history textbook authors to whitewash the former military's actions—which was consequently met with vehement protests from China and South Korea—nationalists could have felt threatened by such foreign intervention into Japan's domestic affairs. They may have also been provoked by incidents such as the trial of Kim Hak-sun and two other Korean survivors, the report on Yoshimi's discovery of the documents proving the Japanese military's involvement in the "comfort" system, and Prime Minister Miyazawa Kiichi's subsequent apologies. Of course, all of this could have been rooted in some underlying prejudice toward Koreans.

By examining the memories of sexual slavery and its survivors over the past seventy years in Japan, we have seen how "comfort women," especially Korean "comfort women," have been "Orientalized" by both Japanese writers and former Japanese soldiers. In the period from 1945 to the 1960s, the women were often exoticized in ways typical for Western Orientalism. Between the 1970s and the 1980s, when the dominant memory was one of victimization, romanticized memories still appeared in the testimonies of former soldiers. Even after the sexual slavery trial, nationalist scholars such as Hata have insisted on depicting Korean and Chinese survivors and Koreans and Chinese in general as irrational, sneaky, and untrustworthy.[5]

Said argues that "the relationship between Occident and Orient is a relationship of power, of domination, of varying degrees of a complex hegemony."[6] He asserts that Orientalism was more than mere scholarly discourse and was an imperial institution.[7] In addition, he claims that it was a way for the Occident to dominate the Orient. Although he refers to the relationship between the colonizing West and the colonized Middle East, his arguments equally apply in this context. Japan was a colonial power, Korea its colony, and the relationship between the two nations was thus based on power and domination. Although postcolonial studies in general tend to focus on Western colonization of the non-West, the evidence presented here strongly suggests that non-Westerners can also "Orientalize" other non-Westerners.

Orientalist memories of sexual slavery may be illustrative of present-day racism toward other Asians, especially Koreans, in Japan as collective memory is influenced by the present. During Japan's modernization and Westernization in the nineteenth century, Westerners became admired, while other Asian nations who could not (or chose not to) industrialize and Westernize fell into disrepute. Certainly, even in postwar Japan, other Asians, and especially Koreans residing in Japan, mostly descendants of those who voluntarily or involuntarily moved to Japan during Japan's colonization, were discriminated against. In recent years, as tensions between Japan and

South Korea have grown because of the Japanese government's treatment of Japanese history, hate speech against Koreans has become an issue in Japan. Said discusses the paternalistic ideology of Western supremacy that supported Western imperialism and colonialism, arguing that "the vocabulary of classic nineteenth-century imperial culture is plentiful with words and concepts like 'inferior' or 'subject' races."[8] Similarly, Korean and Taiwanese colonial subjects were seen as "inferior" in imperial Japan and this way of thinking persists to this day.

In fact, Koreans and Chinese may not be the only Asians exoticized and Orientalized in Japan today. While most Japanese do not consider Japan as part of the West, it seems as if they do not consider themselves to be a part of "Asia," either. Interestingly, a Japanese Internet search for *Ajian* [Asian] restaurants yields a number of results for South Asian or Southeast Asian restaurants, but not Japanese restaurants. Similarly, *Ajian* festivals seem to pertain to festivals that feature *other* Asian nations. In this context, "Asia" is conceptualized as something exotic and foreign. Coupled with Japan's history of Western-centric modernization from the mid-nineteenth century (see chapter 1) and its current internationalization based on *whitenization*, "the process of identifying with white Westerners and privileging white bodies,"[9] the exoticization of other Asian nations, most of which were occupied by Japan during the war, should be critically examined in relation to Japan's discrimination against other Asians.

In my analysis of the collective memories of sexual slavery and its Korean survivors, one constant has emerged throughout the different time periods and that is prejudice against Koreans. Japanese military officials originally targeted Korean women due to their discriminatory feelings toward them. Modern Japanese nationalists refuse to accept the nation's responsibility for past crimes, instead they criticize Koreans and the South Korean government for "falsely accusing Japan for financial gain," stirring up anti-Korean sentiment in the Japanese public. Some Japanese nationalists may argue that they are anti-Korean only insofar as Koreans criticize Japan and are therefore anti-Japanese. However, other nations that have criticized Japan in the past (e.g., the United States during a trade dispute from the late 1980s to the early 1990s) did not have to deal with a similar patronizing and discriminatory backlash (e.g., Hata's "Japan is like a big brother of South Korea"[10]) and it seems plausible that anti-Korean sentiment in Japanese society is what makes the "comfort women" such a persistently controversial issue.

While eradicating prejudice against a certain group is always difficult, I wonder what could have happened if active measures had been taken at the end of World War II when Japan's colonization came to an end. Although Japanese society was exposed to a lot of negative propaganda about the Americans and the British during the war (e.g., *Kichiku Beiei* [Demons and

Beasts, Americans and British]), anti-American and anti-British sentiments were, for the most part, successfully removed through the postwar reeducation program implemented during the Allied occupation of Japan.[11] However, anti-Korean sentiment has always been condoned or even promoted by the Japanese government, as evidenced, for example, by the Japanese government's efforts to repatriate Koreans living in Japan during the 1950s,[12] and by how most Korean high schools in Japan have not qualified for tuition assistance from the Japanese government in contrast to most other international schools. Reflecting on this trend, even educated college professors have made explicitly racist remarks aimed at Koreans and Chinese without any repercussions, as illustrated in chapters 4 and 6.

Hasian calls intercultural memory scholars to link theories to praxis (i.e., practically apply theories) because we will be supporting the status quo unless we reflect more on the politicized nature of even seemingly descriptive studies.[13] Now is the time for us to challenge the discriminatory sentiments embedded in seemingly objective and scholarly studies of sexual slavery under the Japanese imperial military. As Hasian also argues, no human being should be indifferent to the "power and politics of remembering" horrific events and expecting "a single apolitical history" would not work.[14]

DISCURSIVE AMNESIA IN COLLECTIVE MEMORIES OF SEXUAL SLAVERY

I have also examined forgotten memories or discursive amnesia in my analysis of collective memories of sexual slavery and its survivors/victims. As Irwin-Zarecka discusses, an absence of memory is socially constructed[15] and, as Lee and Wander contend, it can privilege a certain group of people.[16]

During the aforementioned postwar period wherein "comfort women" were remembered as romanticized prostitutes, as discussed in chapter 2, the women's pain and suffering were forgotten, which privileged the involved soldiers and officials of the Japanese military by sparing them from being remembered as the perpetrators of the "comfort" system. Furthermore, by forgetting the (Korean) nationality of the "comfort" women/singers in two of the films, discursive amnesia privileged the Japanese by allowing them to evade their imperialist/colonialist past during which they exploited Koreans and other Asians.

Since the 1991 trial by Kim Hak-sun and two other Korean survivors of sexual slavery, "comfort women's" pain and suffering have been forgotten, especially by nationalists. This largely privileges the Japanese government as well as former Japanese soldiers and military personnel because it could potentially exonerate the Japanese government from its responsibility for the women's predicament as it became the main issue in the discourse on "comfort women." In the meantime, the "comfort women" who testified a more or less "romantic memory," albeit small in number, have led to discursive amnesia in progressive circles as the memory contradicts the victimhood of the women.

While I believe that women's suffering needs to be more deeply ingrained in our collective memory, especially in Japan; as Dezaki cautions in his movie *Shusenjō*, the exaggeration of women's suffering could give nationalists a reason to challenge the testimonies and even the issue itself. While forgetting the women's pain and suffering could privilege the former military personnel and government of Japan, forgetting the women who reported more "positive" memories could also privilege a patriarchal ideology that values women's chastity (i.e., "women who are sexually violated must be ashamed and commit suicide. If they are not living in despair, they must not really be victims") and excludes women who do not fit the "model victims" image.

REFLECTIONS ON THE *HALMŎNI* AND MEMORIES OF SEXUAL SLAVERY

Ellis states that autoethnography connects personal stories to cultural, societal, and political contexts.[17] Similarly, Banks and Banks argue that autoethnography is "a critical looking outward at power relations."[18] To conclude this book, I would like to look back and reflect on my autoethnographical trip to South Korea as I spoke about at the beginning as well as my analysis of various artifacts of sexual slavery from the last seventy-five years to consider my reflections in both a societal and political context.

To this day, I still wonder what was so shocking to me and why I felt so exposed when the *halmŏni* accused me of the crimes my country had committed before I was even born. Perhaps I was overwhelmed by the real pain she experienced and expressed. Compared to that, what I had been doing seemed insignificant. It might also have affected me because I had been thinking that I was "one of them," subconsciously and arrogantly thinking that I could understand their pain and feelings from having read their testimonies and books/articles about them, as well as assuming that I could feel and share their pain, agony, and anger as a human being and a woman. Possibly, it was because the *halmŏni* challenged my status as a "good Japanese"; in her eyes, I was simply another one of the Japanese imperialists who have not taken responsibility.

My experience in South Korea, particularly being called out by the *halmŏni*, made me think of the issue of individual responsibility, that is, whether or not individual citizens should be held responsible for their nation's crimes that happened before they were even born. Martin and Nakayama argue that, considering the exploitation and marginalization of the Native Americans in early U.S. history, though the European Americans of today did not partake in said injustice, they are nevertheless beneficiaries of the oppression of Native Americans (e.g., inheriting land that had originally belonged to the Native Americans).[19] Similarly, S. Lily Mendoza contends, when discussing the Australian government's apology to its aboriginal peoples, that the descendants of white settlers are beneficiaries of their ancestors' past exploitation of the aboriginal peoples through the accumulation of economic and political power while aboriginal descendants continue to occupy a disadvantaged position.[20] Likewise, today's Japanese people are beneficiaries of Japan's colonization of Korea and Taiwan. Although Japan and Japanese companies had to leave most of their properties in Korea and Taiwan when colonization ended in August 1945, the companies that benefited from the cheap or free labor of Koreans and Taiwanese prospered during colonization times and continued to do so afterward. In fact, Japanese society's postwar prosperity was largely built on such corporations' success. As the beneficiaries of said society, the Japanese people of today should therefore feel responsible for the suffering of colonized people, including the survivors of sexual slavery.

I also learned the importance of listening to voices critical of Japan's past. Ultimately, regardless of how you remember sexual slavery and its victims and survivors, it is a fact that Japan colonized Korea and Taiwan. Without this colonization, Korean and Taiwanese women would not have become "comfort women." Their voices have to be heard. We must consider what needs to be done and what would be the best for each survivor. It may be impossible to accommodate the needs of every single survivor, but this will serve as a test of the Japanese government's sincerity. The starting point may be the Japanese prime minister showing that the nation is willing to make efforts to "make it right" by entering into dialogue with the survivors, or at least making an effort to do so. Although some of the survivors may have similar experiences, they are all different individuals who need and want different things. For example, some survivors are willing to receive money from the Japanese government as a result of the 2015 agreement, whereas others refuse to do so. As S. Lily Mendoza insists, "the past is not over until the injured party says it's over, and that it's now time to move on."[21] It is not Japan's prerogative to decide whether the matter is settled and "irreversible." She further insists that it is not over "until what's broken is repaired, until what's stolen is given back, and until apologies are in fact backed by the dismantling of the system that perpetuated the violence and injustice in the first place."[22] As the Coomaraswamy report suggests, the Japanese government has never attempted to prosecute those who were responsible for the system. Rather, some Japanese politicians together with nationalist writers have maintained that the "comfort women" were privately recruited prostitutes, therefore exempting the Japanese government from any liability.

It has also led me to begin to think about the connection between how the "comfort women" issue has been handled and how war crimes have generally been dealt with in postwar Japan. Immediately after the war, Japan was tried for its war crimes against the Allied nations at a number of military tribunals headed by the Allies. However, Japan's crimes against those who were from countries other than the Allied nations have not yet been tried, which is in sharp contrast to the ways in which Germany has continued to prosecute former National Socialist crimes to this day. An example of this are the crimes against Okinawan civilians, which include Japanese officers ordering the mass suicides of Okinawan residents or the execution of Okinawan residents as alleged spies. The forced mass suicides of Okinawan residents have been documented as early as 1950 in *Tetsuno Bōfū* [Typhoon of Steel]. They were also written about in *Taiheiyō Sensō* [The Pacific War] (published in 1968) by Ienaga Saburō, a Japanese history textbook author who sued the Japanese Education Ministry three times (chapter 1), and in *Okinawa Nōto* [Okinawa Notes] (published in 1970) by Ōe Kenzaburo, a Nobel Laureate. Evidently, this has been widely known in Japan, yet nobody has been prosecuted for it. Likewise, British historian Anthony Beevor states that some of Japan's reckless military campaigns even without providing its own troops with adequate weapons and food—which consequently caused numerous soldiers to die of starvation—were crimes committed by Japanese military officials.[23] For example, in the battle of Imphal, the Japanese troops were ordered to attack a British base in Imphal, the northeastern part of India, from Burma without an adequate supply of weapons and food. As a result, more than 60,000 Japanese soldiers died, mostly from starvation and illness. However, those who were in charge of these campaigns or the aforementioned atrocities against Okinawan residents have never been tried in postwar Japan, just like those who were in charge of the "comfort" system.

My examination of artifacts related to memories of mostly Korean "comfort women" also made me think about Japanese "comfort women." Nationalist scholars such as Fujioka write that, while they acknowledge that some Korean women had to become "comfort women" due to poverty, many Japanese women from impoverished families also had to become prostitutes against their will under the official prostitution system sanctioned by the Japanese government around the same time. They argue that the Japanese government would also have to apologize to those Japanese women if it had to apologize to Korean survivors.[24] I would argue that the Japanese government should apologize to those Japanese women as well, because their lives were destroyed under the supervision of the Japanese government. Denying the government's responsibility for allowing the exploitation of women under the sanctioned prostitution system and attributing it to individual women's "falling" implicitly endorses classism and sexism (i.e., impoverished women being sold or selling themselves into prostitution, women's lives being sacrificed to take care of men's sexual needs, considering that most prostitutes were unable to get back to normal lives).

Further, Japan's pacifist movement and pacifist education that overemphasize Japanese victimhood need to be reconsidered. While I agree with the main message, "War is terrible; therefore, it should be avoided," as we have seen in chapters 4 and 5, some of the pacifist movement's teachings could be exploited to justify the "comfort" system and exonerate those who were responsible for the system. For instance, chapter 4 presents how some nationalists such as Itō and Kobayashi assert former Japanese soldiers' victimhood. Itō states that "comfort women" lived unreasonable lives, but this was even more true for soldiers.[25] Kobayashi suggests that soldiers fought and died for the nation and their descendants, but now they are being called rapists and, therefore, they are the real victims.[26] The overall message is that "comfort women" may have suffered, but everyone suffered (soldiers suffered the most) during the war because war is inherently tragic. An abstract entity (i.e., war) is blamed for the women's suffering and, ultimately, nobody is held responsible. Likewise, in chapter 5, former Japanese soldiers who were interviewed justified their use of "comfort" stations by blaming war for stripping them of their humanity and thanking "comfort women" for enabling them to regain their humanity. Indeed, one must remember that there is a fine line between Japan's mainstream pacifist discourse and whitewashing Japan's past atrocities.

Moreover, through my visit to South Korea, especially to some of the memory places related to sexual slavery, I was ashamed of myself to realize just how deeply I had internalized stereotypes of (South) Koreans in Japan (e.g., "as anti-Japanese Koreans"). At the Wednesday demonstration I attended, although I was surprised at the generally relaxed atmosphere and smiling participants, what made the strongest impression on me was the female high school student speaker's outpouring of emotion against Japan. Furthermore, although I continued to encounter friendly South Koreans throughout my trip, the ones I remember most tend to be those who expressed anti-Japan sentiments (e.g., the unfriendly man at the information counter over the polite police officers in Busan and the *halmŏni* who criticized Japan over the interpreter who came to talk to me afterward at the House of Sharing). Considering that I selectively went to places where I was more likely to encounter anti-Japan sentiment and that I believe that Japan deserves to be hated by Koreans, I should not have been shocked to encounter these situations. However, after witnessing the *halmŏni*'s outburst at the House of Sharing, I could not stop thinking about her, together with the high school girl and the man at the information counter at the Busan Station. On my return trip to the United States from Seoul Incheon Airport, to Paris Charles de Gaulle Airport, and then to Pittsburgh International Airport, I continued to think about the three of them. When I arrived in Paris, I quickly disembarked the plane because my connecting flight to Pittsburgh was about to take off in an hour. While rushing toward the gate for my Pittsburgh flight, it suddenly dawned on me that I was in France upon hearing an announcement in French. Then, I remember feeling a sudden sense of relief thinking, "I'm finally away from the people who hate me!" Through my examination of the works of Japanese nationalists, I found that this "angry, inherently anti-Japan Koreans" stereotype is something nationalists believe and promote. I was ashamed to find my own internalization of this stereotype that I had seen in Japanese reports.

While I was finishing this manuscript in August 2019, an art exhibition titled *Hyōgen no Fujiyū ten—Sonogo* ["After Freedom of Expression?"] was held during the Aichi Triennale 2019 art festival, in Nagoya, Japan, and it was met with a lot of controversy. In line with the exhibit's intention to celebrate freedom of expression, it included artwork that had been previously excluded from museums in Japan or elsewhere.[27] Ironically, the organizers decided to close down the exhibit after only three days due to the complaints and threats they received. Some of the controversial pieces included the Statue of Peace signifying "comfort women" as well as a film showing the burning of a portrait of the Showa emperor being burned. After much public debate, the organizers decided to reopen the exhibit two months later with heightened security. This incident goes to show how the "comfort women" issue continues to be a highly controversial topic in Japan.

In my collective memory study of sexual slavery in Japan, I have attempted to contribute toward a better understanding of the recent controversy surrounding sexual slavery in Asia and the tensions between Japan and its neighboring countries. The problematic denials of the suffering and trauma of the victims must be challenged. Though many Japanese want to remember the role of Japan as a "victim," of the war, we should also remember those who were victimized by Japan's aggression in the past. Without truly understanding the pain of others and being reflexive of our own country's aggressive past, it will be impossible to prevent future conflicts.

NOTES

1. Ueno, *Nashionarizumu*, 109–110.
2. Blair et al., "Introduction," 6–7.
3. Yoshimi, *Jūgun Ianfu*, 2.

4. Rokurō Hidaka, *Sengoshi wo kangaeru* [Thinking about postwar thought] (Tokyo: Iwanami Shoten, 1980), 4.
5. Hata, *Ianfu*, 179–204.
6. Said, *Orientalism*, 5.
7. Ibid., 95.
8. Said, *Culture*, 5.
9. Etsuko Fujimoto, "Japanese-ness, Whiteness, and the 'Other' in Japan's Internationalization," in *Transforming Communication about Culture: Critical New Directions*, ed. Mary Jane Collier (Thousand Oaks, CA: Sage, 2001), 2.
10. Hata, *Ianfu Mondai*, 100.
11. Etō, *Tozasareta*, 261–312.
12. Morris-Suzuki, "Defining the Boundaries."
13. Marouf Arif Hasian, Jr., "Untimely Meditations: *Praxis*, Critical Intercultural Studies, and Memoricide," *Journal of International and Intercultural Communication* 9, no. 3 (2016): 269–270.
14. Hasian, "Critical Intercultural Communication," 312.
15. Irwin-Zarecka, *Frames of Remembrance*, 116.
16. Lee and Wander, "On Discursive Amnesia," 152–154.
17. Ellis, *The Ethnographic I*, xix.
18. Stephen P. Banks and Anna Banks. "Reading 'The Critical Life': Autoethnography as Pedagogy," *Communication Education 49*, no. 3 (2000): 235.
19. Judith N. Martin and Thomas K. Nakayama, *Intercultural Communication in Contexts* (New York: McGraw Hill, 2013), 144.
20. Bryant Keith Alexander, Lily A. Arasaratnam, Lisa Flores, Wendy Leeds-Hurwitz, S. Lily Mendoza, John Oetzel, Joyce Osland, Yukio Tsuda, Jing Yin, and Rona Halualani, "Our Role as Intercultural Scholars, Practitioners, Activists, and Teachers in Addressing These Key Intercultural Urgencies, Issues, and Challenges," *Journal of International and Intercultural Communication* 7, no. 1 (January 2014): 89.
21. Ibid., 91.
22. Ibid., 91.
23. Misuzu Amano and Yasuji Nagai, "'Shokuryō wo Ataerarenainoni Tatakai Kyōyō' Daihonei Sanbō no Hanzai" ['Forced Troops to Fight without Food' Crimes of Japanese Military Officials], *Asahi Shimbun*, August 1, 2020, https://digital.asahi.com/articles/ASN7W3J28N3SPLZU006.html?iref=pc_ss_date/
24. Fujioka, "Ianfu 'Nikkan Gōi,'" 330.
25. Itō, "Kedakai," chap. 11.
26. Kobayashi, *Shin Gōmanism Sengen*, 88.
27. Motoko Rich, "The Exhibit Lauded Freedom of Expression. It Was Silenced," *The New York Times*, August 5, 2019, ProQuest.

Appendix A
Timeline

1868: Meiji Restoration: Beginning of Japan's modernization—beginning of the Meiji Era (1868–1912)

1895: Japan's victory in the First Sino-Japanese War (1894–1895) and the cessation of Taiwan to Japan as a result

1905: Japan's victory in the Russo-Japanese War (1904–1905) and the cessation of the southern half of Sakhalin Island to Japan

1914–1918: World War I: The Empire of Japan declared war against Germany based on the Anglo-Japanese Alliance (1902–1923)

1915: The twenty-one demands were made by the Empire of Japan to China, demanding special privileges in China. Most of them, such as confirmation of Japan's railroad and mining claims in Shandon Province, were accepted

1919: The Treaty of Versailles: Japan's acquisition of former German territories in Asia including Shandong Province in China, Palau, and the Marshall Islands

1918–1922: The Siberian Intervention

1931: The Mukden Incident: The Imperial Japanese Army's invasion of Manchuria

1932: January: The First Shanghai Incident: a military conflict broke out in Shanghai between the Japanese imperial military and the Chinese military

March: Japan founded the puppet state, Manchukuo, in Manchuria

1937: The Marco Polo Bridge Incident: a military conflict near Beijing between Japan and China, the beginning of the Second Sino-Japanese War

1938: The first confirmed military "comfort" station was built near Shanghai

1941: The Pacific War began

1945: Japan's surrender
1946–1948: The International Military Tribunal for the Far East (Tokyo Trial). Twenty-five Japanese politicians and military officials including Tōjō Hideki, a former prime minister, were convicted for conspiracy to start and wage war (Class A war crimes)
1948: Seven out of the twenty-five convicted at the Tokyo Trial were executed
1965: Ienaga Saburō sued the Japanese Education Ministry (Ienaga lost in 1993)
1967: Ienaga's second lawsuit (Ienaga won in 1989)
1974: Soh's lawsuit against the Japanese government for Koreans left on Sakhalin
1984: Ienaga's third lawsuit (Ienaga's partial victory in 1997, which allowed him to write about human experiments on Chinese and the Nanjing Massacre)
1991: Kim Hak-sun and two other Korean survivors of sexual slavery sued the Japanese government
1992: Historian Yoshimi Yoshiaki's discovery of documents proving the Japanese imperial military's involvement in the "comfort" system; Japanese prime minister Miyazawa Kiichi's visit to South Korea and his apology
1993: The Kōno Statement
2011: The South Korean constitution court ruled that it is unconstitutional for the South Korean government not to secure compensation from Japan
2015: The bilateral agreement between the Japanese government and the South Korean government

Bibliography

Ahn, Yonson. "Japan's 'Comfort Women' and Historical Memory: The Neo-Nationalist Counter-Attack." In *The Power of Memory in Modern Japan*, edited by Sven Saaler and Wolfgang Schwentker, 32–53. Folkestone, UK: Global Oriental, 2008.

Akatsuki no dassou [Escape at Dawn]. Directed by Taniguchi Senkichi. (1950; Tokyo: Shin Toho), Film.

Alexander, Bryant Keith, Lily A. Arasaratnam, Lisa Flores, Wendy Leeds-Hurwitz, S. Lily Mendoza, John Oetzel, Joyce Osland, Yukio Tsuda, Jing Yin, and Rona Halualani. "Our Role as Intercultural Scholars, Practitioners, Activists, and Teachers in Addressing These Key Intercultural Urgencies, Issues, and Challenges." *Journal of International and Intercultural Communication* 7, no. 1 (January 2014): 68–99.

Amano, Misuzu and Yasuji Nagai. "'Shōkuryo wo Ataerarenainoni Tatakai Kyōyō' Daihonei Sanbō no Hanzai." ['Forced Troops to Fight without Food' Crimes of Japanese Military Officials]. *Asahi Shimbun*, August 1, 2020. https://digital.asahi.com/articles/ASN7W3J28N3SPLZU006.html?iref=pc_ss_date.

Aoki, Eric and Kyle M. Jonas. "Collective Memory and Sacred Space in Post-Genocide Rwanda: Reconciliation and Rehumanization Processes in Mureithi's *ICYIZERE*." *Journal of International and Intercultural Communication* 9, no. 3 (2016): 240–258.

Arai, Shinichi, Rumiko Nishino, and Akira Maeda, eds. *Jūgun Ianfu and Rekishi Ninshiki* [Military Comfort Women and History Interpretation]. Tokyo: Shinkō Shuppan sha, 1997.

Arai, Shinichi. "Rekishi wo Mitsumerukoto no Imi" [The Meanings of Reflecting on History]. In *Jūgun Ianfu and Rekishi Ninshiki* [Military Comfort Women and History Interpretation], edited by Shinichi Arai, Rumiko Nishino, and Akira Maeda, 5–14. Tokyo: Shinkō Shuppan sha, 1997.

Babicz, Lionel. "Japan-Korea, France-Algeria: Colonialism and Post-Colonialism." *Japanese Studies* 33, no. 2 (September 2013): 201–211.

Banks, Stephen P. and Anna Banks. "Reading 'The Critical Life': Autoethnography as Pedagogy." *Communication Education* 49, no. 3 (2000): 233–238.

Bar, Cameron W. "US Rushes to Placate Japanese, Angered by rape in Okinawa." *Christian Science Monitor*, September 22, 1995, 6. ProQuest.

Biesecker, Barbara A. "Remembering World War II: The Rhetoric and Politics of National Commemoration at the Turn of the 21st Century." *Quarterly Journal of Speech* 88, no. 4 (2002): 393–409.

Blair, Carole, Greg Dickinson, and Brian L. Ott. "Introduction: Rhetoric/Memory/Place," In *Places of Public Memory: The Rhetoric of Museums and Memorials*, edited by Greg Dickinson, Carole Blair, and Brian L. Ott, 1–54. Tuscaloosa: University of Alabama Press, 2010.

Booth, Wayne C. *The Rhetoric of Fiction*. Chicago: University of Chicago Press, 1961.

Bungei Shunjū, ed. *"Jūgun Ianfu": Asahi Shimbun vs. Bungei Shunjū* ["Military Comfort Women": Asahi Newspaper vs. Bungei Shunjū] (Tokyo: Bungei Shunjū, 2014), Kindle.

Choi, Jung-Bong. "Mapping Japanese Imperialism onto Postcolonial Criticism." *Social Identities* 9, no. 3 (2003): 325–339.

Chong, Young-hwan, "'Sengo Nihon' Kōtei no Yokubou to 'Teikoku no Ianfu'" [Desire to Positively View "Postwar Japan" and "Comfort Women of the Empire"]. In *Q & A Chōsenjin "Ianfu" to Shokuminchi Shihai Sekinin: Anatano Gimon ni Kotaemasu* [Q & A Korean "Comfort Women" and the Responsibility for Colonization: We Will Answer Your Questions], edited by Puja Kim and Ryūta Itagaki, 64–67. Tokyo: Ochanomizu Shobō, 2018.

Dierkes, Julian. *Postwar History Education in Japan and the Germanys: Guilty Lessons*. London: Routledge, 2010.

Dirlik, Arif. "'Trapped in History' on the Way to Utopia: East Asia's 'Great War' Fifty Years Later." In *Perilous Memories*, edited by T. Fujitani, Geoffrey M. White, and Lisa Yoneyama, 299–322. Durham, NC: Duke University Press, 2001.

Drzewiecka, Jolanda A. "Public Memories in the Shadow of the Other." In *The Handbook of Critical Intercultural Communication*, edited by Thomas K. Nakayama and Rona Tamiko Halualani, 286–310. Sussex, UK: Wiley-Blackwell, 2010.

Edwards, Jason A. "Community-Focused Apologia in International Affairs: Japanese Prime Minister Tomiichi Murayama's Apology." *Howard Journal of Communications* 16, no.4 (2005): 317–336.

Ehrenhaus, Peter. "Why We Fought: Holocaust Memory in Spielberg's *Saving Private Ryan*." *Critical Studies in Media Communication* 18, no. 3 (2001): 321–337.

Ellis, Carolyn S. *The Ethnographic I: A Methodological Novel about Autoethnography*. Walnut Creek, CA: AltaMira Press, 2004.

Elllis, Carolyn S. and Arthur P. Bochner. "Analyzing Analytic Autoethnography: An Autopsy." *Journal of Contemporary Ethnography* 35, no. 4 (2006): 429–449.

Etō, Jun. *Tozasareta Gengo Kūkan: Senryōgun no Kenetsu to Sengo Nihon* [The closed language space: The censorship of the occupation force and postwar Japan]. Tokyo: Bungei Shuju, 1994.

Fackler, Martin. "Japan, Seeking Revision of Report on Wartime Brothels, is Rebuffed." *The New York Times*, October 17, 2014, p. 4. LexisNexis Academic.
Fifield, Anna. "An Early Roadblock for Landmark 'Comfort Women' Deal." *The Washington Post*, January 1, 2016, LexisNexis Academic.
Fujiki, Shunichi. "Kokuren de Nihon no Makikaeshi ga Hajimatta!" [Japan's Counterattack Started at the United Nations!]. In *Kokuren ga Sekai ni Hirometa "Ianfu = Seidorei" no Uso: Junēbu Kokuren Hakendan Hōkoku* [A Lie Spread All Over the World Through the United Nations, "Comfort Women = Sex Slaves": Reports by a Team that was Sent to Geneva for the United Nations' Meetings], edited by Nobukatsu Fujioka, 282–296. Tokyo: Jiyūsha, 2016.
Fujiki, Shunichi. "Kokuren Jinken Rijikai ni Norikonde Wakatta koto" [What I Found out by Attending UNHRC meetings]. In *Kokuren ga Sekai ni Hirometa "Ianfu = Seidorei" no Uso: Junēbu Kokuren Hakendan Hōkoku* [A Lie Spread All Over the World Through the United Nations, "Comfort Women = Sex Slaves": Reports by a Team that was Sent to Geneva for the United Nations' Meetings], edited by Nobukatsu Fujioka, 372–386. Tokyo: Jiyūsha, 2016.
Fujiki, Shunichi. "Totsuka Etsurō shi tono Sougū to Taiwa" [Encounter and Conversation with Mr. EtsurōTotsuka]. In *Kokuren ga Sekai ni Hirometa "Ianfu = Seidorei" no Uso: Junēbu Kokuren Hakendan Hōkoku* [A Lie Spread All Over the World Through the United Nations, "Comfort Women = Sex Slaves": Reports by a Team that was Sent to Geneva for the United Nations' Meetings], edited by Nobukatsu Fujioka, 248–280. Tokyo: Jiyūsha, 2016.
Fujimoto, Etsuko. "Japanese-ness, Whiteness, and the 'Other' in Japan's Internationalization." In *Transforming Communication about Culture: Critical New Directions*, edited by Mary Jane Collier, 1–24. Thousand Oaks, CA: Sage, 2001.
Fujioka, Nobukatsu, ed. *Kokuren ga Sekai ni Hirometa "Ianfu = Seidorei" no Uso: Junēbu\Kokuren Hakendan Hōkoku* [A Lie Spread All Over the World Through the United Nations, "Comfort Women = Sex Slaves": Reports by a Team that was Sent to Geneva for the United Nations' Meetings]. Tokyo: Jiyūsha, 2016.
Fujioka, Nobukatsu, Kiyoshi Hosoya, Yumiko Yamamoto, Shunichi Fujiki, Mitsuhiko Fujii, and Michio Sekino, "Itte Wakatta Kokuren Riyou no Karakuri" [Tricks of Utilizing the United Nations We Found Out by Attending]. In *Kokuren ga Sekai ni Hirometa "Ianfu = Seidorei" no Uso: Junēbu Kokuren Hakendan Hōkoku* [A Lie Spread All Over the World Through the United Nations, "Comfort Women = Sex Slaves": Reports by a Team that was Sent to Geneva for the United Nations' Meetings], edited by Nobukatsu Fujioka, 184–246. Tokyo: Jiyūsha, 2016.
Fujioka, Nobukatsu. "'Ianfu = Seidorei' Setsu Netsuzō to Kakusan" [Fabrication and Promotion of the Theory, "Comfort Women = Sex Slaves"]. In *Kokuren ga Sekai ni Hirometa "Ianfu = Seidorei" no Uso: Junēbu Kokuren Hakendan Hōkoku* [A Lie Spread All Over the World Through the United Nations, "Comfort Women = Sex Slaves": Reports by a Team that was Sent to Geneva for the United Nations' Meetings], edited by Nobukatsu Fujioka, 12–52. Tokyo: Jiyūsha, 2016.
Fujioka, Nobukatsu. "Rekishi Kyōkasho no Hanzai" [Crimes of History Textbooks]. In *Rekishi Kyōkasho tono 15 Nen Sensō*, edited by Kanji Nishio, Yoshinori Kobayashi, Nobutatsu Fujioka, and Shirō Takahashi, 44–65. Tokyo: PHP Kenkyūsho, 1997.

Fujioka, Nobukatsu. *Ojoku no Kingendaishi: Ima, Kokufuku no Toki* [Shameful Modern History: Now, Time to Overcome]. Tokyo: Tokuma Shoten, 1996.

Fujitani, T., Geoffrey M. White, and Lisa Yoneyama. "Introduction." In *Perilous Memories*, edited by T. Fujitani, Geoffrey. M. White, and Lisa Yoneyama, 1–29. Durham, NC: Duke University Press, 2001.

"Govt's Stance on Comfort Women Clarified." *The Japan Times*, April 8, 2015. LexisNexis Academic.

Gronbeck, Bruce E. "The Rhetorics of the Past: History, Argument, and Collective Memory." In *Doing Rhetorical History: Concepts and Cases*, edited by Kathleen J. Turner, 47–60. Tuscaloosa: University of Alabama Press, 1998.

Han, Hong-goo. "Jikoku no Kagai no Rekishi to Mukiau" [Confront Your Country's History of Aggression]. In *Q & A Chōsenjin "Ianfu" to Shokuminchi Shihai Sekinin: Anatano Gimon ni Kotaemasu* [Q & A Korean "Comfort Women" and the Responsibility for Colonization: We Will Answer Your Questions], edited by Puja Kim and Ryūta Itagaki, 177–181. Tokyo: Ochanomizu Shobō, 2018.

Handa, Naoko and Takashi Yoshikawa. "Shimai Toshi Kaishō Kodawaru Wake ha Osaka Shichō no 'Orosenu Kobushi'?" [The Reason Why the Osaka Mayor Insists on the Termination of the Sister City Contract is his Criticism that Cannot be Taken back?], *Asahi Shimbun*, November 24, 2017. https://digital.asahi.com/articles/ASKCR4V6BKCRPTIL00L.html?iref=pc_ss_date.

Hang-Sun, Jonathan and Choe Soble. "'Comfort Women' Deal Angers Some." *The New York Times,* December 30, 2015, A07. LexisNexis Academic.

Hariman, Robert and John Louis Lucaites. "Public Identity and Collective Memory in U.S. Iconic Photography: The Image of 'Accidental Napalm'." *Critical Studies in Media Communication* 20, no. 1 (2003): 35–66.

Hasian, Marouf and Carlson, Cheree. "Revisionism and Collective Memory: The Struggle for Meaning in the *Amistad Affair*." *Communication Monographs* 67, no. 1 (2000): 42–62.

Hasian, Marouf and Helene A. Shugart. "Melancholic Nostalgia, Collective Memories, and the Cinematic Representations of Nationalistic Identities in *Indochine*." *Communication Quarterly* 49, no. 4 (2001): 329–349.

Hasian, Marouf and Robert Frank. "Rhetoric, History, and Collective Memory: Decoding the Goldhagen Debates." *Western Journal of Communication* 63, no. 1 (1999): 95–114.

Hasian, Marouf. "Critical Intercultural Communication, Remembrances of George Washington Williams, and the Rediscovery of Leopold II's 'Crimes against Humanity'." In *The Handbook of Critical Intercultural Communication*, edited by Thomas K. Nakayama and Rona Tamiko Halualani, 311–331. West Sussex, UK: Wiley-Blackwell, 2010.

Hasian, Marouf. "Military Orientalism at the Cineplex: A Postcolonial Reading of *Zero Dark Thirty*." *Critical Studies in Media Communication* 31, no. 5 (2014): 464–478.

Hasian, Marouf. "Remembering and Forgetting the 'Final Solution': A Rhetorical Pilgrimage through the U.S. Holocaust Memorial Museum." *Critical Studies in Media Communication* 21, no. 1 (2004): 64–92.

Hasian, Marouf. "Untimely Mediations: *Praxis,* Critical Intercultural Studies, and Memoricide." *Journal of International and Intercultural Communication* 9, no. 3 (2016): 268–271.
Hata, Ikuhiko. *Ianfu Mondai no Kessan* [Settlement of the Comfort Women Issue]. Tokyo: PHP Kenkyūsho, 2016.
Hata, Ikuhiko. *Ianfu to Senjō no Sei* [Comfort Women and Sex in the Battlefield]. Shinchō Sensho: Tokyo, 1999.
Hayashi, Hiroshi and Yoshiaki Yoshimi. "Mun Ok-chu sanha Biruma de Ooganemochi ni natta?" [Did Mun Ok-chu Become Rich in Burma?]. In *Q & A Chōsenjin "Ianfu" to Shokuminchi Shihai Sekinin: Anatano Gimon ni Kotaemasu* [Q & A Korean "Comfort Women" and the Responsibility for Colonization: We Will Answer Your Questions], edited by Puja Kim and Ryūta Itagaki, 42–46. Tokyo: Ochanomizu Shobō, 2018.
Hicks, George. *Comfort Women: Japan's Brutal Regime of Enforced Prostitution in the Second World War.* New York: W.W. Norton & Company, 1995.
Hidaka, Rokuou. *Sengoshi wo Kangaeru* [Thinking about Postwar Thought]. Tokyo: Iwanami Shoten, 1980.
Hirano, Kyōko. *Tennō to Seppun* [The Emperor and Kiss]. Soushi sha: Tokyo, 1998.
Honda, Katsuichi. *The Nanjing Massacre: A Japanese Journalist Confronts Japan's National Shame.* Translated by Karen Sandness. Armonk, NY: Sharpe, 1998.
Hosaka, Masayasu. "Jūgun Ianfu Mondai wo 50 Nengo ni Danzai Suruna" [Do not Prosecute People for the Comfort Women Issue 50 Years Later]. In *"Jūgun Ianfu": Asahi Shimbun vs. Bungei Shunjū* ["Military Comfort Women": Asahi Newspaper vs. Bungei Shunjū], edited by *Bungei Shunjū*, Tokyo: Bungei Shunjū, 2014, Kindle.
"Ianfu Mondai de Kōshiki Shazai" [Official Apologies for the Comfort Women Issue]. *Asahi Shimbun,* January 17, 1992, p. 1.
"Ianfu Mondai: Shusho ga Shazai Hyōmei" [Comfort Women Issue: Prime Minister Expressed Apologies]. *Asahi Shimbun,* January 15, 1992, p. 1.
"Iansho Gunkanyō Shimesu Shiryō" [Comfort Stations Documents that Indicate the Involvement of the Military]. *Asahi Shimbun,* January 11, 1992, p. 1.
"Impasse over Busan Statue Drags on." *The Japan Times,* February 9, 2017. LexisNexis Academic.
Inuzuka, Ako and Thomas Fuchs. "Memories of Japanese Militarism: The Yasukuni Shrine as a Commemorative Site." *The Journal of International Communication* 20, no. 1 (2014): 21–41.
Inuzuka, Ako. "A Dialectic between Nationalism and Multiculturalism: An Analysis of the Internationalization Discourse in Japan." In *Intercultural Communication in Japan: Theorizing Homogenizing Discourse,* edited by Satoshi Toyosaki and Shinsuke Eguchi, 207–223. London: Routledge, 2017.
Inuzuka, Ako. "Memories of the Tokko: An Analysis of the Chiran Peace Museum for Kamikaze Pilots." *Howard Journal of Communications* 27, no. 2 (2016): 145–166.
Inuzuka, Ako. "Remembering Japanese Militarism through the Fusosha Textbook: The Collective Memory of the Asian-Pacific War." *Communication Quarterly* 61, no. 2 (2013): 131–150.

Irwin-Zarecka, Iwona. *Frames of Remembrance: The Dynamics of Collective Memory*. New Brunswick, NJ: Transaction Publishers, 1997.

Itō, Keiichi. "Kedakaki Ianfu tachi" [Proud Comfort Women]. In *"Jūgun Ianfu": Asahi Shimbun vs. Bungei Shunjū* ["Military Comfort Women": Asahi Newspaper vs. Bungei Shunjū], edited by *Bungei Shunjū*. Tokyo: Bungei Shunjū, 2014, chap. 11, Kindle.

Itagaki, Ryūta. "Abe Danwa ha Nani ga Mondai?" [What is the Problem about the Abe Statement?]. In *Q & A Chōsenjin "Ianfu" to Shokuminchi Shihai Sekinin: Anatano Gimonni Kotaemasu* [Q & A Korean "Comfort Women" and the Responsibility for Colonization: We Will Answer Your Questions], edited by Puja Kim and Ryūta Itagaki, 160–176. Tokyo: Ochanomizu Shobō, 2018.

Itagaki, Ryūta. "Nikkan 'Gōi' ha '1miri' mo Ugokasu bekidenai?" [Shouldn't the Japan-South Korea Agreement be Changed even a Little?]. In *Q & A Chōsenjin "Ianfu" to Shokuminchi Shihai Sekinin: Anatano Gimon ni Kotaemasu* [Q & A Korean "Comfort Women" and the Responsibility for Colonization: We Will Answer Your Questions], edited by Puja Kim and Ryūta Itagaki, 185–190. Tokyo: Ochanomizu Shobō, 2018.

Izumi, Mariko. "Asian-Japanese: State-Apology, National Ethos, and the 'Comfort Women' Reparations Debate in Japan." *Communication Studies* 62, no. 5 (2011): 473–490.

"Japan Urged to Set up War-Crimes Tribunal on Forced Prostitution: UN Criticizes Tokyo for Ignoring the Issue of So-Called Comfort Camps." *The Vancouver Sun*, February 7, 1996, A9. LexisNexis Academic.

"Japan's Lack of Apology on War-Time Past to Affect South Korea Ties." *BBC Monitoring Asia Pacific*. April 30, 2015. LexisNexis Academic.

Kamisaka, Fuyuko and Ikuhiko Hata. "Hashimoto Souri ha Dare ni Nani wo Abiruto Iunoka" [To Whom is Prime Minister Hashimoto Apologizing for What?]. In *"Jūgun Ianfu": Asahi Shimbun vs. Bungei Shunjū* ["Military Comfort Women": Asahi Newspaper vs. Bungei Shunjū], edited by *Bungei Shunjū*. Tokyo: Bungei Shunjū, 2014, chap. 5, Kindle.

Kawaguchi Mann, Emi. "Doitsu niokeru Ianfu Hōdō no Ronchō" [The Tone of Media Reports on Comfort Women in Germany]. In *Kokuren ga Sekai ni Hirometa "Ianfu = Seidorei" no Uso: Junēbu Kokuren Hakendan Hōkoku* [A Lie Spread All Over the World Through the United Nations, "Comfort Women = Sex Slaves": Reports by a Team that was Sent to Geneva for the United Nations' Meetings], edited by Nobukatsu Fujioka, 168–182. Tokyo: Jiyūsha, 2016.

Kawata, Fumiko. "'Ianfu' Mondai no Kiten" [The Origin of the "Comfort Women" Issue]. In *"Ianfu" Mondai ga Toutekitakoto* [What the "Comfort Women" Issue has Led us to Question], edited by Noriko Oomori and Fumiko Kawata, 6–14. Tokyo: Iwanami Shoten, 2010.

Kawata, Fumiko. "Kyokasho Mondai" [The Textbook Issue]. In *"Ianfu" Mondai ga Toutekitakoto* [What the "Comfort Women" Issue has Led us to Question], edited by Noriko Oomori and Fumiko Kawata, 27–31. Tokyo: Iwanami Shoten, 2010.

Kawata, Fumiko. "Maegaki" [Introduction]. In *"Ianfu" Mondai ga Toutekitakoto* [What the "Comfort Women" Issue has Led us to Question], edited by Noriko Oomori and Fumiko Kawata, 2–4. Tokyo: Iwanami Shoten, 2010.

Kawata, Fumiko. *Akarenga no Ie: Chōsen kara Kita Jūgun Ianfu* [House with a Red Brick Roof: Military Comfort Women from Korea], Tokyo: Chikuma Shobō, 1987.

Kennedy, Hisae. "2007 Nen Beigikai Ianfu Ketsugi kara Zenbei ni Fukyu" [Spreading all over the United States from the 2007 US Congress Resolution on Comfort Women]. In *Kokurenga Sekai ni Hirometa "Ianfu = Seidorei" no Uso: Junēbu Kokuren Hakendan Hōkoku* [A Lie Spread All Over the World Through the United Nations, "Comfort Women = Sex Slaves": Reports by a Team that was Sent to Geneva for the United Nations' Meetings], edited by Nobukatsu Fujioka, 82–105. Tokyo: Jiyūsha, 2016.

Kim, Il-Myon. *Tenno no Guntai to Chōsenjin Ianfu* [The Emperor's military and Korean comfort women]. Tokyo: Sanichi Shobō, 1976.

Kim, Puja and Ryūta Itagaki, eds. *Q & A Chōsenjin "Ianfu" to Shokuminchi Shihai Sekinin: Anatano Gimon ni Kotaemasu* [Q & A Korean "Comfort Women" and the Responsibility for Colonization: We Will Answer Your Questions] (Tokyo: Ochanomizu Shobō, 2018).

Kim, Puja. "Chōsenjin 'Ianfu' ha Seidorei dehanaku 'Teikoku no Ianfu' datta?" [Korean "Comfort Women" were not Sex Slaves but "Comfort Women of the Empire"?]. In *Q & A Chōsenjin "Ianfu" to Shokuminchi Shihai Sekinin: Anatano Gimon ni Kotaemasu* [Q & A Korean "Comfort Women" and the Responsibility for Colonization: We Will Answer Your Questions], edited by Puja Kim and Ryūta Itagaki, 53–57. Tokyo: Ochanomizu Shobō, 2018.

Kim, Puja. "Shokuminchi Chōsen deha Teishintai to 'Ianfu' wo Kondou?" [In Colonial Korea, Was the Women's Labor Corps Confused with "Comfort Women"?]. In *Q & A Chōsenjin "Ianfu" to Shokuminchi Shihai Sekinin: Anatano Gimon ni Kotaemasu* [Q & A Korean "Comfort Women" and the Responsibility for Colonization: We Will Answer Your Questions], edited by Puja Kim and Ryūta Itagaki, 20–26. Tokyo: Ochanomizu Shobō, 2018.

Kim-Gibson, Dai Sil. *Silence Broken: Korean Comfort Women*. Parkersburg, IA: Mid-Prairie Books, 1999.

Kimura, Kan. "Nihon niokeru Ianfu Ninshiki: 1970 nendai Izen no Jyōkyo wo Chūshin ni" [Perceptions of Comfort Women in Japan: Focusing on the Situations before the 1970s]. *The Journal of International Cooperation Studies* 25, no. 1 (July 2017): 23–44.

Kinkōzan, Masako. "Shimai Toshi Fukkatsu no Hitsuyō Saido Toku" [Arguing for the Need to Sign the Sister City Contract Again], *Asahi Shimbun*, December 12, 2017. https://digital.asahi.com/articles/DA3S13268830.html?iref=pc_ss_dat.

Kitano, Ryūichi and Akira Nakano, "Shokuminchi 'Sōdōin' no Shitade" [Colonies under "Moblization"], *Asahi Shimbun*, November 30, 2016. https://digital.asahi.com/articles/DA3S12682484.html?iref=pc_ss_date.

Kitano, Ryūichi and Tetsuya Hakoda. "Iansho no Seikatsu Tadoru. Ko Mun Ok-chu san no Baai" [Trace the Lives of Comfort Women at Comfort Stations. The Case of the Late Mun Ok-chu], *Asahi Shimbun*, May 17, 2016. https://digital.asahi.com/articles/DA3S12360443.html?iref=pc_ss_date.

Kobayashi, Tetsu, Yoshihiro Makino, and Hajime Takeda "Ianfu Mondai Gōi Shikisha ha Dou Miru? Nichi Bei Kan no 3 nin ni Kiku" [What do Experts Think about the Comfort Women Issue Resolution? Asking 3 Experts from Japan, South Korea, and the United States], *Asahi Shimbun*, December 31, 2015. https://digital.asahi.com/articles/ASHD003SKHDZUHBI028.html?iref=pc_ss_date.

Kobayashi, Yoshinori. *Shin Gōmanism Sengen: Dai 3 Kan* [New Gomanism Declaration: Volume 3]. Tokyo: Shōgakkan, 1997.

"Korega Kankoku da" [This is South Korea], *Sankei Shimbun*, February 1, 2018. https://www.sankei.com/premium/news/180201/prm1802010004-n1.html.

Kurota, Katsuhiro. "Jōcho Jūshi koso Sekiheki Miseshime Bunka ha Tainichi Kankei nimo Oyobu" [Tired of Emotionalism, South Korea's Focus on Setting an Example Can Influence Japan-South Korean Relationships], *Sankei Shimbun*, January 19, 2019. https://www.sankei.com/world/news/190119/wor1901190011-n1.html.

Lee, Wen Shu and Philip Wander. "On Discursive Amnesia: Reinventing the Possibilities for Democracy through Discursive Amnesty." In *The Public Voice in a Democracy at Risk*, edited by Michael Salvador and Patricia M. Sias, 151–172. Westport: Praeger, 1998.

Lee, Woo-young. "[Herald Interview] 'Comfort women' statues magnet for Koreans," *Korean Herald*, March 3, 2016. http://kpopherald.koreaherald.com/view.php?ud=20160303171935265707_2#:~:text=Sculptors%20Kim%20Seo%2Dkyung%20and,comfort%20women%2C%E2%80%9D%20since%202011.

Maeda, Akira. "Seidorei toha Nanika" [What are Sex Slaves?] In *"Ianfu" Mondai ga Toutekitakoto* [What the "Comfort Women" Issue has Led us to Question], edited by Noriko Oomori and Fumiko Kawata, 130–140. Tokyo: Iwanami Shoten, 2010.

Martin, Judith N. and Thomas K. Nakayama, *Intercultural Communication in Contexts*. New York: McGraw Hill, 2013.

Marukawa, Tetsushi. "The Representation of 'Asia,' 'Occupational Forces,' and 'Women' against the Backdrop of Post-War Japanese Culture: from the System of Censorship to the Present." *Inter-Asia Cultural Studies* 6, no. 2 (2005): 274–281.

Matui, Yayori. "'Jūgun Ianfu' to Josei no Jinken, Media no Yakuwari" ["Comfort Women" and Women's Human Rights, Roles of the Media]. In *Jūgun Ianfu and Rekishi Ninshiki* [Military Comfort Women and History Interpretation], edited by Shinichi Arai, Rumiko Nishino, and Akira Maeda, 88–104. Tokyo: Shinkō Shuppan sha, 1997.

McCurry, Justin. "Former Sex Slaves Reject Japan and South Korea's 'Comfort Women' Accord; Deal Made us Look Like Fools, Say Women Forced to Work in Japanese Wartime Brothels." *The Guardian*, January 26, 2016. LexisNexis Academic.

Morris-Suzuki, Tessa. "Defining the Boundaries of the Cold War Nation: 1950s Japan and the Other within." *Japanese Studies* 26, no. 3 (2006): 303–316.

Nagasawa, Kenichi. *Kanko Iansho* [Kanko Comfort Station]. Tokyo: Tosho Shuppansha, 1983.

Nakai, Daisuke, Ari Hirayama, and Yū Miyaji. "Ianfu no Hi Zō Bei no Jijō ha" [Comfort Women Memorials and Statues, What are the Situations in the United

States?], *Asahi Shimbun*, November 18, 2015. https://digital.asahi.com/articles/DA3S12072838.html?iref=pc_ss_date

"Nikkan Shunō Kaidan" [Japan – South Korea Summit Meeting], *Asahi Shimbun*, February 10, 2018. https://digital.asahi.com/articles/DA3S13353327.html?iref=pc_ss_date.

Nishiguchi, Katsumi. *Kuruwa* [Brothels]. Tokyo: Tōhō Shuppansha, 1969.

Nishino, Rumiko. "Gyōsha ga 'Jinshin Baibai' de Chōshū Renkō shitakara Nihongun ni Sekinin ha nai?" [As Proprietors "Human Trafficked" Women, wasn't the Japanese Military Liable?]. In *Q & A Chōsenjin "Ianfu" to Shokuminchi Shihai Sekinin: Anatano Gimon ni Kotaemasu* [Q & A Korean "Comfort Women" and the Responsibility for Colonization: We Will Answer Your Questions], edited by Puja Kim and Ryūta Itagaki, 31–36. Tokyo: Ochanomizu Shobō, 2018.

Nishino, Rumiko. "Shōgen to Shijitsu kara Ukiagaru Nihongun 'Ianfu'" [Japanese Military "Comfort Women" from Testimonies and Historical Facts]. In *Jūgun Ianfu and Rekishi Ninshiki* [Military Comfort Women and History Interpretation], edited by Shinichi Arai, Rumiko Mishino, and Akira Maeda, 72–82. Tokyo: Shinkō Shuppan sha, 1997.

Nishino, Rumiko. *Jūgun ianfu* [Military comfort women]. Tokyo: Akashi Shoten, 1992.

Nishio, Kanji, Yoshinori Kobayashi, Nobukatsu Fujioka, and Shirō Takahashi, eds. *Rekishi Kyōkasho Tono 15nen Sensō* [A 15-Year War with History Textbooks]. Tokyo: PHP Kenkyūsho,1997.

Nishioka, Tsutomu. *Yokuwakaru Ianfu Mondai* [Understanding the Comfort Women Issue]. Tokyo: Sōshisha, 2007.

Okamoto, Yuka. "Nikkan 'Gōi' wo meguru Nihon no Masukomi Hōdō ha Koredeiino?" [Are Japan's Media Reports on the Japan-South Korea "Agreement" Acceptable?]. In *Q & A Chōsenjin "Ianfu" to Shokuminchi Shihai Sekinin: Anatano Gimon ni Kotaemasu* [Q & A Korean "Comfort Women" and the Responsibility for Colonization: We Will Answer Your Questions], edited by Puja Kim and Ryūta Itagaki, 191–195. Tokyo: Ochanomizu Shobō, 2018.

Okinawa Prefectural Government Washington, D.C. Office. "U.S. Military Bases." Accessed June 26, 2020. https://dc-office.org/wp-content/uploads/2018/03/E07.pdf.

Onishi, Norimitsu. "Tokyo Outraged by a Familiar Face: Japanese-American Fights for Apology over 'Comfort Women.'" *The International Herald Tribune*, May 12, 2007, p. 1. LexisNexis Academic.

Oomori, Noriko. "Kokusai Shakai karano Kankoku" [Warning from the International Community]. In *"Ianfu" Mondai ga Toutekitakoto* [What the "Comfort Women" Issuehas Led us to Question], edited by Noriko Oomori and Fumiko Kawata, 43–49. Tokyo: Iwanami Shoten, 2010.

Oomori, Noriko. "Sabakareta Nihongun Seidoreisei" [The Japanese Military Sex Slavery System being Prosecuted]. In *"Ianfu" Mondai ga Toutekitakoto* [What the "Comfort Women" Issue has Led us to Question], edited by Noriko Oomori and Fumiko Kawata, 32–42. Tokyo: Iwanami Shoten, 2010.

Owen, A. Susan and Peter Ehrenhaus. "Communities of Memory, Entanglements, and Claims of the Past on the Present: Reading Race Trauma through the Green Mile." *Critical Studies in Media Communication* 27, no. 2 (2010): 131–154.

Owen, A. Susan. "Expertise, Criticism and Holocaust Memory in Cinema." *Social Epistemology* 25, no. 3 (2011): 233–247.

Ōtaka, Miki. "Ianfu Mondai de Nihon wo Hihan shitekita Kankoku ga Uso Shazaihi wo Fukkatsu saseta Hontō no Riyuu" [The Real Reason why South Korea that Continued to Criticize Japan Restored the Apology Monument based on Lies], *Sankei Shimbun*, February 17, 2018. https://www.sankei.com/politics/news/180217/plt1802170001-n1.html.

Park, Boram. "Deciphering Symbolism of Girl Statue," *The Korean Times*, September 6, 2016. https://en.yna.co.kr/view/AEN20160906000200315#:~:text=%22The%20allusion%20is%20that%20the,Kim%2C%20the%20sculptor%2C%20said.&text=Loaded%20with%20such%20heavy%20symbolism,way%20to%20rebuild%20the%20embassy.

Park, Yuha. *Teikoku no Ianfu* [Comfort Women of the Empire], Tokyo: Asahi Shimbun Shuppan, 2017.

Peterson, Mark. *A Brief History of Korea*, Facts On File, 2009. http://pitt.idm.oclc.org/login?url=https://search.credoreference.com/content/entry/fofbk/south_korea_s_long_road_to_democracy_1953_2009/0?institutionId=1425.

Prosise, Theodore O. "The Collective Memory of the Atomic Bombings Misrecognized as Objective History: The Case of the Public Opposition to the National Air and Space Museum's Atomic Bomb Exhibit." *Western Journal of Communication* 62, no. 3 (1998): 316–347.

Said, Edward. W. *Culture and Imperialism*. New York: Alfred A. Knopf, 1993.

Said, Edward W. *Orientalism*. New York: Vintage Books, 1978.

Sang-Hun, Choe and Jonathan Soble. "Apology, if not Closure, for 'Comfort Women.'" *The New York Times*, December 29, 2015. LexisNexis Academic.

Senda, Kakō. *Jūgun Ianfu Keiko* [Military Comfort Woman Keiko]. Tokyo: Kōbunsha, 1981.

Senda, Kakō. *Jūgun Ianfu: Seihen* [Military comfort women: Main edition]. Tokyo: Sanichi Shobō, 1973.

Senda, Kakō. *Jūgun Ianfu: Zokuhen* [Sequel: Military comfort women]. Tokyo: Sanichi Shobō, 1978.

"Senjichū Ianfu ni Atta 4 Nin no Shōgen" [Testimonials of 4 People Who Met Comfort Women during the War]. In *Jūgun Ianfu and Rekishi Ninshiki* [Military Comfort Women and History Interpretation], edited by Shinichi Arai, Rumiko Nishino, and Akira Maeda, 39–71. Tokyo: Shinkō Shuppan sha, 1997.

"Shimaitoshi Shimin Kōryū wo Tsuzuketekoso" [Sister Cities, It is Important to Maintain Interactions between Residents], *Asahi Shimbun*, November 19, 2017. https://digital.asahi.com/articles/DA3S13234938.html?iref=pc_ss_date.

Shiono, Nanami. "Asahi Shimbun no 'Kokuhaku' wo Koete" [Beyond the Asahi Shimbun's Confessions]. In *"Jūgun Ianfu": Asahi Shimbun vs. Bungei Shunjū* ["Military Comfort Women": Asahi Newspaper vs. Bungei Shunjū], edited by Bungei Shunjū. Tokyo: Bungei Shunjū, 2014, chap. 10, Kindle.

Shunpūden [Story of a Prostitute]. Directed by Suzuki Seijun. (1965; Tokyo: Nikkatsu), Film.

Soh, C. Sarah. *The Comfort Women: Sexual Violence and Postcolonial Memory in Korea and Japan*. Chicago: University of Chicago Press, 2008.

Sugita, Mio. "Furansugo de Kinchou no Supiichi" [French Speech Given While Feeling Nervous]. In *Kokuren ga Sekai ni Hirometa "Ianfu = Seidorei" no Uso: Junēbu Kokuren Hakendan Hōkoku* [A Lie Spread All Over the World Through the United Nations, "Comfort Women= Sex Slaves": Reports by a Team that was Sent to Geneva for the United Nations' Meetings], edited by Nobukatsu Fujioka, 298–318. Tokyo: Jiyūsha, 2016.

Swan, William L. "Japan's Intentions for its Greater East Asia Co-Prosperity Sphere as Indicated in its Policy Plans for Thailand." *Journal of South East Asian Studies* 27, no. 1 (March 1996): 139–149.

Swartz, Omar. *The Rule of Law, Property, and the Violation of Human Rights: A Plea for Social Justice*. London, UK: Foxwell & Davies Scientific Publishers, 2007.

Takagi, Kenichi. *Jūgun Ianfu to Sengo Hoshō* [Military Comfort Women and Postwar Compensation]. Tokyo: Sanichi Shobō, 1992.

Takahashi, Shirō. "Beigikai Ketsugi no Konkyo tosareta 'Tanaka Yuki' shi no Chosho" [The Book by Mr. Yuki Tanaka that became the basis of the US Congress's Resolution]. In *Kokuren ga Sekai ni Hirometa "Ianfu = Seidorei" no Uso: Junēbu Kokuren Hakendan Hōkoku* [A Lie Spread All Over the World Through the United Nations, "Comfort Women = Sex Slaves": Reports by a Team that was Sent to Geneva for the United Nations' Meetings], edited by Nobukatsu Fujioka, 106–123. Tokyo: Jiyūsha, 2016.

Takeda, Hajime. "Ianfu Gōi Hontōni 'Shissei' ka Shienkin Motomeru Moto Ianfu mo" [Is the Comfort Women Resolution Truly a "Failure"? Some Former Comfort Women Ask for the Support Money], *Asahi Shimbun*, July 7, 2019. https://digital.asahi.com/articles/ASM6J7QVLM6JUHBI019.html?iref=pc_rellink

Tamura, Taijiro. *Inago* [The Locust]. Tokyo: Chikuma Shobō, 1964.

Tamura, Taijiro. *Shunpūden* [Story of a Prostitute]. Tokyo: Chikuma Shobō, 1947.

Tharoor, Shashi. "Are Human Rights Universal?" *World Policy Journal* 16, no. 4 (1999/2000): 1–6.

Tokiura, Ken. "Heishi Taikenki, 'Shazaiha' Shōgenshu kara Yomu Ianfutachi no Jisseikatsu Daikenshō" [An Examination of the Lives of Comfort Women by Reading Soldiers Memoirs, "Apology Faction'" Testimonials]. In *Shin Gōmanism Sengen: Dai 3 Kan* [New Gomanism Declaration: Volume 3], 91–106. Tokyo: Shōgakkan, 1997.

Tokutome, Kinuyo. "San Francisco no Ianfu Kinenhi ga Setsuritsu sareta Riyū" [The Reasons why the Comfort Women Memorial was Erected in San Francisco], *Asahi Shimbun*, December 14, 2017. https://webronza.asahi.com/politics/articles/20171 21400006.html?iref=pc_ss_date

Toyosaki, Satoshi. "Toward De/postcolonial Autoethnography: Critical Relationality with the Academic Second Persona," *Cultural Studies/Critical Methodologies* 18, no. 1 (2018): 32–42.

Tsuzuki, Chushichi, *The Pursuit of Power in Modern Japan, 1825 – 1995*. New York: Oxford University Press, 2000.

Turner, Kathleen J. "Rhetorical History as Social Construction: The Challenge and the Promise." In *Doing Rhetorical History: Concepts and Cases*, edited by Katheleen J. Turner, 1–15. Tuscaloosa, AL: University of Alabama Press, 1998.

Ueno, Chizuko. *Nashonarizumu to Jenda* [Nationalism and Gender]. Tokyo: Seidosha, 1998.

Vitello, Paul. "Yoshiko Yamaguchi, 94, Actress in Propaganda Films: [Obituary (Obit); Biography]." *New York Times*, Sep 23, 2014. Late Edition (East Coast). http://pitt.idm.oclc.org/login?url=https://www-proquest-com.pitt.idm.oclc.org/docview/1564106074?accountid=14709.

Wander, Philip. "The Third Persona: An Ideological Turn in Rhetorical Theory," *Central States Speech Journal* 35 (1984): 197–216.

Yamaoka, Tesshū. "Glendale shi Ianfuzō Tekkyo Saiban no Tenkai to Mitōshi" [Development and Prospect of the Trial for Comfort Women Statue Removal in the City of Glendale]. In *Kokuren ga Sekai ni Hirometa "Ianfu = Seidorei" no Uso: Junēbu Kokuren Hakendan Hōkoku* [A Lie Spread All Over the World Through the United Nations, "Comfort Women = Sex Slaves": Reports by a Team that was Sent to Geneva for the United Nations' Meetings], edited by Nobukatsu Fujioka, 136–167. Tokyo: Jiyūsha, 2016.

Yoshida, Seiji. *Chōsenjin Ianfu to Nihonjin* [Korean comfort women and Japanese]. Tokyo: Shinjinbutsu Ōraisha, 1977.

Yoshida, Seiji. *Watashino Sensō Hanzai: Chōsenjin Kyōsei Renko* [My War Crime: Forced Recruitment of Koreans]. Tokyo: Sanichi Shobō, 1983.

Yoshimi, Yoshiaki. *Jūgun ianfu* [Military comfort women]. Iwanami Shoten: Tokyo, 1995.

Yun, Chung-ok, "Yun Chung-ok san ni Kiku" [Asking Yun Chung-ok]. In *Q & A Chōsenjin "Ianfu" to Shokuminchi Shihai Sekinin: Anatano Gimon ni Kotaemasu* [Q & A Korean "Comfort Women" and the Responsibility for Colonization: We Will Answer Your Questions], edited by Puja Kim and Ryūta Itagaki, 27–30. Tokyo: Ochanomizu Shobō, 2018.

Index

Page numbers with "n" refer to endnotes.

Abe Kōji, 137–38
Abe Shinzō, 12, 149, 150, 155, 162, 188, 190–91, 193, 204
Abiru Rui, 181
Abousnnouga, Gill, 163–65
Ahn, Yonson, 19–20
Akarenga no Ie: Chōsen kara Kita Jūgun Ianfu (House with a Red Brick Roof: Military Comfort Women from Korea, Kawata), 25, 61–62, 65–66, 68–69, 75
Akatsuki no Dassou (Escape at Dawn, Tamura), 25, 36, 41, 43, 44, 47, 49–54, 57
American Plan study, 7, 21
An Byeong-jik, 98
anti-American sentiments, 207
anti-Asian sentiment, 207
anti-British sentiments, 207
anti-Chinese sentiment, 174–79
antiforeign sentiment, 109–13
anti-Japanese ideology, 118–19
anti-Japanese sentiment, 187, 211
anti-Japan left-wingers, 166, 168, 170, 172, 183, 204
anti-Korean sentiment, 109–13, 174–79
antiprogressive arguments, 166–70

apology, 21
appellations, 21–23
Arai, Shinichi, 26, 125, 130, 131, 138, 145, 148, 150, 151
Araki Kanichi, 131, 132
Asahi Shimbun, 12, 25, 27, 30n31, 62, 86, 98, 104, 105, 118, 155, 162, 166, 167, 180, 183, 185, 187, 189, 191, 192; attacks on, 168–70; criticism of, 115–16
Asian Women's Fund, 173
Asia-Pacific War, 1, 2, 14, 28n1
Asō Tetsuo, 8, 105, 132
Atarashii Rekishi Kyōkasho wo Tsukurukai (Japanese Society for History Textbook Reform), 120
autoethnography, 27, 208

Babicz, Lionel, 17–18
Bae Jok Gan, 154
Banks, Anna, 208
Banks, Stephen P., 208
Beevor, Anthony, 210
Booth, Wayne, 49
Bungei Shunjū, 92
Bungei Shunjū: "Jugun Ianfu": Asahi Shimbun vs. Bungei Shunju

("Military Comfort Women": Asahi Newspaper *vs.* Bungei Shunju), 26, 91–92, 115
Burma, 82, 85, 93, 132, 144, 210

censorship, General Headquarters (GHQ), 37–38, 44, 45, 53
Chinese comfort woman, 97, 128
Choi, Jung-Bong, 18
Chong Ok-sun, 172–73
chŏngsindae (Women's Volunteer Corps), 22
Chong Young-hwan, 192
Chon Jun-mo, 152
Chosenjin Ianfu to Nihonjin (Korean Comfort Women and the Japanese, Yoshida), 11, 25, 62
Chūgoku no Tabi (Travels in China, Honda), 24, 86
Chun Doo Hwan, 145
Class A War Criminals, 28n3
coerced labor conditions, 144
coerced recruitment of women, 12–14, 20, 116–17, 140–45, 147, 149, 151
Cold War politics, 14
collective forgetting, 52–54
collective memories, 14–16, 204–6; postcolonial analyses, 17; sexual slavery, 21; of sexual slavery, 27
colonization, 16–18; Western, 16–17, 206
comfort stations, 1, 7–8, 10, 41, 47, 55, 66, 68–70, 73–76, 79, 93, 96; for Allied soldiers, 83; categories, 9–10; Japanese imperial military, 103; operation of, 84–86, 104–5, 126; proprietors, vulgar and greedy, 82–84
comfort system, 1, 8, 10, 19–21, 57; American Plan and, 7; common practice of, 102–4; criticism of, 54, 55; facilities, 9; inhumane, 136; Japanese colonization as the cause of, 185–86; Japanese imperial military involvement, 139–40; justification of, 136–37; as military sexual slavery, 144; negative effects on women, 54; reasons for establishing, 5–6; recruitment of minors for, 137–39; romanticized memories, 136; violation of international law, 137–39, 191
comfort women, 5–10, 16, 17, 19–21; appellations, 21–23; categories of, 13–14, 133; characteristics of, 97; Chinese, 7–8; coercive recruitment of, 12–14, 20, 116–17, 140–45, 147, 149, 151, 169–70; collective memory, 204–6; (discursive amnesia in, 207–8); committing suicide, 135; conservative memories, 166–72; Coomaraswamy report for, 11–12; criticism of, 56; deaths of, 64, 65, 131, 135–36; decade-old conflict, 10–13; diseases, 63–64, 129–31; drugs addiction, 127; "final and irreversible" agreement, 12–13; human rights discussion, 13–14; idyllic memories, 72–76; incomes, 93–94; infertility, 64–65, 70, 133; inhumane treatment of, 74; international perceptions of, 171; issue and Japan in international community, 170–72; issue presenting in UN, 170–72; issue, South Korean origin of, 145–47; Japanese. *See* Japanese comfort women; Japanese imperial military's responsibility for, 84–85; as Japanese-made issue, 107–9; Kōno Statement for, 10–11; Korean. *See* Korean comfort women; lives of, 93–94, 96; as paid prostitutes, 39–46, 55; pain and suffering, 207, 208; passionate with insatiable sexual desires, 46–52; payment for, 7–9, 126–27; progressives, 113–19; as prostitutes, 92–96; as public toilets, 22, 56, 64, 67, 96, 132–33, 135; punishment to, 127; recruitment, 84–86; role

Index 231

of apologies in, 21; romanticized memories, 134–37; romantic memories, 72–76, 134–37, 203, 205, 208; as sex slaves, denial of, 172–73, 193; soldiers' gratitude for, 134–37; survivors as victims, 183–85; testimonies, 93–99, 126–32, 142–44, 148, 173; in textbooks, 113, 120, 148, 150; as victims, 63–66, 86, 126–34; violence on, 128; young age, 134
The Comfort Women: Japan's Brutal Regime of Enforced Prostitution in the Second World War in 1997, Hicks), 19
The Comfort Women: Sexual Violence and Postcolonial Memory in Korea and Japan (Sarah Soh), 20
comfort women statues, 163–65, 171, 174–76, 178, 180; erection of, 187–88
concessionary facilities, 9
conservative memories: antiprogressive arguments, 166–70; comfort women: (denial of sex slaves, 172–73; issue presenting in UN, 170–72)
conspiracy theory, 112, 113, 119, 166
Coomaraswamy, Radhika, 11–12, 92; Report, 62, 74, 120, 162, 172, 173, 209; (criticism of, 118–19)
crime against humanity, 138
criminal facilities, 9–10
criticism: of nationalist writers, 128, 147–51, 190–92; *Teikoku no Ianfu* (Comfort Women of the Empire, Park Yu-Ha), 192–93; of 2015 bilateral treaty, Japan and South Korea, 188–90
criticism of progressives, 113–19

"*Daitōa Kyōeiken*" (the Greater East Asia Co-Prosperity Sphere), 5, 17, 51
Datsuaron (*Discussions on Leaving Asia*, Fukuzawa), 4
deceptive or forceful recruitment, 140–45, 191

decolonization, 17
denial of comfort women as sex slaves, 172–73, 193
Dezaki, Miki, 27, 162, 163, 183, 184, 190, 208
Dierkes, Julian, 14
discrimination, 43, 53, 54, 133–34; against Korean comfort women, 43, 53, 63, 67–68, 70, 151–52
discursive amnesia, 52–54, 95, 154; in collective memory, 207–8
drugs addiction, 127
Drzewiecka, Jolanda A., 54
Dutch women, 49

Edwards, Jason A., 21
Ellis, Carolyn S., xi, 208
The Emperor's Forces and Korean Comfort Women (Kim Il Myon), 25, 62–64, 96
ethnic rape, 6–7
exotic comfort women/singers, 42–46, 48–49, 52–54
exoticization, 206

Filipino comfort women, 142
final and irreversible agreement, 12–13
forced mobilization, 162, 168, 172, 191
forced recruitment, 140–45
forceful mobilization, 180–82, 204
foreignness, 42–44. *See also* Koreanness
France, 103
French colonization, 17
Fujii Mitsuhiko, 169
Fujiki, Shunichi, 166–68, 175, 190
Fujimoto, Etsuko, 49
Fujioka, Nobukatsu, 26, 91, 101, 116, 120, 150, 162, 163, 174–75, 177, 180–81, 183, 210; anthology, 166, 168, 169, 171–73, 176; *Kokuren ga Sekai ni Hirometa "Ianfu = Seidorei" no Uso: Junēbu Kokuren Hakendan Hōkoku*, 27, 162
Fujisawa (military doctor), 105
Fukuzawa Yukichi, 4

general antiprogressive sentiments, 166–67
general discrimination against Koreans, 151–52
General Headquarters (GHQ), 47, 49; censorship, 25, 37–38, 44, 45, 53
Germany, 103
GHQ. *See* General Headquarters (GHQ)
Gilbert, Kent, 169, 170

Hakoda Tetsuya, 183–85
halmo ni, 22, 23, 187; memories of sexual slavery, 208–12
Handa, Naoko, 191
Han Hong-goo, 192
Hasian, Marouf, 17, 27, 207
Hata, Ikuhiko, 19, 92–95, 97–99, 102–5, 108, 114, 116–18, 168, 169, 171–74, 181, 187, 205, 206; anti-Korean sentiments, 178–79; criticizing the Kōno Statement, 182; *Ianfu Mondai no Kessan* (Settlement of the Comfort Women Issue), 27, 162; *Ianfu to Senjō no Sei* (Comfort Women and Sex in Battlefields), 26, 91
Hayashi, Hirofumi, 141, 183
Hicks, George, 19, 118
Hidaka, Rokurō, 204–5
Hirahara Kazuo, 141
Hishida Motoshiro, 102
Hitler, Adolf, 148, 192
Holocaust, 147–48, 192
Honda Katsuichi, 24; *Chūgoku no Tabi* (Travels in China), 24, 86
Honda, Michael, 11–12
Hosaka, Masayasu, 92, 96, 102
Hosokawa administration, 117
houses of entertainment, 9
houses of prostitution, 9
The House with a Red Brick Roof (Kawata), 133
human rights: categories of, 13–14; violations, 13
Hwang Kum-ju, 129–31, 134

Ian Buruma, 4
"*Ianfu*" *Mondai ga Toutekitakoto* (What the "Comfort Women" Issue has Led us to Question, Oomori), 26
Ianfu Mondai no Kessan (Settlement of the Comfort Women Issue, Hata), 27, 162
"Ianfu to Byōki" (Comfort women and Illness), 63
Ianfu to Senjō no Sei (Comfort Women and Sex in Battlefields, Hata), 26, 91
Ichikawa Ichiro, 139, 140
ICJ. *See* International Court of Justice (ICJ)
Ienaga Saburō, 2, 24, 86; *Taiheiyō Sensō* (The Pacific War), 210
Im Pan-ge, 153
imperialism, 18
Inago (*The Locust*, Tamura), 24, 36–37, 39, 41, 47, 49, 51–57
Indonesia, 140
infertility, 64–65, 70, 133
inhumane "comfort" system, 74
International Court of Justice (ICJ), 138
International Labour Organization, 138
international law violation, 137–39, 191
irrational and unreliable Korean comfort women, 97–98
Irwin-Zarecka, Iwona, 15, 27, 207
Ishihara Nobuo, 92
Itabe Kosei, 141
Itagaki, Ryūta, 162, 183, 184, 187–88, 191–92; *Q & A Chōsenjin "Ianfu" to Shokuminchi Shihai Sekinin: Anatano Gimon ni Kotaemasu*, 27
Itō, Keiichi, 73–74, 92, 96, 101, 102, 211
Ito Shōzō, 65
Izumi, Mariko, 21, 23

Japan: modernization, 49, 67, 205; (and militarism, 3–5); war memories, 14–15; westernization, 4
Japanese colonization, 18; as cause of comfort system, 185–86

Japanese comfort women, 7, 64–65, 128–29, 132; Korean comfort women versus, 66–71, 85
Japanese imperialism, 18
Japanese imperial military, 57, 86; comfort stations, 103; criticism, 49–53, 56; involvement: (in coerced recruitment of women, 140–45, 147, 149; in comfort system, 139–40); responsibility, 84–85; sexual slavery, 5, 8, 10, 12, 13; (research, 18–21)
Japanese language skills, 42
Japanese soldiers, as war victims, 99–102
Japan's colonization, 205, 206, 209
Jūgun Ianfu (Military Comfort Women, Yoshimi), 21–23, 26, 125, 151
"Jūgun Ianfu": Asahi Shimbun vs. Bungei Shunjū ("Military Comfort Women": Asahi Newspaper *vs.* Bungei Shunjū), 26, 91–92, 115
Jūgun Ianfu Keiko (Military Comfort Woman Keiko, Senda), 25, 61, 70, 79
Jūgun Ianfu: Motoheishitachi no Shōgen (Military Comfort Women: Testimonies of Former Soldiers, Nishino), 125, 151
Jūgun Ianfu: Seihen (Military Comfort Women, Senda), 18, 145
Jūgun Ianfu to Rekishi Ninshiki (Military Comfort Women and History Understanding, Arai), 6, 125
Jūgun Ianfu to Sengo Hoshō (Military Comfort Women and Postwar Compensation, Takagi), 26, 125
Jūgun Ianfu: Zokuhen (Military Comfort Women: Sequel, Senda), 18, 25, 61

Kage Teruo, 67–68, 82
Kamisaka, Fuyuko, 92, 98, 99, 104
Kamiya Shigeo, 85
Kanai Nobutaka, 139
Kato Daisuke, *Minami no Shima ni Yuki ga Furu* (It Snowed on a Southern Island), 100

Kawaguchi Mann, Emi, 169
Kawata, Fumiko, 26, 70, 71, 74–76, 125, 127–28, 133, 142, 146, 150, 153, 154; *Akarenga no Ie: Chōsen kara Kita Jūgun Ianfu* (House with a Red Brick Roof: Military Comfort Women from Korea), 25, 61–62, 65–66, 68–69, 75, 133
Keiko (comfort woman), 70, 132, 144
Kennedy, Hisae, 172, 174, 177–78
Kim Eun-sung, 163
Kim-Gibson, Dai Sil, 19, 21, 52, 79
Kim Hak-sun, 10, 13, 22, 24, 91–93, 97–98, 115, 125, 133, 147, 184, 205, 207; testimony of, 93, 126
Kim Il Myon, 19, 24, 62, 63, 66–68, 73, 74, 77, 78, 83; discrimination against Koreans, 72; *The Emperor's Forces and Korean Comfort Women*, 62–64; *Tennō no Guntai to Chōsenjin Ianfu* (The Emperor's Forces and Korean Comfort Women), 19, 25, 62, 82
Kim Puja, 27, 162, 183–85, 187, 192; *Q & A Chōsenjin "Ianfu" to Shokuminchi Shihai Sekinin: Anatano Gimon ni Kotaemasu*, 27, 162
Kim Seo-kyung, 163–65
Kim Young-sam, 117
Kin Haruko: Chōsenjin Ianfu no Shuki [Kim Chun-ja: A Korean Comfort Woman's Story], 78
kisen, 184
Kishida Fumio, 180
Kitano, Ryūichi, 183–85
Kobayashi, Yoshinori, 26, 91, 94, 95, 97, 100, 101, 105–7, 115, 116, 119, 120, 139, 150, 151, 211; *Shin Gōmanism Sengen* (New Gomanism Declaration: Volume 3), 26, 91, 96
Kojima Takao, 151
Kokuren ga Sekai ni Hirometa "Ianfu = Seidorei" no Uso: Junēbu Kokuren Hakendan Hōkoku (Fujioka), 27
Kon Im-Suk, 147

Kōno Statement of 1993, 10–11, 150, 180; criticism of, 116–17; opposition to the, 182–83
Korean comfort women, 19–20, 39, 40, 42, 46, 53, 65, 94–98, 132, 192–93; coerced recruitment of, 140–45; compensation for, 103; denial of forced recruitment of, 104–7; discrimination against, 67–68, 70–72, 151–52; irrational and unreliable, 97–98; versus Japanese comfort women, 66–71, 85; mistreatment, 66–71, 85; Orientalist depictions of, 48, 55; Orientalist, exotic, erotic depictions, 76–80, 85; "positive" memories, 73; pure, innocent, 80–82; romantic, idyllic memories, 72–76
Korean Council, 178–79, 187
Koreanness, 42–44, 54
Korean patriarchy, 20
Kouminka Seisaku, 152
Kurosawa Akira, 25
Kurota, Katsuhiro, 176
Kuruwa (Brothels, Nishiguchi), 62, 68

Lee Myung-bak, 99
Lee, Wen Shu, 207
Lee Yong-soo, 173
left-wing anti-Japan forces, 119
Li Xianglan, 44

MacArthur, Douglas, 37
Machimura Nobutaka, 150
Machin, David, 163–65
MacKinnon, Catherine, 6
Maeda, Akira, 26, 125, 130, 131, 138, 145, 148–51
maidens auxiliary, 9
Marano, Tony, 190
Martin, Judith N., 209
Masamichi Inoki, 4
masculinist ideology, 53, 54, 102
masochistic view, 20
Matsubara Shunji, 129, 143, 152
Matsui Yayoi, 142, 145, 146, 148, 150

McDougall, Gay, 138
Meiji Restoration of 1868, 3, 4
Mendoza, S. Lily, 209
Mera Koichi, 171, 176
militarism, Japan, 3–5
military supplies, 131–33
Minami no Shima ni Yuki ga Furu (It Snowed on a Southern Island, Kato), 100
Mita Kazuo, 72–73
Miyaji Yū, 188
Miyazawa Kiichi, 116, 117, 169, 205
model victims, 144–45, 154
modernization, Japan, 3–5
Moon administration, 177, 179, 189
Morris-Suzuki, Tessa, 17
Motoyama Toshimi, 134–35
Mun Ok-chu, 93, 94, 98, 143, 183

Nagasawa, Kenichi, 93, 105
Nakai, Daisuke, 187
Nakano Akira, 185
Nakasone Yasuhiro, 177
Nakayama Mitsuyoshi, 135–37, 143
Nakayama, Thomas K., 209
Nakazato Chiyo, 130–31
Nashino, Rosita Bakarto, 142
Nashonarizumu to Jendā (Nationalism and Gender, Ueno), 26, 125
nationalist writers, criticism of, 128, 147–51, 190–92
Native Americans, 209
neo-nationalists, 20
New Jersey, 176, 177, 188
NGOs, 166
nihilism, 49
Nikutai no Akuma (Devil of Flesh, Tamura), 36
Nikutai no Mon (Gate of Flesh, Tamura), 36, 43, 48
Nishiguchi, Katsumi, *Kuruwa* (Brothels), 62, 68
Nishino, Rumiko, 26, 48, 74, 125, 128–40, 143, 145, 148, 151–53, 162, 163, 190–92; *Jūgun Ianfu:*

Motoheishitachi no Shōgen (Military Comfort Women: Testimonies of Former Soldiers), 125, 151
Nishio, Kanji, 26, 91, 100, 103–4, 118, 120
Nishioka, Tsutomu, 92, 97–99, 104, 106, 115, 117, 118, 150; *Yokuwakaru Ianfu Mondai* (Understanding the Comfort Women Issue), 91
No Ching-ja, 143
Nogi Harumichi, 140
non-model victims, 145
non-Western colonization, 17–18
No Ok-sil, 143

Obama, Barack, 178
Ōe Kenzaburo: *Okinawa Nōto* (Okinawa Notes), 86, 210
Okabe Naosaburō, 105
Okamoto, Yuka, 189
Okamura Yasuji, 7, 118
Okinawa Nōto (Okinawa Notes, Ōe Kenzaburo), 86, 210
Oomori, Noriko, 26, 125, 137, 138, 149
oppositional imperialism, 18
Orientalism, 16–18, 205
Orientalism (Said), 16–17
Oriental women, 40, 46, 47, 55, 76, 85
Ōtaka Miki, 177
Ozawa Kazuhiko, 134, 135

Pae Pong-gi, 125, 133, 146, 154
paid prostitutes, 13, 19, 22
paramilitary facilities, 9
Park Chung Hee, 145
Park Geun-hye, 12, 13, 162
Park Yu-ha, 164, 193; *Teikoku no Ianfu* (Comfort Women of the Empire), 82, 161, 192–93
passionate "comfort women," insatiable sexual desires, 46–52
paternalistic ideologies, 20, 105, 206
patriarchal colonial policy, 20–21

patriarchal ideologies, 7, 20, 41, 52, 103, 132, 133, 145, 154
Pe Pongi, 61–62, 65–66, 69–71, 75
Perry, Matthew C., 3
Peterson, Mark, 145
Philippines, 146
postcolonial *Kisen* tourism, 185–86
postcolonial studies, 17–18
The Power of Memory in Modern Japan (Ahn), 20
POWs, 36, 50, 51
progressive activists, 118
progressives' criticisms, 190
prostitutes, relationship with, 41–42, 54
prostitute volunteers, 40
PTSD, 133

Q & A Chōsenjin "Ianfu" to Shokuminchi Shihai Sekinin: Anatano Gimon ni Kotaemasu (Kim Puja), 27, 162
quasi-brothel, 9

RAA. *See* Recreation and Amusement Association (RAA)
racist colonial policy, 20–21
racist ideologies, 54, 132
rape, 6–7
recovery of nationalistic pride, 148
Recreation and Amusement Association (RAA), 83; comfort stations, 103
recreation centers, 103
redress movement, 11–12, 20, 22, 145–46, 186–88, 193
Rekishi Kyōkasho Tono 15nen Sensō (A 15-Year War with History Textbooks), 26, 91
The Rhetoric of Fiction (Booth), 49
romantic, idyllic memories of comfort women, 72–76
romanticized memories, 96; of comfort women, 134–37
Ruff-O'Herne, Jan, 49
Russo-Japanese War, 4

Said, Edward, 16–17, 41, 43, 48, 56, 80, 97, 98, 175, 205–6
Saito Kiri, 64
Sakurai Yoshiko, 92, 117, 138, 150–51, 173
sanctioned prostitution system, 210, 211
San Francisco, 188
Sankei Shimbun, 27, 162, 169, 175–78
Satō Katsumi, 147
Satō Kuni, 12, 162
Seidler, Franz, 103
Senda, Kakō, 18–19, 21–22, 24, 61, 62, 64–68, 72–74, 83–85, 132, 133, 143, 144, 203; *Jūgun Ianfu Keiko* (Military Comfort Woman Keiko), 25, 61, 70, 79; *Jūgun Ianfu: Seihen* (Military Comfort Women), 18, 145; *Jūgun Ianfu: Zokuhen* (Military Comfort Women: Sequel), 16, 25, 61
sexist ideologies, 54
sex slaves, 22, 148–49, 167, 168; defined, 92; denial of comfort women as, 172–73
sex tourism, 186
sexual assault, 146–47
sexual assaults, 6
sexual slavery: collective memories, 21; collective memories of, 27; discursive amnesia in collective memories of, 207–8; forceful recruitment, 10; as human rights violation, 13–14; Japanese imperial military, 5, 8, 10, 12, 13; (research, 18–21); Korean survivors of, 19–20; Korean victims of, 16, 17; memories in postwar period, 38–39; (collective forgetting, 52–54; "comfort women" as paid prostitutes, 39–46; discursive amnesia, 52–54; exotic "comfort women/singers," 42–46, 48–49); memories of, 2, 10, 14; Orientalist memories of, 205; survivors of, 10–11; ("final and irreversible" agreement, 12–13); as war crime, 19
Shimada Kiyoshi, 131, 132

Shimizu Akira, 47
Shimizu Norio, 104
Shina no Yoru (China Nights), 44
Shin Gōmanism Sengen (New Gomanism Declaration: Volume 3, Kobayashi), 26, 91, 96
Shiono, Nanami, 92, 98–99, 116
Shirota Suzuko, 128, 129
Shugart, Helene A., 17
Shunpūden (*Story of a Prostitute*, Tamura), 24–25, 36, 39–40, 42–43, 46–49, 51, 53–55, 57, 145, 203
Shusenjō: The Main Battleground of the Comfort Women Issue, 27, 162, 183, 188, 190–91, 208
Silence Broken: Korean Comfort Women (Kim-Gibson), 19
Sim Mi-ja, 129–30, 173
slaves, 106–7
Soh, C. Sarah, 21, 22
Song Eoun-ok, 184
Song Sin-do, 98, 127–28
South Korea: democracy, 145; democratization movement, 145–47, 186, 193; origin of "comfort women" issue, 145–57; women's movement, 146
Soviet Union, 103
Statue of Peace. *See* comfort women statues
STDs, 5–7, 64, 129–31, 133, 141
Stern, Scott, 130; American Plan study, 7, 21
Sugita, Mio, 169, 190
survivors as victims, 183–85
Suzuki Seijun, 25, 35, 56
Suzuki Takushirō, 139
Swartz, Omar, 13
Syngman Rhee, 145
syphilis, 130

Taiheiyō Sensō (The Pacific War, Ienaga), 210
Takagi, Kenichi, 26, 92, 129, 133, 134, 140, 143, 147, 152, 153; *Jūgun Ianfu*

to Sengo Hoshō (Military Comfort Women and Postwar Compensation), 26, 125
Takahashi, Shirō, 26, 91, 95, 169
Takeda, Hajime, 189–90
Tamura, Taijiro, 35–36, 85; *Akatsuki no Dassou* (Escape at Dawn), 24–25, 36, 41, 43, 44, 47, 49–54, 57; *Inago (The Locust)*, 24, 36–37, 39, 41, 47, 49, 51–57; *Nikutai no Akuma* (Devil of Flesh), 36; *Nikutai no Mon* (Gate of Flesh), 36, 43, 48; *Shunpūden (Story of a Prostitute)*, 36, 39–40, 42, 43, 46–49, 51, 53–55, 57, 145, 203
Taniguchi Senkichi, 25, 35, 53, 56
Tanabe Ryūji, 49
Teikoku no Ianfu (Comfort Women of the Empire, Park Yu-Ha), 82, 161; criticism of, 192–93
Tennō no Guntai to Chōsenjin Ianfu (The Emperor's Military and Korean Comfort Women, Kim Il Myon), 19, 25, 62, 82
Tetsuno Bōfū (Typhoon of Steel), 210
Tharoor, Shashi, 13
Tokiura Ken, 96, 105
Tokugawa Shōgun, 3
Tokutome, Kinuyo, 188
Tomiichi Murayama, 21
Tomokiyo Takashi, 142
Totsuka Etsurō, 166, 191; attacks on, 167–68
transported supplies, 133
Tsuzuki Chushichi, 5
2015 bilateral treaty, Japan and South Korea, 27, 174–79, 193; criticism of, 188–90; mixed evaluations of, 179–81

Uemura Takashi, 109, 115
Ueno, Chizuko, 19, 40, 94, 144–48, 150–51, 153; *Nashonarizumu to Jendā* (Nationalism and Gender), 26, 125

UNCEDAW. *See* UN's Committee on the Elimination of Discrimination against Women (UNCEDAW)
uncontrollable sexual desire, 54
UNHRC. *See* United Nations Human Rights Committee (UNHRC)
United Nation (UN), 172
United Nations Human Rights Committee (UNHRC), 118, 166–69, 172
United Nations Universal Declaration of Human Rights, 13
United States, 102, 103; slaves in, 149
UN's Committee on the Elimination of Discrimination against Women (UNCEDAW), 188, 189
Uwake Tamako, 69–70

Vartabedian, Sarah, 21
VAWW RAC. *See* Violence against Women in War Research Action Center (VAWW RAC)
violation of international laws, 137–39
Violence against Women in War Research Action Center (VAWW RAC), 154–55
Vitello, Paul, 44

WAM. *See* Women's Active Museum on War and Peace (WAM)
Wander, Philip C., 15, 54, 207
war crime, 19, 57
war is tragic, 99–102
war memories, 14–15
Watanabe Mina, 183
Watashi no Sensou Hanzai (My War Crimes, Yoshida), 11, 25, 62, 71–72, 76, 79–80
Wen Shu Lee, 15
Western colonization, 16–17, 205, 206
Westernization, 49, 67, 205
Western Orientalists, 40, 41, 46, 48, 55, 76, 77, 85, 97, 134, 190; perceptions, 176

Women's Active Museum on War and Peace (WAM), 27, 162, 185–87

Yamada Shōzō, 65
Yamaguchi Akiko, 186
Yamaguchi Kazuo, 192
Yamaguchi Yoshiko, 44
Yamamoto Yumiko, 167
Yamaoka, Tesshū, 169–71, 174, 175
Yang Ching-ja, 187
Yokuwakaru Ianfu Mondai (Understanding the Comfort Women Issue, Nishioka), 91
Yomiuri Shimbun, 117
Yorichi, Alex, 94, 95, 148, 168, 173
Yoshida, Seiji, 11–12, 25, 62, 84, 116, 118, 143, 155, 162, 169, 170, 180; *Chōsenjin Ianfu to Nihonjin* (Korean Comfort Women and the Japanese), 62; criticism of, 114–15; *Watashi no Sensou Hanzai* (My War Crimes), 25, 71–72, 76, 79–80
Yoshiike, Toshiko, 133
Yoshikawa Masayoshi, 73
Yoshikawa Takashi, 191
Yoshimi, Yoshiaki, 19, 26, 28n2, 30n31, 40, 104, 106, 118, 125–27, 129, 131, 133–44, 148–49, 162, 163, 166, 168, 169, 183–85, 193, 204, 205; attacks on, 168; *Jūgun Ianfu* (Military Comfort Women), 26, 125, 151
Yoshimura, Hirofumi, 161, 191, 192
Yoshizawa Fumitoshi, 189
Yuasa Ken, 129, 139, 140, 151
Yun Byung-se, 188
Yun Chong-ok, 146
Yun Chung-ok, 184, 185
Yun Doo Ri, 79

Zachmann, Urs Matthias, 4

About the Author

Ako Inuzuka (PhD, Bowling Green State University) is an associate professor of Communication at the University of Pittsburgh at Johnstown. Her areas of research include intercultural/international communication and collective memory. Her essays have been published in *Howard Journal of Communications*, *Journal of International Communication*, *Communication Quarterly*, *Journal of Multicultural Discourses*, and *Intercultural Communication in Japan: Theorizing Homogenizing Discourse*.